NATIONALISM
IN MODERN
ANGLO-IRISH
POETRY

Nationalism in Modern Anglo-Irish Poetry

RICHARD J. LOFTUS

MADISON AND MILWAUKEE, 1964

THE UNIVERSITY OF WISCONSIN PRESS

Published by

The University of Wisconsin Press

Madison and Milwaukee

Mailing address: P.O. Box 1379, Madison, Wisconsin 53701

Editorial offices: 430 Sterling Court, Madison

Printed in the United States of America

by the Kingsport Press, Inc., Kingsport, Tennessee

Library of Congress Catalog Card Number 64–22234

5- 1 u -7 0

TO BEVERLY AND THE TIGER

ACKNOWLEDGMENTS

This book began with the writing of my dissertation for the Ph.D. degree at the University of Wisconsin. Consequently, I wish first to acknowledge my indebtedness to the faculty of the Department of English and the staff of the Library at the University of Wisconsin. I am especially grateful to Professor Paul Wiley, who directed my dissertation and without whose patience and wisdom this book would never have been possible, and to Professor Helen C. White, Professor Alvin Whitley, and Mrs. Barbara Fraser.

I am also indebted to many persons engaged in Irish studies for their generous help and advice. I wish particularly to thank Maurice Harmon, Lawrence J. McCaffrey, Ailfrid Mac-Lochlainn, Roger McHugh, Vivian Mercier, Gearóid Mac-Niocaill, Frank O'Brien, and James O'Brien. My warm thanks go also to Padraic Colum and Austin Clarke for discussing with me their work and to Mrs. Geraldine Plunkett Dillon for her helpful comments on the verse of her brother; to Mrs. Danute (Carl) Ernst and Miss Margo Cummings for their skilled typing; and to the staff of the University of Wisconsin Press, especially Mrs. Rufus (Jane) Blanshard, for whose sensitive and intelligent editing I am deeply grateful.

I wish to acknowledge the generosity of the American

Philosophical Society, the University of Illinois Research Board, the University of Wisconsin Alumni Research Foundation, and the sponsors of the James Campbell Good Will Traveling Fellowship. Their support made it possible for me to visit Ireland in order to gather material for this book. I am also grateful for the assistance and cooperation of the staffs of the National Library of Ireland, the Newberry Library in Chicago, and the libraries of the University of Illinois and the University of Wisconsin.

I warmly acknowledge my indebtedness to the following persons, firms, and institutions for permission to quote from source materials: The Macmillan Company, New York, for *The Collected Poems of W. B. Yeats* (copyright 1903, 1906, 1907, 1912, 1916, 1918, 1919, 1924, 1928, 1931, 1933, 1934, 1935, 1940, 1944, 1945, 1946, 1950, 1956 by The Macmillan Company; copyright 1940 by Georgie Yeats), *The Collected Plays of W. B. Yeats* (copyright 1934, 1952; new edition, 1953), James Stephens' *The Adventures of Seumas Beg* and *The Rocky Road to Dublin* (copyright 1915) and *The Collected Poems* (copyright 1954); Diarmuid Russell, for A.E.'s *Collected Poems* (copyright 1926) and *The House of Titans* (copyright 1934); The Macmillan Company, London, for F. R. Higgins' *The Dark Breed* (copyright 1927) and *The Gap of Brightness* (copyright 1940); Austin Clarke and The Dolmen Press, Dublin, for *The Collected Poems of Austin Clarke* (copyright 1936), *The Vengeance of Fionn* (copyright 1917), *The Cattledrive in Connaught and Other Poems* (copyright 1925), *Flight to Africa and Other Poems* (copyright 1963), *Too Great a Vine* (copyright 1957), *The Horse-Eaters: Poems and Satires* (copyright 1960), and *Ancient Lights: Poems and Satires* (copyright 1955); Padraic Colum and The Devin-Adair Company, for *The Poet's Circuits* (copyright 1961), *The Collected Poems of Padraic Colum* (copyright 1953), and *The Story of Lowry Maen* (copyright 1937); The Bodley Head, John Lane, Ltd., London, for F. R. Higgins' *Island Blood* (copyright 1925); The Talbot Press,

Ltd., Dublin, for *The Collected Works of Padraic Pearse* (copyright 1924); Miss Maeve Donnelly, for Joseph Plunkett's *The Circle and the Sword* (copyright 1911) and *The Poems of Joseph Mary Plunkett* (copyright 1916); Donagh Mac-Donagh, for *The Poetical Works of Thomas MacDonagh* (copyright 1916); and the Trustees of the National Library of Ireland, for manuscript materials.

R. L.

June, 1964

CONTENTS

NATIONALISM
IN MODERN
ANGLO-IRISH
POETRY

II

FOR HOULIHAN'S DAUGHTER

" 'For God's sake,' said the hag, 'leap for us now one of the leaps you used to leap when you were mad.' " [1] With these words the mill-hag of Loingseachan taunts Suibhne, son of Colman Cuar, who, cursed by a holy man, had fled insane from the Battle of Mag Rath and then for seven years wandered restlessly over Ireland until at last his sense and memory returned to him. But the mill-hag taunts Suibhne and he leaps back into his madness and the hag leaps after him; and, matching his prowess leap for leap, she pursues Suibhne through all of Erin and he cannot escape her. Such is the story of *The Frenzy of Suibhne*, one of the most unusual tales to have come down to us from ancient Ireland—with its riddling dialogue, its catalogues of sacred animals and trees, its curious mingling of pagan and Christian lore. Many elements of the story are strikingly relevant to the course of poetry in modern Ireland—the intense love of countryside, the element of bitter political strife, the ideological conflict between druidic and Christian belief, and especially the episode of Suibhne driven to frenzy by the relentless pursuit of the hag.

At the close of the nineteenth century the poets of the Irish cultural revival chose to personify their country as Cathleen Ní Houlihan, the romantic heroine of an eighteenth-century love ballad.[2] In the years that followed, though, the choice must often have seemed a poor one; for modern Ireland, the Ireland to which the poets dedicated their art, at times more closely approximated Suibhne's mill-hag than the oppressed yet queenly heroine of Samuel Ferguson's poem and of W. B. Yeats' play. In the first decade of the twentieth century the Irish people repudiated Yeats and John Synge. Then, a few years later, they abused Lady Gregory's nephew, Hugh Lane, for trying to give them his collection of modern paintings. Afterwards, in the nineteen-twenties, Sean O'Casey discovered how ungracious his countrymen could be when they rioted during the second performance of *The Plough and the Stars*, the women "squealing that Irish girls were noted over the whole world for their modesty" and the men "bawling out *The Soldier's Song*," the Irish national anthem. In *Inishfallen, Fare Thee Well*, O'Casey remarks that on the night of the riots "Sean felt a surge of hatred for Cathleen Ni Houlihan sweeping over him. He saw now that the one who had the walk of a queen could be a bitch at times. She galled the hearts of her children who dared be above the ordinary, and she often slew her best ones. . . . What an old snarly gob she could be at times; an ignorant one too."[3]

The men who helped to shape the Irish cultural revival in the eighteen-nineties, in the years following the death of Charles Stewart Parnell, dedicated themselves to the regeneration of their race and nation. They sought to ennoble the Irishman's soul and by doing so to make him worthy of his ancient heritage. Inevitably, however, they were to be disappointed.

Douglas Hyde and Father Michael O'Hickey, for example, who with a few others established the Gaelic League, saw in the language movement the means of spiritual renewal. They recognized that the culture of the Gaelic people had fallen into a period of decadence in the eighteenth century and believed that the last vestiges of that culture were on the verge of extinction; and certainly their fears had basis in fact. The encroachment of what Hyde terms "West-Britonism" upon Irish life had made considerable headway during the nineteenth century. For one thing, the impoverished people, recognizing the material well-being of the English and Anglo-Irish ruling class, sought to identify themselves with what was clearly a better way of life, at least in terms of creature comforts, by aping English manners and mannerisms and by adopting the English language. At the same time, they came to regard their own language and traditions as stigmata of social inferiority. Daniel O'Connell had pointed the way, warning his countrymen against the old language and customs, and teaching them practical lessons in English sociology, economics, and politics. Indeed, the history of nineteenth century Ireland is a history of sociological, economic, and political struggle and change. The Irishman won the right to vote and, after O'Connell, the right to hold office. Still later, after the Famine and decades of land agitation, he won the right to own his own land. However, Hyde and O'Hickey were convinced that during the same period the essential cultural foundation upon which any claim to independent nationality must rest had been undermined and had begun to collapse. In trying to come to terms with the realities of modern Europe, the Irish people gradually exchanged their Gaelic culture for what Father O'Hickey bitterly describes as "a veneer of spurious cockneyism." "We are doubtless a glorious nation," O'Hickey told his students at Maynooth college, "in our own estimation! Little need we to utter the Scotchman's prayer. 'The Laird gie us a guid conceit o' oursels' for our national self-esteem is quite colossal. Would that it had other than a foundation of sand!" [4]

Nationalism, as Hyde and O'Hickey conceived it, meant a struggle for "racial" survival, and not merely in a political sense. The Irish movement which was then taking shape would involve not simply the struggle of Irish against English politician but also the much more vital struggle of Irish against English culture. In 1892 Hyde explained to a meeting of the

National Literary Society in Dublin what he believed to be the significance of "sentiments of nationality" which were at that time taking hold among the Irish people. "I believe," he said, "that what is largely behind it [nationalism] is the half unconscious feeling that the race which at one time held possession of more than half Europe, which established itself in Greece, and burned infant Rome, is now—almost extirpated and absorbed elsewhere—making its last stand for independence in this island of Ireland; and do what they may the race of to-day cannot wholly divest itself from the mantle of its own past." [5] Hyde urged his countrymen "to cultivate everything that is most racial, most Gaelic, most Irish"; [6] and O'Hickey proclaimed the words of Thomas Davis: "Nationality . . . is the summary name for many things. It seeks a literature made by Irishmen, and coloured by our scenery, manners and character. It desires to see art applied to express Irish thoughts and belief. It would make our music sound in every parish at twilight, our pictures sprinkle the walls of every house, and our poetry and history sit at every hearth. It would thus create a race of men full of more intensely Irish character and knowledge, and to that race it would give Ireland." [7]

The dream shared by Hyde and O'Hickey, and afterwards by Padraic Pearse, the dream of a Celtic people speaking a Celtic tongue, proved illusory. The "race of to-day" had indeed divested itself of "the mantle of its own past"; its cloak of "spurious cockneyism," imported from Victorian England, proved too snug a fit. At first the Gaelic League seemed to prosper; its membership increased as hundreds, then thousands of Irishmen, caught up in the enthusiasm of the revival, sought to demonstrate their patriotism by mastering their native language. But, in the end, they did not learn Gaelic; it was too difficult and, after all the fine speeches had been made, not very practical. James Stephens, who as a young writer preached the League's cause in the columns of *Sinn Féin*, Arthur Griffith's popular newspaper, learned to read Gaelic with passing competence, but he never mastered it as a spoken tongue. Even Pearse, who was editor of the League's official journal, An Claidheamh Soluis (The Sword of Light), was not a fluent speaker of Gaelic.[8] Today, it is true, Irish intellectuals know their Irish and most writers are bilingual. Yet how few use the Gaelic language as a medium of expression and how many treat it as a depository of idiom and anecdote to be drawn upon as their work in English requires! Moreover, in its primary purpose the League failed. The proportion of Gaelic-speaking people in the Irish population has continued to decline; and the Gaeltacht, the area in which Irish is the medium of everyday speech, has continued to shrink. Nor did the movement effect any significant change in the national character; the Irish people persisted in taking for their own the Philistine moral and intellectual values of their middle-class peers in England. At length the Gaelic League became little more than a pawn of the more chauvinistic and insensitive elements of Irish society. The hopes of its founders were soon forgotten. O'Hickey, disillusioned, left the League after only a few years; and even Hyde felt compelled to resign as president in 1915 when extremist members succeeded in transforming the League from a cultural to a militant political organization.

Yeats, too, miscalculated; like Hyde and O'Hickey, he mistook the spirit of the times. After Parnell's death a hush had fallen upon the Irish public scene; and the poet, who already had prophesied an intellectual awakening among his countrymen, was struck by "the sudden certainty that Ireland was to be like soft wax for years to come." [9] With remarkable determination Yeats, romantic aesthete and dabbler in occult lore, set out to remake the Irish nation to fit the specifications of his own aristocratic vision. Like Hyde and O'Hickey, he regarded the cultural movement as a means of reviving and ennobling the race and of saving Ireland from the vulgarity and materialism of nineteenth-century England. He argued the need of a new literature, one which would be free from the saber-rattling and the trite sentimentality that characterized the verse of the "Young Ireland" poets in the *Nation* news-paper in the 1840's and in which artistic values would be given primacy over narrowly nationalistic values.[10] At first he enjoyed a measure of success. His creed of "a nobler form of art" was subscribed to not only by those who were already confirmed in their allegiance to the Muse, not only by such writers as George Russell, Lionel Johnson, and T. W. Rolleston, but also by those whom one might expect to have been susceptible to chauvinistic pressures: Edward Martyn, for example, and Padraic Pearse and Thomas MacDonagh of the younger generation. Yet in the end Yeats lost his struggle to keep the Irish literary revival on a sound aesthetic footing.

Yeats had been wrong to suppose that the ghost of Parnell could be used as a cudgel with which to subdue the Irish Philistines. True enough, they had been stunned. The con-fusion visited upon them by the Parnell affair is given vivid expression in the Christmas dinner scene of James Joyce's *A Portrait of the Artist as a Young Man*. In effect, Joyce pits one kind of provincial ignorance against another. He leaves the reader little to choose between Dante Conway, a woman who blindly justifies her priests as "the apple of God's eye," and John Casey, a man who once spat tobacco juice in the eye of an old woman who had insulted his "king." Joyce's point is simply that as a result of the Parnell debacle the Irish middle class had become a house divided against itself. It was this division into factions, this same persistent wrangle between Parnellite and anti-Parnellite, that enabled Yeats to win his way at the early committee meetings of the National Literary Society, that enabled him to argue successfully the cause of "noble art." Obsessed with their own family quarrel, the Irish Philistines failed to grasp exactly what it was Yeats and his supporters intended. Nevertheless, Yeats was naïve to think that he might convert Irish society to a creed of nationalism founded on values any more noble than Victorian morality and narrow political hatred. That he was able for a time to maintain the artistic integrity of the movement was a feat remarkable in itself. But, in fact, he could not free the new literature indefinitely from the stultifying pressures of a self-righteous and intolerant society. The Parnell affair had rendered the Irish Philistines momentarily inarticulate, but it had not destroyed them.

By the turn of the century the Irish middle class had regained its composure sufficiently to turn a hostile gaze upon Yeats and his movement. In 1899 *The Countess Cathleen* was greeted by a scurrilous pamphlet, *Souls for Gold*,[11] before production, and by "a storm of booing and hissing" at its opening performance.[12] In the years that followed, the Philistines grew in strength and their attacks upon "noble art" became increasingly louder and angrier. They heaped abuse upon John Synge's *The Playboy of the Western World* because of some imagined insult to the Irish people. They clamored against Hugh Lane's proffered gift of modernistic paintings to the city of Dublin—modern art was alien to their narrow conception of nationality—then complained bitterly of British treachery when the offer was withdrawn and the collection went to London.[13] They badgered Sean O'Casey for his Marxism until, at last, he exiled himself from his native land. They objected to the Irish Academy of Letters, founded by Yeats in the nineteen-thirties, because membership depended on other than overtly patriotic criteria. In their journals and newspapers they invariably denounced excellence in art and literature and attempted to drag down poetry, prose, and drama to their own level of mediocrity. Inevitably, they have rejected the best of the modern Irish writers. They would have no truck with Yeats, for example, or with Joyce or A.E.; the work of these artists was "not in any true sense either Irish or a real renaissance."[14]

It is ironical that Yeats, who more than any other man was responsible for the revival of Irish literature, should have become the favorite target of Philistine abuse. The journalistic hacks of *Sinn Féin* and other extremist publications questioned his art, his patriotism, and even his personal character.

For example, less than three months before the Easter Rising of 1916, *Nationality*, the official organ of the Irish Volunteers, published an article, "Down Among the Dead Men," commenting on George Russell's renunciation of violence as a nationalist policy. A.E. is rebuked for his apostasy, but in moderate terms; the writer's most stinging insults are reserved for Yeats and Thomas Rolleston, the poet and critic who had been first secretary of the Irish Literary Society of London:

> It would be inaccurate to bracket A.E. with Rolleston and Yeats. ...Rolleston and Yeats were poseurs in patriotism precisely as Chesterton is a poseur in Catholicism.
>
> Russell was distinct in many ways from these types which an enslaved nation develops.... Unlike Yeats, he was essentially a modest and unselfish man, and did not seek the incense.[15]

A bitter feeling had grown up among the extremists against Yeats, not because he had rejected the ideal of Irish nationality but rather because his definition of that ideal diverged more and more from the narrow, restrictive values of the Irish middle class. Years later, in 1943, Father Patrick J. Gannon, reviewing Joseph Hone's biography of the poet, looks back on the period preceding the 1916 rebellion and notes that Yeats "was always at loggerheads with the Catholic Celtic people of Ireland and lost no opportunity of expressing his contempt for them. Their religion was superstition, their morality hypocrisy or puritanism, their whole culture [except their folklore] stunted." Father Gannon adds that Catholic Celtic Ireland in turn "covered with ridicule" Yeats' "weird conception" of Ireland's sacred myth: "Thus contempt was answered with contempt, and a deep abyss was dug between Ireland and its most distinguished interpreter to the outer world." [16] Father Gannon mixes his chronology—the Catholic Celtic nationalists were surely first with their contempt—but his main point is perfectly true. During the early years of the twentieth century Yeats and the ideal of art which he represented became more and more isolated from the people of Ireland and, what is more significant, from the emerging generation of young poets who would gain prominent place in the movement in the years that followed.

Yeats and the other poets and scholars who founded the movement beguiled themselves with dreams of a new Ireland ennobled by the spirit of the ancient Celt. Ireland's heritage was a great and noble one; and by grasping at that heritage, the Irish people might again achieve the greatness and nobility that was the birthright of their race. In the eighteen-nineties, with the political scene calm and the Philistines muted, the moment for a cultural and spiritual renaissance seemed at hand. Years afterwards, Yeats was to recall the enthusiasm that at the time gripped him and his compatriots: "O what fine thought we had because we thought / That the worst rogues and rascals had died out." [17] But Yeats and the others were wrong. The contemporary Irishman had no desire to be ennobled. The "rogues and rascals" had not in fact died out. The poet's hopes for a great spiritual and cultural awakening were to prove ill-founded.

"Nations, races, and individual men," Yeats wrote in *The Trembling of the Veil* (p. 80), "are unified by an image, or bundle of related images." During the first two decades of the twentieth century, during the years leading up to the struggle for political independence, the people of Ireland were, indeed, joined together by means of a "bundle of related images"; however, these images were drawn not from Yeats' socio-religious vision nor from Hyde's concept of a Gaelic nation but from the body of sterile moral and political abstractions by which the Irish middle class justified its own existence. The people of Ireland responded to the clarion call for cultural revival, but they did so on their own terms. Men and women alike dressed themselves in colorful—at times outlandish—re-creations of traditional Celtic garments.[18] Some made pilgrimages in donkey carts to the western counties to immerse themselves, with a kind of religious fervor, in the native way of life. Some, like "the O'Rahilly," whom Yeats immortalized in a poem, prefaced their surnames with the definite article—in imitation of the old Gaels—to designate themselves chieftains of their clans. The Irish were more than willing to make public display of their nationality. But they were not prepared to engage in any soul-searching or to question seriously their own virtues or values.

It was not the Irish people but the literary and cultural movement that was destined to change. Gradually, inevitably, Irish society, Victorian in its morality, Philistine in its taste, sought to inflict its will upon the new literature; and the demands it made were basic ones. The concept of nationality which informed the movement must be redefined to correspond to the narrow idea of nationality in the popular imagination. Similarly, the poet's attitude and, indeed, even his aesthetic must be shaped to suit the artlessness and ignorance of the popular mind. Such a struggle between artist and society, between aesthetics and ethics, does not, of course, represent a problem peculiar to modern Ireland. Plato banned the poets from his Republic and the convention of Irish kings and clerics at Drumceat in 575 A.D. threatened the ancient Gaelic *filid* with the same fate; Cromwell's "crew" closed down London's theaters in the seventeenth century and so brought to an end one of the world's great periods of dramatic art; a host of contemporary artists of different nationalities have felt compelled to choose exile in order to escape the stultifying pressures of social conformity. What is remarkable about the conflict in modern Ireland, however, is that so many poets and writers not only accepted the restrictions imposed on their art by society but even undertook to enforce the restrictions on those less ready to submit. For a time, for as long as it took the middle class to grasp the significance of the cultural revival, the poet might express his newly discovered sense of nationality in his own way with relative impunity; eventually, however, freedom of expression gave way before a steadily increasing demand for conformity. What had been in the beginning a poetry of revelation, a poetry drawing its strength from the vision of the individual poet, became gradually a poetry of recognition, a poetry bound to a restrictive convention imposed by a society, the appreciation of which was postulated as the sole measure of a poet's worth.

That the society's demands, when they were at last formulated, should have been so inflexible and so restrictive was due in some part at least to the failure of the Gaelic League to gain its primary objective. The founders of the League—Hyde, O'Hickey, Dr. George Sigerson—had envisioned a great popular movement which would restore the Gaelic tongue as the universal spoken and written language of the Irish people. In the early years the League had been uncompromising: Irish nationality without the Irish language would be no more than an empty phrase. But this position became less and less tenable as the years passed; the great majority of the Irish people simply refused to make the effort necessary to relearn a language discarded by their grandfathers. Of necessity some new criterion for nationality had to be defined. In what ways could the Irishman, deprived of his distinctive language, be distinguished from other men, and in particular, from Englishmen? As a matter of fact, throughout the revival the poets had been searching out those peculiarities in their countrymen which were "most racial, most Gaelic, most Irish"; but the poets were vague and some of them—notably Yeats and A.E., who were unorthodox in philosophy and religion—were unreliable. Irish nationalism required a more precise, more literal delineation of the national literary and historical heritage and of the unique character—intellectual, emotional, and spiritual—of the Irish people.

The demand for a new image of nationality became an important factor in the cultural and literary movement after the turn of the century. Arthur Griffith founded his Sinn Féin Party, a political and cultural organization dedicated to the task of reconciling the traditions of Celtic civilization with the morals and mores of the contemporary middle class. Griffith and the journalists who wrote for his popular newspaper became the watchdogs of Irish Philistinism; they revived all the malicious anger and hatred that had swept Ireland during the Parnell controversy and then, like God's avenging angels, turned upon the cultural and literary movement. Sinn Féin, in its editorial columns and in the essays and verse it published, preached a vague creed of sentimentality and puritanism; but most of its efforts were devoted to attacks on Yeats and the Abbey Theatre, on John Synge, and on anyone or anything else Griffith considered offensive. The newspaper's vitriolic campaign against The Playboy of the Western World represents a low point in the national movement. Yeats was entirely justified in the bitter language he used to describe those who were responsible for the narrow, cruel attacks upon Synge: they were "Paudeens" who, when confronted by an image of great passionate art, whether Don Juan in Hell or Christy Mahon in a village in County Mayo, could only "rail and sweat / Staring upon his sinewy thigh." [19] Nevertheless, Griffith and Sinn Féin won wide support in a nation moving steadily toward an armed struggle for political independence. Vituperation became an accepted tool of Irish criticism; and for many years a bigoted, obscurant approach to art and literature—the approach of Sinn Féin—influenced for the worse the course of Irish letters.

More significant than Sinn Féin with regard to the subsequent course of Irish verse was the development of a poetry of "peasant realism" in the early years of the century. Padraic Colum was not the first to traffic in this kind of verse—Ethna Carbery [20] had been writing of country life for some time and even Yeats in certain of his early poems anticipates the genre—but Colum was the most gifted poet to identify himself with the new school and in his work the ideal of a peasant nation is given fullest expression. The term "realism" has validity when applied to Colum's poetry—or to that of Miss Carbery or Joseph Campbell—only in a superficial sense. The props which Colum employs for local color—cottages, fields and roads, cows, donkeys, and gabbling geese—are real in that they are the physical paraphernalia of the country scene; but in Colum's verse the mores and morals of the Irish country people—which in the end are the poet's basic concerns—are obviously subjected to purposeful distortion. Colum employs various means to romanticize the peasant, but his most remarkable technique consists of a rather startling inversion of traditional concepts attaching to human behavior. He equates meanness with nobility, subservience with heroism, sentimentality with intense passion, religiosity and superstition with spirituality, ignorance with wisdom, material greed with honest endeavor, craftiness with creative genius. Colum's definition of what he called the "national character" could not fail to win the acclaim of the patriotic extremists, if only because it gave the lie to the less palatable definition implicit in Synge's plays and to the explicit criticisms of Irish society that Yeats was making in certain of his poems.

It is noteworthy that much of Colum's early verse was first published in *Sinn Féin*. That Griffith and his followers should have admired the young midlander is not surprising; for his poetry of "peasant realism" gave substance to their own notion of what combination of virtues distinguished the true Irishman. The new poetry quickly won popular favor and captured the fancy of a host of lesser rhymesters. The peasant ideal became the dominant theme of Irish verse; and the practitioners of peasant poetry became, as Professor John V. Kelleher has noted, as numerous "as sands of the sea, or stars on a winter's night." [21]

In 1917, with the posthumous publication of Thomas MacDonagh's *Literature in Ireland*, the convention of "peasant realism" was given the imprimatur of scholarly criticism. By then the dream of a Gaelic people with a literature of their own had faded. Hyde, Pearse, Sigerson, Joseph Campbell, and others had composed prose and poetry in Irish; [22] and Hyde's play, *Casadh an tSúgáin* (*The Twisting of the Rope*), performed by members of the Gaelic League, had led to the establishment of a Gaelic theater; [23] but, clearly, the embryonic Gaelic literature could not be compared with the burgeoning Anglo-Irish literary movement. What MacDonagh proclaims in his study is not a revival of Gaelic letters but rather the emergence of a new national literature that "could come only when English had become the language of the Irish people, mainly of Gaelic stock," a literature written in English but devoted to the expression of Irish manners, customs, traditions, and outlook as they affect social manners, religion, and morality.[24] MacDonagh also provides aesthetic justification for the new literature; he discusses at great length the ways in which the peculiarities of Irish speech and the transference of techniques of rhyme and meter from Gaelic prosody give to the new Anglo-Irish poetry distinctive cadences. Unique subject matter and unique sound combine into what he terms the "Irish Mode" of verse.

MacDonagh was not himself a narrow critic; for instance, he recognized Yeats' achievement as a poet and, in fact, cites certain of Yeats' poems—although, significantly, the earliest poems as a rule—to illustrate his own ideas concerning the new literature. Nevertheless, in his book MacDonagh affirms the popular, middle-class attitude toward art. In the context of his essay the assertion that the Irish poets should express various facets of the Irish heritage as "they *affect* social manners, religion and morality" [my italics] comes to mean that the poets should express their heritage as it is *determined* by social manners, religion, and morality. What is most noteworthy about MacDonagh's criticism is that he all but ignores the question of the poet's individual vision. He implies that for the Irish poet both the nature of his vision and the means for giving it expression are predetermined. The poet has only to give himself to the convention and the convention in turn will guarantee his art.

The literary creed formulated in *Literature in Ireland* inevitably led to a further narrowing and hardening of the nationalist approach to literature and criticism. The extent to which the Irish eventually came to equate literary excellence with adherence to the popular convention is suggested in this comment by A.E. in *The Irish Statesman:*

After long despair about the vanishing Irish culture we have come to have power through an Irish state to mould the cultural character of the people. Nothing is more natural or right than that everything possible should be done to blow the dying Gaelic fire into a blaze, and in every way to preserve and intensify those national characters. I do not protest against this. I only assert that we cannot intellectually be self-sustaining any more than England, France, Italy or Germany could be intellectually self-sustaining. We must penetrate the Irish culture with world wisdom, or it will cease to be a culture, and our literature will lose its vitality and become a literature of conventions.[25]

The warning came much too late. By the time A.E. took pen in hand in 1929 Irish poetry and prose had long since become a literature of convention. To be sure, James Joyce, working on *Finnegans Wake*, was attempting to give to human language new mythic dimensions and Yeats was following his artistic vision into "the black mass of Eden" where Crazy Jane promised "Unity of Being" through sexual passion. But Joyce and Yeats were the exceptions. Irish literature had bogged down in a morass of its own choosing; it had surrendered its creative energy to a prefabricated formula, the "Irish Mode" of the peasant ideal. How could one best combine the soft rhythms of Thomas Moore with the primitive chant of Amergin (traditionally the first poet of Ireland)? How could one escape the corruption of alien thought? How could one set forth most convincingly the case for peasant religion, peasant morality, and peasant culture? The recipe for poetry was simple; and almost without exception the poets confined their efforts to finding the right ingredients and mixing them in proper proportion.

The more Irish verse adhered to the aesthetic standard of popular nationalism the more sterile it became. Sound was exalted above sense, artlessness above intellect. Martin Douras in Padraic Colum's play, *The Land*, proclaims what was to become the creed of the Irish poets when he asserts that "a man farming the land, with a few books on his shelf and a few books in head, had more of the scholar's life about him than the young fellows who do be teaching in schools and teaching in colleges." [26] The convention of the peasant ideal inflicted upon Irish letters the peculiar notion that "bog wisdom"—the wisdom of half-learning acquired "by the dim rush-light / In smoky cabins" [27]—was the ideal toward which all Irishmen should strive. Irish literature gradually divorced itself from the mind, and a cult of naïveté gained ascendancy: poets should feel, not think. Such an obscurantist attitude was not likely to engender great art. Popular nationalism had discovered in the artless culture of the country people a kind of literary Pandora's box; Colum and Joseph Campbell dared to open it; and then, in the words of F. R. Higgins,

> out crawled our poetic grubs—
> Those ancient lights from shadowy pubs—
> With rhythms rheumatic and a rub-a-dub-dubs
> Of paralytic rhyming.[28]

Without doubt the popular convention inflicted upon Irish literature an aesthetic paralysis not unlike the sleeping sickness which, according to legend, was visited upon the Red Branch heroes of ancient Ireland in times of impending danger. The creed of mediocrity implicit in the convention could not have done otherwise than inhibit and limit poetry.

In the late nineteen-twenties and early nineteen-thirties, the Irish literati turned against the romantic sentiment of the convention and the narrow puritanism of popular morality; but their revolt, admirable in certain respects, did not in fact revitalize Irish verse. The poets seem to have recognized that something, somewhere, had gone wrong with the literary movement and almost invariably they sought to blame the breakdown on one or another element of Irish society. F. R. Higgins' later poetry, by its repeated demand for "books without censors," implies that the Irish government had crippled Irish verse by legislative act. Patrick Kavanagh, who has made a life's career of complaint and protest, condemns Ireland's romantic nostalgia for the past:

> Culture is always something that was,
> Something pedants can measure:
> Skull of bard, thigh of chief,
> Depth of dried-up river.
> Shall we be thus forever?
> Shall we be thus forever? [29]

Of the more recent Irish poets only one, Austin Clarke, has succeeded in translating his disillusion and anger into an artistic achievement of merit. Clarke directs a relentless, at times savage satire against the Roman Church and the middle-class establishment in Ireland and against Christian morality in general; and the intensity of his wrath gives to his verse a unique if narrow power. But Clarke is an exception. The others have recognized the symptoms of decline and they have tried to place the blame on anything and everything in sight; yet they have ignored the real cause of their failure—their own intellectual laziness. They have repudiated the old romanticism and sentimentality; but they have clung to the most romantic and sentimental illusion of all—the ideal of "bog wisdom," the naïve belief that great poetry is an inevitable by-product of untutored, undisciplined emotion, that great art is a spontaneous expression of racial character. Bent on reform of some sort, the poets have demanded the overthrow of the old order; but quite clearly they have felt no compulsion to establish a new order in its place.

In a sense, the appearance of Sean O'Faolain's magazine, *The Bell*, in the spring of 1940 signaled the end of the Irish poetic revival. Yeats had been dead for a year; and Yeats, of all the Irish poets, had most consistently maintained his integrity as an artist against the threats and blandishments of a Philistine society. All the others, in one way or another, had been subverted by popular pressures. In the initial issue of his magazine, O'Faolain renounces the romantic attitude in which the Irish movement had been conceived; and he rejects all of the "old symbolic words" which he believed were symptomatic of that attitude: "They are as dead as Brian Boru, Granuaile, the Shan Van Vocht, Banba, Roisin Dubh, Fodhla, Cathleen ni Houlihan, the swords of light and the risings of the moon." O'Faolain recognizes that the moment for poetry is past; but, significantly, he has no alternative to offer for the old symbolism he rejects: "THE BELL has, in the usual sense of the word, no policy. We leave it to nature to give the magazine its own time-created character." [30] Inevitably, however, *The Bell* became a vehicle for social criticism and for a prose literature, short story and essay, into which such criticism might be incorporated. The popular convention had deprived Irish verse of its imaginative vitality and its creative intellect; and the best of the new literary artists—O'Faolain himself, Mary Lavin, Frank O'Connor—turned their talents in another direction.[31]

2

THE IRISH HERITAGE

The poets of the literary revival did not suddenly discover that Ireland possessed a cultural heritage of its own. The Irish writer, many critics have pointed out, had always been concerned with questions of national and cultural identity: "He was haunted by history, and his thoughts returned, again and again, to the living bones of the past." [1] One may, indeed, with some justification, go back into the nineteenth century to find the precursors of the revival: to the novels of John Banin, Gerald Griffin, and William Carleton; to the verse of Samuel Ferguson, James Clarence Mangan, and Thomas Moore; to the scholarly work of John O'Donovan and Eugene O'Curry. One might even say that Thomas Davis and the other poets of the *Nation* helped to stir up interest in the myth of nationality, though their motives in doing so were primarily political rather than literary or cultural.

But despite the labors of these few, the old Gaelic heritage was dying; the "living bones" were becoming fossils. During the nineteenth century the Irishman had come to regard his heritage as a curiosity of antiquity, as something to be carefully preserved in library and museum. Daniel O'Connell's famous remark on the decline of the Irish language typifies the ambivalent attitude of nineteenth-century Ireland toward its

own culture: "I am sufficiently utilitarian not to regret its
gradual abandonment. A diversity of tongues is of no benefit; it
was first imposed on mankind as a curse, at the building of
Babel. It would be of vast advantage to mankind if all the
inhabitants of the earth spoke the same language. Therefore,
although the Irish language is connected with many recollections that twine around the hearts of Irishmen, yet the superior
utility of the English tongue, as the medium of all modern
communications, is so great that I can witness without a sigh
the gradual disuse of Irish." [2] The nineteenth century in
Victorian England and on the continent was a period of
pragmatism and materialism, the age of John Stuart Mill and
Thomas Gradgrind; and Ireland did not escape the spirit of the
times. Whatever their nostalgia for the Celtic past—and
whatever their admitted political contributions to Ireland's
history—Daniel O'Connell became an "English" orator and
politician, Thomas Davis an "English" journalist, and even
Charles Stuart Parnell an "English" parliamentarian. When
he was elected Lord Mayor of Dublin, O'Connell pledged
himself not to reviving Irish culture but to "the spread of
teetotalism." [3] One need not be surprised that the average
nineteenth-century Irishman perceived in the old Gaelic culture little more than what Baudelaire found in the ancient art
of Mexico, Egypt, and Assyria—"an ineluctable, synthetic,
childish barbarism." [4]

Fundamentally, the revival of the eighteen-nineties was
meant to counteract this tendency on the part of the Irish
people to regard the Celtic past as a dead letter. The founders
of the language and literature movements wished to take their
heritage out of the libraries and museums and restore it as a
meaningful element in Irish life. This was the gist of Douglas
Hyde's exhortation in 1892 to the members of the National
Literary Society that they should "cultivate everything that is
most racial, most Gaelic, most Irish"; and it was the point, too,
a half century later of Yeats' final admonition to the Irish poets
in "Under Ben Bulben":

> Sing the peasantry, and then
> Hard-riding country gentlemen,
> The holiness of monks, and after
> Porter-drinkers' randy laughter;
> Sing the lords and ladies gay
> That were beaten into clay
> Through seven heroic centuries;
> Cast your minds on other days
> That we in coming days may be
> Still the indomitable Irishry.[5]

The Irish literati, with few exceptions, were quick to respond to the summons; almost self-consciously they sought to recapture and revivify the triumphs and tragedies, the joys and sorrows of their race and nation. Indeed, if the poets of the literary movement had any one thing in common, it was an inclination to turn to the national heritage for subject material and inspiration.

Just what was this cultural heritage of the Irish people? In fact, it defies precise definition. For one thing, as Edmund Curtis observes in his study of Ireland's history, the "traditions of the Irish people are the oldest of any race in Europe north and west of the Alps, and they themselves are the longest settled on their own soil." [6] For another, Ireland's chaotic history has served to tangle and confuse elements of different cultures—Celtic, Danish, Norman, English—so that it becomes almost fruitless to try to decide what is Irish and what is not. Nevertheless, the poets were willing enough to define Ireland's heritage—though they rarely agreed among themselves as to what it should properly include. Moreover, certain strands from Ireland's past held a particular fascination for them and, for that reason, have a special relevance to their verse.

From the very beginning, the poets steeped themselves in their nation's history. Guided by their newly found racial consciousness, they discovered not the official English account of the Crown's patient efforts to civilize an unruly rabble, but rather a moving chronicle of tragic heroism and suffering under foreign oppression. They found, too, a spirit of perseverance

equal to that of the Jews; for in Ireland terror, persecution, and
privation seemed to have followed one upon the other through
centuries without respite—the ravages of the Norse invaders
who extinguished the "light of learning and piety" of the great
Irish monasteries and who for two hundred years were a source
of dread to the native Irish; the coming of the Normans with
their mail shirts and iron helmets, with their impregnable
castles, and with their feudal law that relegated Irish freemen
to the status of serfs; the Elizabethan and Cromwellian planta-
tions that deprived the Irish of almost all their land and
pressed them further into a condition of servitude; the in-
famous penal laws designed to "bar the Roman Catholics from
the land, the army, the electorate, commerce, and the law";
and the "Great Famine" of 1845–48, during which hunger,
fever, and emigration reduced Ireland's population by more
than one and a half millions.

The poets found in their nation's history villains enough
upon whom to heap their scorn—Diarmuid Mac Murchadha
(Dermot Mac Murrough) who brought the first Normans to
Ireland and upon whom the historian Curtis passes judgment:
"This bad man was to be the ultimate cause of the loss of
Ireland's independence"; local tyrants like Sir Richard Bingham of Connacht and his brother, Captain John Bingham,
who indulged in cruelty without restraint and who treacher-
ously murdered Owen, son of Gráinne Ní Mháille (Grace
O'Malley), the famed pirate-queen of the western coast; all of
the English kings, excepting the Stuarts, and most of their
governors, lord lieutenants, and ministers in Ireland; and, most
pernicious of all, Oliver Cromwell, who, after he had put to the
sword the entire population of Drogheda, could pray "that all
honest hearts may give the glory of this to God alone" and who
with his army of Protestant zealots turned Ireland into a land
where one "might travel twenty or thirty miles . . . and not
see a living creature." [7] The Irish people to the present day use
his name for their bitterest malediction, "the curse of Crom-

well," an imprecation which Yeats chose as the title for an equally bitter poem.

Too frequently modern Irish verse and prose are described as a "literature of lamentation," which some Irish commentators ascribe to a "thousand years of persecution and hardship and suffering" [8] and which the American scholar, John V. Kelleher, attributes to "too many failures" by Irish revolutionary and constitutional movements. Indeed, Professor Kelleher, whose point of view is representative of much British and American criticism, argues that defeatism is an essential element in the aesthetic of modern Irish verse. "Poetry in Ireland," he maintains, "would have to accept the atmosphere of defeat as its first ingredient; and out of defeat and melancholy it must somehow make the ultimate victory not only credible but expected." [9] Kelleher's contention represents at best a partial truth. To be sure, one may cite a considerable body of verse that is melancholy in tone; yet modern Irish verse more often proclaims a proud spirit of heroic action than the sadness of defeat. Padraic Pearse hung a picture of Cú Chulainn above the front door of St. Enda's School to inspire his students to heroic deeds, not to stir in them a sense of self-pity. Yeats' Cathleen ni Houlihan asks the Irish peasants to fight and die for her, not merely to weep.

Irish history provided the poets with a list of great heroes who had taken up the cause of the Gael against the foreigner, the Gall—a name successively given by the Irish to the Norse, the original Normans and all subsequent English invaders. There was Brian Boru, who united the Irish septs and who as an old man overthrew the Northmen at the Battle of Clontarf on Good Friday, April 23, 1014, and ended the Viking terror of two hundred years. There was the rash "Silken Thomas," Earl of Offaly and deputy for King Henry VIII in Ireland, who, on hearing a false report that his father had been murdered in the Tower of London, told the Council of State in Dublin: "I am none of Henry's deputies. I am his foe." Offaly's rebellion, hopeless from the start, was short-lived and the young lord was executed afterwards; but his gallant gesture lived on in Irish history.[10] There was the proud Shane O'Neill, who outwitted Elizabeth's courtiers and outfought her generals and who sent back her emissaries with the pronouncement: "My ancestors were kings of Ulster and Ulster is mine and shall be mine." There were Hugh O'Neill and Red Hugh O'Donnell, who led the great Confederacy of the North in the last stand of the old Gaelic order in the Tyrone War of 1594–1603; [11] and there was Hugh O'Neill's nephew, Owen Roe O'Neill, who led the Catholic Confederacy of 1642–49 and who, had he not died, might have championed the Irish against Cromwell. There was Sarsfield, hero of the Irish Jacobites, who after the Treaty of Limerick served the king of France and died in battle against the English in 1693 after having cried out, "Oh, that this were for Ireland." Finally, there were the equally courageous if more pathetic heroes of later years—Wolfe Tone and Robert Emmet of the ill-fated United Irishmen; John O'Leary and O'Donovan Rossa of the Fenians; and, in the midst of the cultural revival itself, the heroes of 1916, among them the poets Pearse, MacDonagh, and Plunkett. What the poets found in their nation's history was a remarkable spirit of resistance against foreign rule, a spirit which centuries of bloodshed and oppression could not quell.

Another important aspect of the national heritage is the history of Christianity in Ireland. Partly because it was isolated from Rome for more than a century as a result of the Anglo-Saxon conquest of Britain and the Frankish conquest of Gaul and partly because of the nature of Gaelic society, the Irish Church evolved as a monastic rather than an episcopal organization. The great saints of Ireland were the founders of monasteries and religious houses for women—Colmcille (Columba), Ciarán, Brendan, and Brigid. Of all the saints, even including Patrick, Colmcille was held in highest esteem by the old Gaelic people; for he was not only a prince of the Church but a prince of the blood as well, a descendant of Niall of the

Nine Hostages. Colmcille established religious communities at Derry and Durrow; afterwards, when he had gone into self-imposed exile for having been the cause of a great battle in which thousands were slain, he founded the great monastery on Iona, which for three centuries was renowned throughout Europe as a center of holiness and learning. From Irish poets Colmcille could claim special allegiance, for in the sixth century he saved the *filid*, the professional poets, from being expelled from the land. Padraic Colum, in his *Legend of Saint Columba*, relates the story, no doubt apocryphal in its details, of the saint's intervention on behalf of the poets at the convention of Drumceat in 575 A.D. A proposal had been made that the poets should be banned from Ireland for abusing their privileges. When a prelate condemned poems as being mere fables, Colmcille replied:

> If the poets' verse be fable,
> Then is all your knowledge fable.
> All your rights and state and power,
> And this drifting world is fable.

Colmcille's words won over the convention; and although certain reforms were imposed on them, the poets remained a privileged class until the final collapse of the Gaelic order more than a thousand years later in 1603.[12]

The lives of the early saints are wrapped about with the trappings of make-believe; the legend inevitably obscures the historical reality. More substantial and equally impressive are the achievements of the monastic system itself. The monasteries were in the Middle Ages the bastions of civilization for Ireland and, during the seventh and eighth centuries, for the entire western world. The Irish monasteries sent to Europe missionaries and learned men—Columbanus, for example, who restored the faith to Lombardy and Burgundy in the seventh century, and John Scotus, the great Neo-Platonist, who in the ninth century became chief professor at the palace school of the Emperor Charles the Bald of France. The monks at

Durrow and Iona and other houses developed manuscript illumination to the level of magnificent art, as certain of the extant Celtic masterpieces, such as the Book of Kells and the Lindisfarne Gospels, vividly demonstrate. The dedicated scribes gave to Ireland another art as well, that of lyric verse, which was probably unknown to the pagan *filid*. Much of this early poetry was written in the margins of manuscripts and some of it has a unique and splendid beauty. The following quatrain, for instance, preserved in the St. Gall Manuscript, was composed by a monk during the Viking terror:

> Fierce and wild is the wind to-night,
> it tosses the tresses of the sea to white;
> on such a night as this I take my ease;
> fierce Northmen only course the quiet seas.[13]

Eventually the bards adopted the genre and in the centuries that followed developed its Latinate technique into increasingly intricate systems of prosody.

The Viking raids of the ninth century ushered in a period of decline for the great Celtic monasteries. The sea-kings from the North plundered Orkney, Shetland, and the Hebrides; and in 830 A.D. the monks of Iona were forced to flee to the mainland of Ireland with the relics of Colmcille. The fortunes of the Irish Church became more and more dependent upon the successes of the Gaelic chieftains. Although the monastic system survived until the time of Henry VIII, its golden age was past. A brief reflowering of art and literature took place in the reign of Brian Boru; but after his death the Irish lords took to squabbling among themselves, and then, in the twelfth century, the Normans landed. Ironically, during the first three centuries of their struggle against English invaders, the Irish often asked for support from the Church in Rome but rarely received it. In 1172 Pope Alexander III sent one letter to the Irish bishops condemning the evil ways of the Gaelic people and another to England's Henry II commending him for the reforms he was carrying out in Ireland. In 1317 a combination

of Irish chieftains, supporters of Edward Bruce, brother of the
King of Scots, sent to Pope John XXII a remonstrance against
English oppression; but their only reply was a bull of excom-
munication against Bruce and all his adherents. At the close of
the fifteenth century the Irish lords supported the Yorkist
pretender against Henry VII, the usurper; but the pope
confirmed Henry's right to the throne. Even in the late
nineteenth century Pope Leo XIII on several occasions pub-
licly condemned the Irish land agitation, and in 1882 he
forbade Catholics to contribute to a "national tribute" for
Parnell.

Despite these occasional rebuffs by Rome, the Irish demonstrated their remarkable loyalty to their religion, as few other
peoples have done, by suffering in its cause for hundreds of
years. Nor would it be just to suggest that the Church of Rome
remained indifferent to their plight. Elizabeth was excommunicated in 1570, the Church having despaired of winning
her back to the fold, and thereafter great efforts were made to
secure the Irish people in the faith. Edmund Spenser in his
View of the State of Ireland testified to the courage and
perseverance of the Jesuits sent to Ireland after the native
clergy had been outlawed: "For they spare not to come out of
Spain and from Rome by long toil and dangerous travelling,
where they know peril of death awaiteth them and no reward
or riches are to be found, only to draw the people unto the
Church of Rome." [14] At Aughrim, the final battle of the
Jacobite War in 1691, there were priests urging the Irish army
"to die or conquer for the Faith." There were priests, too,
Father John Murphy of Boolavogue and Father Michael
Murphy, among the leaders of the Wexford Rising of 1798.
Indeed, even during the land agitation certain of the Irish
bishops supported the peasants despite the pope's admonition
to the contrary.[15] Most important of all, the longer the struggle
against England continued, the more the cause of Catholicism
became identified in men's minds with the cause of Irish
political freedom; the mass of the Irish people clung to their

religion as a mark of nationality and even of race. One need not be surprised that religion was looked upon as an essential part of the national heritage by many of the modern poets and that some of them incorporated the values and beliefs of Irish Catholicism into their verse.

A third major strand of the national heritage of the Irish poets consists of the literature of ancient Ireland, a literature which was written down and preserved for posterity by the monastic scribes but which in many instances finds its origin in the oral tradition of the pre-Christian era. This inheritance from the old Celtic civilization which scholars found in collections of manuscripts is a massive one; the task of editing and translating is still far from complete a century after O'Donovan and O'Curry.[16] The extant manuscripts include great bodies of material that are not specifically literary although valuable for historical and anthropological studies of Celtic civilization; annals, histories, topographies, law tracts, medical and scientific treatises, and works of philosophy. They include also much narrative and elegiac poetry (besides the marginal lyrics), numerous homilies and saints' lives from the early Christian period, many romantic and pseudo-historical tales, and Gaelic renderings of classical and medieval literatures, often freely adapted for local taste.[17] Most significant, however, as far as modern Anglo-Irish verse is concerned, are the three principal cycles of saga material—the mythological, the Ulster, and the Fenian (or Ossianic).

The mythological tales which make up the first cycle are concerned with the struggles of the pre-Celtic races for possession of Ireland and the ultimate conquest of Ireland by the Goidelic Celts under the leadership of the Sons of Mil, who defeated the Tuatha Dé Danann, the tribes of the Goddess Danu, killing the three ruling kings, Brian, Iuchair, and Iucharba, descendants of the Dagda (the Good God), and their queens, Éire, Fodhla, and Banbha, whom Robert Graves describes as the triple goddess of the pagan Irish.[18] Vanquished, the Tuatha Dé Danann took refuge in palaces beneath the hills of Ireland, from which during the centuries that followed they came forth at will to take part in the affairs of men. The cycle also contains several stories which have all the wonder and romance of fairy tales. One of the most charming is that called "The Wooing of Étain," which relates the tribulations and final happiness of a lovely and gentle woman, beloved of both fairy and mortal. At one point, Étain is transformed into a pool of water, from a pool of water into a worm, and from a worm into a beautiful purple fly. In the form of a fly she is carried away by a magic wind to seven years of misery upon the rocks and waves of the sea; afterwards, she falls into a woman's cup, is swallowed, and at length is reborn as the woman's daughter. Another charming story is "The Tragedy of the Children of Lir." Lir's daughter, Fionnguala (Whiteshoulders), and his three sons, Aedh, Fiachra, and Conn, are transformed into swans by their jealous stepmother and must remain in that form until they have spent three hundred years on Lake Derryvaragh, three hundred years by the Mull of Cantre in Scotland, and three hundred years in Erris and around Inish-glory. When the curse at last runs its course, the swans return to their home at Síd Finnachaid only to find it deserted, without house or shelter of any kind, without hounds or women or lords. Fionnguala speaks a lay of sorrow: "Formerly this place was not left to grass and forest. All that we knew are dead, and we are here. It is strange." [19]

The tales of the Ulster cycle, which follow those of the mythological cycle in the pseudo-chronology of Irish legend, are concerned with the heroic deeds of the Ulaid, a warlike race that dwelt in northeastern Ireland in a remote period, traditionally set in the century preceding the birth of Christ. The principal tale of the cycle is *Táin Bó Cúalnge* (*The Cattle Raid of Cooley*), an epic-like narrative written for the most part in prose with verse interspersed for emotional heightening.[20] The central focus of the *Táin* and of the Ulster cycle in general is upon the titanic figure of Cú Chulainn, a reincarnation of the god Lug of the Long Arm. Cú Chulainn, who is capable of prodigious feats of strength, holds off the invading armies of Queen Medb (Maeve) single-handed. At one point in the story Cú Chulainn, angered by the death in battle of the boy-warriors of Ulster, is possessed—as Odysseus was possessed in his fight against the suitors in Homer's epic—and suffers a physical distortion:

He gulped down one eye into his head so that it would be hard work if a wild crane succeeded in drawing it out to the middle of his cheek from the rear of his skull. Its mate sprang forth till it came out on his cheek, so that it was the size of a five-fist kettle, and he made a red berry thereof out in front of his head. His mouth was distorted monstrously and twisted up to his ears....There were seen the torches of the Badb, and the rain clouds of poison, and the sparks of glowing red fire, blazing and flashing in hazes and mists over his head with the seething of the truly wild wrath that rose up above him. His hair bristled all over his head like branches of a redthorn thrust into a gap in a great hedge.[21]

Afterwards, concerned that the frightful shape he wore into battle might dishonor him, Cú Chulainn displays his great physical beauty to the women and the poets.[22]

The Ulster cycle contains more than one hundred tales in all; and in many of them Cú Chulainn does not figure prominently. One of the most impressive of these is the saga entitled "The Destruction of Da Derga's Hostel," which depends for its construction and movement on the Celtic system of *gessa*, prohibitions or taboos which, according to tradition, governed the conduct of Irish kings.[23] Another, "The Death of the Sons of Uisnech," the story of Deirdre's tragic love, proved the most popular of the Irish sagas among the writers of the literary revival. Yeats, Lady Gregory, A.E., Synge, and Stephens, among others, adapted the ancient tale to their own work.

The Fenian cycle, consisting of both prose tales and ballads, became the most widely known of the major cycles among the people of Ireland and, perhaps because of its popularity, includes by far the greatest number of stories. The cycle is concerned with the adventures of Finn MacCumhaill and the hunter-warriors of his *fianna*, a military comradeship which flourished, according to tradition, during the reign of Cormac Mac Airt as high king in the third century. The stories and ballads run the full gamut of narrative categories to which the Gaelic *filid* gave themselves; voyages, courtships, slaughters, pursuits, and all the other classes of tales are represented. The most famous of the prose tales is "The Pursuit of Diarmuid and Gráinne," which is the story of Finn's jealousy, Diarmuid's nobility, and Gráinne's fickle selfishness. The Irish scholar Myles Dillon has shown that the tale is ultimately a variant of the story of Deirdre: both episodes, he notes, involve "the tragedy of a young girl betrothed to an old man and of the conflict between passion and duty on the part of her lover. In both cases death is the price of love." [24]

The sagas represent a literary achievement of some merit. The impartial reader will not discover in them—as Padraic Pearse did—"all the hidden splendours of the world"; [25] but he will certainly find much more than the worthless muddle scoffed at by Professor John Pentland Mahaffy and his colleagues at Trinity College in the early days of the cultural revival. The stories of all three cycles probably find their origin in pagan religious myth. The mythological cycle retains many elements that are magical or supernatural. The Ulster and Fenian cycles, on the other hand, have been subjected to considerable revision and interpolation, the former at the hands of literary craftsmen who apparently sought to convert the saga of Cú Chulainn, Medb, and Conchobhar into a national epic patterned after the *Aeneid*, the latter by popular bards who humanized and romanticized the tales to win greater favor with more vulgar audiences. Perhaps in part because of the nature of their evolution, the sagas are artistically defective. *Táin Bó Cúalnge* for example, in the versions that are extant, certainly lacks unity—according to one prominent scholar, the *Táin* is "jerky and episodic" and "the merest hotch-potch" in its construction. [26] To the original ancient story, which probably centered on the struggle of the dark bull and the white bull, there have been added numerous interpolations ranging from scenes of broad humor to the series of Homeric single combats at the ford.[27] Nevertheless, the very fact that the saga is an admixture of esoteric, heroic, and comic motifs renders it mysterious and, for that reason, fascinating. Certainly the Irish poets found it so.

The fourth aspect of the national heritage of Anglo-Irish verse is the popular tradition which includes both what Thomas MacDonagh termed the "ways of life . . . and ways of thought" of the Irish people and the literature in which those ways of life and thought are given expression. The Gaelic League had chosen as its principal goal the preservation of whatever survived in Ireland of the old Gaelic world; as a result Irish enthusiasts, suddenly conscious of their racial identity, focused their interest on the peasant culture of the Gaeltacht, the Irish-speaking counties in the West and South. Gradually the definition of Irish folk tradition was broadened in order to take in the life and popular literature of other rural areas of Ireland, where the Gaelic origin of customs was less sure and where the spoken and written language of the people was English. One cannot deny that the popular tradition in Ireland has produced some lovely poetry. In Douglas Hyde's translation, "If I Were to Go West," a love complaint from western Ireland, a girl speaks of a faithless lover:

> My heart is as black as a sloe,
> Or as a black coal that would be burnt in a forge,
> As the sole of a shoe upon white halls,
> And there is great melancholy over my laughter.[28]

Hyde's translation, with its homely metaphor and halting rhythm, captures a sense of bare emotion. But the verse of the peasantry is often heavy with sentiment or weighted with one or another affectation; at times it is vulgar.

The popular tradition is related to each of the other three strands of the Irish national heritage. History and religion provide important themes for the folk literature, but in popular poem or story the given historical incident or religious value is invariably simplified, romanticized, and sentimentalized. Again, it must be conceded that the popular tradition is in certain respects derivative from the tradition of old Celtic Ireland embodied in the formal literature of the manuscripts; yet, surely, the gulf between is wide. In both substance and form, the living culture which the poets sought among the Irish peasants was but a decadent survival of the old way. One finds, for example, curious relics of Irish myth and legend in modern folk Ireland. The topography of its rivers, valleys, and hills is resplendent with allusions—the twin mountains in County Kerry, known as the Paps, echo back through the centuries to the Mother Goddess of the pre-Celts—but by the end of the nineteenth century the significance of the place names had been lost or largely dissipated. The banshee and leprechaun are strangely diminished and transfigured descendants of the heroic Tuatha Dé Danann, who, according to the myth, a thousand years before the birth of Christ marched out to battle the invading Milesians:

> White shields they carry in their hands,
> White emblems of pale silver;
> With glittering blue swords,
> With mighty stout horns.[29]

Then, too, the techniques of versification used in the composition of popular ballads and songs represent at best a debasement of the intricate prosody of the bardic schools.

These, then, are the four major strands of the national heritage of modern Anglo-Irish poetry—the political history of Ireland, the Roman Catholic religious tradition, the heritage of ancient Irish literature, and the popular tradition, cultural and literary, of the Irish countryside. Each of the poets included in this study demonstrates what Thomas MacDonagh refers to as "national consciousness" in that each takes much of the substance of his art—theme, metaphor, even technique—from one or more of these areas. However, "national consciousness" is at best a nebulous term; and there are other questions which must be answered before one can measure the real significance of Irish tradition in modern Anglo-Irish verse. What kind of material does the poet take from tradition? What is his attitude toward that material? To what use does he put it in his own work? Invariably, the poets interpreted the national heritage according to their peculiar aesthetic and philosophic conceptions.

For example, each of the poets found in the old saga literature only what he wished to find. Thomas MacDonagh could not comprehend the mystical interpretation which Yeats and A.E. gave to Irish legend and he was frank in his disapproval: "Now new religions are made out of half-understood passages of the old literature, India, of course, contributing whatever is not to be found in these. If anyone has a favorite theory of the invisible world, he can use the translation of an obscure old Irish poem for text." [30] Mac-Donagh, of course, was wrong; the sagas were built upon the foundations of religious meaning—old religions, not new ones—and subsequent scholarship has demonstrated the close relationship between Celtic and Indian literatures, a relationship that Yeats understood intuitively.[31] Yeats and A.E. searched the old sagas for esoteric meanings and found them without difficulty. James Stephens—to judge from his renderings of the old stories in *Irish Fairy Tales* and *In the Land of Youth*—looked for human comedy and found it in abundance. Padraic Colum, seeking popular romance, invariably turns to the more romantic Fenian cycle for material and with equal consistency rejects what is esoteric in the saga in favor of what is prosaic and sentimental. All of the modern Irish poets turned to the old literature and to the other strands of the national heritage; and all purposefully selected those portions that would best serve their particular ends.

The primary focus of modern Irish poetry is not Ireland as it was in the past—not the Ireland of legend, popular myth, or history—but Ireland as it might be in the future. Each of the poets considered in this study attempts to define what it is that he desires for the Irish people. In certain of their works the outlines of an ideal nation are discernible. Yeats, for example, defines in his verse the ideal of an aristocratic society in which nobility and art might flourish side by side. A.E. argues for an Ireland peopled by god-men, seven feet tall. Colum proposes a nation of peasants, a nation founded on peasant values and celebrated by a popular peasant literature. In Higgins' verse one finds two contradictory visions, the first clearly a copy of Colum's, the second a poor imitation of Yeats'. In Stephens' poetry the ideal nation is given only the vaguest outline and in his later verse it is obscured completely; but what he desires for the Irish people, clearly enough, is that they practice the virtue of humane love. The verse of the Rising poets, Pearse, MacDonagh, and Plunkett, is concerned more with proclaiming the need for action to achieve political freedom than with defining the ideal Irish nation which might emerge after sovereignty had been won. Their ideal of Ireland is one of becoming rather than being; their vision is of the Irish people in holy rebellion against English tyranny. James Stephens expressed the attitude of the Irish poets toward their heritage when he wrote in 1922: "The past is a word to conjure with, it is a word to hypnotize with, but it is not a word to evoke reality. Reality is present action." [32]

3

W. B. YEATS: THE NATIONAL IDEALS

To define precisely the genesis of Yeats' attitude toward Ireland is perhaps impossible, but one can distinguish a number of major influences which helped shape his outlook. For one thing, as his autobiographical *Reveries* makes clear, Yeats as a youth formed a close and lasting attachment to the Sligo countryside with its curious mixture of Great Houses and peasant cottages, ancient burial grounds dating from the pagan and early Christian eras, quiet lakes and glens, and wind-swept mountain ranges—the whole scene wrapped about with a romantic cloak of legend and folklore. As a boy he had tramped around Lough Gill and spent a sleepless night in Slish Wood just across from the small island of Innisfree where it was his ambition to live, like Thoreau, in search of wisdom.[1] He had assimilated the local lore of the supernatural, wandered through the ancient raths and fairy mounds, and once, while walking at night with two cousins, had watched as a strange light ascended in five minutes' time the slope of Knocknarea toward Queen Medb's cairn—a feat he knew to be beyond human capability.[2] The place names, the history and folklore, the very way of life Yeats found in Sligo became an essential ingredient of his poetry. His earliest verse, despite its overtones of Indian philosophy, is rooted in County Sligo, and one finds running through it a catalogue of place names—Rosses, Glen-car, Lissadell—and a small anthology of local tales, "The Ballad of Father O'Hart," for example, and "The Ballad of Moll Magee." [3] It is certainly significant that at the close of his *Collected Poems* Yeats returns to Sligo and calls upon the fierce horsemen and horsewomen who "ride the wintry dawn / Where Ben Bulben sets the scene" to bear witness to his final artistic testament.[4]

The political turmoil which enveloped Ireland in the final decades of the nineteenth century also left its mark upon Yeats. Indeed, one commentator goes so far as to suggest that all the writers of the Irish movement, including Yeats, owe their inspiration to the single tragic episode of Parnell's fall and death.[5] Such an interpretation no doubt represents an over-simplification, even though Yeats and many others were deeply moved by the Parnell affair. But Yeats' initial contact with active nationalism came years earlier through his acquaintance with Charles Hubert Oldham, the leader of a political group at Trinity College, Dublin, and one of the founders in 1885 of the *Dublin University Review*, the journal in which Yeats' earliest verse was published.[6] One of his early efforts, "The Two Titans, a Political Poem," appeared in 1886; in it Yeats describes England as a monstrous sibyl with "foam-globes" bursting

> Over her spotted flesh and flying hair
> And her gigantic limbs. The weary thirst
> Unquenchable still glows in her dull stare,
> As round her, slow on feet that have no blood,
> The phantoms of her faded pleasures walk;
> And trailing crimson vans, a mumbling brood,
> Ghosts of her vanished glories, muse and stalk
> About the sea.

Ireland is represented as a "grey-haired youth" who is

> Worn with long struggles; and the waves have sung
> Their passion and their restlessness and ruth
> Through his sad soul for ever old and young,

> Till their fierce miseries within his eyes
> Have lit lone tapers.[7]

"The Two Titans" is, as Richard Ellmann has observed, a "preposterous poem." Somehow the allegory strikes a false note; the obvious representations of England as oppressor and Ireland as oppressed can only be regarded as oratorical, if not insincere. Certainly this kind of blunt sentiment does not reflect the kind of nationalism to which Yeats devoted himself, and one can readily understand his willingness to delete the poem from his canon.

Yeats discovered—perhaps in part created—a more compatible brand of nationalism in the person of the old Fenian, John O'Leary; for O'Leary, in Yeats' estimation, stood apart from the two-headed Cerberus of Irish political life—the Parnellite and anti-Parnellite factions, each seemingly obsessed with devouring the other.[8] Then again, O'Leary's beliefs closely paralleled the poet's own. He abhorred violence and would shun old friends if he suspected them of terrorism; he fought all his life against constitutional politicians who he believed degraded mankind; he "hated democracy ... with more than feudal hatred"; and he rejected the Church. "My religion is the old Persian," O'Leary told the young poet, "to pull the bow and tell the truth." O'Leary had enrolled in the Fenians because he believed the movement would "be good for the *morale* of the country";[9] without doubt, the old man's notion of morale, however vague, helped Yeats to formulate his own concept of nationalism as a search for Unity of Culture.

O'Leary gave Yeats some verse by Thomas Davis and afterwards introduced him to a Young Ireland Society where by joining in debates the poet trained himself in public speaking. "From these debates," Yeats wrote in *Reveries* (p. 119), no doubt exaggerating, "from O'Leary's conversation, and from the Irish books he lent or gave me has come all I have set my hand to." It was through O'Leary, too, that Yeats met many of those who were to be his associates in the following years: Katherine Tynan, who urged him to the writing of "Oisin" and whose own poetry resembles his early work; Douglas Hyde, translator of the remarkable *Songs of Connacht* and founder of the Gaelic League, whom Yeats was later to mourn as "the great poet who died in his youth"; [10] and finally Maud Gonne, who so enraptured Yeats that he followed her blindly into nationalist politics at the turn of the century. Yeats joined the Irish Revolutionary Brotherhood and in 1898 was a member of the Wolfe Tone Centennial Committee responsible for organizing a jubilee observance of the rebellion of 1798. The poet's most significant contribution to the swelling tide of nationalism was *Cathleen Ni Houlihan*, written for Maud Gonne in 1902. The play profoundly impressed the youthful Padraic Pearse; [11] and Stephen Gwynn, after witnessing a performance, wrote: "I went home asking myself if such plays should be produced unless one was prepared to go out and shoot and be shot." [12]

Whatever the consequences of his drama—and there is surely ground for maintaining that it prodded Pearse, MacDonagh, Plunkett, and a few others a step closer to the blood sacrifice of 1916—Yeats did not intend to create an incendiary literature. For his notion of insurrection and upheaval bore little or no relation to practical realities, but in all likelihood evolved from his familiarity with Irish legend and myth, from his acquaintance with MacGregor Mathers who had announced "the imminence of great wars," [13] and from his study of Blake, whose New Jerusalem was to emerge out of chaos and ruin. [14] O'Leary's views on the question of violence would have been sufficient for Yeats. Indeed, in his intellectual development he had been subjected to far too many contrary influences—his father, Arthur Symons, Madame Blavatsky, to mention a few—to identify himself with any kind of overtly propagandistic literature. Yeats' real hope for Ireland was not a politician's platform, it was a poet's dream. He soon grew disenchanted with Irish politics; and, indeed, his disillusionment with the nationalist cabals, as well as his reaction to

Maud Gonne's marriage, gave rise to the bitter tone of his entries in *Estrangement*.

Despite its note of outrage, however, this curious diary does not represent an attempt by Yeats to dissociate himself or his art from the Irish scene. "I shall write for my own people," he had told Miss Horniman, "whether in love or hate of them matters little—probably I shall not know which it is." [15] In *Estrangement* he assumes the role of a surgeon probing for a malignant growth: "The root of it all is that the political class in Ireland—the lower-middle class from whom the patriotic associations have drawn their journalists and their leaders for the last ten years—have suffered through the cultivation of hatred as the one energy of their movement. . . . Hence the shrillness of their voices. They contemplate all creative power as the eunuchs contemplate Don Juan as he passes through Hell on a white horse." [16] Without doubt Yeats is contemptuous and disillusioned, yet his eye is just as closely focused upon what he liked to call "the painted scene" of public life as it was to be years later when, in a more nostalgic mood, he urged his readers to visit the Municipal Gallery in Dublin where "the images of thirty years" hang upon the wall:

> An ambush; pilgrims at the water-side;
> Casement upon trial, half hidden by the bars,
> Guarded; Griffith staring in hysterical pride;
> Kevin O'Higgins' countenance that wears
> A gentle questioning look that cannot hide
> A soul incapable of remorse or rest;
> A revolutionary soldier kneeling to be blest.[17]

As this collage of images suggests, one might compile an anthology of poems by Yeats which could be classified as "occasional," in that they represent the poet's response to specific moments in contemporary Irish life. As early as 1891 he published a poem in a nationalist journal, commemorating the death of Parnell and urging the Irish people to keep faith with his image:

> Mourn—and then onward, there is no returning
> He guides ye from the tomb;
> His memory now is a tall pillar, burning
> Before us in the gloom! [18]

This is a public poem, to be sure, embodying a message for the Irish people. Throughout his career, whenever an event aroused him, Yeats addressed himself, usually through the popular press, to the nation at large. He did so when the patriotic extremists attacked *The Playboy of the Western World* and struck out at the play's critics as "eunuchs" who "longed to look / All their lives through into some drift of wings," [19] and again during the Lane controversy, when he expressed contempt for "the blind and ignorant town." [20] He did so after Easter Week and during "the troubles" of the nineteen-twenties. He did so once again after the British government's publication of the "forged" Casement diaries:

> Afraid they might be beaten
> Before the bench of Time,
> They turned a trick by forgery
> And blackened his good name. [21]

Yeats sent this poem, "Roger Casement," to *The Irish Press*, the popular nationalist newspaper, where it was published twice; and later he was officially thanked by the government of Eamon De Valera. [22] Another late poem, "Cracked Mary's Vision," was provoked by King George's opening of a new wing of the Tate Gallery in London in 1929 to house the "stolen" Lane collection. In his verse Yeats contrasted the English king unfavorably with a king of the Tuatha Dé Danann, and employed the insulting refrain, "May the devil take King George." The poem was never published, although Yeats did try unsuccessfully to have it printed in George Russell's *Irish Statesman*. [23]

There can be no doubt that Yeats was, after his own fashion, a kind of patriot; and it would be quite feasible, if not entirely satisfactory, to trace the relationship between the poet's personal attitude toward Ireland and the changing mood of his verse. One might segment Yeats' career according to his changing reaction to the public scene and examine the poetry of each period from whatever point of view seemed appropriate. One might discuss the early Yeats—until the turn of the century—as a poet expressing Ireland in romantic terms, as an apostle of "A Druid land, a Druid tune"; [24] the Yeats of *The Green Helmet* (1910) and *Responsibilities* (1914) as an angry poet whose energies have been dissipated in a daily "war with every knave and dolt"; [25] Yeats after the Easter Rising as a poet inspired by the manifestation of a "terrible beauty" on the national scene; Yeats during the Black and Tan War and the civil strife as a poet-become-prophet, who perceives in national turmoil the omens—horrible green birds, a rough beast slouching toward Bethlehem—signaling the imminent collapse of civilization; Yeats as a Free State senator whose verse suggests his role as "A sixty-year-old smiling public man"; [26] and finally, Yeats, an old man, as a poet disillusioned with the Irish experiment, who heaps abuse on democracy and flirts with fascism, who sees the nation as a tomb where "the dark grows blacker." [27]

Whatever its value, such an approach to Yeats imposes certain limitations on the reading of the poetry. For one thing, it implies that a biographical frame of reference is sufficient to define Yeats' nationalism as it is expressed in his verse. Yet when special emphasis is placed on the biographical element, one can never be quite sure of his ground. The reader must continually ask himself whether what is manifest in any given poem is representative of the man or the mask. Monk Gibbon, whose study of Yeats, *The Man and the Masterpiece*, suffers from a bias born of personal hostility, argues, not without a measure of justice—that Yeats was a poseur in his life as well as in his art and that the student, however industrious, can never hope to penetrate to the real man or the real beliefs. Certainly Yeats exhibited a studied aloofness in his personal dealings with acquaintances and even with relatives.[28] Nor can there be any doubt that the Yeats who revised his autobiographical writings and even his letters as carefully as he did his verse sought to create for posterity an image of his own personality which would complement and justify his artistic output.[29] The implication is that Yeats so stylized his own personality that what remains more closely approximates "a plummet-measured face" than a sentimental or realistic picture of a human being.[30]

If there is any doubt as to the extent to which Yeats applied his doctrine of the mask to his life, there can be none as far as his poetry is concerned. It was Yeats' purpose to escape from the particular, the personal and objective world of his own experience, into the universal, the essential reality of human nature. His aesthetic is designed to transfigure, and in a sense destroy, what is personal and objective, not simply to hide it behind an artistic screen. A poetic utterance inspired by a public event must indeed have some reference to the actuality of that event, but the artistic embodiment will not be an exact copy, any more than that remarkably ferocious crone, Crazy Jane, is a true likeness of the half-comic peasant woman upon whom Yeats based her. Any biographical examination of Yeats' verse, whether concerned with personal emotional experience or with his attitudes toward public events, must be tempered by a recognition of the poet's aesthetic intent.

Yeats' nationalism, as it is manifest in his art, is determined not by its connections with the realities of the contemporary scene, but rather by a Utopian dream of Ireland as ideal nation; Yeats saw Ireland not as it was in fact, but Ireland as it might become. According to Irish tradition, the ancient *filid* were not only technically accomplished in the art of verse-making, but also were possessed of *imbas forosna*, that is, second sight; and many of the Irish poets, including Yeats, seemed to have believed half-seriously that this unique faculty was theirs by right of inheritance. The poets, each in his own way, invoked a vision of the new Ireland as a model nation that would be "a light to the Gentiles." [31] George Russell believed that the ancient gods had returned to Ireland and that they would "awaken the magical instinct everywhere, and the universal heart of the people will turn to the old Druidic beliefs." [32] Yeats was somewhat more restrained. In a speech in New York in 1904 he foresaw that in the re-emerging Irish nation "there will be an imaginative culture and power to understand imaginative and spiritual things distributed among the people." [33] Yeats' ideal, as it evolved, encompassed much that was not Celtic in origin, yet from the very beginning he sought to embody in his art moral and cultural principles which he believed would guarantee the nobility of the Irish race in the future.

Yeats' nationalism, then, may be regarded as the artistic expression of the ideal Irish nation. This vision evolved in conjunction with Yeats' development as an artist; in *If I Were Four and Twenty* the poet writes that as a young man he had three interests: "interest in a form of literature, in a form of philosophy, and a belief in nationality. None of these seemed to have anything to do with the other, but gradually my love of literature and my belief in nationality came together. . . . Now all three are, I think, one, or rather all three are a discrete expression of a single conviction." [34] In the poetry of his mature period Yeats' nationalism is integrated into a larger symbolic design and becomes, paradoxically, both more precise and more difficult. Nevertheless, it is possible, through an examination of his work, to define the intellectual outlines of his vision of Ireland.

Certainly Yeats' ideal owes much to the classical tradition of pastoral romance with its mixture of aristocratic sentiment and rural simplicity. Like many Irish writers of the period, he glorified the simple culture of the Gaelic-speaking folk of the West of Ireland and condemned the complex industrial society of England. In "Street Dancers," a poem published in *The*

Wanderings of Oisin and Other Poems (1892) but omitted from the definitive editions, Yeats describes the plight of "two ragged children bright" singing in a London street:

> Others know the healing earth,
> Others know the starry mirth;
> They will wrap them in a shroud,
> Sorrow-worn, yet placid-browed.
> London streets have heritage,
> Blinder sorrows, harder wage—
> Sordid sorrows of the mart,
> Sorrows sapping brain and heart.   (*Var.*, p. 733)

Children born into an urban environment can never know the instinctive joy and wisdom of nature that are the right of children who live in the countryside, or (as we learn in the poem) on a South Sea island, or in a Bedouin desert camp. The industrial age had in effect destroyed the natural nobility of mankind.

That Yeats blamed the industrial revolution on the rationalism of the seventeenth and eighteenth centuries, the underlying philosophy of Puritanism, of the middle class, and, eventually, of democracy, is made clear in an epigram included in *The Tower:* "Locke sank into a swoon; / The Garden died; / God took the spinning-jenny / Out of his side."[35] Having adopted Locke's "scientific" point of view, the eighteenth century sought to subordinate to the control of rational intellect the passionate nature of man, designated in Yeats' poetry by the image of the garden, where, according to religious tradition, man was instinctively in harmony with Nature. As far as Yeats was concerned, the Age of Reason marked the beginning of the decline of European civilization, just as the period of the Roman Empire represented the decline of classical culture.[36]

England had exported to Ireland the by-products of rationalism. One of these was the "mechanical logic and commonplace eloquence" which Yeats believed characterized Irish politics during his lifetime. It is against the danger of such

abstraction that Yeats warns in an early poem, "The Two
Trees":

> There, through the broken branches, go
> The ravens of unresting thought;
> Flying, crying, to and fro,
> Cruel claw and hungry throat,
> Or else they stand and sniff the wind,
> And shake their ragged wings.   (*Poems*, p. 48)

Another outgrowth of rationalism was the materialism, denounced so bitterly in "September 1913," that led men, who
were "come to sense," to "fumble in a greasy till" until they
"dried the marrow from the bone." [37] Here again Yeats implies
a repudiation of "sense," that is, the rational approach to life
stressed by Locke and those who followed him; for it is
rationalism that deprives the bones of "marrow," the organic
principle that feeds man's natural instincts. In another poem,
"The Curse of Cromwell," Yeats identifies "Cromwell's house
and Cromwell's murderous crew" with "money's rant" because, in his mind, Puritanism and materialism and rationalism were out of the same package. Just as Locke's rationalism
killed the Garden and just as the Paudeens dry up the marrow
of the bone, so also the Puritans destroyed the lovers and
dancers who represent the natural, instinctive way of life
(*Poems*, pp. 302–3). The antithesis of Yeats' ideal nation is a
compound of these qualities which he attacked bitterly
throughout his life—industrial blight, Puritanism, materialism, and rationalism.

Yeats once wrote that the statue of Artemis in the British
Museum, half animal, half divine, became for him an image of
"an unpremeditated joyous energy, that neither I nor any
man, racked by doubt and inquiry, can achieve; and that yet, if
once achieved, might seem to men and women of Connemara
and Galway their very soul." [38] The Irish peasants, as Yeats
conceived them, knew nothing of urban civilization; they
survived in the rugged countryside, in close union with the wild
landscape, the wind, and the sea. They knew nothing of Locke

or the Age of Reason, but lived their lives simply and without question, following the commands of habit and instinct. Yeats' linking of these people to the goddess of untamed nature was not inappropriate. Their words and deeds were "unpremeditated" and their lives could give the lie to the sterile world of abstraction and materialism:

> 'Though logic-choppers rule the town,
> And every man and maid and boy
> Has marked a distant object down,
> An aimless joy is a pure joy,'

> Or so did Tom O'Roughley say
> That saw the surges running by,
> 'And wisdom is a butterfly
> And not a gloomy bird of prey.' [39]

The butterfly in Yeats' verse symbolizes the natural way of intuition, the hawk the destructive path of logic. In Yeats' ideal nation Irishmen would go the way of the butterfly and of the Irish peasant; they would be "ignorant as the dawn" and in that joyous ignorance would find harmony with nature.

Yeats often uses a peasant mask when arguing his belief in the intuitive way of life. Tom O'Roughley serves such a function. However, where the poet attempts to represent the rustic as a personification of simple nobility and dignity, the result is usually less than satisfactory. "The Fiddler of Dooney" is more ordinary frolic than "pure joy" and "The Ballad of Moll Magee," a poem in which one suspects Yeats intended to embody the image of simple folk dignity in the face of adversity, fails sadly. The central incident, Moll's accidentally smothering her own baby during the night, is pathetic perhaps, but hardly tragic in the classical sense of the word. Aristotle was right to insist that the protagonist of a tragedy should be one who is ennobled above the commonplace and responsible to an elevated norm of values. Yeats might at least have had his protagonist spend her days otherwise than "saltin' herring" in "the saltin' shed" (*Poems*, p. 23).

Yeats discarded the idea of presenting a realistic picture of peasant life, and it is significant that his attempts to do so are found only in his early verse. He did not abandon either the peasant or the ideal of "an unpremeditated joyous energy," but he found more satisfactory images, or symbols, for the expression of that peasant ideal. Yeats, it should be remembered, recognized a basic dichotomy between spirit and flesh in man's nature; and, indeed, in one very important sense, the whole of his work is an attempt to define and reconcile the two extremes. In his mature verse, where the aesthetic doctrine of antithesis has special importance, Yeats identified the peasant with the physical extreme of human nature, with man's animal appetites and instincts. Curiously enough, if this image of the peasant in the later verse is less photographic, it is more convincing. The romantic and sentimental overtones of the early ballads disappear, and the reader is confronted by a powerful, although stylized, symbol of human vigor that seems to penetrate to the center of man's physical being. The fiddle of Dooney and Moll Magee give way to the beggar, the fool, and Crazy Jane.

However deformed they may be, these creatures embody Yeats' affirmation of the physical nature of man. In a poem of the middle period, "The Hour Before the Dawn" in *Responsibilities and Other Poems* (1914), the reader is introduced to "A cursing rogue with a merry face, / A bundle of rags upon a crutch," who rejects the romantic dream in favor of the physical world. Stumbling across Cruachan, the beggar chances upon a hidden cave where "A great lad with a beery face" lies sleeping, a tub of Goban's beer by his side.[40] This young man means to escape from the world of reality and keep to his dreams until "flesh and bone may disappear, / And souls as if they were but sighs, / And there be nothing but God left." The beggar is enraged by this rejection of life: he pummels the senseless youth, seals the cave again with stones, and hurries back into the natural world where "The clouds were brightening with the dawn." At one point in the dialogue, the youth complains that his sleep has been interrupted by "The lapwing at their foolish cries / And the sheep bleating at the wind"; and the beggar rails at him for mocking "everything I love" (*Poems*, pp. 114–17). The beggar, ragged and vulgar though he is, identifies himself with the world of Nature; he is in this—and in his love for birds—like George Pollexfen, Yeats' uncle, who "loved natural things and had learnt two cries of the lapwing, one that drew them to where he stood and one that made them fly away" (*Reveries*, p. 81).

Yeats' peasants, because they live according to instinct, are at one with the natural order of the world; and this is as true of Crazy Jane as it is of beggar or rogue. It is true that Yeats vacillated in his personal attitude toward his remarkable creation—he wrote to his wife that he wished "to exorcise that slut" on one occasion and to Mrs. Shakespear that he approved of her on another.[41] Nevertheless, the sequence of seven poems which he devotes to Crazy Jane in *Words for Music Perhaps* (1932) can only be described as an affirmation of sexuality. An understanding of Yeats' concept of the conflict between flesh and spirit in human nature can help with the reading of these poems; the Crazy Jane sequence certainly exults in complete sexual abandon, but the sequence of seven poems that follows in the *Collected Poems* provides a kind of balance for her erotic image in that it is devoted to the antithetical ideal of Platonic love (*Poems*, pp. 256–59). In any event, Crazy Jane achieves fulfillment of her nature through sexual experience. Her vision in "Crazy Jane Grown Old Looks at the Dancers" identifies the sexual dance with the ultimate reality of human nature, and her closing statement reaffirms her belief in instinctive passion:

> God be with the times when I
> Cared not a thraneen for what chanced
> So that I had the limbs to try
> Such a dance as there was danced.   (*Poems*, p. 255)

The mature Yeats was not content to sketch quaint scenes of peasant life in his verse; he probed much deeper and tried to define the essence of peasant nature. The result was, of course, a fabrication, the product of a poet's imagination; for in reality the Irish peasant was anything but passionate, especially where matters of sex were concerned. In Yeats' ideal Ireland, however, the peasantry would be composed of a race of men which accepted instinct and habit as the driving forces of human existence, a race which surrendered itself to mankind's natural drives, whether of sexual passion, as in the case of Crazy Jane, or physical survival, as with those beggars whose morals and mores are shaped by the hunger pangs in their stomachs. To be sure, the beggar man and Crazy Jane are not to be taken literally. They are symbols of the instinctive passion that would give to the peasantry of Yeats' "Holy Ireland" its racial character. Such a race, Yeats believed, could achieve harmony with the natural world and in that harmony could perceive intuitively the utter reality of their own being and of the universe that surrounded them. Their lives would be guided by a kind of natural religion, and in Yeats' verse it is the half-pagan hermit Ribh and not Patrick who is their prophet:

> Natural and supernatural with the self-same
> ring are wed.
> As man, as beast, as an ephemeral fly begets,
> Godhead begets Godhead,
> For things below are copies, the Great Smaragdine
> Tablet said.[42]

In the context of Ribh's teachings, Crazy Jane deserves sainthood rather than damnation, for she has dedicated her whole being—"body and soul"—to the sexual drive, which is an essential part of man's nature.[43]

But if Ribh provides justification for Crazy Jane, he also establishes for her, and for the peasantry which she represents, a specific place in the order of things. Yeats' reasoning with respect to the natural order is that of the Brahman caste system or of the medieval Great Chain of Being. Mankind has a set station in the order of the universe, and each class of man has a set station in the order of human society. For his conception of social hierarchy Yeats could find precedent in Indian, Celtic, classical, medieval, and Renaissance civilization, as well as in Madame Blavatsky's theory of the spiritual evolution of the soul through eight hundred incarnations to perfection; [44] and he could perceive in the modern movement toward democracy the opposite of his ideal. In Yeats' hierarchical order the peasantry constitutes the base of the social pyramid, and the aristocracy its pinnacle. The simple race of Gaels had escaped the infection of political hatred. The Irish peasant knew his place and accepted it. Like his Gaelic forefathers he could say of his aristocratic masters, "My fathers served their fathers before Christ was crucified" (Var., p. 833).

In his autobiographical Dramatis Personae, 1896–1902, Yeats praises Lady Gregory for "her sense of feudal responsibility," a quality of character which, he says, relates not to any traditional notion of duty but to the voluntary acceptance of those burdens "laid upon her by her station" (p. 13). Yeats regarded equalitarianism in any form as perversion; and his admiration for the Irish peasant class grew from his misconception that they accepted subordinate social status. To this strain of class consciousness one may trace the unreal quality of those parts of Reveries where Yeats rampages through family generations of country parsons, small businessmen, and farmers to discover "a little James the First creamjug with the Yeats motto and crest" upon it or knowledge of some remote great-uncle who had been Governor of Penang (Reveries, pp. 18–20). His obsession with class distinctions certainly gave birth to personal foibles. He asked someone to trace his family tree and was delighted to hear that in the Butler line on his father's side there was noble blood; later, he told friends, including George Russell, that he himself rightfully should be the Duke of Ormonde.[45] According to Lady

Gregory's coachman, Yeats was the "finest gentleman" to visit
Coole Park—because he would never lower himself to so much
as speak to any of the servants.[46] In his age, of course, the poet
engaged in his unfortunate flirtation with General O'Duffy's
fascist "Blue Shirt" movement in Dublin; he composed
"Three Songs to the Same Tune" for O'Duffy's troopers to
march to, but afterwards, having recognized the discordance
between O'Duffy's beliefs and his own, revised the songs so
that "no party might sing them." [47]

Whatever personal absurdities it may have inspired, Yeats'
belief in the aristocratic way of life was motivated not so much
by the desire for self-aggrandizement as by an honest concern
for the cultural welfare of his country.[48] The fact of the matter
would seem to be that he set up his own ideal of artistic
excellence and regarded with scorn that which failed to meet
his standard. He was merciless in his condemnation of the
Philistine insensitivity which he believed had overwhelmed
Ireland. In contrast to the culturally sterile society he saw
about him, the aristocratic societies of the ancient Irish and
Renaissance Europeans, and the one he discovered in Sweden
when he received the Nobel Prize for Poetry, encouraged and
patronized artistic endeavor. Prince Eugene, friend of Swedish
artists and himself a painter whom Yeats admired during his
Stockholm visit, had labored side by side with artists and
workmen for two years in redecorating the Town Hall.[49]
Indeed, Yeats believed the aristocracy gave much more than
mere support to the artist; it provided as well that quality of
human nobility that informed all great art. In the closing lines
of "A Prayer for My Daughter" (1919) Yeats identifies
aristocratic ceremony and custom with "the rich horn" and
"the spreading laurel tree" respectively, the one referring to the
full-uddered goat-goddess Amalthaea, a symbol of abundance,
the other a symbol of sacred prophecy;[50] he then asks rhetorically: "How but in custom and ceremony / Are innocence
and beauty born?" (*Poems*, p. 187).

The Great House, the temple of aristocratic ideals in which

Yeats chose to worship, is at once a receptacle for artistic treasures and a wellspring of creativity. In Lady Gregory's home at Coole Park he found a copy of the Venus de' Medici which a Gregory had had hauled in bullock-carts across Italy; paintings, mezzotints, and engravings, some of them portraits of renowned friends of the family, Pitt, Lord Wellesley, Gladstone; and relics from the East, Persian helmets and "Indian swords in elaborate sheaths." [51] In such a setting the son of a great family might develop a sense of pride in a tradition built up over generations and the poet might find inspiration for the artistic expression of the aristocratic ideal. One might almost say that Yeats believed the aristocracy drew some unique spiritual strength from those heirlooms which linked one generation to another. Deprived of its trappings, in any event, the aristocracy must decline. In *Dramatis Personae* (pp. 3–4) Yeats describes Edward Martyn's home at Tullyra Castle, which had been rebuilt by Martyn's mother in the worst style of the nineteenth century: "A fire had destroyed the old house and whatever old furniture and pictures the family possessed, as though fate had deliberately prepared for an abstract mind that would see nothing in life but its vulgarity and temptations."

What had befallen Martyn was symptomatic of the times, for, as Yeats argues in the fifth movement of "Nineteen Hundred and Nineteen" (1921), the "levelling wind" of mechanical logic and materialism and mob rule had become a "foul storm" which was destroying all that was great and good and wise in human society (*Poems*, p. 207). Yeats had a word to describe the sum total of these evils, "whiggery," which he defines in "The Seven Sages" (1932) as "A levelling, rancorous, rational sort of mind / That never looked out of the eye of a saint / Or out of a drunkard's eye" (*Poems*, p. 236). It was whiggery that had destroyed Parnell and that destroyed Synge and then singled out Hugh Lane for its next victim. In a poem concerned with Lane and the art gallery controversy of 1913, "To a Shade," Yeats warns the ghost of Parnell back to

the safety of the tomb so that it may not witness a shameful
spectacle:

> A man
> Of your own passionate serving kind who had brought
> In his full hands what, had they only known,
> Had given their children's children loftier thought,
> Sweeter emotion, working in their veins
> Like gentle blood, has been driven from the place,
> And insult heaped upon him for his pains,
> And for his open-handedness, disgrace;
> Your enemy, an old foul mouth, had set
> The pack upon him.   (*Poems*, p. 108)

Yeats' belief, almost an obsession, that the worst elements in
society were in the ascendancy remained with him throughout
his life. The "levelling wind" and the "old foul mouth" in the
later poetry become fused with the violence of fratricidal war
and evolve into the Armageddon imagery signaling the collapse
of civilization.

Yeats thought that contemporary art was "powerful but
prosaic" and that it chronicled the "fall into division" of man
and his society. The emphasis upon individuation of character
that he perceived in the grotesqueries of Augustus John's work,
the protruding shoulder blades and oversized noses and stomachs, sacrificed the essential energy of human passion to a cult
of personality. The old aristocratic art, by contrast, celebrated a
"resurrection into unity," and sought after the ideal of human
perfection. The Greeks had been on the right track in seeking
the perfectly proportioned human body in the gymnasium;
their art, "if carried to its logical conclusion, would have led to
the creation of one single type of man, one single type of
woman; gathering up by a kind of deification a capacity for all
energy and all passion, into a Krishna, a Christ, a Dionysus." [52]
The contrast between the old and new approaches to art is the
central theme of "The Statues" (1934):

> Pythagoras planned it. Why did the people stare?
> His numbers, though they moved or seemed to move

In marble or in bronze, lacked character.
But boys and girls, pale from the imagined love
Of solitary beds, knew what they were,
That passion could bring character enough,
And pressed at midnight in some public place
Live lips upon a plummet-measured face.   (*Poems*, p. 322)

Borrowing from Egyptian scholarship, Pythagoras had tried to find the exact mathematical proportions of the human body, for these proportions would permit the representation in art of the perfect man, that is, the image of God. Art directed toward this end would be concerned not with the "character" of individual personality but with human passion, which is, Yeats would have us believe, the source and determinant of life itself. Slaves to mechanical abstraction cannot grasp such art; they can only stare and complain of lack of character; but would-be lovers, given over to their natural passions, can perceive its beauty intuitively.

The aristocrat, in the context of Yeats' verse, is the embodiment of human passion; he becomes a symbol of human perfection and, in a manner of speaking, is deified. Nowhere is this image of the aristocrat more clearly defined than in the poem, "In Memory of Major Robert Gregory" (1918), commemorating the death of Lady Gregory's son, whom Yeats describes as "Our Sidney and our perfect man," one so noble that the poet had supposed him immortal. In the poem Yeats identifies Robert Gregory with images of nature, "old storm-broken trees" and a ford where each night the cattle coming to drink startle the water-hen, and with the image of a man-made tower which has stood for so long by the edge of a stream that it has in fact become an integral part of the natural setting. These things Robert Gregory loved, for each in its own way embodies the passionate spirit of nature—the tree battered and bent by the living fury of ocean gales, the water-hen instinctively giving place to the invading cattle, the untamed race who centuries ago built the tower and whose only law was the law of their own natural passions. Because Robert Gregory was himself a

man of passion, because the passion of his mind was even more
furious than the physical passion of horses taken up in the
animal excitement of the hunt, he could ride after the Galway
hounds with such abandon that those about him closed their
eyes in astonishment. But he was a painter, too, and he was "a
great painter," because the passion that ruled his heart is the
source of all great art; and he had mastered the lesser arts as
well, the "lovely intricacies of a house," for the same reason. In
"An Irish Airman Foresees His Death," the poem immediately
following in the definitive editions, Robert Gregory's heroism
at the moment of death bursts forth from the same instinctive
passion that ruled his life; for courage in the face of danger is
inspired neither by law nor duty nor desire for fame but by "A
lonely impulse of delight" born of human passion. Because he
was the embodiment of passion, Robert Gregory, like the ideal
Renaissance courtier, knew no limitation: "Soldier, scholar,
horsemen, he, / And all he did done perfectly / As though he
had but that one trade alone" (*Poems*, pp. 130–34).

If the simple passion which defines the peasant's nature
marks him for an humble existence, then the nobler passion of
the aristocrat demands "the inherited glory of the rich"; [53] and
if it is the peasant's lot to serve, it is the aristocrat's right to
rule. The order of society was fixed at the dawn of history and
against that order there is no appeal. In *The Dreaming of the
Bones* the Young Man who fought at the Post Office during
Easter Week, a symbol for the emerging Irish nation, *almost*
forgives Diarmuid and Dervorgilla, who betrayed Ireland to
seven centuries of English rule, because their sin was a sin of
passion; but he condemns out of hand Donough O'Brien and
his followers who rebelled against their "rightful master," the
King of Thomond, because theirs was a crime against order.
"My curse on all that troop," the Young Man exclaims, "and
when I die / I'll leave my body, if I have any choice, / Far from
his ivy-tod and his owl." [54] Nature herself devised the hierarchical system along with its inevitable corollary: to each man

according to his birth. In *The Bounty of Sweden* (pp. 19–20)
Yeats cites an old Gaelic poem composed by nuns on the island
of Iona who saved a royal baby from the wreck of a Scandi-
navian ship: "The nuns mothered the baby, and their cradle-
song, famous for generations after, repeated over and over
praising in symbol every great man's child—every tested
long-enduring stock—'Daughter of a Queen, grand-daughter
of a Queen, great-grand-daughter of a Queen, great-great-
grand-daughter of a Queen.' "

It follows, of course, that the aristocrat's pedigree, like that
of a pure-bred dog, must be maintained at all costs, for
cross-breeding must inevitably result in a mongrel litter. The
consequence of polluting noble with base blood provides the
theme for Yeats' most powerfully dramatic play, *Purgatory*.
The Old Man in the play reveals that his mother, a woman of
noble birth, had mated with a drunken gamekeeper and then
died in childbirth. The gamekeeper subsequently "squandered
everything she had" and, in a final drunken fit, fired the Great
House where "Magistrates, colonels, members of Parliament, / Captains and Governors" had lived and died. The Old
Man, at the time a youth of sixteen years, killed his drunken
father with a jack-knife and then fled the scene to become a
pedlar. As the play begins, the Old Man returns to the ruin of
the house with his own son, whom he "got / Upon a tinker's
daughter in a ditch." While they stop there, the soul of the
Old Man's mother relives her marriage night, as she must do
perpetually in consequence of her sin. At last, in a futile
attempt to cleanse the aristocratic line of pollution and win
peace for his mother's spirit, the Old Man slays his son with
the same knife he had used to kill his father. "I killed that lad,"
he mutters, "because had he grown up / He would have struck
a woman's fancy, / Begot, and passed pollution on." But even
this is not enough. He hears hoof-beats signaling the arrival of
the gamekeeper on the wedding night; the horrible cycle has
begun again, and the Old Man cries:

> Twice a murderer and all for nothing,
> And she must animate that dead night
> Not once but many times!   (*Plays*, pp. 431–36)

The play's allegory is clear enough. The drunken game-keeper is a personification of the "old foul mouth" and the "levelling wind" which Yeats believed were replacing all that was great and good and wise in society with all that is mean and vulgar and ignorant. The drunken gamekeeper represents all that is antithetical to Yeats' ideal nation; and when as an old man the poet wrote his play, the gamekeeper's breed were everywhere gaining power. Lady Gregory was gone and Coole Park had fallen into the hands of a government that would one day dismantle the Great House brick by brick in order to build workers' cottages. The aristocratic way of life was indeed dying; but it was Yeats' dream that the old way might again have its day of glory. After quoting the nuns' cradle-song in *The Bounty of Sweden*, Yeats suggests that Nature "may even now mock in her secret way our new ideals—the equality of man, equality of rights—meditating some wholly different end" (p. 20). Surely, as far as Yeats was concerned, that different end was the passionate ideal of the aristocracy with its "ancestral houses," where amid the "flowering lawns" and "planted hills" of the rich "Life overflows without ambitious pains." [55] In such a setting noble life and noble art are possible.

Both the peasant ideal, representing the humble life of service, and the aristocratic ideal, representing the nobler life of wealth and art and rule, are incorporated into Yeats' vision of Ireland as it might someday be. The two ideals are antithetical in that they represent the two extremes of human social existence, servant and master, and the extremes of human nature as well, base and noble, and, in a sense, physical and contemplative. But if they are antithetical, they are also complementary, inasmuch as together they embody the hier-archical ideal of social order which, Yeats tells us, is essential to Nature's design. "The whole state," he argues in *On the Boiler*, "should be so constructed that the people should think it their duty to grow popular with King and Lord Mayor instead of King and Lord Mayor growing popular with them." [56] It is noteworthy that within the context of Yeats' verse both peasant and aristocratic ideals are associated with the imagery of nature, lapwings and trees and water-hens, and both are set in opposition to contemporary civilization with its conglomeration of industrialism, Puritanism, and abstract logic.

If both the peasant ideal and the aristocratic ideal find their source in natural instinct and passion, so also does the heroic ideal, the third component of Yeats' vision of Ireland. It has been noted already that Robert Gregory's heroism in the face of imminent death—as Yeats describes it in "An Irish Airman Foresees His Death"—springs neither from the illusion of righteousness, nor of duty, nor of vainglory, but from "A lonely impulse of delight," that is, from a natural and instinctive response to the threatening situation. Such is the courage of heroic passion, and it is certainly true that Yeats identified this particular human quality with the aristocratic ideal. But in the poetry heroic passion does not remain the exclusive property of the aristocrat. Yeats places special importance upon the heroic ideal in his vision of Ireland and defines it in several contexts. The verse concerned with the Easter Rising, for example, shows clearly that Yeats believed the rebels, all of them commonplace enough, were driven by the same instinctive courage that illuminated Robert Gregory's final moment. In a late ballad Yeats describes the death of the O'Rahilly, a Republican leader, who, doubting the wisdom of the rebellion, kept his men in County Kerry from taking arms but "travelled half the night" to join the hopeless struggle himself. O'Rahilly meets his death in "a doorway / Somewhere off Henry Street" with the same passionate abandon:

> They that found him found upon
> The door above his head
> 'Here died the O'Rahilly,
> R.I.P.' writ in blood.[57]

That final instinctive gesture—scribbling his epitaph in his own blood at the moment of death—defines his heroism.

Yeats experimented with the ideal of heroic passion in his earliest treatment of subjects from Irish myth and legend. In "The Wanderings of Oisin" (1892) the hero fights and slays the "dusky demon" in the Hall of Manannan and then casts the lifeless hulk into the sea. But after three days the demon, like Christ, is reborn and returns, "dropping sea-foam on the wide stair, / And hung with slime"; so, on each fourth day Oisin renews the fight "and for a hundred years / So warred, so feasted, with nor dreams nor fears, / Nor languor nor fatigue: an endless feast, / An endless war" (*Poems,* p. 369). Oisin's instinctive joy in battle for its own sake springs from heroic passion. Such warfare, wrapped about with the forms of ritual, is the opposite of modern warfare, which is fought to achieve some practical end and which results only in terror and human misery. In *The Herne's Egg,* written almost a half century after "The Wanderings of Oisin," Yeats draws the distinction between the subjective warfare of his ideal and the objective warfare of modern reality. Congal and Aedh have engaged in ideal battle, the battle of heroes. They have fought their fiftieth engagement, with each side suffering the same number of casualties, with the leaders receiving complementary shoulder wounds:

> *Congal.*   This is our fiftieth battle.
> *Aedh.*   And all were perfect battles.   (*Plays,* p. 416)

But the kings and their followers feast on the eggs of the Great Herne, a Sphinx-like creature that resembles the "rough beast" of "The Second Coming," and are thrust suddenly into the bitterness of objective reality:

Congal.   They had, we had
Forgotten what we fought about,
So fought like gentlemen, but now
Knowing the truth we must fight like
                    the beasts.   (*Plays*, p. 416)

The heroism of passion is instinctive; its battles are waged without cause or purpose, without knowledge of "what we fought about," its only objective the spontaneous expression of man's noble courage. Joseph Hone, in his biography of the poet, records a conversation in which Yeats, an old man, suggests a solution to the controversy between Moslems and Hindus in India: " 'Let 100,000 men of one side meet the other. That is my message to India, insistence on the antinomy.' He strode swiftly across the room, took up Sato's sword, and unsheathed it dramatically and shouted, 'Conflict, more conflict' " (p. 491). Such a struggle, like that of Congal and Aedh before they ate the Herne's eggs and like that of Oisin against the demon, would be an end in itself. Neither of the symbolic forces, both equal in strength, could conquer. What would result from such a ceremonial struggle would be the passionate joy of battle for its own sake, and that instinctive joy in turn would purge the bitterness of Moslem and Hindu factions.

In his poems and plays concerned with the fabulous hero of the Ulaid, Cú Chulainn, who is the personification of the heroic ideal, Yeats clearly identifies heroic passion with the natural, instinctive way of life. In *The Green Helmet* Cú Chulainn alone of the Ulster heroes is fearless enough to fulfill the pledge of "A head for a head" that Laeghaire and Conall had made with the Red Man. In turn, the Red Man, who is a spirit and "Rector of this land," chooses Cú Chulainn and the passionate life he represents as his champion:

I choose the laughing lip
That shall not turn from laughing, whatever rise or fall;
The heart that grows no bitterer although betrayed by all;
The hand that loves to scatter; the life like a gambler's throw.
                                    (*Plays*, p. 159)

Cú Chulainn is the epitome of heroic courage because his whole life is spontaneous and instinctively in accord with his noble nature. The same point is made in *On Baile's Strand* where the central issue is whether men should be ruled by rational law or by their own natural passions. Conchobhar and the lesser kings demand that Cú Chulainn be bound by oath to order his turbulent life according to rules laid down by the high king. The hero defends the life of passion in which one may see "the heavens like a burning cloud / Brooding upon the world," and condemns those who would do away with that life because "they have no pith, / No marrow in their bones" (*Plays,* pp. 167–68); but at last he gives way and takes the oath of obedience to the king's law. During the remainder of the play, Yeats drives home his moral—that passion is Nature's law and rational logic mankind's blunder—with a vengeance. A Young Man, Cú Chulainn's son by the woman-warrior Aoife, breaks in upon the company and challenges Cú Chulainn to single combat. Cú Chulainn senses a natural affinity for the strange youth—who like the great hero himself is under a *geis* to reveal his name only at sword's point—and seeks friendship with him; but Conchobhar and the kings argue that because the Young Man is from the country of Aoife, their enemy, Cú Chulainn must fight him. They finally convince the Ulster hero that the youth has won his affection by means of witchcraft, and the enraged Cú Chulainn fights his own son. Only after he has dealt the Young Man a mortal blow does he learn the tragic truth; and then, returning to the way of passion, he vents his instinctive fury against the waves.

The song of the First Musician in *The Only Jealousy of Emer* embodies a lyric expression of heroic passion that links the fury of battle itself with the world of nature:

> A strange, unserviceable thing,
> A fragile, exquisite, pale shell
> That the vast troubled waters bring
> To the loud sands before day has broken.
> The storm arose and suddenly fell

> Amid the dark before day had broken.
> What death? What discipline?
> What bonds no man could unbind,
> Being imagined within
> The labyrinth of the mind,
> What pursuing or fleeing,
> What wounds, what bloody press,
> Dragged into being
> This loveliness? [58]

Although the poem has occult overtones that are perhaps beyond logical explication, Yeats intends clearly enough to suggest a metaphorical connection between the images of nature in turmoil—"vast troubled waters," the sands resounding to the crash of breaking waves, the storm in the night—and the violent press of heroic battle. The fierce beauty of an ocean storm breaking upon the coast—perhaps an Atlantic gale moving into the Sligo Bay area between Ben Bulben and Knocknarea—is used to suggest the intense passion, at once terrible and lovely, that overwhelms the warrior, in this instance Cú Chulainn, in the violence of battle.

Yeats' three ideals—the hero's gay, instinctive courage in the face of danger or death, the aristocrat's passionate acceptance of the life that is his by right of birth, the peasant's physical simplicity and spiritual humility—are integrated into his vision of "the Holy Land of Ireland," a place where men could live in complete harmony with Nature's design.[59] During the early years of the revival Yeats had discovered the image of such a nation in the literature of ancient Ireland, and he expressed hope then that consciousness of that past glory might unify Ireland spiritually and politically. He became convinced, too, that his own vision, expressed through his poetry and drama, might become the spiritual inheritance of the Irish people in future generations and that his dream might become reality; for, as he wrote in The Trembling of the Veil (1922), "Nations, races, and individual men are unified by an image, or bundle of related images, symbolical or evocative of the state of mind, which is of all states of mind not impossible, the most difficult to that man, race, or nation; because only the greatest obstacle that can be contemplated without despair rouses the will to full intensity" (p. 80). In Yeats' verse the images of peasant, aristocrat, and hero are intended to suggest that state of mind whereby national unity could be achieved through a universally accepted philosophy of natural passion.

W. B. YEATS:
"THE HOLY LAND OF IRELAND"

W. B. Yeats' vision of "the Holy Land of Ireland" is not communicated directly in his verse but rather is embodied in a cluster of images that are symbolic and evocative of the heroic, aristocratic, and peasant ideals. It is important to note that Yeats rejected the technique of allegory, that he associated it with the mechanical logic of the Age of Reason, and that he devised for himself an aesthetic of symbolism by which visionary art might be created in a kind of "wizard frenzy." [1] If allegory may be defined as the translation of idea into image or as the intellectual process by which idea and image are mechanically joined and therefore separable, then Yeats' symbolism is something different, something more difficult and certainly more powerful. What he achieved, or at any rate hoped to achieve, was a symbol of embodiment not unlike the literary symbol which William York Tindall defines in an essay on modern poetry: "As the spirit or vital principle occupies our bodies and shines out, so thought and feeling occupy the form, shape, or body that we call symbol." [2] One may accept or reject this conception of symbol, but in either event one must recognize that Yeats' notion of symbolism, similar to Tindall's, exerted a considerable influence upon his mature art. Indeed, such an aesthetic is essential to the visionary art Yeats wished to create, for the object of such art is not simply to represent human experience but to move from human experience to a kind of knowledge, emotional and religious, that is beyond purely rational comprehension.[3] This is not to say that intellectual explication of Yeats' verse is impossible or useless, but only to suggest that the reader must be prepared to substitute emotional response and even religious intuition for rational understanding whenever the symbolic pattern or lyric intensity of the verse so demands.

One might even maintain that Yeats sought to create in his poetry and drama a kind of "sacred" literature—"sacred" in the sense that André Malraux uses the word in his provocative, at times disturbingly subjective book, *The Metamorphosis of the Gods*. Malraux argues that in the twentieth century man has become increasingly aware of a "sacred element" in the creative arts and that this awareness has prompted him to question the aesthetic criterion by which earlier ages valued art works according to the pleasure they afforded to the eye and the imagination. So, he says, modern man can sense a strange power in creations of antiquity which a nineteenth century critic would have dismissed as archeological curiosities, wanting in skill and refinement of technique—the Egyptian statue of the Pharaoh Zoser, the Seven Mothers in the Kailasa Temple in India, the grotesque reliefs adorning Romanesque cathedrals, the stylized mosaic works of Byzantium. One's aesthetic response to such works "can hardly be conveyed by words associated with pleasure, even the delight of the eye, or with the traditional idea of beauty. It is obvious that the men who made the figures in the Royal Portal at Chartres and the effigies of Gudea did not do so with a view to giving pleasure, and that the emotions they inspire in us are of a quite different kind." [4] Malraux would have it that the artists who created these works were primarily concerned with the expression of religious truth—a truth having more relevance to the hidden reality of an Otherworld than to the appearances of this world—and that the emotions such works inspire are essentially religious emotions, awe and even fear, but hardly pleasure of a conventional sort.

Malraux suggests that this new aesthetic awareness of the "sacred element" in creativity has exerted a profound influence upon modern art; he points out, for example, the significance of African primitive art in the work of Cézanne and Picasso. Though he limits his discussion to the fine arts and architecture, his argument has a certain relevance for much modern poetry, and for the poetry of Yeats in particular. Early in his book Malraux describes the Sphinx at Gizeh as an example of the sacred art of antiquity. Approaching the complex of pyramids at dusk, he writes, the Sphinx seems at first no more than "an enormous knife-rest." But with sunset the huge paws disappear, the head looms up without a body, the time-ravaged features take on the "accent of 'devil's chimneys' and sacred mountains," the flaps of the headdress become like wings on barbarian helmets. As darkness falls the head takes on the appearance of a "hieroglyph, a trapezoidal sign," hanging in the sky; it grows larger, more immense, and at last seems "like the guardian of a dike set up against the tides of the desert and the encroaching dusk." [5] Malraux's description is romantic and impressionistic, no doubt; yet it represents an emotional response to what is strange and mysterious which is curiously similar to the response of any sensitive reader when confronted by such a poem as Yeats' "The Second Coming":

> somewhere in sands of the desert
> A shape with a lion body and the head of a man,
> A gaze blank and pitiless as the sun,
> Is moving its slow thighs, while all about it
> Reel shadows of the indignant desert birds.
> The darkness drops again; but now I know
> That twenty centuries of stony sleep
> Were vexed to nightmare by a rocking cradle,
> And what rough beast, its hour come round at last,
> Slouches towards Bethlehem to be born? (*Poems*, p. 185)

In its rhythms and language this poem is beautiful in a
traditional sense; but in its emotional mood it is much closer to
the sacred art of Egypt or Assyria than to the sonnets of
Shakespeare or Spenser's *Shepherd's Calendar*.

"The Second Coming" and, indeed, much of Yeats' verse,
especially that written after the turn of the century when the
mature poet left behind the more or less conventional romanticism of his youth, is informed with a religious meaning.
When he was completing *A Vision*, that complex and curious
work in which he tries to define the "system" revealed to him
by Otherworld spirits through the medium of his wife's
automatic writing, Yeats addressed himself to Ezra Pound: "I
send you the introduction of a book which will, when finished,
proclaim a new divinity." [6] In fact, of course, Yeats had been
proclaiming new gods in his poems and plays for many years;
and *A Vision* should be regarded less as a serious theological
work than as an apology, an attempt to justify the "sacred
element" in the poet's artistic creation. The Communicators
themselves had made clear their purpose in revealing to Yeats
their secret knowledge. Early in the period of automatic writing, which began shortly after the poet's marriage in 1917,
Yeats offered to spend the remainder of his life synthesizing the
wisdom of the Communicators into a philosophical treatise.
But they firmly rejected this idea: "No, we have come to give
you metaphors for poetry." [7] *A Vision* is a difficult and often
confused work; yet it attests to Yeats' belief that the function
of poetry is something more than the giving of pleasure, that,
indeed, its function is to reveal through metaphor and symbol
the hidden reality of the Otherworld.

The nature of Yeats' mature aesthetic perhaps can best be
seen within the framework of his changing attitude toward
myth and its function in poetry. As a young man Yeats drew
heavily from the material of Celtic mythology to provide a
setting for his poetic expression. He professed belief that his
work at the time was in the tradition of Mallarmé and that the
images he drew from the old tales were symbols that could

evoke an unseen reality. But in practice, as Richard Ellmann observes, "Yeats used symbols primarily to hide this world rather than to reveal another one." [8] A change was to come in the poet's aesthetic, however, a hardening of his language and imagery and a deeper insight into the human situation. There is more than a hint of Yeats' emerging aesthetic in "Adam's Curse," first published in 1902, in which the colloquial tone of intensified conversation is clearly manifest.[9] *On Baile's Strand* (1904) was conceived in the old aesthetic, born in the new; Yeats wrote concerning the play: "The first shape of it came to me in a dream, but it changed much in the making, foreshadowing, it may be, a change that may bring a less dream-burdened will into my verses" (*Var.*, p. 814). By the time of *The Green Helmet and Other Poems* (1910) the transformation of Yeats' poetics had been completed.

Most commentators agree that the mature Yeats rejected the Celtic legend that absorbed his youth in favor of myth-symbols that might serve his new objective to write poetry "as cold / And as passionate as the dawn" (*Poems*, p. 146). T. R. Henn observes that the obscurity sometimes found in *The Green Helmet and Other Poems* stems from the fact that Yeats had replaced the "vague historical symbols" of the Celtic world with "a more personal set of images, sometimes set in a grammatical compression of language which is new." [10] Richard Ellmann takes much the same view but relates the rejection of Celtic legend to Yeats' increasing awareness of the mythologies of other cultures.[11] Both of these observations are in some measure apt. Yeats' mythological symbols in his mature verse are indeed "personal" to the extent that he picks and chooses only those mythological images that serve his purpose. He does delete considerable allusion to Celtic legend, but it is noteworthy that he retains much and adds some as well. Mr. Henn points out that in the second version of *The Countess Cathleen* Kevin becomes Aleel and the image of the harp with torn wires is expunged; and no doubt the changes were made because of the sentiment attached to the image of

the harp and the name Kevin. But during this same period
Yeats introduced the image of Cú Chulainn into his canon as a
symbol for the heroic ideal. It is equally true that Yeats began
to draw imagery from the mythologies of other cultures; in *In
the Seven Woods* he uses Adam from the Hebraic-Christian
tradition and in *The Green Helmet* Homer's Helen of Troy.[12]
But the fact that he increased the range of his myth-symbols
does not necessarily mean that he was exchanging one set of
myth-stories for another, nor that he was replacing his Irish
allegory with an international allegory.

The truth of the matter would seem to be that Yeats had
always been somewhat casual in his handling of mythological
materials. For example, in the poem "Cuchulain's Fight with
the Sea" (1892), he did not hesitate to alter the legend,
substituting Emer, wife of the promiscuous hero, for Aoife, a
mistress who years before the episode of the poem had borne
him a child, in order to achieve greater simplicity and perhaps
to intensify the tragic implications by legitimizing the slain
son.[13] Yeats sought in mythology, whether of the peasant, the
old Celtic literature, or the comparative mythologists, not
what was significant but what might be suggestive; not substantive material but emblems that could be employed to
evoke the hidden reality. Aesthetically he identified poetry
with myth; he was concerned not with retelling myths for their
own sake but with assimilating the religious magic of the
mythopoeic process. When he had mastered the art of myth-
making he moved away from the world of allegory into the
realm of visionary symbol and sacred art.

Yeats' symbolism in fact represents an attempt, whether
conscious or unconscious, to duplicate the religious act of
myth-creation. In *The Trembling of the Veil* (1922) Yeats
writes that in the "species of man, wherein I count myself,
nothing so much matters as Unity of Being," and then offers
this definition: "true Unity of Being, where all the nature
murmurs in response if but a single note be touched, is found
emotionally, instinctively, by the rejection of all experience not

of the right quality, and by the limitation of its quantity" (p. 227). Ernst Cassirer, who a year later published the first volume of his theory of the human mental process, provides the following description of what he calls the mythico-religious protophenomenon of the "momentary god." The primitive ego, Cassirer suggests, was dominated by a mythico-religious sensitivity, so that when confronted and overwhelmed by a single object of experience it could perceive in that object the nature of the deity: "When, on the one hand, the entire self is given up to a single impression, is 'possessed' by it and, on the other hand, there is the utmost tension between the subject and its object, the outer world; when external reality is not merely viewed and contemplated, but overcomes a man in sheer immediacy, with emotions of fear or hope, terror or wish fulfillment: then the spark jumps somehow across, the tension finds release, as the subjective excitement becomes objectified, and confronts the mind as a god or a daemon." [14] Yeats' language may be that of the layman who has dabbled in occult lore, Cassirer's that of the philosopher, but they are saying the same thing. Mythopoeic vision is achieved through experience so intense and so immediate that it overwhelms the human consciousness with powerful emotion. It was toward such visionary perception that Yeats directed his art. "The imagination," he wrote to George Russell, "deals with spiritual things symbolized by natural things—with gods not with matter." [15]

Yeats was not familiar with Cassirer's work; it is therefore especially interesting that he should include a detailed rendering of the phenomenon of the momentary god in *The Herne's Egg*. In the fifth scene of that remarkable play the priestess Attracta, promised bride of the Great Herne, calls on her god-spouse to "Let the round heaven declare" that their marriage was consummated in the night and that King Congal and his men have lied in claiming to have ravished her. The heaven responds with "low thunder growing louder" and all the soldiers except Congal kneel and recant their claims of having raped her. Attracta then calls upon the god to provide "a most memorable punishment" for the repentant blasphemers and the thunder replies as before. The six soldiers prostrate themselves and Congal half kneels, but then stands upright. Finally, Attracta announces that the six soldiers will be reincarnated after death into "cat or rat or bat / Into dog or wolf or goose," but that Congal's ultimate fate has not been settled. The thunder sounds a third time, proclaiming the truth of Attracta's pronouncements; and this time all the men, including Congal, prostrate themselves.

> *Attracta.*   What has made you kneel?
> *Congal.*   This man
>   That's prostrate at my side would say,
>   Could he say anything at all,
>   That I am terrified by thunder.
> *Attracta.*   Why did you stand up so long?
> *Congal.*   I held you in my arms last night,
>   We seven held you in our arms.
> *Attracta.*   You were under the curse, in all
>   You did, in all you seemed to do.
> *Congal.*   If I must die at a fool's hand,
>   When must I die?
> *Attracta.*   When the moon is full.
> *Congal.*   And where?
> Attracta.   Upon the holy mountain,
>   Upon Slieve Fuadh, there we meet again
>   Just as the moon comes round the hill.
>   There all the gods must visit me,
>   Acknowledging my marriage to a god;
>   One man will I have among the gods.
> *Congal.*   I know the place and I will come.
>   Although it be my death, I will come.
>   Because I am terrified, I will come.[16]

Congal's conversion satisfies all the conditions for the phenomenon of the momentary god. During the play he has been in continuous conflict with the god's will. At the moment of conversion his attention is wholly taken up with the violent natural disturbance which is the manifestation of the divinity.

He is overwhelmed by fear, not merely because he is "terrified by thunder," but because he has identified the thunderclap with the godhead itself. His subjective fear is objectified into a god-image, which Yeats represents in the play as the Great Herne. It is noteworthy that Yeats chose as the outward sign for the deity that natural disturbance, thunder, which is associated with the greatest of the gods, the Greek Zeus, the Roman Jupiter, the Norse Thor, and, in Celtic mythology, the hero-god Lug, who is Cú Chulainn's supernatural father.

The momentary god, as the designation suggests, exists in the immediacy of the visionary experience itself. But the god may survive the subjective state of inner excitement and be given the objective form of myth.[17] He may be given existence apart from the particular experience and he may be named. Yeats objectifies the Great Herne in this manner, and does so also with the "rough beast" of "The Second Coming" and Christ in *The Resurrection*.[18] But it is the initial visionary perception that is most important to his aesthetic, what may be termed the principle of *pars pro toto*—sensing in the experience of the moment the totality of being.[19] This mythopoeic principle is basic to Yeats' symbolism; and, indeed, the purpose of that symbolism is identical to the purpose of myth: that is, by intensifying selected human experiences to achieve visionary perception of the godhead in nature and to suggest an instinctive knowledge of the total reality.

This myth-making aesthetic of Yeats' mature period must be considered in any final estimate of his vision of "the Holy Land of Ireland," because the three ideals—heroic, aristocratic, peasant—which are components of his image of the perfect nation are subjected to symbolic intensification that elevates them from the level of mundane reality to the spiritual permanence of a visionary Otherworld. The initial step in the elevation is closely related to the principle of *pars pro toto*; for, within the context of Yeats' poetry, that kind of experience which is identified with each of the three ideals is represented as being sufficiently intense or sufficiently passionate to result in that instinctive perception of the totality of being that is essential to the mythopoeic process.

In "Easter 1916" Yeats applies his mythopoeic art to the heroic ideal. The 1916 insurrection by a small force of Irish Volunteers deeply moved Yeats; he felt personal involvement in the violent events and a strong enough sense of personal responsibility to ask in his verse years later: "Did that play of mine send out / Certain men the English shot?" [20] The poet numbered several of the rebellion's leaders among his acquaintance and shared with them a faith in the re-emergence of an Irish racial heritage. He had exchanged letters with Thomas MacDonagh and had found in the younger man's poetry ideas both "daring and sweet"; he had visited St. Enda's School where Padraic Pearse blended heroic idealism into a Gaelic curriculum; he had shared public platforms with Pearse and Connolly, the labor leader the British shot tied to a chair because he was too weak from wounds to stand. When news of the Easter Rising reached him in England, Yeats spoke to his host, Sir William Rothenstein, of "innocent theorists" who were convinced they must sacrifice themselves to an abstraction; indeed, the poet tended to identify himself with the rebels and "fretted somewhat that he had not been consulted." [21] Twenty years later he would have the O'Rahilly utter much the same complaint in a poem:

> Am I such a craven that
> I should not get the word
> But for what some travelling man
> Had heard I had not heard? [22]

It is true that in the context of "Easter 1916" there are manifest two unresolved attitudes toward the rebellion: a sense of awe inspired by the martyrdom of the sixteen leaders and an inclination to condemn the hatred to which their action gave birth. This conflict within the poet certainly finds expression in the verse, but it is less an end in itself than a functional device, for it helps to establish an undercurrent of emotional turmoil which is essential to mythic perception. The key to the central intent of the poem is to be found in the third movement, where the calm, objective tone of the introductory passages gives way to an intense lyricism. It is by means of this lyric movement that Yeats tries to suggest the nature of the heroic passion which drove "MacDonagh and MacBride / And Connolly and Pearse" to make their blood sacrifice:

> Hearts with one purpose alone
> Through summer and winter seem
> Enchanted to a stone
> To trouble the living stream.
> The horse that comes from the road,
> The rider, the birds that range
> From cloud to tumbling cloud,
> Minute by minute they change;
> A shadow of cloud on the stream
> Changes minute by minute;
> A horse-hoof slides on the brim,
> And a horse plashes within it;
> The long-legged moor-hens dive,
> And hens to moor-cocks call;
> Minute by minute they live:
> The stone's in the midst of all.   (*Poems*, p. 179)

What Yeats means to suggest here is the transformation of the rebels and their action from the commonplace scene of "grey / Eighteenth-century houses" into the immortal world of myth. That the nature of the phenomenon is magical, or mythico-religious, is suggested by the use of the word "Enchanted" in the third line of the passage, and again, at the beginning of the second eight lines, by the powerful image of the changing "shadow of cloud on the stream," which, in its metaphysical texture, anticipates the ghost who can "drink

from the wine-breath" in "All Soul's Night" (1921).[23] The
images of "horse" and "rider" and "birds" are, in the context of
Yeats' verse, symbols of passionate nature. Horse and rider
evoke both the selfless aristocrats of Ireland's Great House
tradition and the fierce specters from Irish legend that people
Ben Bulben and Knocknarea.[24] The tumbling birds suggest
both the mystical Loves which circle the Sacred Tree in an
early poem, "The Two Trees," and the strange creatures who
greet Cú Chulainn after death in a poem Yeats wrote as an old
man.[25] Finally, there is a burst of apocalyptic imagery, the
horses sliding and the moor-hens diving and calling their
mates—like the crowing cockerel in "Solomon and the Witch"
(1921); these are omens of break-up. An epoch is ending; a
new god has been born. The stone symbol, which recurs in the
passage, has a special function in the mythopoeic process. On
the uppermost level it does suggest the hatred which Yeats
foresaw would be a consequence of the Easter revolt. But the
stone also embodies the meaning of permanence, of immortality, and encompasses allusions both to the magical stone
that the Tuatha Dé Danann of Irish mythology carried into
battle and to the philosopher's stone—the key to all knowledge—of medieval alchemy.[26] The stone, therefore, serving as a
catalyst within the pattern of imagery, effects the transformation of the act of revolt into the momentary perception of
"terrible beauty," that is, the vision of totality, the manifestation of the godhead.

   If "Easter 1916" is meant to suggest visionary perception
equivalent to the phenomenon of the momentary god, Yeats'
other verse concerned with the Rising carries the mythopoeic
process a step further and effects the deification of its heroes.
The rebel leaders, like the "men of the old black tower" who
stand "on guard oath-bound" to their rightful king and the old
way of life,[27] reject by the nobility of their death the meanness
of modern life. Pearse and Connolly, in particular, were taken
up into the poet's heroic symbolism of Ireland's greatness
along with Parnell, Wolfe Tone, Robert Emmet, and, most

important of all, Cú Chulainn. Yeats was aware that some of "the best known men who got themselves killed in 1916 had the Irish legendary hero Cuchulain so much on their minds that the Irish government celebrated the event with a local statue. For us a legendary man or woman must still be able to fight or dance." [28] So, Yeats tells his readers, Pearse summons Cú Chulainn to his side at the General Post Office and through the inspiration of the *Táin's* hero is able to climb from "this filthy modern tide" to find wisdom and heroic passion in "The lineaments of a plummet-measured face." [29] Yeats elevates the insurrectionaries to a mythological world where the battle is identical with the dance, where swords flash but never strike home, where every movement has symbolic meaning. Within this framework the Rising becomes a kind of national ritual.

Having transformed the Cú Chulainn legend into a sacred drama from which the Irish people might take spiritual nourishment, Yeats gives similar treatment to the Rising and its heroes—and to the other modern Irish hero, Parnell, as well—blending dramatic technique and national idealism into ritual. That his nationalism bears a relationship to his dramatic art is made clear in a note appended to "Three Songs to the Same Tune": "A nation should be like an audience in some great theatre—'in the theatre,' said Victor Hugo, 'the mob becomes a people'—watching the drama of its own history . . . that sacred drama must to all native eyes and ears become the greatest of parables" (*Var.*, p. 837). In the poetry of the Rising, theatrical imagery tends to establish a stylized tone, thereby removing the poetic substance from commonplace reality to a ceremonial plane where the effect of a dramatic, liturgical ritual is possible. In "Three Songs to the One Burden, III," a late poem, the imagery is applied specifically to the Rising:

> Come gather round me, players all:
> Come praise Nineteen-Sixteen,
> Those from the pit and gallery
> Or from the painted scene

> That fought in the Post Office
> Or round the City Hall,
> Praise every man that came again,
> Praise every man that fell.

The same metaphor is used, with reference to Parnell, in "Parnell's Funeral" (1932).

The rebels of 1916, taken up in the flow of mimetic action, are transfigured; they become Messianic figures:

> Some had no thought of victory
> But had gone out to die
> That Ireland's mind be greater
> Her heart mount up on high.   (*Poems*, p. 321)

There is evidence that the poets of the insurrection—Pearse, MacDonagh, and Plunkett—did in fact conceive of rebellion as an act of spiritual importance, a necessary purgation for the shame of Ireland's servitude, a blood sacrifice to restore Ireland's racial integrity. Behind the Republican movement there existed an overwrought sense of national pride—even, perhaps, fanaticism—that Yeats and most other prominent figures of the literary movement shared. Yeats was aware that the Rising poets held a common faith in the ritual of blood sacrifice; and he made reference to the ominous tone of prophecy in Pearse's poetry:

> For Patrick Pearse had said
> That in every generation
> Must Ireland's blood be shed.   (*Poems*, p. 321)

These self-appointed victims Yeats gathered up into his hagiology of Irish heroes, with "Lord Edward and Wolfe Tone," with Charles Stuart Parnell at whose death the sky brightened with light and flames, and with Cú Chulainn who fastened his belt to a pillar-stone that he might die heroically upon his feet. The mystical force of the blood sacrifice—set into this racial dream of heroic virtue—is far more powerful than any appeal to discursive reason, for no logic can "outweigh / Mac-Donagh's bony thumb." [30] The sacrifice is, indeed, strong enough magic to elevate the willing victims to the status of demigods.

The process of deification is suggested in "The Rose Tree." On one level, the poem clearly represents an allegorical comment on the Irish struggle for political sovereignty. But Yeats' artistry penetrates much deeper. Through the medium of an overtly patriotic ballad he seeks to "communicate" an intense, spiritual message to a people whose racial heritage renders them receptive:

> 'O words are lightly spoken,'
> Said Pearse to Connolly,
> 'Maybe a breath of politic words
> Has withered our Rose Tree;
> Or maybe but a wind that blows
> Across the bitter sea.'
>
> 'It needs to be but watered,'
> James Connolly replied,
> 'To make the green come out again
> And spread on every side,
> And shake the blossom from the bud
> To be the garden's pride.'
>
> 'But where can we draw water,'
> Said Pearse to Connolly,
> 'When all the wells are parched away?
> O plain as plain can be
> There's nothing but our own red blood
> Can make a right Rose Tree.'   (*Poems*, pp. 180–81)

The Rose Tree itself is a symbol of multiple reference, if, indeed, its limitations can be fully defined. It echoes back, first of all, to the image of Róisín Dubh in traditional Irish protest literature and represents the Irish nation in the pre-Rising period. Parnell had been dead more than two decades; O'Leary was "in the grave," and with him the heroic tradition of Romantic Ireland. But Pearse and Connolly, along with their ill-fated comrades, burst upon the scene to renew for Ireland—and for Yeats—the tradition of heroic gesture. The symbolic meaning, however, extends much further. The Rose, for example, carries suggestions of Shelley's Neo-Platonic concept of intellectual beauty and, on yet another level, of the flower of the Rosicrucians. Most important of all to our full appreciation of the poem is Yeats' identification of the Rose Tree with the archetypal Sacred Tree. The reference to "the garden's pride" in the second stanza recalls Yeats' note to *The Wind Among the Reeds* in which he describes an Irishman's vision in the Garden of Eden: near the top of the Tree of Knowledge, a beautiful woman, like the Goddess of Life associated with the Tree in Assyria, gives him a rose (*Var.*, p. 811); the Rose Tree, considered in this context, becomes a symbol for the ideal of the passionate life which had been swept away by the bitter wind of abstract rationalism and which Pearse and Connolly seek to return to its place in the "garden" so that Irishmen may live as men lived before the Fall, in instinctive harmony with nature.

But the relationship between the Rose Tree and the archetypal Sacred Tree is not simply a matter of allusion, for the mythological Tree provides an essential frame of reference for the poem and, indeed, helps to determine its very form. Yeats was certainly familiar with the essential characteristics of the Sacred Tree in ancient Mesopotamian pictorial art. First, the arrangement of the Tree's branches is often symmetrical. Second, two acolytes, or genii, identical in expression and attitude, almost always flank the Tree. In most Assyrian art, the acolytes hold toward the Tree conical objects which some scholars believe are cones of pine or cedar used in magical ceremonies of exorcism to sprinkle the Tree with lustral water taken from containers in their other hands.[31] Although Yeats imposes symmetrical arrangement on his Sacred Tree symbol elsewhere, in "The Two Trees," for example, formal harmony in "The Rose Tree" is confined to the structure of the poem, with its carefully worked out stanzaic pattern and versification. But the stylized figures of Pearse and Connolly are certainly meant to represent acolytes. They are no longer political leaders but consecrated priests performing a mystical ritual,

that of exorcising the Sacred Rose Tree of the Irish race and
nation with a lustral liquid—in this instance their own blood.
By creating his Rose Tree symbol, then, Yeats gives to Pearse
and Connolly and to the ritual sacrifice in which they shared a
new meaning within the context of his own *anima mundi*, that
peculiar Celtic Otherworld.

Yeats' *anima mundi* and Carl Jung's collective unconscious
are similar in that both can affect the emotional and imaginative aspects of human life; however, certain important distinctions between the two must be made. Jung's conception of
racial memory is essentially biological and its archetypes were
formed in that remote prehistoric period when mankind was
emerging from the animal to the human state. Yeats' Great
Memory, on the other hand, is spiritual in nature; and its
power to absorb the images of human experience is not limited
in time. Any experience may be gathered up, provided only
that it is sufficiently intense or passionate. The nature of the
anima mundi can best be understood by reference to the poet's
theory of the daemon, which owes something to the influence
of Blake and something again to the poet's study of Plotinus.
The primary source, however, is Plutarch (*Morals*, IV, 4), who
held that good spirits are transformed into angels or daemons.[32]
For Yeats, as for Plutarch, it is the daemon's task to care for
and encourage humanity, to serve as a guardian angel for
mankind, or, in the case of Yeats' hagiology, for the Irish race;
so "When Pearse summoned Cuchulain to his side," a dae-
monic power "stalked through the Post Office"; and so the
sixteen leaders executed for their part in the Rising "are
loitering there / To stir the boiling pot." [33] The heroic images
of the *anima mundi*, like the magical race of Tuatha Dé
Danann who took refuge in Ireland's fairy mounds after their
defeat by the Milesians, can help to shape the fates of
individuals or even a race of men, provided that race "first find
philosophy and a little passion." [34] Yeats' vision of Ireland,
then, has a vitality of its own, just as had the natural
mythologies that man created before the dawn of history; his

vision is a kind of mythico-religious force that could one day give to the poet's own people what he called "Unity of Culture."

If the heroic ideal is invested with a special spiritual significance, so also is the aristocratic ideal. The effect of Yeats' mythopoeic aesthetic upon the ideal of noble passion can be seen through an examination of "Coole Park, 1929" and "Coole Park and Ballylee, 1931," companion poems in which Yeats comments on the passing of that gentle way of life he associated with Lady Gregory and her home in County Galway.[35] The first of these poems is relatively explicit. In the opening lines Yeats identifies the aristocratic tradition with images of nature—the swallow in flight, the sycamore and lime-tree at sunset—and attributes to the dying way of life artistic achievement of "a dance-like glory," a figure which suggests both order and natural passion. In the second stanza Yeats mentions five men who had found inspiration at Coole Park: Douglas Hyde, whose *Songs of Connacht* captured the instinctive passion of the western Gaels; Yeats himself; John Synge, who, like Lady Gregory, remained isolated "from all contagious opinions of poorer minds"; [36] John Shawe Taylor, Lady Gregory's impetuous nephew, who Yeats believed guided his actions by a kind of divine intuition; [37] and Hugh Lane, whose attempt to introduce modern art to Dublin stirred a furor. In the final two lines of the stanza Yeats suggests what is essential to the aristocratic ideal: arrogant pride of family balanced by personal humility, and the physical and intellectual luxury that is the right of inherited wealth. In the third stanza Yeats personifies in Lady Gregory those concepts of permanence and order that are inherent in the aristocratic tradition [38] and in the final eight lines of the poem he urges those who retain some connection with the old way of

life—"traveller, scholar, poet"—to keep faith with the ideal
(*Poems*, p. 238).

If "Coole Park, 1929" defines the aristocratic ideal by means
of restrained imagery, "Coole Park and Ballylee, 1931" does
much more. In the first half of the latter poem, the theme of
the passing of the aristocratic way of life is couched in the
intense language of visionary symbol. The opening stanza is
dominated by the metaphor of the stream which in fact passes
Yeats' tower at Ballylee, then flows underground through
"Raftery's 'cellar' "—a sinkhole named after a blind Gaelic
poet of the early nineteenth century—before emerging again as
a source for one of Coole Park's lakes:

> Under my window-ledge the waters race,
> Otters below and moor-hens on the top,
> Run for a mile undimmed in Heaven's face
> Then darkening through 'dark' Raftery's 'cellar' drop,
> Run underground, rise in a rocky place
> In Coole demesne, and there to finish up
> Spread to a lake and drop into a hole.
> What's water but the generated soul? [39]

The central metaphor of flowing water may hint of Yeats'
belief in the soul's progress from the light of life into the
darkness of death and then into the renewed light of reincarnation, but such a reading does not fit well into the context of the
entire poem, which, after all, is concerned not with the
individual but with the aristocratic tradition. The essential
reference for the metaphor is to Yeats' theory of recurring
cycles in history—a theory which operates on the same general
principles as that of reincarnation—the great aristocratic ideal,
which had thrived "undimmed in Heaven's face" for centuries
(which is but a "mile" in the great span of eternity), was dying
out, or rather was sinking into the darkness of the racial
memory. But in the inevitable flow of history the ideal would
someday re-emerge and flourish and then again disappear as an
antithetical epoch gained ascendancy. The analogy of the last
line of the stanza, then, identifying the water of the stream

with "the generated soul," refers not to the individual spirit, but to the *anima mundi*, that vast reservoir in which experiences of human passion are preserved. The allusion to Raftery in the fourth line supports this reading. For the blind poet, fabled in the West of Ireland during his lifetime, was forgotten after death (*ca.* 1840). But his songs remained in the "racial memory" of the peasantry; and a half-century afterwards Douglas Hyde rediscovered both Raftery and his Gaelic songs when a beggar, who, like the poet, was blind, directed him to the locale where Raftery died.[40]

The occult symbolism of the initial stanza prepares the way for the poet's vision that follows:

> Upon the border of that lake's a wood
> Now all dry sticks under a wintery sun,
> And in a copse of beeches there I stood,
> For Nature's pulled her tragic buskin on
> And all the rant's a mirror of my mood:
> At sudden thunder of the mounting swan
> I turned about and looked where branches break
> The glittering reaches of the flooded lake.   (*Poems*, p. 239)

The images of "dry sticks" and "a wintry sun," signifying the declining seasons in nature, point up the tragic passing of the old way of life, which like the seasons is subject to Nature's cyclical law; just as the trees must wither beneath the harsh glare of the winter sun, so also must the aristocratic tradition decline before the destructive force of rationalism and materialism. And again, the fury of the winter in the natural scene is like the poet's own anger that the swan, the pure image of the aristocratic ideal, should be driven to flight. But this poetic protest is not the limit of Yeats' art in this stanza; for he contrives to elevate his aristocratic ideal to the realm of myth by symbolically identifying it with the godhead. It is noteworthy that a state of tension exists between the poet and the object of his contemplation, the image of decline in nature on one level of meaning, the fact of decline of the aristocratic ideal which the image represents on another level. Then, too, the impact upon the poet of the swan's "sudden" flight is immediate and overwhelming. What follows is revelation in the "thunder of the mounting swan" of the momentary god, that is, the glimpse into the underlying reality. "Mounting swan" is a pun; it embodies both a reference to the disappearing aristocratic way of life and an allusion to the rape of Leda by Zeus in the form of a giant swan, an event which, in "Leda and the Swan" (1924), signals the end of one cycle and the beginning of another (*Poems*, pp. 211–12). The appearance of the deity is proclaimed by thunder, the voice of Zeus by tradition and of Yeats' Great Herne as well. Indeed, in the opening lines of the poem there is an augury of the god's coming in the image of the moor-hens caught up in the turbulence of the rushing waters.

In the first stanza Yeats defines the aristocratic ideal in terms of its relationship to the cyclical theory of history and to the *anima mundi* that transcends history's limitations of time and mutability. In the second stanza he identifies the ideal with the visible manifestation of divinity in nature, with that peculiar kind of passionate beauty—"thunder of the mounting swan"—that can strike the "single note" in man's religious imagination and engender visionary perception. The third stanza relates the passing of the tradition to the life and death of the individual human being. The "stormy white" image of the swan, "arrogantly pure" in keeping with its suggestion of the aristocratic ideal, "like the soul . . . sails into sight / And in the morning's gone, no man knows why." It is noteworthy that the "logical" structure of the poem's imagery seems to involve a gradual lessening of esoteric symbolism: so Yeats progresses from the realm of pure spirit, the *anima mundi*, to the physical manifestation of the deity, to the basic human predicament of mutability, and then, for most of the final three stanzas, to a direct commentary on the aristocratic society, its decline, and its relationship to the artist. The ideal is personified in the aged figure of Lady Gregory passing amid books and busts and pictures, relics of past glory. The estate itself,

with its "ancestral trees" and "rich gardens," also is suggestive
of the antiquity and grandeur of the family line. Out of such
surroundings, Yeats adds in a final stanza, the poet may draw
the "Traditional sanctity and loveliness" of the aristocratic
ideal that "most can bless the mind of man." Only in the last
lines of climax does Yeats return to the world of vision with the
myth-symbol of riderless horse and the image of the drifting
swan "upon a darkening flood" (*Poems*, p. 240).

In his Coole Park poems Yeats presents a lyric protest
against the social and cultural visitations—rationalism, materialism, democracy—that were destroying the way of life he
believed to be the noblest form of civilization achieved by
mankind. But in "Coole Park and Ballylee, 1931" his aesthetic
purpose extends beyond the expression of indignation. By
using the occult symbolism of his mystical system, Yeats seeks
to elevate the aristocratic ideal into his national mythology; in
other words, the overlay of spiritualism is meant to transform
the ideal into a racial archetype that could become a living
force in the life of an Utopian Irish nation ruled by the law of
human passion.

It may seem unkind, not to say indecorous, that Yeats should
place Lady Gregory and Crazy Jane in the same Heaven, but
that he did so seems quite certain from the evidence of the
poetry. For, like the mistress of Coole Park, Crazy Jane is
emblematic of that human passion through which human
sanctification may be achieved, and in Yeats' treatment of her
unladylike antics one finds the same esoteric ingredients as in
"Coole Park and Ballylee, 1931": the *anima mundi*, the
appearance of the god, and the vision. The sequence of seven
poems concerned with Jane in *Words for Music Perhaps*
constitutes a kind of sensual "Pilgrim's Progress" in which
Everywoman successfully resists the blandishments of the

Bishop, with his creed of sterility and abstraction, and ultimately identifies her whole being with the instinctive drive of sexual passion that is inherent in her nature. Crazy Jane therefore represents an affirmation by Yeats of the peasant ideal, that is, the physical nature of man, and implies also that complete abandonment to the dictates of that nature can bring man into harmony with the invisible forces that sustain the universe. In a letter to Mrs. Shakespear, Yeats comments on the genesis of one of the poems, "Crazy Jane and Jack the Journeyman"; the poet had been walking along a dark path when suddenly two "excitements" fused together: "The autumnal image, remote, incredibly spiritual, erect, delicate featured, and mixed with it the violent physical image, the black mass of Eden" (*Letters*, p. 785). What Yeats perceived was an archetypal image of the union of spirit and flesh, and in his verse he attempts to recreate that image for the reader by merging Crazy Jane's sexual promiscuity with the symbolism of his occult system.

On the uppermost level of meaning, the sequence is concerned with the choice between asceticism and sensuality. The conflict between the two is made explicit in the first poem, "Crazy Jane and the Bishop" (1930), in which Jane comments on the relative merits of the Bishop and her lover, Jack the Journeyman. The poet's verdict in favor of Jack as an image of physical instinct is spelled out through the changing sense of the refrain. In the opening stanza, Jane reveals that the Bishop has denounced her lover: "Coxcomb was the least he said." The meaning of the refrain that follows—"*The solid man and the coxcomb*"—is clear: the "solid man" is the righteous Bishop; the "coxcomb" is the sinner, Jack the Journeyman. However, in the second stanza Jane undercuts the Bishop's position by observing that he was not even an ordained priest when he drove Jack out, and that his only authority was "an old book," a reference to the Bible no doubt, but with the implication that it had long since outlived its usefulness. In the next stanza the two men are judged by their physical merit:

> The Bishop has a skin, God knows,
> Wrinkled like the foot of a goose,
> (*All find safety in the tomb.*)
> Nor can he hide in holy black
> The heron's hunch upon his back,
> But a birch-tree stood my Jack,
> *The solid man and the coxcomb.*   (*Poems*, p. 251)

The Bishop and his sterile dogma are depicted as decrepit and deformed and are found lacking entirely when measured against the physical standard of Nature. But Jack, described by a single phallic image from the natural scene, epitomizes both "solidness" and sexual potency. In consequence, the meaning of the refrain is reversed; Jack is now the "solid man" and the Bishop the "coxcomb."

The basic conflict between sensuality and asceticism is continued intermittently in the poems that follow—in what could be described as a debate between Jane and the Bishop—until in "Crazy Jane Talks with the Bishop" (1933) Yeats' heroine has the woman's last word:

> 'A woman can be proud and stiff
> When on love intent;
> But Love has pitched his mansion in
> The place of excrement;
> For nothing can be sole or whole
> That has not been rent.'   (*Poems*, p. 255)

The affirmation of man's physical nature is unqualified; for the poet links together the physical function of love, which has often been idealized into something more ethereal than fleshly, with another physical function that defies idealization. In the final two lines Yeats integrates man's animal and spiritual natures by means of a remarkable and, in some measure, repulsive pun; for while both "sole" and "whole" convey notions of unity and harmony, each has another reference, the former to "soul," that is, the spiritual nature of man, the latter to "hole," associated with the physical function of sex and that of excretion. The collage of suggestion is synthesized by the image of violent passion—the act of tearing asunder—in the final line.

The Bishop's point of view, expressed in the second poem of the sequence, "Crazy Jane Reproved" (1930), is not likely to convert Jane. What the Bishop offers is defined in the second stanza:

> To round that shell's elaborate whorl,
> Adorning every secret track
> With delicate mother-of-pearl.

There is a contrived beauty here, but more noteworthy is the fact that the imagery is highly artificial; the metaphor, like the Bishop's philosophy, is an abstraction. Crazy Jane rejects this world of austere contemplation with the derisive nonsense refrain, *"Fol de rol, fol de rol."* She applies the same phrase of ridicule to the Bishop's plea against the life of physical passion in the opening stanza of the poem; the deformed cleric exclaims:

> All those dreadful thunder-stones,
> All that storm that blots the day
> Can but show that Heaven yawns;
> Great Europa played the fool
> That changed a lover for a bull.   (*Poems*, p. 252)

But what the Bishop denounces is precisely what Jane seeks; for the "bull" is the natural divinity that reveals itself in the moment of passionate experience which is, like human copulation, so immediate and intense that it overwhelms the consciousness. In this instance, because his appearance is heralded by "thunder-stones" and because of the reference to the Europa legend, the bull-god is Zeus, who, disguised as a bull, carried Europa to Crete where she bore him three children. The choice of divine animal is appropriate for Jane, who is an image of the peasant ideal, inasmuch as bull-worship was almost certainly part of the heritage from pagan Ireland.[41] In any event, Crazy Jane already had dedicated herself to the pagan gods of passion; her first utterance in "Crazy Jane and the Bishop" makes her position clear: "Bring me to the blasted oak," she says, to that tree which is traditionally sacred to witches and thunder-gods (*Poems*, p. 251).

The instant of sexual release is for Crazy Jane the moment of the god, and the moment of vision as well. When the human consciousness is utterly absorbed in a single passionate experience, then it is possible, as Jane suggests in "Crazy Jane on the Day of Judgment" (1932), to escape from time into eternity where knowledge of the ultimate reality may be achieved.[42] Crazy Jane's mythic vision is defined in the last poem of the sequence, "Crazy Jane Grown Old Looks at the Dancers" (1930), in which Yeats treats of sexual passion in the language of destructive violence. In the poem Jane watches the "ivory image" of a sexual dance in which the passion of each of the dancers evolves into a desire to destroy and consume the partner in a kind of ritual sacrifice; Yeats implies that love and hate, fascination and terror are combined in the sexual act, just as they are embodied in the refrain image of the rhetorical "lion's tooth." The object of sexual passion is suggested in the rhetorical questions at the beginning of the final stanza: "Did he die or did she die? / Seemed to die or died they both?" Participation in the sexual act involves the death of the individual ego; and because this is so, because personal consciousness is destroyed, the dancers may be absorbed into the occult world of the unconscious—the "black mass of Eden"— where ultimate knowledge is possible. The dominant dance image of the poem has a double function in the process of mythic vision: it is, of course, an agent of synthesis and intensification; but it also conveys an allusion to the spinning gyre, which served Yeats as a Mandala-like symbol for the nature of the deity.

The peasant ideal centers on man's physical nature and finds its source in the same principle of human passion that determines both the heroic and aristocratic ideals. Yeats' approval of this ideal of physical passion is implicit in Crazy Jane's visionary perception which it inspires, and in the fact that her promiscuous relationship with Jack the Journeyman is assimilated into the myth-world of the *anima mundi*. If the leaders of the Easter Rising can evoke from mythology the spirit of Cú Chulainn as hero, and the aristocrats that of Cú Chulainn as one whose only law is his own noble will, then it is only fitting that Crazy Jane, in "Crazy Jane on the Mountain" (1939), should encounter the spirits of Cú Chulainn as violent lover and the "Great-bladdered Emer," his spouse. The Bishop had cried that Jane and Jack the Journeyman "lived like beast and beast" (*Poems*, p. 251); but, in the context of the sequence, their having done so becomes a virtue rather than a vice, for the instinctive sexual urge is its own justification. Indeed, because of the intensity of their passion, Crazy Jane and her lover achieve immortality; Jane promises in "Crazy Jane and Jack the Journeyman" that should Jack's ghost pass her grave and turn his head, then her own spirit "must walk when dead" (*Poems*, p. 253).

The fifth poem in the sequence, "Crazy Jane on God" (1932), is important in several respects. For one thing, it defines Yeats' conception of deity as the *anima mundi*, the world-spirit which he believed to be the fountainhead of all myth. For another, it chronicles the elevation of Crazy Jane's physical passion into that storehouse of archetypes. But its central significance is that it incorporates into a single vision the three ideals of Yeats' "Holy Land of Ireland." In the second stanza Yeats suggests the heroic ideal through the imagery of "the great battle" fought "In the narrow pass," referring to Thermopylae, but suggesting also Cú Chulainn's singlehanded stand against Maeve's armies in the *Táin* and the fight of Ficna, Innsa, and Diarmuid against the powers of the King of the World in the Fenian Cycle.[43] In the third stanza Yeats presents the image of a house, "Uninhabited, ruinous, / Suddenly lit up / From door

to top," alluding to the theme of aristocratic decline that is
treated fully in *Purgatory*. The final stanza depicts the passion
of Crazy Jane and Jack the Journeyman:

> I had wild Jack for a lover;
> Though like a road
> That men pass over
> My body makes no moan
> But sings on.

Their passion had been so intense, and because intense so pure,
that its image cannot be defiled by subsequent experience. The
poem's refrain—"*All things remain in God*"—serves to elevate
and integrate the heroic, aristocratic, and peasant ideals; all
three are taken up into the godhead, and Yeats' national
vision is thereby given divine sanction (*Poems*, pp. 253–54).

The same principles of sublimation and synthesis are at work
in "Three Songs to the One Burden" (1939). The first poem
suggests that the Roaring Tinker, Mannion, who conjures up
the image of Crazy Jane, is distinct from the "common breed"
because of the ferocity of his nature. At the center of the
second poem is the image of the old order, Henry Middleton,
who locks his gate against the world's degeneracy and each
Sunday walks "On the Green Lands," reflecting on the past
glory of the aristocratic tradition. The third song defines the
heroic ideal through the images of Pearse and Connolly and
their selfless sacrifice in the Easter Rising. All three ideals,
peasant, aristocratic, heroic, are transformed by means of the
common refrain, "*From mountain to mountain ride the fierce
horsemen*," which carries an allusion to the myth-world of Ben
Bulben and Knocknarea where the passionate spirits of Cú
Chulainn and Medb and Diarmuid abide and "ride the wintry
dawn" (*Poems*, pp. 319–21; 341).

"Crazy Jane on God" and "Three Songs to the One Burden"
illustrate the final step in the mythopoeic process. Through
this synthesis within the animating force of the natural godhead, the *anima mundi*, the heroic, aristocratic, and peas-

ant symbols are given the archetypal status of myth and are therefore infused—or so Yeats believed—with a vitality of their own that would permit their existence independent of the temporal experience from which they were drawn. Such symbols are functional in that they can unify individuals, races, and nations. Thus Yeats' three ideals are meant to exert a very real influence upon future generations of Irishmen; for, as archetypes, they can elicit the same immediate response that characterizes the phenomenon of the momentary god and they can thereby invest the Irish race with a deep-rooted sense of the spiritual passion that permits men to live in harmony with Nature's grand design. There is little need to add that a society ruled by such natural passion would be in its social organization hierarchical, would provide physical and intellectual luxury for aristocrats and humble service for the baseborn, and would foster once again the noble art of Phidias and Michelangelo and Botticelli, an art devoted to the unity and perfection of man and not to his division and degradation.

In his mature verse Yeats kept faith with the pledge, made in New York in 1904, to work toward the creation in Ireland of "an imaginative culture and power to understand imaginative and spiritual things distributed among the people." He tried to create a national mythology that would embody the image of the Garden before the Fall, a mythology that might inspire each man as an individual and the race and nation as a whole to live according to the law of instinctive passion. In "Under Ben Bulben," the last poem in the definitive edition, Yeats bequeaths the burden of this task to the Irish poets of coming generations. He urges them to devote their song to the expression of whatever embodies the passionate ideal—the simple peasants, the country gentlemen, the lords and ladies "That were beaten into clay / Through seven heroic centuries." Most important of all, he asks that they renew that tradition of art, born in antiquity and fostered in aristocratic societies before the "levelling wind" brought confusion upon the world, which sought to create the image of perfect human nobility. To this end he gave to the poets his mythopoeic aesthetic by means of which they might achieve visionary perception of the hidden reality and create for Ireland a sacred literature:

> Poet and sculptor, do the work,
> Nor let the modish painter shirk
> What his great forefathers did,
> Bring the soul of man to God.

(*Poems*, pp. 342–43)

5

A.E.: THE LAND OF PROMISE

In almost every critical commentary on modern Irish verse
A.E. (George Russell) is singled out to share credit with W. B.
Yeats for having breathed life into the embryonic literary
revival of the eighteen-nineties. It is certainly true that A.E.
contributed much to the movement, taking on himself the role
of prophet and patriarch, advising and encouraging innumerable young poets and writers for a period of forty years; yet,
relatively speaking, he was a late-comer to the cause of literary
renaissance and at first a somewhat reluctant apostle. Yeats,
indeed, had encouraged the youthful Russell in his painting
and poetry and had brought him into his circle of literary
friends in the later eighteen-eighties; but Yeats also introduced
him to Charles Johnston, who had founded a branch of
Madame Blavatsky's Theosophical Society in Dublin; and for
the moment the lure of occult wisdom proved stronger for A.E.
than the lure of literary fame. He turned his back on artistic
ambition and for almost a decade was obsessed with the notion
that he himself was chosen of the Mighty Mind (i.e., God) to
evangelize the religion of theosophy. He published *Homeward:
Songs by the Way* in 1894, but did so only after he was
convinced by friends that poems might work spiritual good and
after one of those friends, Charles Weekes, turned publisher in

order to produce the small volume.[1] Soon afterwards A.E. came under the influence of James Pryse, an American theosophist, who decided that the young Irishman's special aptitude was in the area of "psychic vision" and who helped him master the difficult art of conjuring up the spirits which inhabited Ireland's ancient ruins.[2] That Russell took himself seriously as a medium is clear from his own testimony and from such evidence as George Moore's comic picture of him calling up the gods at Dowth and New Grange, squatting on the ground like a Yogi, muttering incantations, waiting for his vision.[3]

A.E. remained the dominant spirit of the Dublin theosophical movement until 1897, a critical point in his life and career, a year of apostasy. First of all, he published a second volume of poems, *The Earth Breath*, noticeably more secular in content and tone than the earlier *Homeward*; and he produced two pamphlets, *The Awakening of the Fires* and *Priest or Hero?*, by means of which he certainly intended to create a public stir. Concerning these pamphlets he wrote to Yeats: "I will say things in fierce print to make people's hair stand up." [4] Second and no doubt more significant, in 1897 A.E. accepted employment as a field representative for Sir Horace Plunkett's Irish Agricultural Organization Society and toured the countryside by bicycle preaching the advantages of co-operative farming—a curious occupation, to say the least, for a dedicated mystic. In the following year A.E. completed his secularization. He flouted one of theosophy's cardinal rules, that of celibacy, by marrying and, to make matters worse, took as his bride Violet North, herself a student of the "secret doctrine" and Pryse's assistant in editing *The Irish Theosophist*. In the same year, after an argument over the leadership of Dublin's theosophists, he formally resigned from the Point Loma Universal Brotherhood, as the Theosophical Society was formally designated.[5]

A.E. did not renounce his theosophical beliefs nor the practice of psychometry,[6] nor did his verse become noticeably less mystical, yet he gave up the ascetic disciplines associated

with occult studies and with the passing years devoted more
and more of his time to worldly pursuits, especially literature,
economics, and political journalism. He made a name for
himself as a writer with an outpouring of poetry and prose. The
production of his play, *Deirdre*, along with Yeats' *Cathleen Ni
Houlihan*, by W. G. Fay's National Dramatic Company,
marked the beginning of the Irish dramatic movement.[7] The
play was heralded as a significant event and its author won
acclaim as a literary lion. Young people gathered about the
bearded poet, who, next to Yeats, was held in greatest esteem
and who, unlike Yeats, was profuse in advice and encourage-
ment. Much more than Yeats he became a popular public
figure. Then he took up journalism, as editor of *The Irish
Homestead* (1905–23) and *The Irish Statesman* (1923–30),
and for many years in the columns of these two newspapers he
tried to influence the course of Irish affairs. During the labor
strife of 1913 in Dublin, A.E. sided with the workers and
delivered a speech on their behalf at a mass rally in London;
but he found himself castigated in Ireland by the press, the
Catholic Church, and the middle-class nationalists for espous-
ing "Bolshevism" and thereafter was more restrained in his
social criticism.[8] In 1917 he argued the nationalist point of
view at a fruitless Home Rule convention, of which Horace
Plunkett was chairman. He became an important public figure,
even in his own estimation, and when in 1919 Sinn Féin won
the general election, he wrote to a friend: "The coming
national policy will be a blend of Pearse, Connolly and AE."
What was possibly his greatest public performance came late
in life when Henry Wallace invited him to Washington, D.C.,
to speak with President Franklin Roosevelt and to indoctrinate
American agricultural experts with the underlying spiritual
truth of the co-operative movement.[10]

A.E.'s attitude toward the national political movement in
Ireland, like that of Yeats, passed through various phases. At
the turn of the century—and, indeed, until the nineteen-
twenties when a self-governing Ireland proved him wrong—he

was confident that his country would soon emerge as a great "rural civilisation," founded upon spiritual beliefs which A.E. himself and the ancient Celts held in common. He shied away from the popular bitterness against England in the years prior to the 1916 rebellion; and in *The National Being* he warned his countrymen that hatred of the British would be self-defeating: "Race hatred is the cheapest and basest of all national passions, and it is the nature of hatred, as it is the nature of love, to change us into the likeness of that which we contemplate." [11] The Easter Rising stirred A.E., as it did almost every Irishman; but the subsequent Black and Tan War and civil strife saddened and angered him, for they involved a useless shedding of blood and the dissipation of creative energy necessary to the building of a nation. His anger turned slowly to disillusion in the nineteen-twenties as he watched unfolding events in the Irish Free State. The intensity of his bitterness is expressed in two letters written in the spring of 1932; in one he writes to Kingsley Porter, an American friend: "I rage and gesticulate and curse the fools who run my country," [12] and in the other, even more incensed, to Pamela Travers: "I would like to fly from Dublin, even from Ireland, so much do I dislike the new generation of bigoted Catholics and political louts who are dominant. . . . Ireland as a nation I have no further interest in." [13]

Occasionally A.E.'s public attitudes find expression in his verse. "On Behalf of Some Irishmen Not Followers of Tradition," for example, like Yeats' "To Ireland in the Coming Time," is a defense of an aesthetic grounded in the unorthodoxy of theosophy. In his poem A.E. exhorts the youthful poets of Ireland to reject "the sceptyred myth" of conventional belief and to dedicate themselves to "The golden heresy of truth." [14] The Easter Rising of 1916 inspired A.E. to compose a most moving poem, "Salutation," addressed to Padraic Pearse, James Connolly, Thomas MacDonagh, Countess Markievicz, and those other rebels whom he did not know personally:

Your dream had left me numb and cold
But yet my spirit rose in pride,
Re-fashioning in burnished gold
The images of those who died,
Or were shut in the penal cell—
Here's to you, Pearse, your dream, not mine,
But yet the thought—for this you fell—
Turns all life's water into wine.[15]

A.E. composed "Salutation" shortly after the abortive rebellion and had it privately printed and distributed. The poem has often been anthologized, yet A.E. omitted it from the final selection for the collected edition. Deeper and more lasting, perhaps, was his response to the death of Terence MacSwiney, the mayor of Cork, after a sixty-nine-day hunger strike in Brixton Gaol during the Black and Tan War. In a sonnet, "A Prisoner," A.E. compares MacSwiney to the "fabled Titan chained upon the hill" (*Poems*, p. 354). MacSwiney's act of passive heroism demanded and won the poet's admiration; whereas his response to deeds of violence was ordinarily characterized by indignation and regret. So, in "Waste," A.E. decries the slaughter of the Irish Civil War as a "sacrifice / For words hollow as wind" (*Poems*, p. 352), an allusion in general to the emptiness of political oratory and, perhaps, in particular to the fact that Eamon De Valera rejected the Free State Treaty and thereby precipitated the year-long fratricidal struggle because he objected to the *phrasing* of the oath of allegiance to the English king.

A.E.'s attempts at public rhyming are remarkably few. He was moved by the events of World War I to compose a series of poems which have frequently been praised for their humanity but which in fact are characterized by a kind of smug exultation—unusual in A.E.—that the poet's prophecies have been borne out.[16] Except for the war poems and the handful of Irish poems mentioned above, one will find very little in the canon of A.E.'s verse that is directly relevant to the chronicle of public affairs in Ireland. The reason for this poetic aloofness is a matter for speculation. Perhaps, for one thing, he was lacking in suitable technique; for A.E. never mastered the ballad form which Yeats employed so effectively in writing of the Parnell debacle, the Easter Rising, and the controversy surrounding Roger Casement. Again, A.E. had available for his public comments a prose outlet in the columns of *The Irish Homestead* and *The Irish Statesman,* so perhaps he felt no need to assume the role of bard. In his prose A.E. expounds endlessly on the day-to-day affairs of Ireland, but in his verse his attitudes and opinions remain fragmentary and ill-defined.

The nationalism expressed in A.E.'s verse, more so even than that of Yeats', is subjective rather than objective, romantic rather than realistic, ethereal rather than material. It proclaims an inner state of being rather than an outer actuality. "Nationality," he writes in *The National Being,* "is a state of consciousness, a mood of definite character in our intellectual being, and it is not perceived first except in profound meditation; it does not become apparent from superficial activities any more than we could, by looking at the world and the tragic history of mankind, discover that the Kingdom of Heaven is within us." A.E. believed, as did Yeats, Douglas Hyde, and most of the writers of the eighteen-nineties, that the people of modern Ireland possessed the same racial and spiritual characteristics as the ancient Celts: "Races which last for thousands of years do not change in essentials. They change in circumstance." [17] In the spirit of the times, A.E. found it a simple matter to ignore the fact that wave after wave of invaders and conquerors had made the Irish anything but a "pure race." As far as he was concerned, the spark of greatness remained. All that was needed was spiritual regeneration, and that, surely, the poet could bring about. Like Yeats, A.E. attempted to express in his verse a vision of the ideal Irish nation, a Utopian dream which he conceived in his own imagination and which he hoped would inspire his countrymen to put on once again the mantle of grandeur that belonged to the ancient Gaels.

In certain ways A.E.'s approach to poetry resembles that of
Yeats. Both professed faith in an ennobling art that might
inspire Irishmen to reject modern materialism in favor of a
more profound spiritual culture. Both turned to the doctrines
of theosophy and to the religious and philosophical writings of
the East for wisdom and inspiration. Both recognized ancient
Celtic tradition as a unique heritage that could give a distinctive character to the new Irish literature. Indeed, there is a
remarkable affinity—in theme, rhythm, and image—between
A.E.'s verse and that of the younger Yeats. However, when the
two are measured in terms of total artistic achievement,
Russell's work does not stand up well. As a poet Yeats succeeds
as very few others have done; but A.E. fails—and, considering
his pretensions, fails rather badly. Except for a handful of
poems scattered here and there through his canon, his work
lacks vitality and, what is worse, lacks significance for modern
man. Having examined his collected poems, one finds it
difficult not to conclude that A.E.'s development as an artist
was stunted, that in the end his aesthetic, in Yeats' words,
"surrenders itself to moral and poetical commonplace," and
that his verse remains soft and fleshless, a survival of
nineteenth-century romanticism.[18]

His failure may be blamed in part upon the dissipation of his
talents in the practical work of agricultural reorganization and
journalism. Irish critics have been curiously oblivious to the
difficulties that must have beset a poet committed to devote a
large proportion of his time to commonplace affairs. Ernest
Boyd, for example, in an essay published in 1917, argues that
A.E. "has gained enormously by this diversity of occupation,
which has saved him from exhausting his artistic faculty by
writing in order to live, while poetry and painting prevent him
from forgetting the aesthetic in economic man. His spiritual
sense has been all the more sharpened by the correlation of the
superhuman with the all-too-human." [19] Boyd's strange logic is
typical. His implied major premise—that concentrated effort
exhausts artistic genius—is hardly justifiable; and his applica-

tion of that premise to A.E. is certainly wrong, if one considers the poet's repeated complaint that his economic and journalistic activities kept him from his creative work. At any rate, after the death of *The Irish Statesman* in 1930 he wrote to an American professor of his "hope to start writing books I have long wanted to write, but could not find time or energy to undertake while I was an editor." [20] Yeats, thanks to Lady Gregory's generosity, was able to devote himself to the development of his art; A.E. had no such patron. Sir Horace Plunkett lured the poet into the busy world of economics and politics, a world in which poetic creation could be little more than an avocation. Indeed, so demanding was this new world and so conscientiously did Russell give himself to its causes that a Dublin wit, when asked the meaning of "A.E.'s" pen-name, replied, "Agricultural economist." [21]

Yet difference in circumstance does not begin to explain the disparity between the quality of Yeats' mature art and that of A.E., even if one takes into account the contrast between Yeats' rather stimulating youth, years spent alternately with relatives in the romantic Sligo countryside and with his father among the literati and artists of Bedford Park and London, and A.E.'s middle-class upbringing and comparative isolation from intellectual influences. The fact of the matter would appear to be that A.E.'s genius was of a lesser sort and that he was from beginning to end Yeats' inferior creatively, if not intellectually.

A.E. regarded himself as a kind of prophet. He was obsessed with the idea that he had been singled out from the rest of humanity for special treatment; despite this, however, his whole approach to mysticism was remarkably naïve. Just how naïve is suggested by the anecdote concerning his choice of a pseudonym. He had painted a picture of "the apparition in the Divine Mind of the idea of the Heavenly Man" and was struggling to choose a title for it when a voice whispered in his ear, "Call it the birth of AEon." The next day he experienced a vision of the myth; and two weeks later at the National Library in Dublin his eye fell upon the word "aeon" in an open book lying upon the counter. He "trembled" with foreknowledge and thought his pen-name had been chosen for him. But again the Divine Mind intervened, this time through a compositor who, unable to make out the signature affixed to an article, spelled it "AE." Russell accepted the change, recognizing the work of supernatural forces.[22] Despite such signs of divine favor, however, A.E. was never moved to practice seriously the esoteric religion in which he professed faith. He was not an ascetic in any real sense, even though Irish writers habitually use the word when writing of him. As far as one can determine, he never indulged in the kind of bodily mortification one usually associates with holy men, whether Christian or Hindu; nor did he engage in the practice of spiritual exercises with any consistency. In a letter dated in 1932 he wrote: "I have read accounts of Hindu yogis and I cannot with my temperament see myself with a beggar's bowl following after Buddha. I love his wisdom but not his manner of living." [23] The truth of the matter is that A.E.'s relationship with the gods was a casual one. He was not required to purify himself or to make any special preparation for their coming; and for their part the gods might visit him or not as they chose.

There is no need, though, to deny A.E. his visions. His claims for them are too intense, too persistent, too obviously sincere to permit much doubt. St. John Ervine describes an incident which took place at the poet's house. Ervine and an unnamed lady were admiring a landscape by A.E. in the center of which stood a strange dancing figure, when the poet turned to them and said suddenly, "That's the one I saw." The dancer was a fairy creature he had seen in a vision and not an invention of his fancy. Both lady and Ervine were astonished by A.E.'s remark; yet Ervine, who was as skeptical of spiritual phenomena as it is possible for an Irishman to be, goes on to comment that "while I do not believe that 'A.E.' saw a fairy, otherwise than in his imagination, I am certain that he believes he saw one, not as a creature of the mind, but as having flesh and blood." [24] A.E.'s own attempts to describe his experiences, in *The Candle of Vision* and elsewhere, suffer from inflation and vagueness—"I would be living in the Mother's being in some pure, remote, elemental region of hers"—nevertheless, they are in a way convincing enough. Christian priests would no doubt condemn A.E.'s visions as manifestations of Satan; and Brahman holy men would probably dismiss them as Kharmic illusions; yet in certain respects, especially in the use of imagery—"sky of rarest amethyst," "divine wilderness," all things "rapt, breathless and still" [25]—his descriptions echo traditional accounts of mystical religious experience. Moreover, modern psychology has uncovered sufficient evidence to demonstrate the psychic reality (if not the metaphysical truth) of such experience as seems on occasion to have overwhelmed A.E.'s consciousness.[26]

A.E. certainly saw things. But to grant this is not to say that he understood his visions, any more than normal people understand their dreams, or that he was competent to give them expression in verse or painting. For one thing, his knowledge of eastern religious literature, in terms of which he tried to express himself, was superficial and at times confused. There is at least some reason to believe that Russell was not as serious a student of the occult as he is often thought to have been. H. M. Magee, A.E.'s roommate at the Theosophical Society Lodge in the eighteen-nineties, has noted that Russell's favorite pastime during that period was the study of Madame Blavatsky's *Secret Doctrine*; but, he adds, "I'm bound to say I don't remember seeing him 'study' for long without breaking off for argument or discussion." [27] More pertinent perhaps is Yeats' comment that when A.E. turned to Madame Blavatsky and to such classic Indian works as the *Upanishads* his mind already was impregnated with the sanguine ideologies of certain nineteenth-century writers, especially Emerson and Whitman.[28] Yeats' judgment strikes close to the mark. A.E. was surely influenced by the two romantic poets from America.

In Emerson the young Russell discovered a faith in the individual, in Whitman a faith in democracy; from the two together he acquired an attitude of confidence with regard to mankind. A.E., says Yeats, like Emerson and Whitman (and like a great many writers of the nineteenth century), lacked "the Vision of Evil." A.E. himself in a letter to an angry young poet says as much: "I am a gentle creature and look with terror on the wrath of God, which is the attitude of deity you feel inspired by." He admits the existence of evil—"I have no doubt that there is a divine wrath"—but he rejects it as a proper subject for the artist. In the same letter he cautions his young correspondent that "there is the depth in us which we never speak of for pity's sake; 'it must never, never be sung.' " [29]

What is awkward about these predispositions—for the individual, for democracy, and for moral and spiritual good—is that they are alien to the eastern religious philosophy which A.E. expounds. In "Krishna," a poem about the eighth Avatar (i.e., reincarnation) of the supreme Hindu deity, Vishnu, A.E. tries to express the concept that in God all human opposites are reconciled. In a series of stanzas he observes that Krishna, "the King of Kings," enshrines in his own being both age and youth, lust of body and purity of spirit, blustering drunkenness and sober tranquility, repulsive ugliness and perfect beauty, miserliness and generosity, and, finally, death to mortal life and life eternal. In a general way this is sound enough Brahmanism; and as a poem "Krishna" is fairly effective, even though A.E.'s language tends to be overwrought. On close examination, however, one discovers a small but significant discrepancy:

> I heard the passion breathed amid the honey-
>   suckle scented glade,
> And saw the King pass lightly from the
>   beauty that he had betrayed.
> I saw him pass from love to love; and yet the
>   pure allow His claim

> To be the purest of the pure, thrice holy,
> stainless, without blame.   (*Poems*, p. 61)

A.E. is defining the twofold nature of God in man; yet, although perhaps unintentionally, he shows his preference for Good over Evil by capitalizing the third person of the personal pronoun, "His," when referring to God as pure and using the lower case, "he," when describing god as the embodiment of bodily lust. He maintains similar distinctions throughout the poem: the "Ancient and Unborn God" is "It," the mortal child-god playing at the cabin door is "it"; the beautiful God is "He," the ugly god is "it"; the divinely silent God is "the Prince of Peace," the drunken god is an "outcast." What emerges is not really a reconciliation of opposites, but rather the exaltation of what A.E. admired in man and the subordination, if not outright rejection, of what he found distasteful. In a way Good conquers Evil.

Yeats struck closer to the essence of Hindu thought in that he recognized the conflict between Good and Evil as part of the nature of being and sought reconciliation in the intense passion generated by that conflict. For A.E., on the other hand, the struggle between Good and Evil was confined to this world; strife and evil together would be "Overthrown ... in the unconflicting spheres" of the world to come (*Poems*, p. 132). Yeats' myth-god is an organic synthesis of the twofold nature of man; A.E.'s, like the conventional Christian conception of God, is a thing undefiled. Both Russell and Yeats attempted to create in their verse a mythology that would propagate religious "truth" among their countrymen. That neither succeeded as an apostle of theosophy among the Irish people is perfectly obvious. As a poet, however, Yeats succeeded in blending together Irish tradition and eastern occultism into a unified artistic creation of major proportions. A.E., despite his psychic disposition and power of vision (or perhaps because of them), failed to achieve the permanence of art and, considering the claims he sometimes made for his poetry, failed rather badly.

More than any other Irish writer, A.E. is the poet of the Celtic Twilight. He believed—quite literally—that "Earth's faery children . . . roam the primrose-hearted eve" (*Poems*, p. 218). Twilight was the magic hour, the time of day when the spiritual world was most likely to reveal itself and therefore a time especially suitable for visionary experience. So, for example, in "The Fountain of Shadowy Beauty," a long, dull, epistolary poem, he writes of his vision:

> Even then a vasty twilight fell:
> Wavered in air the shadowy towers:
> The city like a gleaming shell,
> Its azures, opals, silvers, blues,
> Were melting in more dreamy hues.
> We feared the falling of the night
> And hurried more our headlong flight.
> In one long line the towers went by;
> The trembling radiance dropt behind,
> As when some swift and radiant one
> Flits by and flings upon the wind
> The rainbow tresses of the sun.   (*Poems*, p. 206)

This is a bad poem. The rhythm is singsong. The diction is so cluttered that, despite the list of colors, A.E.'s vision remains drab and vague and lifeless. Yet in its imagery, its rhythms, its tone, in its contrived atmosphere of soft, dreamy shadows, the poem is characteristic of much of A.E.'s verse. For the world of his vision, the world of the Mighty Mind and the Thrice Great Hermes, was hidden behind the veil of Maya (the illusory reality of this world), glimpsed only momentarily in the half-light, never really in focus for either the poet or his readers.

A.E.'s obsession with the remote, the obscure, the unknown, is evident in his earliest poetry, the esoteric verse of *Homeward*. That he should have turned for the inspiration and subject matter of his art to the oldest and most obscure of the national traditions, the mythological lore of prehistoric, pagan Ireland, is not surprising. When he addressed himself to his

countrymen, it was to urge them to return with him to the
mysterious twilight era of Ireland's remote past:

> Come, acushla, with me to the mountains old.
> There the bright ones call us waving to and fro—
> Come, my children, with me to the ancient go.
>
> (*Poems*, p. 105)

The old mythological tales, quite clearly religious allegories,
however inscrutable their meaning, inevitably attracted the
poet-seer. Here was a vehicle for his theosophical creed. No one
was really sure what exactly the people of Druid Ireland
believed in—no one, that is, except A.E., who had conjured up
the old gods—Lir and Angus Óg and the Dagda—and had
talked with them in the twilight zone of vision.[30] Having seen
and spoken with the ancient gods, he *knew* with absolute certainty that his own beliefs and those of the pagan Celts were
identical. Not only that, but although "the modern degenerate
English-speaking nation" no longer recognized the old gods,
the gods had not deserted the Irish but continued to watch
over the "destinies of a favored race." [31] And the gods were at
work, too. They were responsible for the cultural movement
and for the Gaelic revival, and, indeed, for A.E.'s own wisdom.
A.E. was even convinced that the Avatars, the reincarnated
Druid gods, would soon appear in Ireland to restore their
spiritual power among humankind:

> I think that in the coming time
>   The hearts and hopes of men
> The mountain tops of life shall climb,
>   The gods return again.   (*Poems*, pp. 198–99)

One cannot say that A.E.'s approach to Irish legend was
scholarly; he played freely with the ancient myths, turning and
twisting them to his own purposes. Nevertheless, now and then
his rendering of one or another old story is strangely convincing. In "The Children of Lir," for example, one of his most
beautiful poems, A.E. tries to define the religious meaning
hidden in what he believed to be a myth from pagan Ireland:

> We woke from our sleep in the bosom where
> cradled together we lay:
> The love of the dark hidden Father went with
> us upon our way.
> And gay was the breath in our being, and
> never a sorrow or fear
> Was on us as, singing together, we flew from
> the infinite Lir.

In the next two stanzas A.E. follows in general the chronology of the traditional tale. Lir's children are enchanted and transformed into swans; they are forced to fly to the far corners of the earth where they learn "unspeakable things"; and eventually they pass "from the vision of beauty to the fathomless beauty of love." At last, their trials over, the children speak:

> Still gay is the breath in our being, we wait
> for the bell branch to ring
> To call us away to the Father, and then we
> will rise on the wing.
> And fly through the twilights of time till the
> home lights of heaven appear;
> Our spirits through love and through long-
> ing made one in the infinite Lir. (*Poems*, pp. 160–61)

The story of "The Children of Lir" is very likely a modern invention by an anonymous author of the fifteenth or sixteenth century and its form is that of a simple, charming fairy tale.[32] Clearly A.E. has informed the original with an esoteric message of his own. He identifies the "children" of Lir with mankind and Lir himself with the Mighty Mind, and he relates the transformation of Lir's children, their wanderings, sufferings, and eventual return home to man's mortal incarnation, his journey through life, spiritual sufferings, and ultimate return to union with the divinity. One cannot deny that story and message blend together to give to A.E.'s poem a curious potency.

In "The Children of Lir" and a few other poems A.E. treats of old Irish legends and myths with remarkable sensitivity. In much of his verse, though, he is less successful. Frequently his readings of the old saga materials lack sophistication and suffer distortion as a result of his predisposition for good and against evil, for love and against hate, for joy and against terror and fear. At times he misses the point entirely. In "Dana," for example, his speaker is the mother-goddess of pre-Christian Ireland:

> I breathe
> A deeper pity than all love, myself
> Mother of all, but without hands to heal:
> Too vast and vague, they know me not.
> But yet,
> I am the heartbreak over fallen things,
> The sudden gentleness that stays the blow,
> I am in the kiss that foemen give
> Pausing in battle, and in the tears that fall
> Over the vanquished foe, and in the highest,
> Among the Danaan gods, I am the last
> Council of mercy in their hearts where they
> Mete justice from a thousand starry thrones.
>
> (*Poems*, p. 38)

Plainly A.E. has softened and sentimentalized the old goddess. True enough, Danu in Irish legend is the beneficent earth goddess, the giver of life and sustenance; but she is also the maleficent goddess of the grave and death. A.E.'s attributing to her influence the "sudden gentleness that stops the blow" in battle would seem an arbitrary perversion of her nature; for Danu, or Ana, as she is sometimes referred to, is one of the three fate-goddesses that appeared before battles to foretell (with considerable relish) the gore and horror of the coming slaughter.[33] In this poem and, indeed, in his verse generally, A.E. excluded the "divine wrath" from his vision; and his doing so can only be regarded as an escapist gesture. Christ may properly be regarded as a God of love and pity, perhaps; but the gods of Druid Ireland were no such thing. A.E. claimed intimate knowledge of those ancient gods and, in fact, thought of himself as the prophet of their return; yet the gods and goddesses who stalk gently through his verse more closely approximate nineteenth-century reformers like General William Booth and Florence Nightingale than they do pagan deities. One is tempted to apply the phrase of Swift's wise horse to A.E.'s handling of Irish myth—that he "said the thing which was not"; and such purposeful distortion as he engages in cannot be entirely excused in one self-dedicated to "the golden heresy of truth."

Modern Celtic scholarship, in particular the work of the late T. F. O'Rahilly, has demonstrated convincingly that the ancient sagas, and the stories of the mythological cycle especially, originated in the rituals and beliefs of pagan Ireland. A.E., like Yeats, sensed the religious significance of the old legends and turned to them, almost instinctively, as a source of secret wisdom that might be used to effect the spiritual regeneration of the Irish people. A.E. was concerned not so much with restoring Druidism as with justifying his own preconceived theosophical beliefs. What is given expression in his verse is not the old religion of pagan Ireland but a new religious conception which John Eglinton has aptly termed "AEism." A.E. expounded his peculiar creed at every opportunity—in his organizational work for the Irish agricultural co-operative movement and his political and economic journalism as well as in his avowedly literary works, prose and poetry. His occult doctrines impressed many of his contemporaries but won few real followers, perhaps because no one could comprehend them. Nor did A.E. himself make the task of understanding an easy one; for he was remarkably vague and, as Yeats observed of the young George Russell he knew at art school in Dublin in the eighteen-eighties, when holding forth on the Mighty Mind and the Thrice Great Hermes he was "almost unintelligible" and at times seemed "incapable of coherent thought." [34] Only when as an old man he undertook to write an epic poem, *The House of Titans*, did A.E. manage to define his religious creed with much success. "AEism," as it turned out, was not particularly complex or difficult; nor, unfortunately, did it seem to justify the grandiloquence with which the poet had espoused it for some forty years.

The House of Titans is not really a poem of epic proportions; yet it represents A.E.'s only sustained effort in verse to impose an order upon the mythic vision which had obsessed him through his entire creative life.[35] It is a national poem in that it represents a final attempt by A.E. to teach his countrymen what they must believe in and to what course of action they must devote themselves if they would maintain faith with their ancient heritage and achieve spiritual nobility in the future. *The House of Titans* is not a good poem. It has all the characteristic weaknesses of A.E.'s verse—pomposity of tone, exaggerated imagery, vagueness of language and phrasing. But it has a story, too; and in the unraveling of that story A.E.'s idea of man—his origin, his condition, his destiny—gradually emerges and becomes intelligible.

In his poem A.E. fills out the vague pattern of Celtic mythology with substantive details from Greco-Roman tradition and philosophic concepts from the East. The story begins with a reconstruction of the legendary Battle of Mag Tuired between the Tuatha Dé Danann and the race of giants, the Fomorians.[36] In A.E.'s account the Tuatha Dé Danann are represented as spiritual beings, the overlords of the universe; the Fomorians, renamed "Titans," are children of the earth and, hence, creatures of flesh and passion. Nuada, high king of the spirit world (in the saga high king of the Tuatha Dé Danann) and his fellow gods—Ogma, the Celtic equivalent of Heracles; Dana, the magician; Angus, the poet; Diancecht, the healer; Manannan, the shepherd and son of the great Lir—descend to the chaos of earth to struggle against the Titans, the

powers of gloom and darkness, who are led by Balor of the Evil
Eye (in the saga leader of the Fomorians). Nuada and the gods
of spiritual light are victorious and become lords over the
Titans. But in the ages following the conquest "evil sorcery
worked on the gods" so that they forgot their divine origin and
at last came to believe "the bodily form to be / Themselves.
And earth had lost its first / Impenetrable strangeness and
grew dear / As hearth and home." Their divine knowledge
forgotten, the gods took wives from among the children of
earth and at last "the being of the gods was changed / To be
but lordlier titan." Only Nuada, the king, retains a vague
half-memory of ancient glory and only he struggles to regain
the lost knowledge of things divine; to the others he seems "a
madman dreaming of lost worlds."

One young woman, Armid, believes in Nuada's dreams and
listens enrapt as he recounts what he can remember of the
ancient myth of the gods. When he has finished, Armid rushes
in ecstasy to the cold waters of the sea; and, as she stands in the
water, there descends from the sky "a tall warrior" on a winged
horse, a warrior who seems "a pillar of flame, his eyes so still
/ They might have watched only eternities." The stranger
sends Armid to announce to the king the presence of "a
champion of the Land of Promise" and to ask an audience.
The girl does as she is told; but Nuada, hearing her story,
recalls that his own champion, Ogma, had been the mightiest
warrior in heaven but had become corrupted and forgotten his
own nature:

> Now he leads the giants in war.
> Tell that champion to fly his winged horse,
> Swift as its frantic plumes may carry, before
> The sorcery overcomes him and he forgets.

Then, in succession, the stranger claims to be "an enchanter"
(like Dana), a poet (like Angus), a historian and prophet (like
Fintan), a healer (like Diancecht), and a "shepherd ... To
guide the starry flocks (like Manannan); however, Nuada

replies that each of these had been in his divine company but each in turn had been overcome by sorcery. The stranger sends Armid to the king yet once more: "Ask the high king has he in that dark house / One who is master of so many arts."

In the context of the poem it becomes clear that Nuada and the corrupted gods are meant to represent the race of men who had once known the heavenly regions of immortal light but who now must endure the "dark house" of mortal existence on earth. A.E. maintained as one of his fundamental doctrines a kind of inverted theory of evolution; men were not, as Darwin would have it, improved apes, but rather degenerate gods. Twenty years before *The House of Titans* George Moore in *Hail and Farewell* recalled how once, when on a bicycle tour of ancient holy places in the vicinity of Dublin, he and A.E. had become involved in "a learned discussion regarding the antiquity of man, myself muttering that about a million years ago man separated himself from the ape, AE repudiating the ape theory strenuously all the way down the hillside, saying that the world was not old enough to make the theory of evolution possible. At least a billion more years would have to be added to the history of our planet, so it could not be else than that man had been evolved from the Gods—there could be no doubt about it, he said; and we sat down in front of the temple to munch bread and butter." [37] A.E.'s insistence upon the literal truth of his own point of view, no matter how peculiar, no doubt invited Moore's irony; yet the concept of the fall of man which he espoused recurs with such remarkable persistency in the history of religious thought that it would seem to warrant serious consideration, if only as a phenomenon of human psychology. At any rate, the first half of *The House of Titans* is devoted to the study of man's decline from the divine to the human state.

In the second half of his poem A.E. provides a rationale for man's fall and attempts to define the means by which he may again attain to the divine state. The stranger from the Land of Promise is probably the Mighty Mind, for he em-

bodies the divine perfections of all the lesser gods. He announces that Nuada and his followers are "but shadows of
immortals" and then invokes a vision of "a lordlier company /
Of the star-crested Ever-Living Ones." Each of these true gods
reveals to Nuada a portion of the divine wisdom. The "poet of
heaven," for example, states that to achieve spiritual perfection
man must practice "selfless" love, a love founded upon sacrifice. Most significant are the words of the true Son of Lir, for he
explains why gods must become men to dwell in darkness and
to seek again the light:

> those who sat on thrones
> And shone like gods at dawn of the great day
> I bring to the abyss where they are dimmed,
> But not for their abasing. Those who know
> The heavens only are but slaves of light,
> Mirrors of majesties they are not, shining
> In beauty given to them, not their own,
> Nor born from their own valour. For to be
> True gods, self-moving, they must grow to power
> Warring in chaos with anarchs.

True gods must suffer first, must earn their divinity. (So, too,
Christians tend to exalt themselves above the angels.) The Son
of Lir promises Nuada that when he "knoweth all" he will
become a "counsellor with the high gods / Who pass remembering through the nights and days / Of the All-Father."

This, then, is the theme of *The House of Titans*: that the
spirit of man must be swallowed up by the "titan" of flesh and
passion; that the spirit must suffer the Titan's "brute despair
and the descent to hells / Earth had not known before the
spirit came"; and that somehow in the depths of the Titan's
heart the spirit must discover the truth of selfless love and the
"magian mind" that can transform sorrows into blessings and
agonies into joys. When these things have transpired, man will
progress toward union with the All-Father in the Feast of Age
(i.e., eternity). So, at the end of the poem, Nuada is left by the
Gods,

> rapt in his vision, dreamed
> Of that great hostel at the end of time
> When all the cycles sleep; and came at last
> To open his eyes upon the brazen gloom
> To know the labour before him, and to hear
> The titans raving madly in the hall.

The task, then, for such enlightened ones as Nuada and A.E. is to awaken the Titans, that is, men in general and Irishmen in particular, to their noble spiritual destiny.

That *The House of Titans* is an Irish poem and that its message was intended for the edification of Irishmen is evident from the use of Celtic myth-figures as dramatis personae. For A.E., even more than for Yeats, mysticism and nationalism were joined inseparably. John Eglinton observes in his memoir of the poet that A.E. believed literally in "a localised Earth-memory of spiritual happenings" and that as a result he was convinced that the esoteric wisdom of the Druids could still exert an influence upon the course of events in Ireland. Apparently he felt that the Easter Rising of 1916 was the handiwork of the ancient gods: "There was a point in AE's mind," writes Eglinton, "in which the mystical nationalism of Pearse met and blended with . . . [his own] beliefs." [38]

In a second long poem, "Michael," the concepts of vision and selfless sacrifice, both of which are defined in *The House of Titans*, are specifically related to the Easter rebellion (*Poems*, pp. 358–69). The hero of the poem, Michael, is a boy from the rugged coast of County Donegal (where A.E. spent his summers) in the West of Ireland, an area where "fisher folk" sat and "listened to old tales / Or legends of gigantic gales." Michael, a sensitive, imaginative youth, experiences a vision of "palaces of light" and "towers that faded up in the air"

> And casements lit with precious fires,
> And mythic forms with wings outspread
> And faces from which light was shed
> High upon gleaming pillars set
> On turret and on parapet.

Like most Irish mystics, Michael cannot define his vision—
"What there beyond the gate befell / Michael could never
after tell"—and is left with only a vague sense of something
profound and limitless. Soon afterwards the young man leaves
Donegal to find work in Dublin; and, oppressed by "the city's
dingy air," "the black reek of chimneys," and "the dark
warehouse where he drudged," he begins to forget the wonder
of his vision.

Happily, however, the youth encounters in Dublin another
native of Donegal, one who still holds fast to the "spiritual
heritage" of the ancient Gaels and who introduces Michael to
the traditions and legendary heroes of Ireland's past, from the
great Cú Chulainn, "who with his single sword / Stayed a great
army at the ford," to the impoverished, wandering bards of the
seventeenth and eighteenth centuries, "Who gave their hearts
to the Dark Rose." The legends of Ireland seem to Michael
"the story of the soul" and those who made those legends seem
"warriors of Eternal Mind." Then on Easter Monday—when
"The lord in man had risen here, / From the dark sepulchre of
fear"—Michael goes to the barricades to give himself to
Ireland's holy cause. An enemy bullet wounds him mortally;
but even as death takes hold of his body, he feels "The rapture
that is sacrifice" and the vision he had experienced in the
mountains of Donegal returns to him—in A.E.'s words: "lofty
forms of burnished air / Stood on the deck with Michael
there." Michael's visionary experience and his sacrifice in the
cause of nationalism both find their meaning in the sacred
truth which the Druid gods brought with them when they
descended to struggle against the Titans. Michael has fulfilled
the Son of Lir's conditions for true divinity; so, as the presence
of "lofty forms" suggests, he will become "counsellor with the
high gods" and dwell in the being of the All-Father.

Michael's curious mixture of occultism and patriotism is
what A.E. desired for the Irish people. A national vision based
on the idea that men can and should become gods is noble
enough, certainly; but it is also a romantic vision, perhaps

much too romantic for a modern world in which men seem intent on being anything but godlike. More than that, however, it is the pomposity of A.E.'s vision—the hyperbolic abstractions, the unrestrained diction—that renders it unconvincing. It seems almost incredible that he should have expected the average Irishman—a prosaic, middle-class creature at best—to comprehend and to accept his creed of nationalism; yet that is precisely what he did expect; and he was bitterly disappointed and disillusioned when his countrymen ignored his wisdom.

At one point in *The National Being,* a treatise in which he proposes an economic and political policy for the emerging Irish nation, A.E. writes: "No policy can succeed if it be not in accord with national character. If I have misjudged that, what is written here is vain." [39] What A.E. advocated in *The National Being* was a kind of rural socialism motivated by selfless love; what Ireland became was a nation of shopkeepers and land-hungry farmers. A.E. did indeed misjudge the national character, and no less in his poetry than in his prose writings on economic and political questions. Eventually he seems to have recognized his mistake, and now and then in the work of his mature period a note of frustration, a sense of failure recognized, is apparent. In "Promise," for example, a poem published in 1925 in *Voices of Stone,* A.E. attempts to reconcile himself to his loss of vision:

> Be not so desolate
> Because thy dreams have flown
> And the hall of the heart is empty
> And silent as stone,
> As age left by children
> Sad and alone.   (*Poems,* p. 320)

There may well be reference intended here to the course of events in Ireland after independence, the fratricidal violence of civil strife, the narrow, unenlightened rule of the Free State government. Certainly the reality of the Irish nation fell far short of the poet's dream. More than this, even, the poem expresses the poet's dissatisfaction with his own achievement as an artist. In a subsequent stanza A.E. reassures himself that his verses have "become immortal / In shining air"; yet there remains about the poem a sense of doubt as to the validity of his poetic vision. At any rate, there is evident in much of the verse of *Voices of Stone* an attempt by A.E. to reshape his aesthetic, to find a new direction for his poetry.

One of the poems included in this volume, "Mutiny," is of interest primarily because it may well have provided a model for Yeats' "Sailing to Byzantium." A.E. writes of a voyage upon a "sea of glass" rimmed by "perilous magic mountains"; both the poet and his "dusky coracle" and the "blazing galleon the sun" set sail for a holy city:

> Come, break the seals and tell us now
> Upon what enterprise we roam;
> To storm what city of the gods,
> Or—sail for the green fields of home.
>
> (*Poems*, p. 306)

More relevant is A.E.'s attempt to imitate the peasant poetry which by this time had become the dominant genre of Anglo-Irish verse. The dedicatory verses of *Voices of Stone* are entitled "To Padraic Colum" and celebrate the union of Colum's peasant realism and A.E.'s pontifical vision: "Only the humble stones have kept / Their morning starriness of purity / Immutable" (*Poems*, p. 301). Another poem, "Exiles," is more closely modeled upon Colum's verse. A.E. writes that "peasants driving swine" embody in their humble being

> The majesty of fallen gods, the beauty,
> The fire beneath their eyes.
>
> They huddle at night within low, clay-built cabins;
> And, to themselves unknown,
> They carry with them diadem and sceptre
> And move from throne to throne.   (*Poems*, p. 304)

By 1925 peasant verse had become a sterile convention; if A.E. hoped to find renewed inspiration in the commonplace world of hearth and barn, he was to be disappointed. In his last poems, published with *The House of Titans*, he returned to his own ethereal world, the world of the Earth-Mother, the Mighty Mind, and the Ever-Living Ones.

One is most reluctant to term A.E. a failure. Yet, although he wrote a number of poems that have charm and grace and that no doubt will survive as anthology pieces, his total achievement as a poet is of a minor sort. More than anything else, he was lacking in art. Ernest Boyd, writing as early as 1917, observed: "Form has never been a preoccupation of 'AE'; his verses are sometimes marred by clumsiness and obscurity of phrase, and he openly avows his inability to remould them before giving them definite arrangement." [40] Three decades later Robert Farren came to much the same conclusion with respect to A.E.'s total creative production: "A.E. the poet was incurious in matters of craft; his technical armature was simple, the same, you might say, at the end as it was at the start." [41] No doubt Farren's statement is somewhat too strong; yet the promise of the poet's first, in many ways remarkable volume, *Homeward*, was never really fulfilled. A.E.'s importance in the cultural movement was, perhaps, more as a personality than as an artist; for he served as a kind of All-Father for three generations of young Irish writers, encouraging them, helping them, printing their formative efforts. Of the poet-seer's relationship to the aspiring poets who followed him, Robert Farren comments: "A.E. may be called the careful midwife who delivered them alive, and the wet-nurse who suckled them to strength. He even had by him the sheets on which to lay them: the sheets of his *Irish Statesman*." [42] Farren's metaphor is immoderate; but, then, for A.E., perhaps, such a metaphor is fitting.

PEARSE, MacDONAGH, AND PLUNKETT:
THE MESSIANIC IDEAL

Of Padraic Pearse, Thomas MacDonagh, and Joseph Mary
Plunkett, it may be said that they became by their "blood
sacrifice" in the Dublin insurrection of 1916 symbols of
fulfillment for the Irish national revival in both its cultural and
political frameworks.[1] For the intense sense of racial pride that
found expression in Irish literature and art, in political journals
and pamphlets, and on public speaking platforms, from the
early eighteen-nineties onward, seems, in retrospect, almost to
have demanded translation from words into deeds. But the fact
that the three are so closely identified with the cause of violent
rebellion against English rule in Ireland has made difficult the
task of appraising their merit either as men or as poets. The
native Irish critic almost inevitably regards them simply as
martyrs for the cause of Irish political freedom.[2] The patriotic
Briton, at the opposite extreme, is apt to concur in the
judgment of the Anglicized St. John Ervine, who singled out
Pearse and described him as "an incompetent schoolmaster"
who taught only "riot and disturbance"[3]—a smug misstate-
ment at best. Whether one labels Pearse, MacDonagh, and
Plunkett as saints or rabble rousers, the implication is that they
were fanatics; and although there may be some truth in such a

charge, it nevertheless involves oversimplification of a flagrant kind.[4]

The Rising poets were young men at the time of the 1916 rebellion, but each one had already achieved distinction in Irish intellectual circles. Pearse was a playwright, storyteller, and poet of some fame, a literary critic, a Gaelic scholar and translator, an essayist on topics of contemporary concern, an educator, a social reformer whose creed mixed Marx with Pope Leo's encyclicals on labor, a lawyer (who refused to practice in His Majesty's courts), a political leader, and finally a soldier and revolutionary. MacDonagh wrote considerable verse, tried his hand at drama and contributed to the literary criticism of his time through his essays and reviews and the study, *Literature in Ireland*, published posthumously. He studied in the libraries of Paris, mastered four languages, and, at the time of the Rising, was a lecturer in English literature at the National University.[5] Plunkett was the youngest of the three. Educated at Dublin's Belvedere College and at Stonyhurst in England, where he studied Scholastic philosophy, he published his first volume of poetry in 1911 at the age of twenty-four, and thereafter became active in Dublin's literary life.[6] In failing health, Plunkett was confined to a nursing home in April, 1916, to recover from an operation; he left his bed to take part in the Rising.[7]

All three devoted most of their adult lives to the cause of Irish nationality. Each was an active member of the Gaelic League—and Pearse edited the League's journal, *An Claidheamh Soluis* (*The Sword of Light*), and devoted much of his personal literary effort to the task of creating a modern Gaelic literature.[8] Like Douglas Hyde, the founder of the Gaelic League, Pearse, Plunkett, and MacDonagh (until the writing of *Literature in Ireland* at any rate) regarded the language revival as essential to the revitalization of the Irish racial character. Above all, a knowledge of Gaelic would help save the Irish people from what they believed was an insidious conquest of mind and spirit by the materialistic and "intellectual" culture of England, a culture that had—to use MacDonagh's words—"Withered the light like a summer flower / And hearts went cold and souls went blind." [9] Even for Irishmen whose everyday language was English, knowledge of their native tongue would be living proof of their superiority to their British peers; to those who derided their Anglo-Irish dialect they could answer as Douglas Hyde, when a schoolboy, had answered an English youth who called him "an Irish paddy" because of his brogue: "You little divil, I speak English as well as you do, even if I have a brogue, and I speak my own language as well. I am twice as good a man as you, for you have only one language." [10]

But, for the Rising poets, Gaelic was only a means to the ultimate goal of Irish sovereignty, as, indeed, was almost everything else that figured in their lives. MacDonagh, it is true, both in his lectures at the university and in his criticism, kept his literary values relatively free from political bias. But Joseph Plunkett, having assumed the editorship of *The Irish Review*, gradually transformed that publication from a cultural review into a political journal.[11] And Pearse founded his Gaelic school, St. Enda's, in order "to create and perpetuate" in Ireland "the knightly tradition of the *macradh* [i.e., "boycorps"] of Eamhain Macha, dead at the ford 'in the beauty of their boyhood'; the high tradition of Cuchulainn, 'better is short life with honour than long life with dishonour,' 'I care not though I were to live but one day and one night, if only my fame and my deeds live after me.' " He also was pleased that the site of his school was Cullenswood House in Rathfarnham, Dublin, because three centuries before "the Wood of Cullen still sheltered Irish rebels. That Wood was famous in Dublin annals, for it was under its trees that the Irish, come down from the mountains, annihilated the Bristol colonists of Dublin on Easter Monday, 1209; whence Easter Monday was known in Dublin as Black Monday and the fields on which our schoolhouse looks down got then the name of the Bloody Fields." [12] In time, Pearse, MacDonagh, and Plunkett turned away from their civilian pursuits and devoted more and more of their energies to the work of the Irish Volunteers.

Because of the roles played by the three poets in the Irish revolution, their verse rarely has been subjected to objective criticism. Even four decades after the Easter rebellion, Irish writers are likely to invoke the excuse—"It is too early for anything in the nature of literary criticism"—coined by James Stephens in writing of MacDonagh,[13] or, failing that, swallow whole the formula implied in a Dublin street ballad: "Plunkett, MacDonagh, and Pearse, / Sweet was the sound of their verse. . . ." Too frequently critical commentary consists of little more than a series of self-propagating superlatives; and when Irish writers attempt to measure one poet against the others according to artistic merit, the result is confusion. "Popular opinion gives Pearse the highest place," Professor Arthur Clery observed in an article on the Rising poets; "and one skilled in all the technique of verse, and himself no mean poet, agreed with this judgment. To me the vision of Plunkett, his breadth of imagination, the intensity of his passion makes the strongest appeal; the expert, however, set him down as wanting in the skill of the art. As a poet MacDonagh perhaps receives least praise. Yet Yeats is said to put him in first place." [14] English and American critics have an easier time with the poetry of Pearse, MacDonagh, and Plunkett; they simply ignore it. Yet a careful and objective reading of their verse, a reading free from political bias for or against their revolutionary activities, will show clearly that although the aesthetic sound of their verse is often less than sweet, it is not wholly without merit.

Pearse's published works are the most extensive of the three Rising poets. They include plays, stories, translations of Gaelic verse, lectures on literary subjects, political tracts, and fragments of an unfinished autobiography; his collected poems, however, number only twenty. In his verse Pearse attempts to

recreate the naturalness and simplicity which he believed
characterized the Irish-speaking peasantry of Connacht. He
does, in fact, manage to convey in some poems a convincing
image of peasant naïveté, at times even a sense of simple tragic
dignity. The final stanza of "A Woman of the Mountain
Keens Her Son," for example, has a quiet emotional power:

> Grief on the death, it cannot be denied,
> It lays low, green and withered together,—
> And O gentle little son, what tortures me is
> That your fair body should be making clay! [15]

Pearse's handling of the keening motif is in keeping with the
traditional Irish theme of womankind oppressed by suffering
and sorrow. Over and over again, from the tenth-century
Deirdre of the Ulster cycle of sagas to Synge's Maurya in
Riders to the Sea, the Irish woman, in poem, story, and play,
keens her menfolk gone to the grave. For men, death can be a
moment of stoic triumph; for women it represents torment
extended in time. Pearse's treatment of the Woman of the
Mountain's sorrow is characterized by restraint, even though
there is more than a trace of effusiveness in the fourth stanza
where he uses the diminutives "little" and "narrow" to describe the grave and substitutes the euphemistic "treasure" for
corpse, evoking a morbid kind of sentiment.[16] Nevertheless, the
poem as a whole manages to express a genuine sense of pathos.

However, the sentimentalism becomes almost oppressive in
"The Mother," an autobiographical poem in which the poet's
own mother repeats his name and that of his brother, William,
"to my own heart / In the long nights; / The little names that
were familiar once / Round my dead hearth." [17] Pearse's
treatment of children is similarly strained. They are forever
prancing with "bare feet upon the strand," or confessing their
"fault truly," or "watching the wee ladybird fly away." [18] Pearse
professed a belief in the child's "inner life" from which adults
are excluded—and he had read Wordsworth [19]—but except
perhaps in his plays, *The King* and *The Master*, where his
austerity of language in dramatic dialogue limits the frequency

of offending modifiers, the point is generally drowned in
excessive sentiment.

Thomas MacDonagh, of the three, published the most
verse, six volumes in all. His earliest work shows a strong
influence of Yeats' poetry; it is romantic and vaguely mystical,
and invokes the spirit of ancient Ireland to help regenerate the
soul of the Irish race. But MacDonagh soon rejected Yeats'
occult "unearthiness" and chose instead for his model William
Wordsworth.[20] In *Literature in Ireland* MacDonagh suggests
that Anglo-Irish poetry should be "the record of speech of the
people, the living word—sometimes, no doubt, heightened to
use the old phrase, but of a directness that Wordsworth would
have adored. Indeed, it would seem that the desire of Wordsworth for a literature written only in the common language of
the people is best fulfilled in the work produced in Ireland." [21]
MacDonagh proposed to carry to fulfillment the revolution
against poetic diction which Wordsworth proclaimed in his
preface to the *Lyrical Ballads* in 1798. But although he avoids
luxuriant imagery in his verse, he rarely achieves the effect of
"common language"; for in rejecting one form of affectation,
he thrives on another.

The essential weakness of his poetic technique is evident in
the rambling poem, "A Season of Repose":

> David is dead long time, and poets here
>   Sell their rich souls upon more sordid marts;
>   And as a grape is crushed all human hearts
> Are trampled of the Beauty they held dear,
> Their wine soon quaffed, their Memory but a tear
>   Dried by new Passion ere another starts—
> Dream not of David thou in human fear.
>
> All souls are lost in the vain world of noise;
>   All gifts of God are bartered for that pelf
>   And every angel soul will change itself
> To serve a brutish idol which destroys
> The sacred spirit's mortal equipoise,
>   Eternal Calm—to serve an evil elf
> Who traffics but Life's lust for Cherub joys.

> Here, in a Summer of sweet Solitude,
>> Oblivion lives gentlier than Thought,
>> Which pains the spirit anxious and distraught,
> Hissing harsh names of disillusions rude—
> Blind Apathy of men, Ingratitude,
>> And Gain for loss of noble kin dear bought—
> Here, 'mid the rose, let Envy not intrude.[22]

The passage begins in language that is colloquial enough, and the omission of the indefinite article in the initial phrase, if an affectation, provides a kind of rhetorical power.[23] But after the first two lines MacDonagh moves steadily away from the world of commonplace reality into that of artifice. The metaphor of grape and wine is effective, although hardly the stuff of everyday conversation. Even in this first stanza, however, Mac-Donagh is guilty of that same stylistic sin, poetic diction, that he condemns in his criticism. The euphuistic "quaffed" and the archaic "ere" anticipate still more precious language—"pelf" and "elf" and "equipoise"—in the following stanza.[24] But what is most destructive to the aesthetic effect of the poem is the piling up of sterile abstractions—"Eternal Calm," "Solitude," "Oblivion," "Thought," "Apathy," "Ingratitude," "Envy." MacDonagh occasionally achieves a lyric charm, such as one finds in his simple song, "The Coming-in of Summer," inspired by a thirteenth-century lyric:

> Corncrake's ancient sorrow
>> Pains the evening hush,
> But the dawn to-morrow
>> Gladdens with the thrush—
> And summer is a-coming in.[25]

He is at his best when he attempts, as he does here, to recapture the simplicity of another age in unaffected songs and in translations of simple Gaelic poems. But these are the exception rather than the rule in his work; his favorite vehicle is that of "A Season of Repose," the philosophical epistle, and his language in the genre suggests not the utterings of an unspoiled child of nature but the jargon of a logician.

Plunkett's reputation has suffered more from the tributes of his admirers than from destructive criticism. The favorite point of departure is a comparison between Plunkett and Francis Thompson, whose poem on God as hunting dog is frequently anthologized. Both poets, the argument goes, are difficult because they are concerned not with physical beauties, but with "the light which blinds the eyes of us ordinary men, and, added to this, their subjects are of the empyrean, their veils are themselves too bright, they are poets' poets. We are bats; they are eagles. While they are circling in the azure of the sky we are blinking at our hearths." [26] One commentator strangely reshuffles the hierarchy of English literature to find what he believes is a suitable place for Plunkett: "Though his life was brief and the grave received him twenty years earlier than Thompson, competent critics concede him an easy second place to the great English mystic whom, in his best moment, some would reckon next to Shakespeare." [27] Such exaggerated claims are more likely to alienate than to win readers for Plunkett; and, indeed, they do him a disservice; for, although his achievement is a limited one, he was nonetheless a gifted man, competent at his craft, and certainly the best of the three Rising poets.

Plunkett's verse can be tedious; and this is especially true where, apparently following MacDonagh's lead, he attempts discursive verse. In "Heaven and Hell," for example, he presents for the reader an extensive description of his visionary experience, but the poem fails to convey the sense of intensity one associates with vision and is, indeed, often amateurish in its fundamental technique. Plunkett treats of his spiritual struggle by means of an extended metaphor of "the clanging wars / 'Twixt Hell and Heaven"; and the theme only serves to invite an unfortunate comparison with Milton. But there is no sublimity of style in Plunkett's verse, no flowing grandeur; nor is there anything resembling profound vision; all one finds is the singsong of rhymed tetrameter couplets, together with incompetent phrasing and awkward transitions of thought. Such

lines as "I took the challenge straightaway / And leaped—and
that was yesterday / Or was last year" may fill out the four
beat measure, but one suspects a schoolboy could have managed the problem of scansion as well.[28]

Even in "Heaven and Hell," which is a bad poem, Plunkett
manages an occasional perceptive image, such as his descriptive
analogy for the concept of "Immortality": "More wondrous
than the wonder-birth / Of the white moon from the dark
rock." At any rate, Plunkett usually confines himself to short
lyric forms—sonnets and songs—and in his handling of these
he is much more successful.

The conception of art which the Easter Rising poets shared
was not a narrowly pragmatic one. Yeats and his colleagues of
an earlier generation had broken with the tradition of overtly
political verse established by the poets of *The Nation* in the
eighteen-forties, and most of the younger poets, including
Pearse, MacDonagh, and Plunkett, accepted that judgment.
Plunkett did indeed compose ballads in the Young Ireland
tradition of Thomas Davis and John Mitchel, but he was
careful to exclude them from the formal body of his poetic
works.[29] MacDonagh had written a marching song for the Irish
Volunteers and other patriotic verses, but he, too, was careful
to keep this kind of public rhyming apart from the canon of his
poetry. Pearse came closest to identifying the cause of poetry
with that of political emancipation in some of his plays and in
such poems as "The Rebel" and "The Mother," but even his
verse cannot be judged propagandistic if one accepts the
criteria set forth by MacDonagh in a lecture on Irish poetry at
St. Enda's: "The collective is enemy to true sincerity. Propaganda has never produced a poem. A great hymn, whether of
religion or patriotism, is rarely other than the cry of a poet,
calling to his god or to his country as if he first and alone felt it,

and utter it unconscious of propaganda, for himself. If others afterwards come and share his joy, the gain is theirs." [30]

But if the verse of Pearse, MacDonagh, and Plunkett is not chauvinistic, in that it was not written with the express intention of stirring up public support for the cause of Irish political freedom, it does not follow that their poetry is not nationalistic in a deeper sense. Professor Clery argues that "God and Love and Beauty are the subjects of their verse. It is only occasionally, as intertwined with these ideals, that their national aspirations appear in their writing." [31] Such a statement is misleading. Much of their poetry is concerned with God and Love and Beauty; but their national aspirations are not merely or incidentally "intertwined" with these ideals. Rather their national aspirations are born of their ideals and emerge naturally and inevitably from them. All three were, by their own claim, "visionary" poets, and the ideals, if one may call them that, which they celebrate in their verse, are meant to invoke a spiritual vision that is not only personal—although for each it is that, to be sure—but also national and racial.

Pearse devoted much of his poetic effort to the exaltation of the ideals of naturalness and simplicity which he found embodied in the peasantry of the West of Ireland. Poems such as "A Woman of the Mountain Keens Her Son" and "Lullaby of a Woman of the Mountain" are attempts to depict in verse aspects of the simple, natural life which he regarded as good and noble. [32] A cult of primitivism flourished during the Irish revival and Pearse was one of its staunchest advocates. The treatment of children in his verse serves to reinforce this ideal of simplicity, for, as one writer notes, his children "are the children of a perfectly natural civilisation, untouched and unspoiled by the artifice and conventions of modern days, presented to us as Pearse found them in the islands of the west, and the 'little towns of Connacht.' " [33] Plunkett and MacDonagh drew upon the peasant tradition as well, although not so heavily. [34] All three also made use of their knowledge of the old Celtic sagas and invoked, as Plunkett proclaims, the heroic

inheritance of "The hands that fought, the hearts that broke /
In old immortal tragedies" to succour modern Ireland.[35] But
MacDonagh and Plunkett and, to a lesser extent, Pearse,
subordinated both peasant and heroic ideals to a third tradition which they regarded as most important to the integrity of
the Irish national character—the Roman Catholic religious
tradition that had survived despite centuries of persecution.

For each of them a deep sense of religious conviction was the
informing strength of poetry and, indeed, of nationalism as
well. The spirit of Christianity had been brought to Ireland in
the fifth century by St. Patrick, who, according to legend,
would plead on the day of judgment for the whole of the
people of Ireland, sinless and sinners alike; and in the centuries that followed Patrick's coming, the Irish racial soul had
become impregnated with Christian belief.[36] The peasant
culture, its literature and its customs, took for itself an
aesthetic of Christian sentiment, and even the Gaelic language
became so conjoined with the Roman Catholic religion that in
the middle of the twentieth century one Irish speaker in
greeting another may invoke the names of God and Mary, and
at times those of St. Patrick and St. Brigid as well, to bless the
meeting.[37] For Pearse even the old pagan sagas had a Christian
flavor; he believed that "the story of Cuchulainn symbolizes
the redemption of man by a sinless God" and he saw running
through the *Táin* an unconscious "retelling (or is it a fore-
telling?) of the story of Calvary." [38] He was convinced that
both pagan and Christian traditions in Ireland provided the
same inspiration for the Irish people: "Colmcille suggested
what that inspiration was when he said, 'If I die it shall be from
the excess of love that I bear the Gael.' A love and a service so
excessive that one must give all, must be willing always to make
the ultimate sacrifice—this is the inspiration alike of the story
of Cuchulainn and the story of Colmcille, the inspiration that
made the one a hero and the other a saint." [39]

The Rising poets sought to vindicate the tradition of
Christianity in Ireland, and each of them turned to that

tradition as a source of poetic inspiration. That they chose to exalt the religious orthodoxy of their country can be attributed, in part at least, to a concern at the growing influence among their contemporaries of the non-Christian, basically pagan poetry of George Russell and Yeats. Plunkett in his essay, "Obscurity and Poetry," describes Russell as a self-confessed heretic and calls him "the prophet of pantheism" who sees "the universal in the smallest things and the immortality of Nothingness at the end of all." [40] MacDonagh wrote a play attacking the doctrine of reincarnation espoused by Madame Blavatsky and taken up into the poetic creed of Russell and Yeats,[41] and afterwards in *Literature in Ireland* criticized the treatment of the ancient Irish sagas by the two older poets. Pearse, too, attacked what he believed was a perversion of the saga material: "Either Mr. Russell or Mr. Yeats discovered a certain symbolism in certain white birds spoken of in connection with Angus in one particular passage of early Irish literature. They straightway let loose those birds upon Anglo-Irish poetry, and for many of us since the music of Anglo-Irish poetry has almost been drowned by the needless flapping of those white wings." [42] It was not that they thought Yeats and Russell bad poets; on the contrary, they admired them as artists—and MacDonagh clearly recognized Yeats as the foremost Anglo-Irish poet—but the Rising poets thought that both Yeats and Russell were sadly lacking as theologians. If such fine verse as that of Yeats and Russell could be created from the error of heresy, how much greater and more noble would be a poetry founded upon religious truth? Pearse, MacDonagh, and Plunkett determined to create such a poetry.

Although the Rising poets gave themselves to the advocacy of Roman Catholic theology, they did not always subscribe to the overweening social morality of the Irish Catholic Church. At the height of the controversy over *The Playboy of the Western World*, Pearse defended Synge against the vicious righteousness of his fellow Irish Catholics; [43] and in a political tract he castigates for their "crime against manhood" those

who in the name of morality hounded Parnell to his grave.
Pearse asks rhetorically: "Does the ghost of Parnell hunt them
to their damnation?" [44] In another essay he indicts the entire
structure of moral conformity in Ireland:

> Our Christianity becomes respectability. We are not content with
> teaching the ten commandments that God spake in thunder and
> Christ told us to keep if we would enter into life, and the precepts of
> the Church which he commanded us to hear: we add thereto the
> precepts or commandments of Respectable Society. And these are
> chiefly six: Thou shalt not be extreme in anything—in wrongdoing
> lest thou be put in gaol, in rightdoing lest thou be deemed a saint;
> Thou shalt not engage in trade or manufacture lest thy hands become
> grimy; Thou shalt not carry a brown paper sack lest thou shock Rath-
> gar; Thou shalt not have an enthusiasm lest solicitors and their clerks
> call thee fool; Thou shalt not endanger thy Job. One has heard this
> shocking morality taught in Christian schools, expounded in Chris-
> tian newspapers, even preached from Christian pulpits. Those things
> about the lilies of the field and the birds of the air, and that rebuke
> to Martha who was troubled about many things, are thought to have
> no relevancy to modern life. But if that is so Christianity has no rele-
> vancy to modern life, for these are the essence of Christ's teaching.[45]

The Rising poets did not, of course, reject the formal practices
of the Roman communion; but they were concerned less with
the forms of public profession than with the exaltation of the
inner man. All three of them were led by religious conviction to
espouse (and to celebrate in their verse) the Christian concept
of *contemptus mundi*—rejection of the natural world for the
supernatural—and to attempt to give artistic representation to
the ideal of mystical union with the Godhead. Each of them
dedicates his poetry to the task of defining the nature of God
and the place of man in the divine scheme.

In Catholic mysticism the key to the aesthetic creed of the
Rising poets may be found, and the key to their nationalism, as
it is expressed in their verse, as well. One may find there also

the source of a basic weakness in their poetry. Following the Christian mystics, all three sought to express in their verse the experience of union with the Divine Essence. Such religious experience, however, may be achieved only in the complete rejection of the world of the senses; and this rejection must encompass all human knowledge as well, as Johann Tauler makes clear in *The Following of Christ*:

> Several say that the highest poverty and the most entire withdrawal consist in this, that a man becometh as he was when he did not yet exist. Then he understood nothing and willed nothing, then was he God with God.... What is the knowing of man? It is the images and forms which man draws in through the senses, and otherwise he is not able to know through nature. And if he wisheth to be blessed and saved he must be lacking in this knowledge and stand on the ground of genuine poverty.[46]

That the three Rising poets attempted to apply something resembling Tauler's formula for beatitude to their poetic expression is suggested by their emphasis upon simplicity and clarity in language. They were, indeed, confronted by a paradox; for if they carried out the aesthetic doctrine of vision to which they subscribed, they must inevitably have denied the very efficacy of language; and language is, of course, the basic tool of poetry. Father Cassidy has noted in his essay on Plunkett that the young poet developed "an attitude of distrust of verbal expression.... Could he find some medium of expression kindred in nature to thought and worthy of it his soul would have clung to it as the key to the success of his apostolate. Such he did not find in language." [47] MacDonagh recognized the enigma with which he and his friends were faced; in an essay in *The Irish Review* he wrote of the difficulties of "the mystic who has to express in terms of sense and wit the things of God that are made known to him in no language." [48]

By adhering to this ascetic stricture against temporal knowledge, the Rising poets severely limited the means by which they might communicate their vision in verse. Exotic and lush imagery were anathema to them, and even the simplest allusions to nature's glories they used cautiously for fear of pantheism. Too frequently in their verse they are forced to admit their inadequacy to commit to paper words that convey a sense of their vision. Pearse in "Renunciation" covers his eyes against the light, closes his ears against the music, hardens his heart against the sweet taste of his visionary experience; for the light is too bright for human comprehension, the music too beautiful, the taste too sweet.[49] Plunkett confesses in "Aaron" that he is a poet who "cannot sing / Of your dear worth, or mortal or divine; / No music hidden in any song of mine / Can give your praise." [50] At other times the Rising poets seem to confuse the mere claim of mystical experience with the artistic representation of vision. MacDonagh, for example, writes in his poem "Images":

> The phases of the might
> Of God in mortal sight
>   I saw, in God's forethought
>   Fashioned and wrought,
>
> Now wrought in spirit and clay,
> In rare and common day,
>   And shown in symbol and sign
>   Of power divine.[51]

Of MacDonagh's art in these two stanzas, Plunkett comments: "He is like Blake, holding infinity in the palm of his hand. He is stating his Vision of all Being in eight short lines. He makes a verse of the Universe. He fills all the heavens with a syllable and with a word holds the gates of hell." [52] This is eloquent enough rhetoric. But in fact MacDonagh's eight lines do none of the things Plunkett claims for them; they state that the poet has experienced a vision, but they do not in any way define that vision.

All three poets are guilty of occasional circumvention and evasion in treating of their claimed visions, and all three tend toward abstraction as a substitute for knowledge obtained through the senses. There were certain kinds of imagery, however, which they regarded as proper and admitted to their verse. All three of them drew material, in some measure, from the Gaelic lyric verse of Christian Ireland; they found there, for example, a body of nature imagery, simple and restrained yet beautiful in its severity, a body of imagery in which the natural scene was praised not for its own sake but because it reflected the glory of God. They drew also upon the verse of pagan Ireland, but to a lesser extent and then only with care. But their primary source of inspiration and language was the tradition of Christian mystical literature, from which they borrowed themes, images, signs, and symbols.

Of the three, Plunkett identified himself most closely with the literature of apocalypse. At school he studied Thomas Aquinas and the other Schoolmen and found in them justification for his faith and also a philosophic foundation upon which to build his creative achievement. More important, he steeped himself in the literature of Christian mysticism, especially the works of Tauler, St. John of the Cross, and St. Theresa of Jesus; and from their writings, it would seem, with some reference to the English poet, Francis Thompson, and to the life and thought of St. Francis of Assisi, Plunkett drew both the inspiration for his poetry and most of the traditional symbols that he uses to communicate, or at least to suggest, the nature of his vision.[53]

In the opening selection of his *Poems*, "Seals of Thunder," Plunkett addresses himself directly to God—"to you the stars belong / And all the glowing splendours that I seek"—Who alone can understand his secret songs.[54] It was his belief that for the truly mystical poet the understanding and sympathy of men are not essential, for the Divine Essence is his chosen subject and chosen audience as well; and he could prophesy the ultimate vindication of his poetic vision not by coming generations but by the Divine Will itself on the day of judgment:

> My songs shall live to drive their blinding cars
> Through fiery apocalypse to Heaven's bars!
> When God's loosed might the prophet's word fulfills,
> My songs shall see the ruin of the hills,
> My songs shall see the dirges of the stars.[55]

Such claims may seem outrageous; nevertheless, they are in keeping with the pose of mystic that Plunkett assumes in his verse. At any rate, in Plunkett's poetry the thought and language of orthodox mysticism are more consistently and more effectively employed than in the verse of either Pearse or MacDonagh.

His poem, "Prothalamion," for example, is concerned not with any worldly marriage between man and woman, but rather with the ultimate spiritual marriage of the human soul with the Divine Essence:

> Now a gentle dusk shall fall
> Slowly on the world, and all
> The singing voices softly cease
> And a silence and great peace
> Cover all the blushing earth
> Free from sadness as from mirth
> While with willing feet but shy
> She shall tremble and draw nigh
> To the bridal chamber decked
> With darkness by the architect
> Of the seven starry spheres
> And the pit's eternal fires
> Of the nine angelic choirs
> And her happy hopes and fears.
> Then this magic dusk of even
> Shall give way before the night—
> Close the curtains of delight!
> Silence is the only song
> That can speak such mysteries
> As to earth and heaven belong
> When one flesh has compassed me.[56]

The theme of spiritual betrothal is commonplace enough in the Hebraic-Christian mystical tradition and Plunkett had certainly encountered it in *The Song of Solomon*, in the Gospels and the *Book of Revelation*, and in his reading of Christian mystics. His intention in this poem is to suggest the nature of the mystic's experience of spiritual elevation into union with the Godhead after continued spiritual exercises. According to St. John of the Cross, with whom Plunkett was familiar, at the moment of elevation "the soul not only ceases from its anxieties and loving complaints, but is, moreover, adorned with all grace, entering into a state of peace and delight, and of a sweetness of love . . . in which it does nothing else but recount and praise the magnificence of the Beloved, which it recognizes in Him, and enjoys in the union of the betrothal." The images of "gentle dusk" and "darkness" and "night" with which Plunkett cloaks his poem are meant to suggest that serenity which St. John calls the "spiritual sleep in the bosom of the Beloved." The poet tries to justify man's desire for mystical marriage to the Divine Essence; for human nature is an integral part of the divine creation, and man's "hopes and fears" are as much the handiwork of God as heaven and hell and the angels surrounding the heavenly throne. The final lines of the poem, in which Plunkett attempts to suggest spiritual consummation, also gather their meaning from the Catholic mystical tradition. Silent music, John of the Cross asserts, is the "marvellous arrangement and disposition of God's wisdom in the diversity of His creatures and operations. All these, and each one of them, have a certain correspondence with God, whereby each, by a voice peculiar to itself, proclaims what there is in itself of God, so as to form a concert of sublimest melody, transcending all the harmonies of the world." [57]

Plunkett incorporates the themes and imagery of ascetic mysticism into his verse consistently and skillfully. What his art lacks, perhaps, is originality, for his poetry is too consciously imitative of the kind of medieval occultism that one finds in the spiritual canticles of St. John of the Cross, and, in consequence, it may have little relevance for modern man.

That his verse has at times a cold, mechanical quality may be attributed to the fact that his inspiration owes more to bookish research than to personal experience.

Both Pearse and MacDonagh took material from the tradition of Christian mysticism, but not so extensively nor with as much success. MacDonagh's approach to visionary art is different from Plunkett's; and one might define the difference by saying that Plunkett assumed the pose of a Christian ascetic who already had achieved mystical union with the Godhead and MacDonagh the pose of a Christian struggling to achieve spiritual perfection, but still pressed by doubts concerning his own unworthiness, still torn between the opposing claims of flesh and spirit. These inner doubts are given expression in the poem "A Dream of Being," which consists of a dialogue between a virginal nun and the dream-image of the child whom she will never bear. The nun tries to reconcile the conflict in her heart by arguing that the son who pleads for life exists only in her dream and "not in eternity"; but in the end her doubts return and her unborn child—from whose point of view the poem is written—leaves her pondering.[58] In "Of My Poems" MacDonagh expresses the desire to perceive the ultimate meaning of man's existence just as once "we saw with Adam's eyes / In the first days of Paradise." One suspects the influence of Yeats in this poem; but whereas Yeats would blame man's fall from natural unity of being upon the destructive influence of rationalism, MacDonagh adheres to the Christian tradition and attributes man's corruption to Original Sin. His hope is that the spiritual knowledge that was Adam's before the fall might afford proof of the immortality of the human soul; for when the poet is able to see with uncorrupted vision he will know "the single bond / Of life with life here and beyond," and that certain knowledge will "lift my deeds the grave above / And give a meaning to my love." [59]

It is significant that as a young man MacDonagh had passed through a period of spiritual doubt.[60] In "The Tree of Knowledge" he traces the journey of one, "Untroubled by knowledge" and in harmony "With the stars of morning and God," who listens to "the serpent's constant call" and eats of the Tree of Knowledge in order that he might "be as a god." But instead he becomes "a man / Upon a bare hill side, / For the tree has withered up / And the ancient life has died." It is only after he has "toiled to the full" that the vision of Paradise may be regained. The substance of MacDonagh's poem is meant on one level to suggest the mystical journey of mankind from the light of grace in the Garden to the darkness of sin and finally, through *imitatio Christi*, into divine light again. But the primary reference for the poem is autobiographical; Mac-Donagh himself had fallen from the light of simple faith into the shadow of doubt and he could hope to achieve spiritual reconciliation only after a long inner struggle.[61] The struggle to regain spiritual innocence is a recurrent motif in MacDonagh's verse. Like his nun in "The Dream of Being," he could not finally choose between the human and the divine, and this inner ambivalence extends not simply to the subject matter of his poetry, to which it sometimes contributes the effect of dramatic conflict, but to his poetic technique as well. Where the latter is true, the poet's indecision only serves to weaken and at times even to confuse the symbolic texture of his verse.

For Pearse, who also laid claim to the mystic's "clear vision" of the "beauty of beauty," there were no struggles, no torments, no doubts concerning his religious belief, if one is to judge by the numerous testimonials concerning his personal life. At the age of ten, having improvised a priest's vestments from his mother's nightdress and a piece of twine, he "said Mass," with his brother acting the role of altar boy and his sisters that of congregation.[62] Pearse deliberately cultivated Christlike virtue. He never married and apparently saw in all women only those virtues of purity and fortitude usually associated with Christ's mother.[63] He had a deep sympathy for the weaker and more helpless of God's creatures. His love for children is chronicled again and again in his plays, stories, and poems, and he so pitied the poor that when a grown man he would masquerade as a pauper and walk the streets in order to find out "how it felt to beg." [64] He also professed sympathy for God's beasts and birds and once angered a Gaelic League audience by accusing the Irish-speaking people of being more cruel to animals than even the English.[65] Pearse sought sanctification in his everyday life; not surprisingly, the "vision" one finds in his poetry is a mixture of gentleness and anger (at injustice), born of Christlike simplicity and overlaid with pious sentiment.

In "The Wayfarer," for example, he chooses a variation of the concept of *contemptus mundi* for his theme:

> The beauty of the world hath made me sad,
> This beauty that will pass;
> Sometimes my heart hath shaken with great joy
> To see a leaping squirrel in a tree,
> Or a red lady-bird upon a stalk,
> Or little rabbits in a field at evening,
> Lit by a slanting sun,
> Or some green hill where shadows drifted by
> Some quiet hill where mountainy man hath sown
> And soon would reap; near to the gate of Heaven;
> Or children with bare feet upon the sands
> Of some ebbed sea, or playing on the streets
> Of little towns in Connacht,
> Things young and happy.
> And then my heart hath told me:
> These will pass,
> Will pass and change, will die and be no more,
> Things bright and green, things young and happy;
> And I have gone upon my way
> Sorrowful.[66]

The poem consists of a catalogue of the images which Pearse associated with the simple peasant ideal, the first half celebrating the romantic beauty of the natural scene, the latter half the human innocence that can thrive in such a setting. At the center of the poem is the informing observation that this innocent world of nature is "near to the gate of Heaven"; in other words, that the hand of the divine creator is everywhere manifest. This notion is in itself orthodox enough, and, indeed, is not unlike the belief of John of the Cross that each item of the creation corresponds in some particular to the nature of the divinity. Similarly, the underlying theme of the poem, that in accordance with the divine scheme these physical beauties of nature must pass away, also is sound enough theology. But the poet's pose of nostalgic sadness at the plight of these natural glories—worldly vanities for all their simplicity—is at least questionable from the point of view of Christian mysticism. For although Pearse subscribes to the doctrine of mutability, he does so only reluctantly and regretfully; and in his sentimental attachment for the natural universe which inevitably must pass away, he tends to ignore the supernatural word of God that shall never pass away.

In the verse of all three of these poets the tradition of religious belief and the ideal of *imitatio Christi* are celebrated as essential elements of Irish nationality. It may be argued with some justice that the Christian cult of ascetic mysticism is not specifically an Irish heritage; and it is certainly true that the three, and Plunkett especially, borrowed from a literature written by European holy men and, in the case of the Apocalypse, by a Jew who took much of his symbolism from eastern rather than western civilization. But Ireland could make some claim to the tradition. St. Patrick, St. Colmcille, and other early saints had submitted to ascetic discipline and had been granted visionary experience. Even in modern Ireland the cult of religious self-mortification is widespread; each year thousands of barefooted pilgrims seek spiritual regeneration through prayer and fasting on the island of Lough Dergh and the mountain Croagh Patrick where centuries before St. Patrick had mortified his body to strengthen his spirit during his missionary work in Ireland.[67]

More important as far as Pearse, MacDonagh, and Plunkett were concerned was the parallel, which they certainly recognized, between the religious persecution of the Irish people by their English rulers and the Roman persecution of the early Christians. Just as the Apocalypse emerged as a mystical affirmation of Christianity during Nero's oppression of the early Church, so too a powerful visionary literature might speak for the Irish race and nation that had held to its faith despite centuries of oppression. The Rising poets and, indeed, many of their contemporaries seem to have considered the Irish to be a kind of chosen people, like the early Christians and the Jews of the Old Testament, a people who had suffered in God's cause and who therefore could expect a lion's share of God's glory. Padraic Pearse had written that "the soul of the enslaved and broken nation may conceivably be a more splendid thing than the soul of a great free nation." [68] It is not surprising that Pearse, MacDonagh, and Plunkett should have turned for inspiration to the Christian tradition of ascetic mysticism in their attempt to give expression to their vision of the Irish nation.

For the Rising poets the cause of nationalism was as much a spiritual consideration as it was a political one. One of them, probably Plunkett, believed that the soul of Ireland was "a mystical entity"; and Pearse maintained that every "true nationality" had its own "spiritual tradition," and of this tradition he wrote: "This spiritual thing is distinct from the intellectual facts in which chiefly it makes its revelation, and it is distinct from them in a way analogous to that in which man's soul is distinct from his mind. Like other spiritual things, it is independent of the material, whereas the mind is to a large extent dependent upon the material." [69] MacDonagh's nationalism, too, had an ethereal quality; and he could write of the "great informing soul of a large body of our lyric poetry, of our oratory, and of much of the rest of our literature—'the cause that never dies,' the ideal held always by the Gaelic race that once dominated Europe—now held by the heir and successor of that race here, the Irish." [70] As far as these three poets were concerned, the cause of Irish sovereignty demanded no less zealous advocacy than the cause of Christ's religion; and each of them would surely have subscribed to the creed of nationalism set down by Pearse: "Like a divine religion, national freedom bears the marks of unity, of sanctity, of catholicity, of apostolic succession. Of unity, for it contemplates the nation as one; of sanctity, for it is holy in itself and in those who serve it; of catholicity, for it embraces all the men and women of the nation; of apostolic succession, for it, or the aspiration after it, passes down from generation to generation from the nation's fathers." [71] The poet who writes poems to or about his homeland is not unlike the holy man who writes hymns to or about God. Having accepted this point of view, the Rising poets took the paraphernalia of mysticism—themes, images, symbols—and used them to express in their verse the sacred truth of Irish nationalism. Pearse, for example, in "The Rebel," gives to the cause of revolution an implied religious sanction by taking his theme, imagery, and even rhythm from the Old Testament:

> I am come of the seed of the people, the
>   people that sorrow,
> That have no treasure but hope,
> No riches laid up but a memory
> Of an ancient glory.
> My mother bore me in bondage, in bondage
>   my mother was born;
> I am the blood of serfs;
> The children with whom I have played, the
>   men and women with whom I have
>   eaten,
> Have had masters over them, have been
>   under the lash of masters,
> And, though gentle, have served churls;
> The hands that have touched mine, the dear
>   hands whose touch is familiar to me,
> Have worn shameful manacles, have been
>   bitten at the wrist by manacles,

> Have grown hard with the manacles and the
> task-work of strangers,
> I am the flesh of the flesh of these lowly,
> I am bone of their bone,
> I that have never submitted;
> I that have a soul greater than the souls
> of my people's masters,
> I that have vision and prophecy and the
> gift of fiery speech,
> I that have spoken with God on the top of
> His holy hill.[72]

Pearse's theme is, of course, drawn from *Exodus*: the Irish rebel (no doubt Pearse himself), like Moses, has spoken with God on the mountain and has received a divine command to free his people. Like Moses, he will lead the Chosen People, the Irish—who have endured captivity under the English just as the Israelites endured it under the Egyptians—out of bondage and into the Promised Land of a free and sovereign Ireland. The tone of Pearse's poem is Biblical and some of his language—"people," "bondage," "task-work," "masters"—is copied directly from the story of Moses and Pharaoh.[73] The reference to "seed" in the opening phrase and the powerful, if rhetorical, line, "I am flesh of the flesh of these lowly, I am bone of their bone," are taken from Genesis and are meant to suggest that the rebel is a racial and national archetype, symbolic of the God-given natural desire of the Irish race for independence, just as Adam is the archetype of mankind, symbolic of God-given human nature.[74] What is wrong with Pearse's poem—aside from its overwrought melodrama and its too apparent note of political hatred—is that the Biblical motif, which by rights should be no more than a secondary frame of reference, is much too obvious and too self-conscious in its implementation. One is tempted to ask just how much credit for the poem should go to Pearse and how much to the Biblical scribes.

The fusion of religious fervor and nationalism in Plunkett's verse is much more subtly expressed than in Pearse's; at times, indeed, it becomes obscure. The mixture is clear enough in such a poem as "The Heritage of the Race of Kings," in which the poet foretells that so long as the Irish people are subject to foreign rule they will "have their hearts volcanic burn / With anger of the suns of God." The ambiguity of "suns," with its twin allusions, the one equating the Irish with the Chosen People of the Old Testament, the other invoking the brightness of the sun to suggest for them a spiritual link with the divinity, is clever without being difficult.[75] More often, however, Plunkett's message is hidden in a complex of mystical symbolism.

MacDonagh, too, informs his poetic expression of nationalism with religious symbolism. In "Barbara" he contrasts Ireland's thriving Christian faith with the godlessness of the rest of Europe:

> When the life of the cities of Europe goes
>   The way of Memphis and Babylon,
> In Ireland still the mystic rose
>   Will shine as it of old has shone.
>
> O rose of Grace! O rare wild flower,
>   Whose seeds are sent on the wings of Light!
> O secret rose, our doom, our dower,
>   Black with the passion of our night.[76]

The allusions to Memphis and Babylon—Biblical cities of idolatry and degradation, both of which enslaved God's Chosen People—are clear enough in their meaning. But the rose symbol in MacDonagh's verse has multiple significance. Through his association with Yeats, MacDonagh no doubt knew that the rose was the flower of the Rosicrucians; but certainly more important to him was its use as a symbol for Christ—"the rose of Sharon"—in the Song of Solomon [77] and as an image in Christian mystical literature for God's gift of grace to men. The rose in the tradition of Irish protest literature—which MacDonagh knew well—has yet another meaning as a symbol for the Irish nation.[78] In "Barbara" MacDonagh employs the image of the rose in order to synthesize the ideals of religion and nationalism. In the second stanza the "rose of Sharon," that is, the flower of Roman Catholicism which bloomed in Ireland for centuries, is related to the divinity by means of the mixed metaphor of mystical imagery—"seeds" and "wings" and "light." The final two lines suggest that the Irish people, blessed with the "dower" of the Catholic faith and doomed to suffer because of it, harbor a black passion of anger born of centuries of English persecution.

The Rising poets were not oblivious to the contradiction involved in justifying militant nationalism by reference to a religion that urged men to the practice of meekness and long-suffering. The problems posed by Christian pacifism on the one hand and the concept of *contemptus mundi* on the other seem especially to have bothered MacDonagh, and his inner doubts found frequent expression in his verse.[79] The hero of "The Poet Captain," for example, is three times called upon to lead his people in battle, once for the sake of national triumph, again to save his race from destruction, and a third time to preserve the language and manners of his people. But each time "the sorrow of life" mocks him for seeking after worldly victories: "—O little soul, striving to little goal! / Here is a finite world where all things change and change!" [80] In "Wishes for My Son" the conflict is made more personal. MacDonagh prays that his child will inherit all of his own gifts except the religious experience which so filled him with love that he could find "no enemy, / No man in a world of wrong, / That Christ's word of charity / Did not render clean and strong"; what he most desires for his son is not this sense of divine love but rather a sense of divine justice:

> Wild and perilous holy things
> Flaming with a martyr's blood,
> And the joy that laughs and sings
> Where a foe must be withstood,
> Joy of headlong happy chance
> Leading on the battle dance.[81]

This poem was composed in 1912; in the following year the dilemma remains for MacDonagh, but the tone of his verse becomes distinctly more decisive, and it is clear that he will turn inevitably from the world of contemplation to the world of action. In "Postscriptum" he asserts that he had renounced the tyranny of worldly desire—to which all men became subject when Adam and Eve ate the apple from the tree of knowledge of good and evil—and rewon for himself the innocent peace of Eden before the Fall; but in the final stanza MacDonagh cries out that personal salvation is not enough:

> And though my tyrant days are o'er
> I earn my tyrant's fate the more
> If now secure within my walls
> I fiddle while my country falls.[82]

Plunkett's verse suggests the same sense of conflicting values and the same inevitable decision for Irish nationalism. In the first and second stanzas of "Before the Glory of Your Love," Plunkett remarks the "silent witness" to God's glory which is given by each part of the creation; but in the final stanza he makes clear that his own witness must be different: "Only this madman cannot keep / Your peace, but flings his bursting heart / Forth to red battle." [83] Pearse, too, makes his choice. In "Renunciation" he pointedly rejects the way of contemplative vision:

> I blinded my eyes,
> And I closed my ears.
> I hardened my heart
> And smothered my desire[;]

and chooses instead the path of militant nationalism, a path that will lead him "To the deed that I see / And the death I shall die." [84]

Each of the Rising poets chose the deed—and the deed for Pearse, MacDonagh, and Plunkett meant violent insurrection —and each of them set about to justify that deed by invoking the sanction of religion. The cause of the Irish people was a holy cause and their war would be a holy war. John Mitchel, the Fenian, had said as much in his *Jail Journal* a half century earlier; and Pearse, in an essay, quotes from that work a passage in which Mitchel's "Ego," using the language of Armageddon, describes for "Doppleganger" the coming upheaval in Ireland:

"Who is this that cometh from Edom: with dyed garments from Bozrah? This that is glorious in his apparel, travelling in the garments of his strength? Wherefore art thou red in thine apparel, and thy garments like him that treadeth in the wine vat? I have trodden the wine press alone, and of the people there was none with me: for I will tread them in mine anger and trample them in my fury, and their blood shall be sprinkled upon my garments, and I will stain all my raiment. For the day of vengeance is in my heart." Also an aspiration of King David haunts my memory when I think of Ireland and her wrongs: "*That thy foot may be dipped in the blood of thine enemies, and that the tongue of thy dogs may be red through the same.*" [85] [Mitchel's italics.]

Mitchel's call for holy vengeance and before him Wolfe Tone's cry for justice—" 'Dieu et nos Droits' " [86]—were part of a tradition of rebellion in God's name from which the Rising poets could take inspiration, and no doubt this tradition was running through Plunkett's mind when he promised in "The Heritage of the Race of Kings" that the Irish people, filled up with God's holy anger, would "fulfill their prophecies in deed / Of terrible and splendid things." [87]

But although the Armageddon motif of climactic struggle between the forces of good and evil is evoked in the verse of each of the Rising poets, it is generally subordinated to another theme, similarly grounded in religious tradition but more appropriate to the imbalance of military power between the Irish revolutionaries and their English antagonists—that is, the theme of sacrifice. They found in Irish history a tradition of heroic gesture, of dedication and courage in the face of overwhelming odds. Indeed, one need not be sentimentally biased in favor of Irish revolutions to perceive the dignity with which Wolfe Tone and Robert Emmet, and, as a matter of fact, Pearse, MacDonagh, and Plunkett themselves accepted the consequences of military defeat. Certainly, as far as the Rising poets were concerned, the only danger that threatened Ireland was that its people might at last submit to the inevitability of foreign rule. In his poem, "I Am Ireland," Pearse alludes to the historical episode in which Diarmuid and Dervorgilla brought the Normans to Ireland and writes of the "shame" of a country whose "own children sold their mother"; [88] to atone for that crime against race and nation, Pearse believed, every Irishman had the sacred duty to renew periodically the cause of rebellion, however hopeless the odds. Yeats was later to immortalize this sense of national shame that so weighted Pearse's mind: "Patrick Pearse had said / That in every generation / Must Ireland's blood be shed." [89] MacDonagh had the same idea in mind when he told the court martial which condemned him that the "resurgent pride" that brought him and his fellows to rebellion "may one day cease to throb in the heart of Ireland—but the heart of Ireland will that day be dead." [90]

A corollary to the theme of sacrifice in the verse of the Rising poets is an obsessive concern with death. A psychologically morbid attitude is expressed by Pearse in such poems as "Long to Me Thy Coming," in which the poet addressed God's "henchman" as his "friend of all friends," and "A Rann I Made," where he affirms that death's house, "tho' black clay," is for him brighter than daylight and sweeter than the sound of trumpets. [91] MacDonagh manages to exult—although not very convincingly—in a "child with rapturous voice / Singing, Farewell! Rejoice! / Singing the joy of death"; [92] but more characteristically his verse embodies a note of human uncertainty with respect to death, such as is manifest in "To Eoghan":

> Will you gaze after the dead, gaze into
> the grave?—

Strain your eyes in the darkness,
  knowing it vain?
Strain your voice in the silence that never
  gave
To any voice or yours an answer
  again? [93]

Plunkett rarely addresses himself directly to the subject of death; and even when he does so, in such poems as "When I am Dead," the result has neither the grisly exuberance of Pearse nor the hesitancy of MacDonagh. Death, says Plunkett, balancing religious belief and human apprehension, is "The ultimate Victory that stings and sears." [94]

For the Rising poets, however, it was not so much the fact of death itself as the kind of death one died that mattered. Death was not for them a nightmare vision; Pearse described a dream in which he saw a boy from his school standing upon a scaffold above a huge crowd.

I understood that he was about to die there for some august cause, Ireland's or another. He looked extraordinarily proud and joyous, lifting his head with a smile almost of amusement; I remember noticing his bare white throat and the hair of his forehead stirred by the wind, just as I had often noticed them on the football field. I felt an inexplicable exhilaration as I looked upon him, and this exhilaration was heightened rather than diminished by my consciousness that the great silent crowd regarded the boy with pity and wonder rather than as a martyr that was doing his duty. It would have been so easy to die before an applauding crowd or before a hostile crowd: but to die before that silent, unsympathetic crowd! [95]

Pearse's dream has a special significance because it helps to define the ideal of sacrifice which informs the verse of the Rising poets. The young man's smile—"proud and joyous"—suggests that he is a willing, even eager, victim. Yet his pose of nonchalance emerges neither out of a desire for the praise of his countrymen (or those for whom his sacrifice is offered) nor out of defiance for the hatred of his enemies; for the crowd is neither applauding nor hostile, but only silent and skeptical.

Personal motivation has no meaning for the youth. His pride and joy are born of an awareness—which is independent of praise or blame—that the cause to which he gives himself is a cause more important than life or death.

Such an ideal of selfless sacrifice that is its own reward implies an inspiration that is something more than patriotism, and in their verse Pearse, MacDonagh, and Plunkett attempt to relate that ideal to the Christian religious tradition. Just as the cause of Ireland is a holy cause and the war of Ireland is a holy war, so also is the sacrifice of the Irish a holy sacrifice. In Pearse's play, *The Singer,* the protagonist, McDara, tells the village elders (after they had dissuaded all but fifteen of their young men from fighting a hopeless battle against the English army): "The fifteen were too many. Old men, you did not do your work well enough. You should have kept all back but one. One man can free a people as one Man redeemed the world. I will take no pike, I will go into the battle with bare hands. I will stand up before the Gall as Christ hung naked before men on a tree." [96] In McDara's brief speech the sacrifice of the Irish rebel is given a special religious significance by means of the analogy with the Messianic sacrifice of the cross; similarly, the Rising poets chose as the informing image of their vision of the Irish nation the supreme point of the Christian religious tradition of contemplation, that is, the redemption symbol of Christ crucified upon Calvary.

The symbolism of the divine passion is at the center of Plunkett's aesthetic; its influence is therefore not limited to the expression of the nationalist ideal of sacrifice but extends to much of his verse. Plunkett had read Johann Tauler's *The Following of Christ* and certainly was aware of the mystic's precept that in order to escape the limitations of the flesh men should contemplate Christ's suffering and death. "If a man immerse himself in the passion of our Lord," Tauler had written, "he is purified and in this purity a light is kindled that burneth and killeth all luring of the body, a spiritual divine rapture is begotten which surpasseth all bodily lust. Whoso wisheth to have this divine rapture, let him lay his mouth at the wounds of our Lord and suck them in." [97]

It is this kind of contemplative experience that Plunkett tries to embody in his verse. In his sonnet, "Arbor Vitae," for example, he relates that "Beside the golden gate there grows a tree / Whose heavy fruit gives entrance to the ways / Of Wonder." The tree is Christ's cross; he who is willing—in Tauler's phrase—to "suck in" the fruits of that tree (i.e., the wounds of Christ) will find them "Sweet-bitter, red and white, / Better than wine—better than timely death / When surfeited with sorrow." And the reward for him who eats is the "Song of Songs with Love's tumultuous light" in "Mansions beyond the gate!" [98] In another poem, "The Living Temple," Plunkett relates the imagery of "proximate apocalypse" to the "strong cross" and the "blood from wounded brows and side." [99] And in a third, "The Splendour of God," he claims that his poetic vision makes him "like God"; for just as "God crushes his passion-fruit for our thirst / And the universe totters," so in his mystical verse Plunkett has "burst the grape / Of the world." [100] The image of the wine of passion used here is drawn from the tradition of the Christian mystics; according to John of the Cross, first God tastes the wine (through Christ's passion) and then "He gives it to the soul to taste, and when the soul tastes it, the soul gives it back to Him, and thus it is that both taste it together." [101] By means of the wine of passion—a sacrificial symbol of passionate suffering grounded in spiritual love—man can achieve union with the Godhead.

In "The Little Black Rose Shall Be Red at Last" Plunkett employs the religious symbolism of Christ's passion to give artistic expression to a different kind of mystical experience. In this sonnet it is not the holy man's union with the divine essence that concerns him, but the patriot's union with the national and racial soul. Plunkett's transference of the trappings of contemplative vision to inform the theme of Irish nationalism is evident even in the title of the poem itself. The "little black rose" is an emblem in Irish protest literature for the Irish nation under foreign rule. The red rose, however, while it is certainly expressive of the idea of revolution, also embodies an allusion to the blood passion of Christ.[102] The ordeal which Ireland must suffer in the cause of justice is thereby infused with a religious meaning. In like manner, in the poem itself Plunkett develops his statement of nationalism within the framework of mystical symbolism:

> Because we share our sorrows and our joys
> And all your dear and intimate thoughts are mine
> We shall not fear the trumpets and the noise
> Of battle, for we know our dreams divine,
> And when my heart is pillowed on your heart
> And ebb and flowing of their passionate flood
> Shall beat in concord love through every part
> Of brain and body—when at last the blood
> O'er leaps the final barrier to find
> Only one source wherein to spend its strength
> And we two lovers, long but one in mind
> And soul, are made one only flesh at length;
> Praise God if this my blood fulfils the doom
> When you, dark rose, shall redden into bloom.[103]

Two themes are interwoven in the poem. One is embodied in the image of battle that is born of dreams that are divine—as the use of the Biblical "trumpets" in the third line rather than commonplace bugles suggests. Ireland's holy war will be like the final apocalyptic battle between the powers of good and evil where God's right will prevail and after which will follow the day of reckoning. But the central movement of the poem is patterned after the theme of lover and beloved that one finds in Solomon's Song of Songs, as well as in the spiritual canticles of St. John of the Cross and numerous other Christian mystical works. Plunkett develops the theme fully; like the mystic's love for God, the poet's love for Ireland must envelop mind and soul and body. The union of mystical love must be in every way complete and irrevocable; for only from such love can the Messianic ideal emerge. Just as Christ's sacrifice of love redeemed the world, so also the poet's sacrifice will redeem Ireland.[104]

In MacDonagh's verse the ideals of nationalism and Messianic sacrifice are nowhere so successfully merged as in this poem by Plunkett. Both themes are present, to be sure; but they are never really synthesized into a single artistic expression. MacDonagh writes often enough of the "passionate proud woes of Roisin Dubh" (i.e., dark rose) and the cause of Irish nationality; [105] and he frequently makes use of the image of Christ upon the cross. However, the symbolism of crucifixion is usually associated with the poet's personal spiritual agony rather than with the national cause. In the poem, "In an Island," for example, MacDonagh writes:

> 'Mid an isle I stand,
> Under its only tree:
> The ocean around—
> Around life eternity:
> 'Mid my life I stand,
> Under the boughs of thee.[106]

The poet here identifies himself with the cult of the cross, but the emphasis is too personal to have any special significance as far as his attitude toward Ireland is concerned. He comes much closer to the motif of Messianic nationalism in "Envoi," where he renounces the sorrows and joys of his youth in order that he may start on "another journey":

> For I am the lover, the anchoret,
>   And the suicide—but in vain;
> I have failed in their deeds, and I want them yet,
>   And this life derides my pain.
>
> I suffer unrest and unrest I bring,
>   And my love is mixed with hate;
> And the one that I love wants another thing,
>   Less unkind and less passionate.
>
> So I know I have lost the thing that I sought,
>   And I know that by my loss
> I have won the thing that others have bought
>   In agony on this cross.

But I whose creed is only death
  Do not prize their victory;
I know that my life is but a breath
  On the glass of eternity.[107]

There is good reason to believe that MacDonagh's newly chosen "journey" is the journey of militant nationalism. During the period in which this poem was written, he was helping Pearse in the task of preaching heroic idealism to the students at St. Enda's school. In the poem itself, he confesses that his "love" is now "mixed with hate"—hatred most likely directed against Ireland's enemies; and that his "creed is only death," a phrase which can reasonably be interpreted to mean that he is determined on martyrdom in his country's cause. However, as such poems as "The Poet Captain" and "Wishes for My Son" make clear, MacDonagh experienced great difficulty in reconciling the concept of *imitatio Christi* with the cause of violent revolt. The same indecisiveness that characterizes those poems is at work here; for MacDonagh's new journey of nationalism is at odds with the old one of contemplation. He tells his reader that because of his choice in favor of the new journey he has lost "the thing that I sought" in the cult of the cross. MacDonagh simply could not convert Christ, as Plunkett did, into a God of vengeance; for him Christ remained a figure of gentle love and therefore represented an ideal "Less unkind and less passionate" than that which the poet had chosen to follow. MacDonagh belatedly argues that his new journey will win for him the same reward "that others have bought / In agony on this cross." Martyrdom for Ireland, in other words, will bring salvation just as certainly as *imitatio Christi*. But this argument is not very convincing, for he already has admitted that hatred has infected his love. Nor does he win the reader's sympathy in the final lines with the muttered slur—which is out of keeping with the tone of the poem—on the brevity of the mortal existence in which Christlike virtue can be practiced.

MacDonagh does not achieve a satisfactory synthesis of the

concept of Christian sacrifice founded upon love and that of violent rebellion either in this poem, or, indeed, elsewhere in his verse. His plays, however, do give expression to the ideal of Messianic nationalism. In John Fitzmaurice's final words to his wife in *Pagans,* the quarrel between contemplation and insurrection is still in evidence, but the decision at least is clearly for the latter course: "I am going to live things that I have before imagined. It is well for a poet that he is double-lived. He has two stores of power. You will not know yourself in the Ireland that we shall make here—when I return to you." [108] Fitzmaurice suggests that he intends to take the role of savior of the nation, even though he does not specifically mention the need for blood sacrifice as essential to that role and, in fact, promises to return. The hero of *When the Dawn Is Come,* Turlough MacKieran, is a Messiah figure in every respect. He is subjected to dishonor and disgrace by his own comrades, but finally vindicates himself and his ideals by dying to give Ireland victory over her foes. After his death, Ita MacOscar, a woman and the only sympathetic member of the Army council that had repudiated Turlough, describes the treatment he has received from the Irish people in a way that begs comparison with the treatment of Christ by the Jews: "Ireland has waited long, waited the man—the man of her far promise and her hope. He comes, and oh, you do not know him." [109]

In Pearse's attitude toward the joining of the Messianic and nationalist ideals there is nothing of the artistic detachment one finds in Plunkett's verse, nor is there any hint of the doubts that so bothered MacDonagh. For Pearse the passion of Christ on the cross was the focal point both of his life and of his work, and, indeed, there is good reason to suspect that he looked upon himself as a kind of national redeemer whose mission had received the seal of divine approval. His sister, Mary Brigit Pearse, has testified to his "deep religious feeling" and has noted that "his greatest devotion was to the tragedy of Calvary—to Christ Crucified, and to the Crucifix." [110] He was a frequent communicant at the Mass, which in Roman Catholic ritual is the bloodless renewal of the sacrifice of Calvary, and he composed a poem, "Christ's Coming," expressing his religious emotion at receiving the communion host.[111] At St. Enda's he displayed for the edification of his students a picture, "The Child Jesus," in which Christ is portrayed as a boy standing serious and erect between two trees with his arms spread-eagled in the pose of crucifixion;[112] and he wrote a passion play which the children of his school performed in the Abbey Theatre during Holy Week, 1911.[113] To instill in his students the idealism of Christ's sacrifice—along with the heroic ideal-ism of Cú Chulainn—was Pearse's primary objective in his experiment with an Irish school.

Pearse frequently informed his polemics on Ireland's revolu-tionary cause with imagery drawn from the Catholic ritual commemorating Christ's sacrifice: "Time after time we have lifted the chalice of victory to our lips; time after time we have essayed to quaff its delicious contents; yet time after time it has been dashed to the ground!"[114] In his poem, "The Fool," Pearse writes of his dream of a free Ireland:

> The lawyers have sat in council, the men
> with the keen, long faces,
> And said, "This man is a fool," and others
> have said, "He blasphemeth";
> And the wise have pitied the fool that hath
> striven to give a life
> In the world of time and space among the
> bulks of actual things,
> To a dream that was dreamed in the heart,
> and that only the heart could hold.
>
> O wise men, riddle me this: what if the
> dream come true?
> What if the dream come true? and if
> millions unborn shall dwell
> In the house that I shaped in my heart, the
> noble house of my thought?
> Lord, I have staked my soul, I have staked
> the lives of my kin

On the truth of Thy dreadful word. Do
    not remember my failures,
But remember this my faith.[115]

In these stanzas Pearse clearly defines the Irish rebel as a
Christlike victim taking part in a ritual that has religious as
well as political significance. Like Christ, the revolutionary
"fool" consecrates himself to the sacrifice of his physical life in
order to achieve a spiritual end—that which Pearse designates
as a "dream." But the parallel in the poem between the fool
and Christ extends further. Both are motivated by divine
revelation: the fool by "the truth of Thy dreadful word,"
Christ by the conviction that the Biblical prophecies must be
fulfilled; and both are condemned for their "blasphemy": the
fool by the lawyers "with the keen, long faces," Christ by the
high priest in the temple.

Just as the rebel in "The Fool" is given the status of a
redeemer, so the Irish people in Pearse's verse are represented
as a people chosen of God and therefore worthy of redemption.
In the poem entitled "The Rebel," Pearse asserts that his
people "are holy, that they are august, despite their chains, /
That they are greater than those that hold them, and stronger
and purer." Then, significantly, he adds that to win their
freedom this people need only "call on the name of their
God, / God the unforgetting, the dear God that loves the
peoples / For whom He died naked, suffering shame." [116] Just
as God sent His Son to win spiritual salvation for the world, so
God will send another, a national redeemer, to win cultural
and political salvation for Ireland. The only trouble with all
this—as poetry—is that Ireland's redeemer, as he is manifest in
these poems, is too obviously, too self-concsiously Pearse
himself. In "The Mother" an Irish woman speaks of "two
strong sons that I have seen go out / To break their strength
and die, they and a few, / In bloody protest for a glorious
thing." [117] Pearse's own mother had "two strong sons," Padraic
and William; and both went out to fight for Irish freedom on

Easter Monday, 1916, and both were subsequently shot by the British. The identification is unmistakable. It is equally apparent that the "fool" is Pearse, and the "rebel" is Pearse, and the "wayfarer" who goes "upon my way / Sorrowful" is Pearse. The poet celebrates himself as Messiah, and although this celebration may be a source of inspiration for generations of patriotic Irishmen, it is not necessarily good poetry.

Historians have not found agreement on the question of whether or not Pearse and his friends in fact went out on Easter Monday, 1916, with the intention of offering themselves and their comrades as a sacrifice to Ireland's "cause that never dies." Desmond Ryan, who had been a student at St. Enda's and whose book *The Rising* provides the most authoritative account of Easter Week, seems to believe that the leaders of the rebellion had a reasonable hope of success; Pearse, he writes, "thought that the people once in insurrection would fight as well as in '98. Ceannt told his wife: 'If we last a month, the British will come to terms.' Connolly said . . . that if they won they would be all great fellows, and if they lost they would be the greatest scoundrels of all history." [118] Pearse, during the years preceding the rebellion, concerned himself with practical social and economic considerations relevant to the governing of an independent Ireland. In lectures and essays he thoroughly expounded his theories of Irish education, and in "The Sovereign People," a pamphlet published two weeks before the rebellion, he argues the intrinsic morality of national socialism (with emphasis, however, on the nationalism) if not its inevitability. Pearse left a considerable body of published works having to do with the mechanics of government, and such materials may be marshaled to support the view that for him the Easter Rising meant much more than a gesture of defiant sacrifice.[119] But, on the other hand, one must also take into account Pearse's speech to the court martial that sentenced him to death: "I have helped to organize, to arm, to train, and to discipline my fellow-countrymen to the sole end that, when the time came, they might fight for Irish freedom. The time, as it seemed to me, did come and we went out to fight. I am glad we did, we seem to have lost, we have not lost. To refuse to fight would have been to lose, to fight is to win, we have kept faith with the past, and handed a tradition to the future." [120]

Pearse's final utterance is consistent with the ideal of nationalism that is given expression in his own verse, and in the verse of MacDonagh and Plunkett as well. Any or all three of them may indeed have nourished hope for military and political success—in all likelihood they did; but if one is to judge by the evidence of their poetry, the question of success or failure was a secondary matter. It is true that their ideal of a free Irish nation is given cultural definition in certain respects. Pearse and MacDonagh champion the virtues of simplicity and naturalness, and all three exalt the Irish heritage of Roman Catholicism; and one may assume, perhaps, that these qualities would characterize the sovereign Irish nation which the poets foresaw. But the vision of Ireland which dominates the verse of each of them is rather a vision of becoming than one of being. To Pearse, MacDonagh, and Plunkett, what was essential was the act of rebellion itself; for the very gesture of insurrection against foreign rule could renew the spiritual integrity of the Irish race and nation. Christ had sacrificed Himself on Calvary in the cause of mankind's salvation; so, too, Irishmen must sacrifice themselves in Ireland's cause. The spirit of Cathleen Ní Houlihan speaks in the verse of the Rising poets; and her message, however clouded by abstractions in MacDonagh's verse or obscured by symbols in Plunkett's, is much the same as that uttered by the Old Woman of Yeats' play: "It is a hard service they take that help me. Many that are red-cheeked now will be pale-cheeked; many that have been free to walk the hills and the bogs and the rushes will be sent to walk hard streets in far countries; many a good plan will be broken; many that have gathered money will not stay to spend it; many a child will be born and there will be no father at its Christening to give it a name. They that have red cheeks will have pale cheeks for my sake, and for all that, they will think they are well paid." [121]

7

PADRAIC COLUM: THE PEASANT NATION

Padraic Colum champions the cause of peasant Ireland. The nationalism which informs his verse bears little resemblance to the nationalism given expression by Yeats, A.E., or the Rising poets. He is concerned neither with creating a national mythology from which his countrymen may draw spiritual strength nor with justifying Ireland's sacred cause of rebellion against the Gall. Ultimately, Colum's nationalism derives from the stuff of everyday existence, from the simple people and the homely properties of the Irish country scene. To be sure, until his departure for America in 1914, Colum participated in a more militant kind of nationalism and had his hand in the curious mixture of cultural and political agitations that constituted Irish public affairs. He served on committees dedicated to the promotion of one or another nationalist scheme and was a member of the Irish Volunteers. He was a close friend of Pearse and MacDonagh and an intimate of Arthur Griffith, whose demagoguery in his newspaper, *Sinn Féin*, inspired the crude attacks on Synge's *Playboy of the Western World* and who after the Black and Tan war became head of the provisional government of the Irish Free State.[1] The names mentioned in dedications to his numerous books comprise a kind of litany of Irish patriots—Pearse, MacDonagh, Griffith,

Michael Collins. In his *Collected Poems* one finds a number of poems that are specifically topical: an elegiac panegyric on Arthur Griffith's death,[2] another on the execution of Roger Casement:

> They've ta'en his strangled body from the gallows
> > to the pit,
> Ochone, och, ochone, ochone!
> And the flame that eats into it, the quicklime,
> > brought to it,
> Ochone, och, ochone, ochone! [3]

Colum's lines have the same bitter ring one notes in Yeats' Casement poems; like most Irish poets, Colum has been moved to respond to the stimuli of contemporary events. Yet significantly, his topical poems are omitted from *The Poet's Circuits*—which Colum describes as his "collected poems of Ireland" [4]—for they are only incidental to the central statement of his nationalism.

Mary C. Sturgeon, writing in 1916, suggested what is essential in Colum's nationalism when she observed that in his poetry and in the poetry of Joseph Campbell one can distinguish "the almost subconscious influence of race. . . . Whether from inheritance or environment, it [racial influence] has 'bred true' in these poets; and it will be found to pervade their work like an atmosphere . . . it is the essence of their genius, and it is revealed everywhere, in little things as in great, in cadency and idiom as well as in attitude to life and a certain range of ideas." [5] Miss Sturgeon's comments ring true. But one need not search for any mysterious subconscious origin of the influence; it is perfectly clear that Colum deliberately chose as his objective the representation of the Irish racial character and that, having done so, he consciously sought out the means by which that racial character might best be expressed. He translated Gaelic verse and he imitated the English songs and ballads that were popular among the Irish people; he copied the verse rhythms of Thomas Moore and James Clarence Mangan because he believed those rhythms to be somehow specifically Irish; and he wrote frequently in the language of the Anglo-Irish dialect with its peculiarities of Gaelic origin. Most important of all, he turned to the Irish countryside and attempted to recreate in his poetry what he found there: the simple, homely life of the peasant, his surroundings, his beliefs, his joys and sorrows and sufferings. The result of all this— Colum's "collected poems of Ireland"—is a kind of illustrated chronicle of the life of the Irish peasantry at the turn of the twentieth century.

In an essay on Colum's poetry, L. A. G. Strong, having noted that Colum was raised not in the remote regions of the West of Ireland but in a suburb of Dublin where his father was stationmaster, argues that the poet's formative environment was urban rather than rural and then concludes: "It is necessary, I think, to stress this question of background and inspiration, since so much has been talked about his so-called peasant quality. Those who most readily detect this legendary quality are usually the last to know what it is in fact; the sort of well disposed visitors who call turf peat, and find what they are looking for." To support his thesis Strong cites a notice, written by Yeats in 1905, in which the subject matter of Colum's verse is described as being closer to the people of the town than to the peasantry. Then Strong suggests that although Colum eventually turned his "direct and simple power" away from the peculiar problems of the townsman, his new themes were concerned not merely with the peasant's lot, but with those "problems that are the same for townsman, peasant, and all classes of human being. It is his simplicity that has earned him the label 'peasant.' " [6]

Whatever his knowledge of the fine distinctions between peat and turf, the reader is not apt to find confirmation of Strong's thesis in Colum's poetry. There is some justification for Yeats' comment, for in his earliest work Colum draws upon experience that is perhaps closer to town than to countryside— although one could not specifically describe that experience as urban. But one cannot examine the whole of the collected poems without recognizing that the simplicity which Colum proclaims is rural, agricultural, and Irish. What is one to make of the woman in the fifth poem of "Reminiscence" who comes "out of the wood" carrying a bundle of sticks or of "Nell the Rambler" in the next poem who comes "down to our houses bird-alone, / From some haunt that was hers"? [7] What is one to think of Downal Baun, the farmer who tries to win a treasure on Saint Brigid's Night by drawing it from a bog "By rushes strung to the yoke of an ox / That had never a hair of white"? (*Poems*, pp. 50–55; *Circuits*, pp. 22–26). What is one to think of Colum's ploughers and sowers and drovers, or of his cottage scenes where "On the floor the chickens gather, / And they make talk and complain"? (*Poems*, p. 91; *Circuits*, p. 109). These are peasant characters, peasant stories, and peasant scenes; and one finds this same "peasant quality" invoked in a hundred other poems, stories, and plays written by Colum during a productive life of more than half a century.[8]

Strong is, in fact, wrong in asserting that Colum was a child of the town rather than the countryside. It is true that he resided for a number of years in Sandycove near Dublin. But much of his early life was spent in the agricultural midlands of Ireland, and, indeed, for a considerable period his home was a traditional peasant cottage, complete with thatched roof and turf fire. In any event, however, for Colum himself the question of personal background is of secondary importance. What matters most as far as his poetry is concerned is his "decision" to become the poet of the field, of the fair, and of the rural Irish people for whom field and fair are the centers of daily life. Colum has spent by far the greater portion of his adult life in exile from his native land, yet by deliberate choice he has kept his poetic vision focused upon the "characters and situations" of the Irish countryside and the peasant hearth.[9] He describes the contents of his recent volume, *The Poet's Circuits* (1961), in which his Irish verse is collected, as "representative of a countryside," and he arranges the poems into eight categories, each having to do with a specific aspect of rural Irish life. In a foreword to the book, Colum gives his reason for calling the first section of verse "The House": "The tradition has its centre there. By the turf fire on the hearthstone, stories, poetry, local history were repeated; around it occurred the exchanges of the *ceilidhe* which had kept pointed discourse alive in Ireland; and the hearth was the centre of such learning as was, at a certain period, obtainable by the people." [10]

The Poet's Circuits includes several previously unpublished selections, the most significant of which is "Fore-Piece," a discursive and autobiographical poem in which Colum attempts to define for the reader the underlying inspiration for his work and by implication its purpose. Significantly, the speaker of the poem finds his way to the hearth of the country cottage, the meeting place for various elements of the popular peasant tradition. When the neighbors have left and the family has gone to bed, the speaker remains by the fire:

> I was alone.
> Yet there were people with me, men and women
> Who had abodes, who had a history,
> And work, and humours, and the moiety
> Of poetry tradition keeps in trust.
> And I could hear
> The door being open, certain birds that flew
> Between the clouds and bog, and I could hear
> The cattle stirring in the byre, the horses,
> Moving in their short sleeps, and while I stayed there
> My mind took to itself a murmuring,
> And there were words that it was fitted to,
> Words that turned in furrows or in verses,
> And took a shape, and went with certainty
> Among surprises, and became a poem.   (*Circuits*, p. 14)

The men and women who lived on the land, the birds and the beasts, the fields and the bogs: these are the images of the countryside; and with these images Colum identifies himself and his work.

As early as 1913, in his introduction to the anthology,

Broadsheet Ballads, Colum commented on the nature of the popular tradition of folk songs and ballads: "There is an idea that popular poetry is an impersonal thing, an emanation from the multitude, but I think this is an illusion. The multitude may change or may interpolate, may coarsen or may improve, but the song has been made by an individual." [11] It is as just such a poet of the people that Colum regards himself. In his attempt to create a popular Irish epic, *The Story of Lowry Maen,* he assumes the role of a storyteller of old Ireland, stopping on his way to the fair to recite his tale in the house of an aristocrat.[12] Similarly, in most of his poems he puts upon himself the robes of the popular bard; his songs and ballads are concerned with the problems of the country folk and, in an important sense, they also are addressed to an audience composed of country folk. Colum intended that his poems should be recited aloud and even sung—as indeed they are—by the people of the Irish countryside.[13]

Colum's poetry, like much of his early drama, represents an attempt to achieve "expression of the national character" as he perceived it in the people of the countryside (*Poems,* p. v). His verse is crowded with what Strong terms the "common furniture" of life, or, more specifically, the common furniture of Irish peasant life—the quaint (one cannot avoid the word) characters, the homely proprieties of hearth and pasture.[14] But his art embodies more than realistic detail, for Colum, more than any modern Irish poet writing in English, with the possible exception of Joseph Campbell, captures in his verse the underlying spiritual naïveté of the peasantry. In this respect, his portrayal of the Irish peasant is more accurate, more true to life, than either Yeats' portrayal or that of Padraic Pearse. Yeats employed folk materials to give substance to his occult vision and Pearse used them to support his own peculiar belief in mystical nationalism. Colum, on the other hand, is innocent of any extrinsic design; the attitudes and beliefs of the peasantry are presented in his verse for their own sake and are recorded in the form in which he found them among the people. Mary Sturgeon perceived this quality in the early work of both Colum and Campbell: "they are innocent of ulterior purpose and free from the least chill of philosophical questioning into origin or ends." [15]

There is nothing of the visionary in Colum; indeed, he sometimes seems deliberately to dissociate himself and his art from unusual insight into the nature of being. So, in "Plougher," he addresses himself to the solitary farmer, standing amid savage and broken land:

"Surely our sky-born gods can be naught to you,
    earth-child and earth-master—
Surely your thoughts are of Pan, or of Wotan,
    or Dana?

Yet why give thought to the gods? Has Pan
    led your brutes where they stumble?
Has Dana numbed pain of the child-bed, or
    Wotan put hands to your plough?

What matter your foolish reply! O man standing
    lone and bowed earthward,
Your task is a day near its close. Give thanks
    to the night-giving God." (Poems, p. 79; Circuits, p. 37)

The essence of Colum's aesthetic point of view is implied in these stanzas. Quite clearly he rejects the pagan gods, whether those of Greece, or of Scandinavia, or of ancient Ireland; and he rejects also the more sophisticated rationales for human existence that western civilization had devised, including Christian theology and philosophy, but not—if one judges by the evidence of his verse—simple Christian faith. For Colum's plougher the old gods have proved worthless, the new ones— theorems and theories—are meaningless. All that matters for him is the pre-ordained physical journey which each man must make and which the images of the brute stumbling and the woman in pain of giving birth and the man at labor in the field suggest is characterized by work and suffering. This struggle from birth to death is the challenge which must be met by Colum's plougher and by the race of men he represents. The poet's task is not to ask why, but only to show how—that is, to compile a faithful chronicle of the journey that is life.

Colum's attitude toward the supernatural reveals much concerning his art. Oddly enough, in a poet who renounced metaphysical speculation, manifestations of the supernatural are not uncommon in his verse. In "Reminiscence, I," for example, the swallows are portrayed as creatures possessing power to revenge themselves on those who would disturb their nests. In the poem the swallows threaten the weathercock, which represents the human world, with the curse of "un-earthbound beings" should harm come to their "brood" of young: "Your temples would fall, / And blood ye would milk from your beeves" (*Poems*, p. 4). In the fourth act of *The Fiddler's House*, Conn Hourican, the fiddler, has a dream in which the ghosts of his wife and his mother-in-law appear, and in the same act Conn's daughter, Maire, discovers the head and wing of a wild goose, in which is manifest a prophetic sign that she will be reunited with the man she loves (*Three Plays*, pp. 79–86, 89–91). What is important to note is that these manifestations of the supernatural are not metaphysical by any strict definition of the word. In Yeats' verse, images and symbols have a mystical flavor and are meant to convey, by their richness and intensity, some insight into the secret of being; because these symbols and images are employed for the purpose of escaping momentarily from the human limitations of time and space, they may be termed metaphysical. Similarly, in Joseph Plunkett's verse symbols and images are used to define the nature of mystical union with the divine essence. But, in contrast, Colum's signs and omens and dream visions have nothing of this mystical quality; they have significance only within the framework of time and space and only with reference to the physical world. Conn's dream-vision serves the function of advising him as to what course of action he should take—to go off alone in search of an audience which will properly appreciate his fiddling—in *this* world; it does not provide any kind of insight into the next world. The head and wing of the goose have relevance only with respect to Maire's romance with Brian McConnell. The swallows' threat is directed not at man's spirit but at his physical possessions.[16] Inevitably in Colum's writings the supernatural is tinged with materialism.

Colum's aesthetic is characterized by a bias in favor of what is tangible and against what is intangible and by a bias in favor of the commonplace and against the exotic. A useful comparison in this regard may be made between the treatment of the old Irish story of the Banquet of Dún na nGédh and the Battle of Magh Rath by Yeats in *The Herne's Egg*, on the one hand, and Colum's version of the saga in his volume, *The Frenzied Prince*, on the other.[17] The Battle of Magh Rath was fought *ca.* 637 A.D. between the High King Domhnall, son of Aedh, and Congal Caech (i.e., dim-sighted) or Congal Claon (i.e., squinting).[18] According to the saga, Congal, a descendant of the kings of Ulster, kills Domhnall's predecessor in the hope that the new king—his foster father—will name him to the vacant kingship of Ulster. Domhnall, having been named high king, sends his stewards in search of eggs to be served at a feast for all the kings of Ireland. The stewards seize a tub of large goose eggs from a woman, despite her protests that the eggs belong to a holy man, Bishop Erc, whose daily meal consists of a single goose egg and a leaf of watercress. When he learns of the theft, Bishop Erc pronounces a most vehement curse upon Domhnall and those attending his feast. The bishop's curse is followed by a series of marvelous happenings, the most noteworthy of which occurs when Domhnall has the goose eggs served in golden dishes to the assembled kings. The goose egg and golden dish set before Congal are strangely transformed—as a result of Bishop Erc's curse—into a hen's egg and a dish of wood. Because of this unintentional slight,

Congal storms from the hall with his followers, raises an army
in Scotland and Britain, and returns to defeat and death in the
Battle of Magh Rath, one of the most famous battles in Irish
history and one especially remembered for the terrible shedding of blood.

As might be expected, Yeats in his play, *The Herne's Egg*, is
not concerned with retelling the story faithfully. Domhnall's
name is changed to the more suggestive Aedh (i.e., fire). The
woman who guards the eggs is transformed into a priestess, the
bishop into the Great Herne, a god. The tale, which is fabulous
enough in its original form, is thoroughly reworked and made
still more fabulous in order to provide a more suitable vehicle
for the expression of the poet's peculiar theology.[19] Colum's
version of the tale follows the original much more closely.
Nevertheless, he does make changes that are significant.
Whereas in Yeats' version the Bishop Erc is elevated to the
status of a god, in Colum's he is lowered to the level of a
simple hermit. Similarly, there is evident in Colum's retelling a
tendency to make more prosaic the fabulous material of the
saga. In the original, for example, after the bishop has delivered
his curse, there appear before the palace of Domhnall two
strange creatures:

a woman and a man; larger than the summit of a rock on a mountain
was each member of their members; sharper than a shaving knife was
the edge of their shins; their heels and hams in front of them; should
a sackful of apples be thrown on their heads not one of them would
fall to the ground, but would stick on the points of the strong, bristly
hair which grew out of their heads; blacker than the coal or darker
than the smoke was each of their members; whiter than snow their
eyes; a lock of the lower beard was carried round the back of the head,
and a lock of the upper beard descended so as to cover the knees;
the woman had whiskers, but the man was without whiskers. They
carried a tub between them which was full of goose eggs.[20]

These two supernatural beings enter the palace, foretell the
advent of great evil, and then vanish. Colum's version of the
same episode reveals a striking difference in tone:

The guards before the ramparts of Dun na Nee saw a company approaching, two of them carrying a tub between them. They were the stewards, but the guards and the doorkeepers saw them as frightening people, with bristling hair on their heads, with faces that looked as if they were smoke-blackened, with eyes in their heads that were white like snow.   (*Frenzied Prince*, p. 112)

Certain details from the original have been retained: the bristling hair, the white eyes, the quality of blackness, which is, however, employed to describe the creatures' faces rather than their members. Yet, on the whole, the bizarre effect has been tempered considerably. The description of the two creatures in the original resembles both in its general effect and in certain of its details the remarkable distortion of Cú Chulainn as he prepared to avenge the slaughter of the boy-princes of Ulster in the *Táin*. Just as Cú Chulainn's frenzy is a sign of his godlike nature—he is the son of the hero-god Lug—so the distorted appearance of the gigantic creatures who approach Dún na nGédh testifies to their supernatural origin. In Colum's version, however, the strange beings are humanized, that is, they are reshaped so that they reflect more closely the appearance of mortal man. Even so, they remain so distinctly unnatural that Colum finds it necessary to add to his account an explanatory statement—"They were the stewards, but the guards and doorkeepers saw them as frightening people"—a statement which effectively dissociates the two creatures from the supernatural. In Colum's account they are the products of the guards' and doorkeepers' imaginations; they are illusions.

It must be noted that Colum compresses the long original of the tale of the Banquet of Dún na nGédh and the Battle of Magh Rath into a few pages, and that his rendering was intended for a youthful audience. Yet the tendency—so clearly manifest in his treatment of the story—to make more credible that which is extraordinary is characteristic of his art. There is more than a trace of the euhemerist in Colum. John O'Donovan, who translated and edited the text of the historical saga more than a hundred years ago, said of the story that "it is evidently interpolated with fables, from the numerous pieces in prose and verse, to which the battle, which was one of the most famous ever fought in Ireland, naturally gave rise" (*Banquet of Dun Na N-Gedh*, p. vii). Colum certainly would subscribe to this point of view. He has devoted a considerable portion of his creative life to the retelling of myths and legends—in particular, Irish, Greek, and Hawaiian—and in every instance his aesthetic intent appears to have been to render the story more intelligible to the ordinary person of his own generation, to simplify what is confused or difficult, to eliminate what is esoteric.

The self-dedicated popular poet has no business trafficking in the artifice of mysticism or even the artifice of sophisticated literature; his task is to find inspiration in everyday life itself, in what one critic of Colum's poetry calls "the stuff of existence." [21] Colum has written enthusiastically of the "symbolism" of Irish protest literature and has claimed for the creators of that literature a unique insight into "the rare, the difficult, the esoteric"; but in fact there is in Irish protest verse no more than the simplest kind of allegory employed for the single purpose of avoiding suppression by sensitive English authorities. [22] In any event, one finds little trace of even this simple artifice in Colum's verse. His poetry is characterized by directness of statement and photographic realism of detail. His purpose is to present a convincing account of life among the simple race of men who lived and died in the Irish countryside. In his "Fore-Piece" to *The Poet's Circuits* (p. 15) he makes clear his aesthetic intent: "Out of glimpses / Of days and nights of women and men, / And often with the words they spoke to me, / Or verses they delivered, I made poems."

In his verse Colum sought to achieve simplicity and directness because he believed both qualities were essential ingredients of

Irish popular poetry. A considerable portion of his work consists of poems written in conscious imitation of popular genres. He composed *The Story of Lowry Maen* in what he conceived was the form used by Gaelic storytellers who competed for honors at fairs and festivals. A number of poems, for example "May Day," "Queen Gormla" and "Autumn," are translations from Gaelic originals (*Circuits*, pp. 52–53, 55–57). "The Poor Girl's Meditation" is a reworking of the folk song, "The Brow of the Red Mountain," which had been collected and translated earlier by Douglas Hyde in *Love Songs of Connacht*.[23] "She Moved Through the Fair" is a restoration of a traditional song of which only one or two lines had survived (*Poems*, p. 97; *Circuits*, p. 97). The conventional ballad stanza is used for Colum's retelling of the popular tale of "Downal Baun" and for "The Terrible Robber Men," another traditional story of the Irish Midlands:

> Oh I wish the sun was bright in the sky,
> And the fox was back in his den O!
> For always I'm hearing the passing by
> Of the terrible robber men O!
> Of the terrible robber men.   (*Poems*, p. 100)

Colum himself has claimed that his poetic technique, more than that of any other modern Irish poet, brings together what he conceives to be the three strands of Irish popular tradition: "the English, the Gaelic and the Classic."[24] By English he means the tradition of ballads and songs that grew up in Ireland when English began to replace Irish as the language of the people at the end of the eighteenth century. This is not to say that English culture exerted no influence upon Ireland, nor even that Colum's poetry has remained free from that influence. For one thing, his ballads, despite their Irish subject matter, clearly owe much of their technique to the tradition of English balladry; for example, "The Terrible Robber Men" and "Jacobite Song" ("Seumas-a-ree") manifest a literary artistry similar to that which characterizes much of the verse of Percy's *Reliques* (*Poems*, pp. 11–12; *Circuits*, pp. 138–39).

Even in its subject matter Colum's verse takes account of the long, if undesirable, presence of the Englishman on Irish soil. Like many other Irish writers, he was concerned with the problem of Jonathan Swift and wrote a verse play about that curious figure, who remains for Irishmen a symbol of the paradox of the Pale, the embodiment of the perplexing problem of the Anglo-Irishman and his place in the Irish nation (*Poems*, pp. 38–43). But these considerations are secondary as far as the expression of nationalism in Colum's poetry is concerned—the play, "Swift's Pastoral," is omitted from *The Poet's Circuits*. What are important are those elements of theme and prosody and language which were unique to Irish poets writing in English and which eventually find their source in the Gaelic tradition. The English strand of the tradition is of value for whatever of the native Irish tradition it retains; Colum's first two strands, the English and the Gaelic, are really one.

One could hardly overestimate the extent to which Colum's technique has been shaped by Gaelic language and literature, whether directly through his study of Irish language poetry and prose or indirectly through his familiarity with the popular tradition of Anglo-Irish verse.[25] For one thing, Colum, like most other modern Irish poets, tried to affect in his verse a peculiarly Irish rhythm that characterized the work of certain nineteenth-century Anglo-Irish poets and that ultimately found its source in older Gaelic poetry. The credit for successfully translating this unique quality into English verse Colum gave to James Clarence Mangan, of whom he wrote in an early essay: "To the Irish poet who must write in English he has given a form that is distinctly Gaelic." [26] The prosody of Old and Middle Irish verse was based upon a syllabic discipline, rather than an accentual one, and upon increasingly intricate systems of primary and secondary rhyme. Similarly, Mangan's poetry takes its dominant rhythms not from the conventional accentual meters of English versification but rather from patterns of rhyme and alliteration. Colum, too, consistently attempts to achieve this kind of rhythm. For example, in the second stanza of "I Went Out in the Evening" he writes:

> Fine colour had my darling though it wasn't me was there:
> I did not sit beside her, but inside there was a pair!
> I stood outside the window like a poor neglected soul,
> And I waited till my own name was brought across the coal!
>
> (*Circuits*, p. 128)

The rhythm of these lines depends not upon stress but, as in Mangan's verse, upon the pattern of sounds: the consonance of "colour" and "darling" and the repetition of "was" in the first line, the secondary rhyme of "beside" with "inside" in the second line and with "outside" in the third, the correspondences between "stood" and "soul," "waited" and "was," "till" and "coal," the recurrence of "l" and "s" and vowel sounds throughout the stanza, and, of course, the rhyming of the couplets. Irish poets make much—perhaps too much—of the peculiar rhythms of their verse; but that Colum, in these lines and, indeed, in most of his poetry, places greater emphasis upon sound patterns than an English poet ordinarily would, and less emphasis on accentual metrics, is certainly true.

The same stanza from "I Went Out in the Evening" illustrates another characteristic influence of the Gaelic tradition upon Colum's versification; for its four lines contain a number of peculiarities of idiom and syntax which may be traced through the popular Anglo-Irish dialect to the Gaelic language. For one thing, the first line includes several grammatical vagaries, all of which typify the dialect and represent the literal translation of Gaelic constructions into the English language. The inversion in the initial clause, that is, the placing of the descriptive complement, "Fine colour," in a more emphatic position at the beginning of the sentence, is not simply an affectation; for its reflects the native Irish habit of ordering word according to intended meaning rather than syntactical rules. The use of the verb "to be" for periphrastic effect in the subordinate clause—"though it wasn't me was there"—represents the direct translation into English of a

standard Gaelic construction. Similarly, the omission of the
relative pronoun in the same clause is proper usage in Gaelic.[27]
The grammatical distortion in the second line also may be
attributed to the Irishman's genuine expertness in the art of
dyslexicology; and the two phrases, "a poor neglected soul" and
"my own name brought across the coal," in the third and
fourth lines respectively, if they are not specifically Gaelic in
origin, are at any rate so indigenous to ordinary Anglo-Irish
speech that they may properly be regarded as clichés. There is
evidence of the influence of Gaelic idiom in the verse of most
of the major poets of the Irish revival, but in Colum's verse the
syntax and idiom of the Gaelic language and of the Anglo-
Irish dialect are employed systematically and therefore must be
regarded as essential elements of his art.

The strands of Gaelic and Anglo-Irish tradition in Colum's
verse are easily recognizable; that of the classical tradition—by
which Colum means the tradition of Homer and Virgil—is less
apparent and, indeed, less convincing. Colum suggests that the
heritage of Greco-Roman literature survived in the remote
Irish countryside through the efforts of hedgerow scholars who
continued (despite hardship and persecution) to spread learning through Ireland after the British authorities had denied the
Irish people education. Colum commemorates the dedication
and forbearance of these teachers in his poem, "Poor Scholar,"
in which a hedgerow schoolmaster relates that his "eyelids red
and heavy are" from reading by the peat fire, that he knows his
Virgil off by heart, and that "I know Homer, too, I ween, / As
Munster poets know Ossian." One may well admire and
sympathize with the weary souls who in the nineteenth century
carried a little learning with them along country roads " 'Twixt
bog and bog" and far from the great city with its "treasures
open to the wise"; but one must nevertheless question just how
much of the rich tradition of classical culture could survive in
such circumstances. Colum's "poor scholar" himself provides
the answer when in a final couplet he defines what he seeks to
achieve in teaching Latin and Greek "by the dim rush-

light / In smoky cabins night and week." His goal is a modest one: "Years hence, in rustic speech, a phrase, / As in wild earth a Grecian vase!" (*Poems*, p. 120; *Circuits*, p. 27).

What the "poor scholar" says of the survival of classical culture among the Irish peasantry may be said as well concerning the influence of the classical tradition upon Colum. One finds in his verse no renaissance, no reflowering of the literary glories of Greece and Rome, but only the vestigial remnants of a lost heritage—a half-understood allusion, a quaintly pedantic phrase. Nor should one expect to find more. Colum's first loyalty is to the popular tradition; consequently, what Yeats would call, derogatorily, the "leveling wind" is basic to Colum's aesthetic point of view. Homer and Virgil, like the Battle of Magh Rath, must be made more prosaic so that they may conform to the cultural standards of the peasantry. The sublimities of Greco-Roman literature must undergo transformation and become, like the plougher and the drover, like the turf fire and the cackling hens, part of the "common furniture" of life. The ideal of the hearthstone and the world it represents inevitably emerges as the determinative factor in the making of Colum's aesthetic; for it is by the hearthstone that the poet's mind begins to murmur and it is there that words come to him and take shape "in furrows or in verses" and become poems.

Despite its graphic, almost physical, use of detail and its dramatic presentation of character, despite all its "common furniture," Colum's verse chronicle of the Irish peasant nation should not be confused with modern realism. Colum read and admired Ibsen and, indeed, claims inspiration from the Norwegian poet-playwright who revolutionized European dramatic art and shocked European morality in the last decades of the nineteenth century; but Colum's art, dramatic and poetic, resembles Ibsen's only in certain technical respects (Ibsen, he

says, mastered the art of constructing plays).[28] As far as basic
attitudes toward life and toward art are concerned, there are
few, if any, similarities between the two writers. Ibsen
preached social revolution, his eye to the future; Colum argues
implicitly for the status quo (except in political matters), his
eye fixed always upon the past. The Harper Croftnie in *The
Story of Lowry Maen* speaks for Colum when, having recognized the signs of change about him, he looks nostalgically
back to the passing Age of Bronze in Ireland and back to the
long, untroubled reign of Ugony the Great, who had "set a
mould of custom round men's ways" and "broken Change to
be a household beast" (p. 4).

Colum's vision (if one may use the word with reference to
his work) of the Irish nation is essentially romantic and, in a
restricted sense, pastoral as well. In "Interior," a charming
poem, an old woman sits by the fire and dreams aloud, in a
voice "low like the chickens'," of the simple and happy life of
another era:

> "In the old, old days upon Innish,
> The fields were lucky and bright,
> And if you lay down you'd be covered
> By the grass of one soft night.
>
> And doves flew with every burial
> That went to Innishore—
> Two white doves before the coffined—
> But the doves fly no more!" [29]

The two stanzas celebrate the physical contentment and "the
spiritual greatness," to use the words of Father James Cassidy
in his study of Colum, "of a people on whom no materialistic
gods have smiled." [30] So close to nature were the Irish peasants
in the past that the grass itself would cover them in their sleep
on a hillside. So close to God were they that He would assign
two doves to escort the corpse of each person who died to its
grave and from there, presumably, to Heaven.

Unlike Yeats' peasants, who know their place in the hierarchical order, the rustics who wander through Colum's verse

and prose have an alarming sense of their own importance. For example, when the basket weaver of "In the Market Place" told of his travels across Ireland with his asses and his goods, "There was dominion in the way he said it" (*Circuits*, p. 86). As far as the *Spadesman* is concerned, his shovel is a noble instrument; for in ancient times, he says, when the swordsmen had fled Ireland (i.e., the Flight of the Earls), "the whitesmiths put / Their art into the making of the spades" (*Circuits*, p. 119). These country people may be humble in material possessions, but there is nothing humble about their self-estimate or, Colum would have us understand, about their inner spirit. In his novel, *Castle Conquer*, Colum goes to considerable lengths to define the peculiar relationship between Sir John Seagrave, the Ascendancy landlord, and David Moore, his agent, on the one side, and the peasants, notably Owen Paralon, on the other.[31] At one point in the story, Moore is sent to the farm of Honor Paralon to deliver an ultimatum to her brother, Owen. Moore intends to remain seated on his horse while having his say; in that way he hopes to make clear the difference between his own station in life and that of the peasants. Happily, however, he suffers a fall from his horse just after he has entered the farmyard and is carried—muddied and bruised—into the house of Honor Paralon: "The moment that Sir John Seagrave's agent was to be brought into the house the peasants became at once nobles: they listened to him with consideration, and it was all done as if a whole stately tradition was embodied in the brother and the sister [i.e., Owen and Honor] and the two young girls."[32]

The underlying purpose of *Castle Conquer* is to justify the cause of the Irish peasants against their English rulers and especially their English landlords. Colum is not, however, sowing the seeds of a revolution based upon universal liberty, equality, and fraternity, but simply raising a question of pedigree. The Irish peasants are proud and unsubmissive for very good reason; they are themselves of noble stock, descendants every one (excepting tinkers) of the high Milesian race and therefore the rightful rulers of Ireland. The ascendant Anglo-Irish lords, on the other hand, are interlopers and, like Cavach in *The Story of Lowry Maen*, usurpers. That Colum should champion his own people against the foreigner is understandable enough; but in his enthusiasm for the peasant he rejects the traditional attributes of nobility, as set down by a Castiglione or a Spenser, and substitutes a new set of attributes more closely reflecting the manners and mores of the peasantry. One may accept as virtuous the long-suffering of the peasants through centuries of oppression. But one may well hesitate to accept as virtuous the questionable avariciousness of the peasant for material possessions, especially land; yet clearly enough Colum presents his wandering *suiler*, who longs for "the good red gold," and his tenant farmers in *The Land*, who scheme and haggle in order to cut a few pounds from the purchase price for their holdings, as objects for the reader's admiration.[33] In general, Colum demands a curious inversion of traditional standards, so that what is menial, sentimental, even in rare instances vulgar is to be regarded as admirable and noble. The pastoral theme, as it is developed in his verse, implies the glorification not so much of what is simple as of what is lowly. His peasants, whether plougher or pedlar or Nell the Rambler, bear little resemblance to Strephon and Claius in Sidney's *Arcadia*. Indeed, were one to judge by manners alone, he must conclude that in Colum's verse Demagoras and his Helots have won a war without having had to fight a battle.

In "Fore-Piece" to *The Poet's Circuits* Owen Paralon's wife, Johanna, makes a quilt of red and white patches of cloth and uses for tufts scraps of paper that catch the young poet's eye; the scraps contain lines in Latin which he recognizes as Virgil's even though they are about "the bulls and cows, / Their mating and the cleaning of their byres" (*Circuits*, p. 6). The discovery of lines of Virgil's verse—and, at that, appropriate lines having to do with life in the farmyard—in the peasant cottage is meant to suggest the noble heritage which belongs to the race of Irish peasants. But is the reader to regard as praiseworthy or indicative of nobility the fact that the only apparent use Colum's peasants have for Virgil's writings is as filling for a patchwork quilt? There are implicit in the situation a want of learning and a want of taste that give the lie to the very point that Colum wishes to make.

Perhaps it would be unfair to say that Colum admires lowliness indiscriminately; yet certainly he tends to exalt what is humble and to give significance to that which others may think insignificant. In "The Poet" Colum's bard explains the secret of his art to the peasants about the turf fire:

> "Your houses are like the seagulls'
> Nests—they are scattered and low;
> Like the blackbirds' nests in briars," he said,
> "Uncunningly made—even so.
>
> But close to the ground are reared
> The wings that have widest sway,
> And the birds that sing best in the wood," he said,
> "Were reared with breasts to the clay."
>
> (*Poems*, p. 127; *Circuits*, p. 28)

At the beginning of *The Big Tree of Bunlahy*, Colum writes:

Bunlahy calls itself a village, but it isn't a village at all. What is it, then? Just a single row of houses facing a wall that shuts in the wood and pasture belonging to an old, deserted mansion.... And yet it is because Bunlahy has but one row of houses (and you might count them on the fingers of your hands) that it got part of the great fame it has. For they used to say of anything that was one-sided, "It's all on one side like the town of Bunlahy."... And this will show you that fame is not only for the big and stirring things of the world; things that aren't big and aren't stirring get a share of it too, just as little pools in grassy borders of the road are lighted by the same sun as the great rivers going through the land.[34]

Both Colum's aesthetic and his nationalism emerge from this ideal of littleness; an Irishman and poet, he strives to brighten with fame the small and inconsequential details of the Irish countryside, the "common furniture" of everyday life; he celebrates in his art the "nobility" of field and barn and hearth, of *suiler* and drover and weaver. Even in the animal world he tends to favor the humbler creatures.[35] He writes poems not about lions and tigers, but about pigeons and bats and monkeys. In "Asses" Colum tells of a country fair in Ireland at which all the donkeys are shamed by the proud horses with their streaming manes and tails. But there is one peasant woman at the fair who sits in her cart "Like a queen out of Connacht / From her toe to her tip, / Like proud Grania Uaile / On the deck of her ship." This woman has with her two asses, a dam and her foal, both of which are such noble beasts that "Horses might not surpass"; mistress and animals alike hold their heads high: "There kind was with kind / Like flowers in the grasses / If the owner was fine, / As fine were her asses" (*Poems*, pp. 158–61; *Circuits*, pp. 87–90).

For Colum the peasant is hero.[36] Quite clearly, the heroism that may be discerned in beggar-women and drovers and weavers cannot be equated with the warlike virtue one associates with the heroic champions of classical tradition or, indeed, with the champions of Old Irish tradition, such as Cú Chulainn and Finn Mac Cumhaill. The heroism of the peasant is that kind of inner courage which enables the persecuted to bear up under chronic adversity, courage not so much like the demonstrative self-sacrifice of the Christian martyrs as like the irrepressible patience of Chaucer's Constance. One finds little of the militant courage of the great warrior in battle in Colum's work; and this is true despite the fact that most of his prose and some of his verse is concerned thematically with mythological and historical subjects which in their original versions are often remarkable for the attention given to details of battle: blood-drenched fields, single combats, and all the rest. In Colum's attempt at epic verse, *The Story of Lowry Maen*, for example, the strands of the tale come together in the epochal battle between Lowry Maen, whose men have weapons of iron, and the usurper, whose men have only bronze weapons. However, Colum's narrator fails to include any account of the battle, much to the dismay of his listeners (and Colum's readers) and to the plea, "O Storyteller, tell of triumph gained," he replies:

> You who have lived with parting and with death
> Need not hear now about the reddened spears,
> Need not hear now about defenders slain,
> Need not hear now about the roofs in flame.
> Now is a horse being shod with shoes of iron,
> A burning and a piercing and a weight
> Being put on hoofs that left hardly a track
> On plain and hillside.

What is important for Colum's storyteller and for the poet himself is not the awesome spectacle of great conflict but the effect the battle has on the everyday existence of ordinary people, the fact that thereafter horses will be iron-shod. The point made here is the same as that made in *The Big Tree of Bunlahy*: the little things in life are just as important as the big things, if not more important. The entire tale of Lowry Maen is flavored with details drawn from the life of the peasantry. Seoriah's people are "Men of the spade, sickle and pasture-field, / And the assembling-place." The first romantic exchange of glances between Lowry and Miria is given a domestic turn by the lines which follow immediately: "The goose that has been turning / Before the fire was placed upon the board." In the camp of the victorious Gaulish Celts "mules and horses stood beside the outposts / Swinging their tails against the swarms of flies." As if to stress this idea, Colum concludes his long and at times prosy saga on a homely note: Lowry and his beloved, Miria, both laugh heartily when Miria's father, King Seoriah, now an old man, mutters his favorite complaint, " 'Tis time I had a grandson"; and the happy couple promise to fulfill his wish (*Lowry Maen*, pp. 50, 71, 75, 80–81).

Of particular note with regard to Colum's treatment of heroic and romantic materials is the fact that, by and large, his prose collections of old stories, legends, and myths are in-

tended for an audience of children. These tales are carefully
prepared for the purpose of communicating with a child and of
entertaining him, but quite clearly they have also the purpose
of instructing him. Colum's intention to teach as well as to
please is demonstrated in *A Boy of Eirinn*. The boy-hero of the
book, Finn O'Donnell (named after the Fenian hero), travels
the length and breadth of Ireland with his uncle in a donkey
cart. In the course of his adventures the boy attains an
awareness of life's joys and its sorrows, including the sorrow
involved in the death of one who is close to him, his grand-
father; in short, he grows up. Stories, heroic and pious, are an
essential part of Finn's life during this period, for the uncle
with whom he travels and every Irishman they encounter on
the roads happen to be incorrigible storytellers, and each adds
to the repertoire of tales about famous men and women from
Ireland's past: Finn Mac Cumhaill, Brian Boru, St. Patrick,
St. Colmcille, St. Brigid, the fairy people (who are treated
comically), Daniel O'Connell, Red Hugh O'Donnell, and so
forth. Each story, like each of Finn's personal experiences, is
meant to contribute something to the formation of his character; and the book, taken in its entirety, is a kind of case study of
the process by which noble and heroic virtues are instilled in
the soul of every Irish peasant.[37]

Except for *The Story of Lowry Maen*, a few Fenian lays in
the popular mode, and a handful of Jacobite ballads, Colum
seems to avoid the direct treatment of heroic themes in his
verse, although in his prose he has done so on numerous
occasions. Of the ten poems, excluding the "Fore-Piece,"
which are gathered together under the heading "Things More
Ancient" in *The Poet's Circuits*, four are nature poems, four
are religious or Biblical in their themes, and only two—both
laments—are concerned with what might be described as the
Irish heroic tradition. In one of these two, "Oisin Gormlai,"
Colum celebrates the heroism of the *fianna*; one should note,
however, that Colum chooses his subject from the more
popular of the two major Irish sagas and that the episode he

treats is not an epical battle but rather the hunt of the stag. More significant is the fact that the second half of the poem emphasizes the illusory nature of even this lesser kind of physical daring:

> The hours have stolen flesh and bone,
> And left a changeling here:
> And where is he who had the pride
> To chase the bounding deer?   (*Circuits*, p. 54)

Colum never endorses the old heroism without qualification; one would not, for example, expect him to urge, as Yeats did, that the Moslems and Hindus of India solve their religious strife by means of a pitched battle between armies of equal size.

Nevertheless, if one approaches Colum's verse as the celebration of what he regards as the Irish national character, then the heroic tradition must be recognized as an important factor in his definition; for Colum carefully identifies the ancient virtues of heroes and saints and scholars with the humble men and women of the Irish countryside. In his "Fore-Piece" to *The Poet's Circuits* the Ogham stone reminds the ploughman that he is descended from a high-king of Ireland, Conn of the Hundred Battles:

> . . . he remembers
> The Ogham stone,
> And knows that he is
> Of the seed of Conn.[38]

The lines are a variation of an earlier poem, "A Mountaineer," in which a peasant from the mountains "remembers / The pillar-stone / And knows that he is / Of the seed of Eoin" (*Poems*, p. 105). Eoin, the early Irish form of John, echoes back to the coming of Christianity to Ireland, Conn to the heroic era of pagan Ireland. In both versions Colum transfers the noble virtue of the past to his peasant hero of the present. Similarly, the mistress in "Asses" is likened to Gráinne Ni Mháille, the "queen out of Connacht" (*Poems*, p. 159;

Circuits, p. 88). Colum's romantic tapestry of peasant virtue is spun of other threads as well. In "Girls Spinning," a young man sings, "Once I went over the ocean, / On a ship that was bound for proud Spain" (*Poems*, p. 66; *Circuits*, p. 78), and in another poem, the drover, driving his cattle to "Meath of the pastures," daydreams "on white ships / And the King o' Spain's daughter" (*Poems*, p. 84; *Circuits*, p. 41). Spain has always been a symbol of romance in the Irish popular imagination. For one thing, in the distant past the Milesian race had journeyed from the Iberian peninsula to settle Ireland. For another, Spain had always been at one with Ireland in its advocacy of the Roman Church and in its political antagonism to England. Mention of the name Spain might conjure up in the popular mind visions of the Armada or of the Flight of the Earls. Spain was at once a possible source of help for the oppressed Irish race and a land in which an Irishman might be treated as an equal, in which he might rise to power, and in which he might even—if fate was kind—marry the king's daughter. Because of these associations, the allusions to Spain by the drover, by the young man, and by other of Colum's peasants testify to a noble desire for high adventure in their characters and, more than that, to a vitally imaginative spirit.

Colum does not suffer any illusions—such as one might attribute to Yeats or A.E.—that the ancient heroic period might someday reappear. Maurice in the poem, "The Hearthstone and the Loom," speaks for Colum when he observes that "We'd see in every age if we went back, / Some heritage destroyed or else forsaken, / And we would know how change makes way for change." Old virtues, like old stories, must take on new shapes in keeping with new circumstances. Nor would Colum be pleased by a return to the old, willful ways of Conn or Cú Chulainn. His hopes for the Irish nation of the future are summed up by Terence, the second speaker of "The Hearthstone and the Loom":

> Bread eaten without debt to harden it,
> Space in a house, no cark to waken to,
> And no word said that brings an inner moan
> And not a faithful answer; over these,
> Work of the day that brings enough to keep
> Brave an innocence in its walks and ways,
> And festivals from time to time that mean
> A share in revelry or in devotion,
> And friends to take one out of the four walls
> To some enjoyment that is like a ransom.
>
> (*Circuits*, pp. 135–36)

This statement of Colum's national ideal, with its stress on the day-to-day "stuff of existence," may embody a kind of popularized Utopia; but there is nothing in it that hints of heroic aspiration in a classical sense. The heroism which Colum celebrates in his verse is a heroism of little people.

Much the same may be said of the religious ideal which is given expression in Colum's poetry. His verse is, to be sure, religious and, more specifically, Roman Catholic, but it is not religious in the same sense that the poetry of MacDonagh, Pearse, and Plunkett, or, for that matter, the poetry of Yeats and A.E. may be described as religious. These poets attempt to express, in one way or another and with varying degrees of success, a kind of religious experience that is introspective and subjective, and they place emphasis upon what may be termed spiritual values as opposed to material values. Colum's religion, on the other hand, is objective, almost materialistic, and it is concerned almost exclusively with the outward signs of God's revealed truth and with the human acts of faith that affirm those signs. For example, in "Fuchsia Hedges in Connacht" Colum defines the religious inspiration which the poet's imagination discovered in the brightly colored hedgerows of the West of Ireland:

I think you came from some old Roman land—
Most alien, but most Catholic are you:
Your purple is the purple that enfolds,
In Passion Week, the Shrine,
Your scarlet is the scarlet of the wounds:
You bring before our walls, before our doors
Lamps of the Sanctuary;
And in this stony place
The time the robin sings,
Through your bells rings the Angelus!   (*Poems*, p. 190)

Christian poets traditionally have sought the reflection of God in the wonders of nature, and, indeed, the occult symbolism of Christian mysticism depends largely upon imagery drawn from nature to communicate its vision of God. Joseph Plunkett's verse, for instance, is consistent with the dictum, set forth by such mystics as Johann Tauler, that every part of the creation embodies in some specific the divine nature. However, what Colum perceives in the "fuchsia hedges" is not God but rather the institution which Catholics believe to be God's agent on earth, the Roman Church, and what the poet ponders are not the attributes of God but the attributes of the Church: Passion Week, the altar, sanctuary lamps, and the Angelus. The allusion to "the scarlet of the wounds" seems to suggest that kind of ecstatic contemplation which is manifest in Plunkett's "I See His Blood Upon the Rose"; but the next lines—"You bring before our walls, before our doors / Lamps of the Sanctuary"—suggest that Colum has in mind the quasi-realistic pictures and plaster statues (made in Belgium and popular in Ireland) in which quite often the stigmata are displayed prominently. The frame of reference for the poem is not Christ's suffering on Calvary but the re-enactment of that suffering, a re-enactment which the peasant himself may witness directly each year during Passion Week. Similarly, in another religious poem, "David Ap Gwillam at the Mass of the Birds," Colum celebrates the Roman Catholic Mass rather than the event which that ritual commemorates. The lark sings the Kyrie, the nightingale the Consecration, and the thrush the Orate Fratres. Finally, "The Thrush it was who, as the sun appeared, / Held up the Monstrance, a dew-circled leaf!" (*Poems*, p. 152). The kind of faith that is manifest in these poems, simple and pious and strengthened by the evidence of material signs, is not only in keeping with Colum's peasant ideal but also essential to it. For Colum's Irish country folk the mysteries of religion must be given concrete form; they must be made as real as the gabbling geese and the cackling hens; they must, in other words, become part of the "common furniture" of life.

By various means Colum attempts to portray the Irish Catholic, especially the Irish Catholic of the countryside, as the embodiment of the kind of piety that is expressed in such poems as "Fuchsia Hedges of Connacht." Such an idealized portrait of Irish Catholicism is not likely to convince anyone who has read Joyce's A *Portrait of the Artist as a Young Man*, or Honor Tracy's *The Straight and Narrow Path*, or any of Sean O'Faolain's essays in *The Bell* concerning the influence of the Irish clergy on Irish life; [39] yet it is certainly true that life in Ireland, at least as far as its externals are concerned, is strongly affected by religious belief and practice. In many ways, as the episodes of Parnell and Synge make clear, not to mention the history of the Irish Free State and Republic, the Catholic Church in Ireland has concerned itself, often with what appears to have been a studied maliciousness, with imposing a code of social conformity as much as with the propagation of childlike virtue. Nevertheless, Ireland is a country where almost every passenger makes the sign of the cross when a bus passes a church, where many thousands participate each year in penitential pilgrimages, and where daily attendance at church is not uncommon. That in such a country a mother should invoke the name of Mary, mother of Christ, as the peasant woman does in Colum's "Cradle Song," is natural and convincing:

> O men from the fields!
> Soft, softly come through—
> Mary puts round him
> Her mantle of blue.
>
> (*Poems*, p. 111; *Circuits*, p. 107)

That an "old woman of the roads" should pray to God—"And I am praying him night and day"—for a little house of her own is just as convincing, if less admirable (*Poems*, p. 90; *Circuits*, p. 110).

At times, however, what Colum seems to exult in is social and moral conformity rather than genuine religious virtue. The Irish peasant, he seems to tell his reader, is pure, even puritanical, in thought and deed. The Irish peasant never takes the name of the Lord in vain. The Irish peasant never blasphemes. In general, Colum distorts his picture of the peasantry in order to make it conform to the Irish Catholic ideal. In "A Poor Girl's Meditation," for example, he is guilty of sentimentalizing his presentation of a young woman's emotional suffering. Colum's poem, a translation of a traditional Irish song, may be compared with Douglas Hyde's "The Brow of the Red Mountain," a literal rendering of the same poem, published in *Love Songs of Connacht*.[40] The two versions are remarkably similar. Colum's diction is more polished, although not in every instance more effective. But the principal difference between the two is that Colum omits from his version a stanza in which the girl's complaint is given passionately bitter expression. Hyde faithfully translates these lines:

> The grief (*or black ale, a play on words*)
>   I myself make
>   I cannot drink any of it;
> It is worse as I am
>   I cannot get the sleep;
> The curse of the Son of God upon that one
>   Who took from me my love
> And left me by myself
>   Each single long night in misery.

Invoking the Son of God to damn a faithless lover may indeed
be impious, even sacrilegious; yet the girl's dramatic curse is
the informing strength of the original folk poem. Colum, by
excluding the stanza in which it is uttered, alters the tone of
the poem and reduces the girl's complaint from a cry of intense
human passion to a sigh of homely sentiment.

One cannot generalize a charge of puritanism against Colum's verse. His young woman in "A Poor Girl's Meditation"
and his young women in other poems are willing enough to
give themselves physically to their true loves, although they
invariably do so with an eye to the propriety of marriage and
never in wanton physical abandonment. His old woman in
"Girls Spinning," a crone who embodies something of the
passionate nature of Crazy Jane, exults in the sexuality of her
youth:

> 'Carricknabauna, Carricknabauna,
> Would you show me Carricknabauna?
> I lost a horse at Cruckmaelinn,
> At the Cross of Bunratty I dropped a limb,
> But I left my youth on the crown of the hill,
> Over by Carricknabauna! [41]

But this ribald old lady is rather a startling exception among
the women of Colum's verse. At any rate, what is implicit in his
"collected poems of Ireland," in his attitudes toward sex,
toward religion, and toward life that are given expression in
these poems, is a peculiar morality of littleness in the context
of which humility, even meanness, is represented as nobility,
religiosity as spirituality, and sentimentality as passion.

In his introduction to *The Poet's Circuits* (pp. v–vi) Colum
writes of his Irish verse: "In so far as they have a succession,
continuity, in so far as they are representative of a countryside,
these poems of men and women make a sequence, or, to leave

aside a word that has become technical, a saga. It is as a saga
and not as separate pieces that they should be presented.
Professor Kelleher in his essay on the Celtic revival cites (pp.
213–14) Colum's saga as an example of "peasant realism"; and
in a restricted sense the term is appropriate, for Colum
consciously has exploited the "common furniture" of rural
Ireland in order to affect a convincing picture of the Irish
nation as he envisions it. But Colum goes further than this. His
verse is intended not only as a saga of Irish life but also as a
defense of the commonplace values which he believed endemic
to that life; to defend these values he inevitably embarks on a
peculiar kind of romantic distortion, and he frequently infuses
traditional concepts with new, sometimes contradictory, meanings. Pedlar and ploughman, cackling hens and gabbling geese,
bulls and cows mating in their byres become images of what is
grand and noble. The "lowest common denominator" of Irish
life is exalted as the ideal toward which the Irish nation must
strive.

The nationalism which is given expression in Colum's verse
provides a kind of antithesis for the nationalism in Yeats'
verse. Yeats in his poems and plays argues the case for an
aristocratic society in which men are ruled by the law of
natural passion; and Yeats justifies his plea by appeal to traditional cultural and literary values that have found acceptance
in western civilization from the age of Plato and Aristotle
and by appeal to the esoteric symbolism of occult mysticism.
Colum, on the other hand, defends the social ideal of the
Irish peasantry—and by implication the social ideal of the
Irish middle class—and glorifies the humble life of a people
whose moral code centers on the suppression of natural passion. He rejects both traditional aristocratic values and the
validity of mysticism—whether, as with Yeats, founded on
occult tradition or, as in the case of Plunkett, on orthodox
Christian tradition; to substantiate his eulogy of the peasantry
Colum invokes the physical realities of everyday life. Yeats
"discovered" Colum in 1904 and certainly Yeats' early, senti-

mental verse on peasant life—for example, "The Ballad of Moll Magee"—influenced the younger poet in the formulation of his artistic objectives. But Yeats and Colum soon came to the parting of the ways. Yeats fought for the survival of the Abbey Theatre; Colum dissociated himself from the Abbey and turned to Arthur Griffith and the zealous patriots who were to beleaguer the theater movement in the name of nationalism. In certain respects, the national ideal which finds expression in Colum's poetry fits too well Yeats' definition of "whiggery": a leveling mentality "That never looked out of the eye of a saint / Or out of a drunkard's eye." [42] The image of passionless moderation is not inappropriate, for Colum seems to advocate the kind of moral values which Pearse condemned as incompatible with Christ's teachings—"Thou shalt not be extreme in anything—in wrongdoing lest thou be put in gaol, in rightdoing lest thou be deemed a saint"—and which the contemporary Irish novelist, Honor Tracy, ridicules by quoting this supposed fragment of an Irish sermon: "What we have to do, my dear brethren, is stay on the straight and narrow path between right and wrong." [43]

Perhaps this is too harsh a judgment of Colum; yet too frequently his verse sounds a note of complacency. Too frequently he tells his readers that man should neither strive nor question, but should be content with his daily lot, however lowly it may be. This is the theme of "The Knitters," a poem in which Colum praises the womenfolk of the country whose work and conversation are endlessly the same:

> Since we who deem our days
> Most varied, come to own
> That all the works we do
> Repeat a wonted toil:
> May it be done as theirs
> Who turn the stocking-heel,
> And close the stocking-toe,
> With grace and in content,
> These knitters at their door.
>
> (*Poems*, p. 98; *Circuits*, p. 45)

In his volume, *Personal Remarks*, L. A. G. Strong comments (p. 79): "The work of Padraic Colum has had little critical attention, not through neglect or ignorance, but because its central quality is one with which literary criticism has had little to do. Simplicity cannot be analysed. No critical instrument has been invented which will react to Colum's poetry." Strong's arguments in defense of Colum are evasive; yet there is a measure of truth in what he says. The collected Irish poems which Colum presents as a saga of the countryside do not stand up well to close analysis when read as an artistic unity, nor does the social ideal of an Irish nation that is implicit in that saga; but, at the same time, close analysis of his total output is apt to ignore or underrate the central merit of Colum's art. Miss Sturgeon recognizes in his verse the blending of three diverse strands: "the individual, the national, and the universal"; she notes also that in certain poems the third element, the universal, is dominant: "Then it follows that the poet is at his best, for he has forgotten the immediacy of self and country and the world of men and things in the joy of singing." [44] When Colum escapes the "common furniture" of Irish peasant life, then he is capable of attaining a lyric universality, or, as Strong would have it, a simplicity, that does indeed defy analysis:

> She stepped away from me and she moved through the fair,
> And fondly I watched her go here and go there,
> Then she went her way homeward with one star awake,
> As the swan in the evening moves over the lake.
>
> (*Poems*, p. 109; *Circuits*, p. 97)

Colum's attempt in *The Poet's Circuits* to give to his verse the unifying framework of a social philosophy is self-defeating; in the end, perhaps, his lyric gift, as it finds expression in individual poems such as "She Moved Through the Fair," provides the best defense of his art.

JAMES STEPHENS: THE NATION OF LOVE

The founders of the Irish literary revival, Yeats and Douglas
Hyde and George Russell, freed those Irish writers who
followed them from the need to abide by a strict creed of
political nationalism such as that which both informed and
limited the Young Ireland movement of the eighteen-forties; [1]
but if political dogmatism was held in check, another kind of
conformity, in some ways more restrictive and stultifying in its
effects upon art, evolved gradually. Yeats and Hyde and
Russell convinced Irish intellectuals that, as far as literature
was concerned, pragmatic political considerations should be
subordinated to a romantic creed of racial destiny that was
somewhat vague and, because vague, less restrictive. Their
motives in doing this, in preaching a Celtic mystique in much
the same manner that Goethe had preached a Germanic
mystique, are above question; they saw Cathleen Ní Houlihan
dead in spirit and they sought to breathe into her new vitality.
Inevitably, however, the racial romanticism of Yeats, Hyde,
and Russell became diluted in the popular imagination with
the commonplace values of contemporary Irish society, and
there evolved from this unlikely mixture a Philistine image of
Ireland and of the Irish people, a compound of religiosity,

puritanism, and sentimentality, an image which in certain respects proved more restrictive in its effects upon literature than the jingoism of Davis and Mitchel. By the turn of the century a new kind of conformity had begun to inflict itself upon Irish letters. Pearse, MacDonagh, and Plunkett were not altogether free from its pressures; Colum succumbed to them and dedicated his considerable talents to the celebration of the popular image of nation and nationality. There emerged two conflicting schools of thought concerning the relationship of the artist to his social and ethnic group. On the one side were those who believed that the artist must have complete freedom of expression; during his years as manager of the Abbey Theatre, Yeats championed this belief. On the other side, ranged against Yeats and the Abbey, were those who believed the popular image to be sacrosanct; these were the Irish Philistines and their most noteworthy advocate was Arthur Griffith.

Paradoxically, the young poet James Stephens found himself betwixt and between the two contending factions of the cultural movement, and in the development of his art each of those factions exerted a significant influence. Stephens became known in the literary circles of Dublin in the months immediately following the production of Synge's *Playboy of the Western World* in the winter of 1907, a critical period in the vendetta between Griffith and the nationalist extremists on the one hand and Yeats and the Abbey Theatre on the other. George Russell is said to have found Stephens at work in a solicitor's office in Dublin and from the beginning to have encouraged and aided him; certainly the elder poet's influence was profound and lasting, and, like many other young Irish poets, Stephens dedicated his first volume of poetry, *Insurrections* (1909), to A.E. In fact, however, it was not A.E. but Arthur Griffith who "discovered" Stephens and who published his earliest prose and verse in the pages of *Sinn Féin*, the popular nationalist newspaper.[2] In the years that followed, Stephens became a close associate of Griffith. He joined the

Sinn Féin political party; he enrolled in the Gaelic League and studied Irish; [3] he wrote a poem, "Epithalamium," to celebrate Griffith's marriage in 1910.[4] Years later, when Griffith died, Stephens described the Sinn Féin movement and Douglas Hyde's Gaelic League as the two essential forces in the creation of modern Ireland: "These movements were actually one, and where Dr. Hyde supplied the ideal motive, Mr. Griffith supplied the driving intelligence." [5]

Stephen's earliest essays in *Sinn Féin* treat of typical nationalist themes with typical enthusiasm. One article, "Irish Idiosyncracies," consists of a mild attack on the Abbey Theatre.[6] Others, "The Seoinin" and "Irish Englishman," deal harshly with the Irishman who mimics English morals and manners: "This miracle is known as a West Briton. He stands fore-front to God and man square, squat, saturnine, and silly, and doesn't appear to know that he is sufficiently funny to tickle the risibility of the equator." [7] Stephens' prose in these journalistic efforts is not remarkable, although one finds an occasional hint of the rhythmical irony which informs *The Crock of Gold* and *The Demi-gods*. In "Builders," for example, he castigates the Irish people for failing to give proper respect to their Gaelic past: "I have heard of a yacht called Oscar, of a horse called Finn, and of a dog called Oisin. 'Alas, alas, and alas! / For the once proud people of Banba.' " However, the essay ends in a conventional flourish that might have been written by any one of *Sinn Féin's* contributors.[8]

Despite his early patriotic enthusiasm, Stephens shied away from the kind of militant sentiment which Pearse already was preaching in nationalist circles and to which Plunkett would soon give prominent place in *The Irish Review*. In his prose essays for Griffith's journal he tends to neglect political matters in favor of social and cultural considerations, and a similar emphasis is evident in his early verse. In "College Green," for example, a poem published in *The Rocky Road to Dublin* but omitted from the *Collected Poems*, Stephens tells his countrymen that

> ...King Billy's horse will start
> From our street and from our heart,
> When each Irishman shall be
> Perfected in courtesy.[9]

His first published poem, "The song of Ossian," an atrocious work in every way, is noteworthy only for the utterly incongruous question addressed by the poet to the warlike heroes of the *fianna*: "What good's thy war? It kills and nothing more, / It kills and there's an end," and for his final plea that they give up their "butcher's trade." [10] There was in Stephens' character an inherent gentleness that shows forth clearly in all his work; and one may more easily imagine his sharing the fate of the pacifist Francis Sheehy-Skeffington (murdered by the British while protesting against the brutal treatment of another) than that of the rebels who took up arms against English rule in 1916. When in the years before the Easter Rising other Irish intellectuals were training themselves in the soldier's trade, Stephens remained dedicated to the task of saving Ireland from the tyranny of British culture.

In certain respects Stephens' development as an artist followed the normal pattern for Irish writers who emerged during the revival. For instance, he sang the glories of the Irish countryside, a natural paradise where a sensitive Irishman like Stephens could escape the mundane horrors of a solicitor's office and where

> There was grass
> On the ground;
> There were leaves
> On the tree;
>
> And the wind
> Had a sound
> Of such sheer
> Gaiety,
>
> That I
> Was as happy
> As happy could be.[11]

He wrote poems, too, of Irish country life and country people—of one old man sitting so motionless beneath a tree "That, if he had been carved in stone, / He could not be / More quiet or more cold" (*Seumas Beg*, p. 27); of another ancient creature mumbling ironically to himself that if he were young again, "I'd jeer at people groaning, and I'd try / To pinch them ere they'd die!" (*Poems*, p. 163). Like many other Irish poets he tried his hand at retelling the Old Irish sagas, although he told them in prose rather than in verse or dramatic dialogue. Finally, like Pearse and Colum and Frank O'Connor, like almost every Irishman who since Douglas Hyde has studied the Gaelic language, Stephens composed translations and "adaptations" of Gaelic verse. Nature poems, character sketches, reworkings of myth and legend, translations—these were the usual things. But Stephens did things that were unusual too, and he often did the usual in a different way; it is these divergencies from the norm that give to Stephens' verse and prose and to the expression of nationalism implicit in his verse and prose a unique and original quality.

When he turned to the old Irish sagas, Stephens set out to retell the *Táin Bó Cúalnge* along with numerous related tales and to incorporate them into a single unified story. It was a formidable task he set for himself and one which he left unfinished after having published *Irish Fairy Tales* (based mainly on the Fenian cycle), *Deirdre*, and *In the Land of Youth* and before beginning the central saga of the great cattle raid of Cooley. Dorothy M. Hoare in her *Works of Morris and Yeats in Relation to Early Saga Literature* claims for Stephens the distinction of having captured in his published volumes the true flavor of the original sagas: "Stephens . . . tells the old story, not *his* story, and manages to retain the old atmosphere because of his knowledge and understanding of the sources. Both the courtly talk and the roughness of action are given. . . . He is quite unaffected by the glamour which A.E., Yeats, Synge, all, in one way or another, cast over the sources. As distinct from them, he sees clearly, with an appreciation at once humorous and poetic, what the underlying situation might have been. It is a signal feat of the historical imagination." [12] Miss Hoare in effect praises Stephens for achieving that which such a scholar of ancient Irish literature as T. F. O'Rahilly would condemn as the fallacy of euhemerism. Even so, her observation is only partly accurate. Stephens does indeed humanize the shadowy heroes of Ireland's remote past as neither Yeats nor A.E. could have done; but he is not at all concerned with recreating the situations of the sagas as they actually happened and the characters as they actually were—if, indeed, the situations did in fact occur and if the characters were real—and such a term as "historical imagination" is really irrelevant to his art.

Stephens makes clear his attitude toward Ireland's Celtic inheritance in his essay, "Outlook on Literature," in which he writes: "It is certain that Ireland will revisit her past with vast curiosity and reverence, but she will not remain there long enough to eat a railway sandwich. She will return with her booty to the eternally present time of an eternally modern world." [13] The focus of Stephens' art is always on the present rather than the past, and this is just as true of his retelling of the ancient saga stories as it is of his essays and poems which are concerned specifically with contemporary Irish life. He views the old tales, certainly, with "vast curiosity," although with something less than reverence, and the tone of *Irish Fairy Tales*, *Deirdre*, and *In the Land of Youth* is light and ironic, and quite clearly the work of the same man who wrote *The Crock of Gold* and *The Demi-gods*. Vivian Mercier in his essay, "James Stephens: His Version of Pastoral," is much more accurate than Miss Hoare when he describes Stephens' *Deirdre* as a "flapper" rather than the *femme fatale* of the original. [14]

The individual character of Stephens' approach to the saga material may be demonstrated by a comparison of his renderings of the old tales with the originals. One of the stories included in *In the Land of Youth* is *Echtra Nerai*, which consists of an episodic account of a young man's adventures in the world of men and in the world of the fairies. The tale begins on a Samhain night at Rath Cruachan where Medb and Ailill and their household are gathered. Ailill offers a reward to that man who is brave enough to tie a withe around the foot of one of two prisoners left for dead on the gallows outside. After a number of warriors have gone out into "the horror of that night" and returned in terror, Nera takes his turn. He reaches the gallows, but is unable to fasten the withe until the corpse tells him how to do so properly. When Nera has completed his task, there follows a remarkable conversation. The corpse speaks first:

> "For the sake of the truth of your valour, take me on your back that I may drink a drink with you. There was a great thirst on me when I was hung." "Come on my back then," said Nera. Then he went on his back. "Where shall I carry you?" said Nera. "To the house that is nearest us," said the captive.
> They went to that house. Then they saw something—a lake of fire round that house. "Our drink is not in this house," said the captive. "There is never a fire without smooring in it. Let us go to the next house (that is nearest us)," said the captive. So they went to it. Then they saw a lake of water round it. "Do not go to that house," said the captive. "Not customary in it (is) washing-water or bathing-water or slop-pail at night after sleeping. Go before us to yet another house," said the captive. "In this house indeed there is my drink," said the captive. He let him down on the ground. He went into the house. Washing and bathing (tubs) (are) in it, and there is a drink in each of them. A slop-pail (is) also on the floor of the house. Now he drinks a drink from each of them, and scatters the last sip from his lips on the faces of the men that were in the house, so that they all died. It is after that then (it is) not good (to have) washing- or bathing-water; or a fire without smooring or a slop-pail in the house after sleeping.[15]

In Stephens' version there are both additions and deletions. For one thing, Stephens is concerned with filling out the skeleton of the original; consequently, what in the old story is a simple exchange becomes a fully developed dialogue. There is

something more to his method, however, for the additions he
makes completely alter the tone of the original. For example,
after Nera has fastened the withe, he speaks with the man on
the gallows:

> "You are not dead?" said he to the man above him.
> "Not out and out," the man replied.
> "How does it happen that you are alive?"
> "It happened this way," replied that creaky and rusty tone; "when
> they were hanging me I was very thirsty, and ever since have been
> too thirsty to die."
> "It is a hard case," said Nera.

Stephens' deletions also are significant. He omits mention of
the first two houses and the enigmatic comments by the corpse
in urging Nera to avoid them. Nera takes "his man" into the
first house they come to, props him up against the door, and
helps him to quench his thirst with three buckets of water. Nor
does the corpse scatter death in the form of water from his lips,
but rather permits himself to be carried quietly back to his
gallows:

> As he [Nera] strung him up he asked:
> "Do you feel any better now, my darling?"
> "I feel splendid," said the outlaw. "I'll be dead in a jiffy."[16]

The contrast between the uncanny original and Stephens'
comic version is obvious; yet it would be a mistake to conclude
that Stephens did not take his saga stories seriously. He
believed that the Old Irish literature could have great importance for contemporary Ireland provided that it were reshaped
so as to embody more effectively those human values which
would be meaningful for modern man. The humor which
infects Stephens' Celtic stories is entertaining; but it is more
than just entertaining, for in Stephens' peculiar philosophy of
life laughter is akin to joy and joy is akin to love and love is
the ideal toward which all men must strive.

Certainly Stephens' treatment serves to deflate the superhuman characters of Irish legend. His Conchobhar and Medb

and Deirdre have little in common with A.E.'s titans or Yeats' myth-figures; they are neither gods nor demi-gods nor, indeed, even heroes in the traditional sense, for Stephens has stripped them of the pomp and dignity that are the accouterments of noble heroism. However, it would be wrong to equate Stephens' treatment of Celtic legends with Colum's; for, although Colum euhemerizes the sagas and turns their poetry into prose, he always presents them seriously and incorporates into his renderings of the old stories the popular reverence for Ireland's past. On the other hand, Stephens' irrepressible sense of the comic, when applied to the popular conception of Ireland's sacred history and legend, is liable to the charge of blasphemy; and it is at least noteworthy that non-Irish readers almost invariably are more enthusiastic in their response to *Irish Fairy Tales, Deirdre,* and *In the Land of Youth* than native Irishmen. There is something incongruous about Stephens' continuing friendship with Arthur Griffith and about his membership in the Sinn Féin Party and the Gaelic League; for all of these inclined toward an ever narrower and more restricted definition of national cultural ideals, and Stephens was, by his very nature, a nonconformist. The poet's early development presents a singular paradox in that he remained outwardly loyal to the popular movement by retaining his connection with it, while at the same time his art diverged more and more from the standard of nationalism which the popular movement insisted upon.

Stephens' independence of spirit found expression in different ways. For one thing, in *The Rocky Road to Dublin* he attempted to create a kind of urban pastoral verse concerned with life in Dublin; the contents of the slender volume, poems with such titles as "Mount Street," "O'Connell Bridge," "Custom House Quay," and "Dunphy's Corner," provide a

literary guide to the city. These are not very good poems, just as
The Charwoman's Daughter is not a very good prose work by
comparison with *The Crock of Gold* or *The Demi-gods*; and it
is significant that of the thirty-six poems originally published
in *The Rocky Road to Dublin* barely a third are included in the
Collected Poems and that of those included most are nature
poems. As Professor Mercier has pointed out, there is probably
an inevitable contradiction involved in idyllic verse about life
in a crowded city; [17] Stephens himself suggests as much in "The
College of Surgeons," one of the poems in the original collection. He describes a "Withered leaf" lying in a "dim gloomy
doorway":

> With thin pointed claws
> And a dry dusty skin,
> —Sure, a hall is no place
> For a leaf to be in!
>   (*Seumas Beg*, p. 76; *Poems*, p. 118)

—and the narrow, grey streets of Dublin were no place for
Stephens' peculiar genius, however important they may have
been in his own life and in the development of his personal
philosophy.

   Like Yeats, Colum, and Pearse, Stephens turned away from
the city to the countryside and the people of the countryside
for the substance and inspiration of his poetry; nevertheless, his
verse retains its distinctive character. "Spring 1916," for
example, Stephens' tribute to the heroes of the Easter Rising
and a poem frequently singled out for praise by Irish critics, is
classical in its conception and derives in certain respects from
the tradition of Milton's *Lycidas* and Shelley's *Adonaïs* rather
than from Irish tradition. The poet mourns the untimely death
of the rebels and claims that Nature itself shares his sense of
loss:

> Then you went down! And then, and as in pain,
> The Spring, affrighted, fled her leafy ways!
> The clouds came to the earth in gusty rain!

And no sun shone again for many days!
And day by day they told that one was dead!
And day by day the season mourned for you!

Finally, the poet finds reconciliation and hope in the inevitable rebirth of the seasons (*Poems*, pp. 33–37). What is remarkable about the poem is that it lacks the violent energy which characterizes the many other elegiac poems, including Yeats' "Easter 1916" and A.E.'s "Salutation," written to honor Pearse, MacDonagh, Plunkett, and the other rebels who died in the insurrection. Easter Week filled Ireland with an infectious nationalist fervor that found expression, in one way or another, in almost every poem that it inspired. Stephens, however, abhorred violence and brutality. His poem honors the fallen heroes, but at the same time it implicitly argues the cause of peace and reconciliation.[18]

"Spring 1916" is an exceptional poem written to commemorate an exceptional event. Nevertheless, one may learn from it much concerning Stephens' deep feeling for the natural beauty of the countryside and of the Irish countryside in particular. For Stephens Nature meant much more than a catalogue of images. He felt a profound kinship for the world of birds and trees and flowers, and he sensed in that natural world a reciprocal empathy for mankind and his plight. The quivering life of the Irish countryside—the "mirth of wind and eager leaf," the "scampering feet," the "reaching out of wings"—that Stephens evokes in "Spring 1916" is not simply fare for the elegiac convention; it is fundamental to the poet's aesthetic and to his philosophy of life as well.

Stephens' attitude toward the people of the Irish countryside to a certain extent echoes Padraic Colum and the doctrinaire view of the popular nationalist movement. Like Colum, he occasionally tends to preach a philosophy of littleness. In "The Paps of Dana," for instance, he rebukes the mountains for their pride and notes that a lark or a linnet can soar just as high as the mountains and yet "can sing / As if he'd not done anything." However, the tone of Stephens' poem is good-natured and light, for his sense of humor will not permit him the pomposity that sometimes dulls Colum's verse; Stephens concludes "The Paps of Dana" with an aphorism that—by its very rhythm and turn of phrase—cautions the reader not to take the matter too seriously: "I think the mountains ought to be / Taught a little modesty!" [19] In rare instances, more often in his prose than in his verse, Stephens describes the humblest of men and women in the language of heroic epic. For example, his description of Mary MacCann in *The Demi-gods* would make a suitable companion piece to Colum's romantic picture of Owen Paralon in the "Fore-Piece" to *The Poet's Circuits*: "She was big in build and bone, and she was beautiful and fearless. Framed in a rusty shawl, her face leaped out instant and catching as a torch in darkness; under her clumsy garments one divined a body to be adored as a revelation; she walked carelessly as the wind walks, proudly as a young queen trained in grandeur." [20]

However, an important distinction must be made between Owen Paralon and Mary MacCann. The one is representative of the land and the peasant cottage, and of the mentality land and peasant cottage imply; the other is representative of the landless and homeless of Ireland, and consequently of an entirely different mentality. Although Colum in his verse and prose defends his peasant hero against the oppression of the British Establishment in Ireland, he invariably does so in full confidence that his peasant hero inevitably will come into his own and will dominate the new, native Irish Establishment when the foreigner at last has been cast off; and historically this is precisely what has happened. For Stephens' rootless wanderers, on the other hand, the very concept of Establishment is anathema; they will be persecuted by the new, native Establishment just as inevitably as they were persecuted by the old, foreign one. In *The Demi-gods* Patsy and Mary MacCann and the angels meet many people—strolling musicians and ballad-singers, weavers who sell rootless ferns "to people from

whose windows they had previously stolen the pots to plant
them in," and "hairy tinkers" who speak a "language composed entirely of curses"; but they have nothing whatever to do
with the peasant folk who till the fields and whose lives center
around the conventions of the hearthside in the scattered
cottages of the country: "for the vagabonds these people did
not count; MacCann and his daughter scarcely looked on them
as human beings, and if he had generalized about them at all,
he would have said that there was no difference between these
folk and the trees that shaded their dwellings in leafy spray,
that they were rooted in their houses, and that they had no idea
of life other than the trees might have which snuff forever the
same atmosphere and look on the same horizon until they
droop again to the clay they lifted from." [21]

Stephens looks at Ireland through the eye of a beggar, and
the resultant image of the nation that is given expression in his
prose and poetry reflects this peculiar point of view. The
vagabond's response to a given situation is direct and immediate, whereas the response of Colum's peasant is invariably
calculated and shrewd. The sentiment which informs Colum's
verse gives way to a more vigorous, if more primitive, emotion
in the verse of Stephens. Nowhere in Colum's verse does one
find the undercurrent of violent passion that is characteristic of
so much of Stephens'. Nowhere in Colum does one find the
earthy vigor of these lines from "Righteous Anger" in which
the poet spits out his anger at the woman of an inn who refused
him a glass of beer: "May the devil grip the whey-faced slut by
the hair, / And beat bad manners out of her skin for a year." [22]
In another poem, "Blue Blood," Stephens relates how the
"good men of Clare" wait upon a "princely lad" and ask one
another,

> from what bluest
> blueness of blood
> His daddy was squeezed, and the pa of the
> da of his dad?

> We waited there, gaping and wondering,
>   anxiously,
> Until he'd stop eating, and let the glad
>   tidings out;
> And the slack-jawed booby proved to the
>   hilt that he
> Was lout, son of lout, by old lout and was
>   da to a lout! [23]

The tumbling rhythm, the rabid language, the coarsely eloquent curse—all these represent a genuine aspect of Irish tradition—indeed, both poems are adaptations of equally bitter satires by the Gaelic bard, David Ó Bruadair [24]—but violent passion of this kind had no place in the sentimentalized image of Ireland and the Irish people which Arthur Griffith and other popular nationalists equated with literary merit.

Ironically enough, the poetry of James Stephens, a friend of Arthur Griffith, is similar in important respects to the poetry of John Synge, the victim of Griffith's righteousness. For one thing, Synge was a master of the Irish satiric tradition to which Stephens' "Righteous Anger" belongs; the poet-playwright's lines, "To a sister of an enemy of the author's who disapproved of The Playboy," for example, embody the same explosive ferocity:

> Lord, confound this surly sister,
> Blight her brow with blood and blister,
> Cramp her larynx, lung, and liver,
> In her guts a galling give her.[25]

Identification of the two poets is valid, in a more general sense, with regard to their attitudes toward language, toward poetry, and toward life. Synge's frequently quoted statement in the prefatory note to his *Poems and Translations*—"before verse can be human again it must learn to be brutal" [26]—might aptly have been incorporated into a preface for Stephens' *Insurrections*, published in 1909, the year in which Synge's volume appeared. What could be more brutally full of life (perhaps too full of life to be convincing) than the rage of Stephens' dancer who refuses to subject her personal sorrow to the demand by her audience that she perform?

> Sleek, ugly pigs! Am I to hop and prance
> As long as they will pay!
> And posture for their eyes! And lay
> My womanhood before them! Let them drain
> Their porter-pots and snuffle—I'll not stay! [27]

Robert Farren, whose useful if sketchy book, *The Course of Irish Verse*, is written from a nationalist point of view, recognizes the relationship between Synge and Stephens. Having quoted these lines from Synge's "Queens"—"Queens whose fingers once did stir men, / Queens were eaten of fleas and vermin" [28]—he notes their connection with the older Gaelic satiric verse; but he insists that the lines were not appropriate to the particular period in which they were written: "no other Irishman—except it were Stephens—either could or would have written [them] at the time; which time was 1908–1909." That Farren should so link Stephens and Synge takes on added meaning from his conclusion that "*Queens were eaten of fleas and vermin* were not quite vestal virgins for the temple of art. Synge did his singing a bit crudely!" [29] Farren's comment is, of course, priggish (and in its priggishness is typical of the main line of modern Irish criticism); nevertheless, he is correct in detecting the same rebellious tone in the poetry of Synge and in that of Stephens. Why did not Griffith recognize the similarity? One can only speculate uncharitably that Griffith did not really understand much about literature or care much about it and that the motive for his attack on *The Playboy of the Western World* may have had more to do with his enduring personal antagonism for Yeats than with any real moral scruples concerning Synge's treatment of Irish womanhood and the Irish peasantry.[30]

What is still more difficult to comprehend is that Griffith and others who insisted upon artistic conformity to a popular, sentimental image of Ireland and its people should find it

possible to tolerate Stephens' unorthodox, Hardyesque treatment of the Christian concept of a personal God. In "Where
Demons Grin," for example, an early poem included in
Insurrections, the poet encounters on a barren hill by the sea
an old man whom life has treated badly, whose children are
starving and whose wife is dead: "He muttered low and
sneered at God, / And said He sure was deaf or blind, / Or
lazing on the sod!" (*Insurrections*, pp. 44–45; *Poems*, p. 158).
In another poem, "Mac Dhoul," Stephens' hero, a ragged,
whisker-blackened man, hides in a rose tree in Heaven and
laughs at the sight of a "serious, solemn-footed, weighty,
crowd / Of Angels—or, say, resurrected drapers" standing in
awe before God's throne. At last Mac Dhoul jumps from his
hiding place, rushes

> to the throne, and, nimble as a rat,
> Hopped up it, squatted close, and there I sat,
> Squirming with laughter till I had to cry,
> To see Him standing there,
> Frozen with all His angels in a stare!

God picks the wretch up with "half a finger" and throws him
down "heels and head, / A chuckle in the void!" down to
earth, where, still overwhelmed with mirth, Mac Dhoul offers
to sing the comic Irish song, "The Peeler and the Goat." [31]

Stephens' earliest verse and prose betray a tendency toward
nonconformity that must inevitably have led him to break with
the artificial restraints imposed upon intellectual and artistic
endeavor by the popular nationalist movement. His personal
approach to life and to art was too honest to permit him any
compromise for the sake of Irish patriotism. He believed in
Irish nationality deeply, but not blindly or fanatically. In his
diary of the Easter Rising, for instance, he records an incident
which indicates that he could not accept any concept of
nationalism which was not firmly rooted in genuine humanity.
In the early hours of the rebellion the poet stood across from
Stephen's Green in a cluster of people watching a man attempt
to remove his lorry from a barricade. The Volunteers in the

Green ordered the man to replace the vehicle, and at length he dropped his hold on it and walked toward the armed men to argue with them:

> "Go and put back that lorry or you are a dead man. Go before I count four. One, two, three, four—"
> A rifle spat at him, and in two undulating movements the man sank on himself and sagged to the ground.
> I ran to him with some others, while a woman screamed unmeaningfully, all on one strident note. The man was picked up and carried to a hospital beside the Arts Club. There was a hole in the top of his head, and one does not know how ugly blood can look until it has been seen clotted in hair. . . .
> At that moment the Volunteers were hated.[32]

Stephens describes in detail the bitterness of the group of onlookers toward the Irish rebels "at that moment" and— there can be little doubt—his own bitterness as well. Some of the leaders of the Rising, most notably Thomas MacDonagh, were Stephens' friends and the cause for which the Volunteers fought, the cause of Irish freedom, was essentially Stephens' cause also. But for Stephens an act of brutality must be abhorrent no matter in whose name or in what cause it was perpetrated.

The biography chronicling Stephens' disaffection from the popular Irish movement has not yet been written, but certainly his development as a writer involved a gradual rejection of the narrow definition of nationalism espoused by Sinn Féin and by the Gaelic League. In his essay, "Outlook for Literature," published in 1922, Stephens has moved away from the insular point of view advocated by Sinn Féin, by the Gaelic League, and, indeed, by Stephens himself in his early essays for Griffith: "Irish national action and culture can no longer be regarded as a thing growing cleanly from its own root." In the same essay he writes concerning Ireland that "in a very few years our national action will tell us what it is we may hope for culturally, or what it is that we may be tempted to emigrate from" (p. 813). Stephens' judgment on the subsequent course of national action is implicit in the fact that less than three years later he gave up his position at the National Gallery in Dublin and left Ireland. During his years in exile he rarely broke a self-imposed silence concerning his attitude toward Ireland. Perhaps he left the damp Irish climate for the damp English climate for reasons of health, as many Irishmen suggest, or perhaps he left Ireland because his wife preferred London to Dublin.[33] There is not as yet available sufficient biographical information to be certain. However, it is not likely that he could have lived content in modern Ireland. Certainly Stephens had his native land in mind when in a radio broadcast for the B.B.C. he rejected nationalism as a determining influence for art. "A country is in a pretty serious condition," he wrote, "when its poetry has to become national; when it has to become, that is, political and angry and defensive. The poets of such a country are almost prohibited from producing poetry. They have to produce instead the anger or the discomfort of the day." [34]

In any event, in the poet's later work a strong note of disillusionment is now and then apparent. The course of "national action" with regard to culture in the Irish Free State and the Irish Republic ruled by Irishmen did not take the direction that Stephens had hoped it would when he wrote "Outlook for Literature" in 1922, the year in which Irish freedom had been won. "To Lar, with a Biscuit," published in 1938 in *Kings and the Moon*, suggests in a few words the extent to which Stephens had become alienated from his homeland:

> No watch
> Is on the household now!
> Penates, Lares,
> Emigrate,
> Begone!   (*Poems*, p. 297)

Another poem in *Kings and the Moon* has for its title the word, "Tanist," which was used in the Old Irish law of succession to designate the heir to a kingdom.[35] In Stephens' poem the word probably refers to the modern rulers of Ireland. Stephens indicts the narrow righteousness of Irish nationalism when he compares the tanist to "the spider / Weaving a snare," to "the cat / Tormenting the bird," to "the fool / Frustrating the good," and to the devil with all his treachery; the poet's concluding lines have a particularly bitter ring to them:

> Remember all ill
> That man can know
> —And that you did it
> When you were so:
>
> And then remember
> Not to forget,
> —That you did it,
> And do it yet.   (*Poems*, pp. 316–17)

George Moore records in *Vale* how A.E. searched through the pages of Griffith's *Sinn Féin* each Thursday in the hope of finding a new literary talent and how, having recognized "a new songster" in some verse by Stephens, he "put on his hat and went away with his cage, discovering him [Stephens] in a lawyer's office. A great head and two soft eyes looked at him over a typewriter, and an alert and intelligent voice asked him whom he wanted to see. A.E. said that he was looking for James Stephens, a poet, and the typist answered: 'I am he.' " [36] Russell introduced Stephens to the literati of Dublin and introduced him also to the spiritual "truths" which he and Yeats had found in theosophy and in eastern philosophy and had infused into their own poetics. It was no doubt inevitable that A.E.'s gospel of heterodox occultism should exert an influence upon Stephens' work, yet it is noteworthy that this influence is least apparent in Stephens' early period and that it grew more and more significant, in the end becoming the dominant factor in his aesthetic, as Stephens himself drew further and further apart from the popular nationalist movement.

One finds a sprinkling of occult material in *The Demi-gods*, but it is almost invariably treated humorously. For example, Stephens satirizes Madame Blavatsky's doctrine of reincarnation in the episode of Brien O'Brien, who, determined to have a "cosmic" joke, tries to disrupt the divine process of creation. The angel Art says of the remarkable O'Brien: "He was a magician, and he was one of the most powerful magicians that ever lived. He was a being of the fifth round, and he had discovered many secrets." But in the end, adds the angel, "O'Brien destroyed himself, he forfeited his evolution and added treble to his karmic burden because he had not got a sense of humor" (p. 187). The comic allusions to theosophy are easily recognizable. Madame Blavatsky described the "cycle of conscious life" as consisting of seven rounds and seven races through which the Ego must evolve by means of reincarnation. Modern man, she said, is in the fourth round and fifth race. O'Brien, "a being of the fifth round," is therefore an advanced being. His inferior contemporaries cannot appreciate his humor, and, for this reason, he determines to try a practical joke on the Almighty—with disastrous results to himself. The Karma in Madame Blavatsky's creed consists of the causes which accompany the Ego from one incarnation to another and "which cannot be eliminated from the universe until replaced by their legitimate effects, and so to speak, wiped out by them." There are two types, the Karma of merit and the Karma of demerit. In Brien O'Brien's case, presumably, the Karmic burden consists entirely of demerits.[37]

As a satire upon theosophy, Stephens' *The Demi-gods* may be compared to Thomas MacDonagh's "Metempsychosis." [38] However, MacDonagh was motivated in making his attack on the theory of reincarnation by a desire to defend the Catholic religion against the incursions of an alien system of thought. Stephens, on the other hand, for whom orthodox Christianity had no appeal, could have had no such purpose in mind when he wrote *The Demi-gods*; more than likely, the weighty profundities of the theosophical cult struck him as grotesquely

absurd and, because absurd, as a source of humor. Nevertheless, many of Stephens' early poems, "Where Demons Grin,"
for example, and "Mac Dhoul," with their emphasis upon
mankind's pitiful condition and their implicit rejection of the
Christian concept of a beneficent personal God, suggest a
sensitive human mind groping for some satisfactory answer to
the problem of being; one need not be surprised that Stephens
in the end turned to theosophy with serious intent. According
to his diary, *Insurrection in Dublin*, on Easter Sunday, 1916,
the day before the rebellion, Stephens was reading Madame
Blavatsky's *The Secret Doctrine*, "which book interests me
profoundly" (p. 4). In the years that followed Stephens directed his attention more and more to the East, so much so
that by 1932 he regarded the practice of Yoga "seriously, as an
approach to the divine." [39]

The acceptance of eastern religious thought worked a
marked change upon Stephen's poetry. His earlier work draws
its substance and its inspiration from life itself; like Colum and
Joseph Campbell, he concerns himself with the "stuff of
existence," with the Irish people and with the environment in
which they live, even though Stephens' point of view is
certainly different from theirs. In some ways, the early volumes, *Insurrections, The Adventures of Seumas Beg, The
Rocky Road to Dublin*, and *Reincarnations*, together comprise
a chronicle of Irish life comparable to Colum's *The Poet's
Circuits*. Eventually, however, Stephens came to equate the
poet's function with that of the magician:

> By magic he transforms to
> A better sound, a finer view:
> And—loveliest tale of all that's true!
> He tells that you come to the spring,
> And that the spring returns to you.
>
> (*Poems*, pp. 290–91)

The poet becomes the oracle for the same kind of nature
religion that one finds in A.E.'s verse and, in more austere
form, in Yeats' verse. In another late poem, "Demiurge,"

Stephens defines the creative act of poetry in the language of theosophy:

> The living, ever-waking Will:
> The ever-spacious, ever-still:
> Wherefrom, as from a fountain, springs
> All that praises, soars, and sings:
>
> All that is not dull and dense,
> Bogged in thought, and clogged in sense,
> Comes unbid, and surge on surge,
> From the Will, the Demiurge.   (*Poems*, p. 265)

The Will as "demiurge" is a concept which Stephens apparently found in Madame Blavatsky's *The Secret Doctrine*, where it is used to explain the Yogi's power of wonder-working as resulting from *Itchasakti*, or the Will, and *Kriyasakti*, or the inherent power of thought. *Itchasakti* Madame Blavatsky defines simply in terms of the physical generation of nerve currents; *Kriyasakti* she describes as a more mystical power, by which thought itself can "produce external, perceptible, phenomenal results by its own inherent energy. The ancients held that *any idea will manifest itself externally if one's attention is deeply concentrated on it*. Similarly *an intense volition will be followed by the desired result*." [40] [Blavatsky's italics.]

Stephens incorporates into his mature poetry many of the same esoteric beliefs which one finds in the verse of Yeats and A. E. The "Theme" of "Theme and Variations," for example, celebrates the concept of *anima mundi*; "All the store / Of all that ever was before" remains teeming in the racial memory, Stephens says,

> All the wit
> Of holy living, holy writ,
> Waiting till we remember it,
> Is dreaming in it!   (*Poems*, p. 277)

In "The Fulness of Time" Stephens affirms the theory of antithesis by reconciling good and evil; Satan is welcomed to

Paradise by his nemeses, Gabriel, Uriel, and Raphael, and is seated "beside / One who had been crucified!" [41] In "Psychometrist" the poet weaves into a single lyric the notion of antithesis, the concept of Karma, and the doctrine of reincarnation:

> —Linnets shall for joy atone
> And be fastened into stone;
> While, upon the waving tree,
> Stones shall sing in ecstasy!   (*Poems*, p. 147)

The very title of the poem, "Psychometrist," with its suggestion of empathetic identification with the object (in this instance the stone) in order to divine its nature provides a hint of Stephens' mystical intent as an artist. In *On Prose and Verse* (1928) he defines the function of the poet in language similar to that used by Yeats to explain "unity of being": "His prime aim is to identify himself, first, with the matter under description, ultimately with everything that is." [42]

Much of Stephens' mature verse, like that of Yeats, is concerned with the problem of unity of being, that is, with discovering the means by which mankind might achieve harmony with the natural universe. The underlying theme of the poem "Barbarians," for instance, is that of man's fall from grace and unity into degradation and division. A stream, a tree, and a wind speak to the poet, but he, as a human, is "deaf and dumb and blind" and cannot understand their message. Every wind and every tree and every stream knows directly and immediately its reason for being; only man is constrained to ask why, for man, having lost unity of being, has fallen into ignorance (*Poems*, p. 228). What would be man's condition were unity of being achieved? In "The Voice of God" Stephens suggests that it would involve a mystical and joyful comprehension of self-embodied divinity. The poet hears the "quiet sound" of the grasses in the countryside and listens to their exclaiming voices: "—*We are the voice of God!*" He bends his head low to make certain that the grasses have indeed addressed him:

But, around me, everywhere,
Grass and tree and mountain were
Thundering in mighty glee,
—*We are the voice of deity!*—

And I leapt from where I lay:
I danced upon the laughing clay:
And, to the rock that sang beside,
—*We are the voice of God!*—I cried.

(*Poems*, p. 233)

There is an affinity between the sound of Stephens' grass, tree, and mountain, at once "quiet" and "thundering," and Joseph Plunkett's cry that "Silence is the only song," an exclamation which owes its strength to the Christian mystical concept of silent music by which every part of the Creation proclaims what there is in itself of God. However, where the Christian poet might find resemblance, Stephens discovers identity; where the Christian sees the reflected glory of God, Stephens perceives Divinity itself. In "The Voice of God" Stephens draws his meaning from eastern occultism rather than orthodox Christian mysticism. Of central importance to this poem, and to Stephens' mature aesthetic generally, is the mythopoeic principle of *pars pro toto*. God is embodied in each blade of grass, each tree, each mountain. It remains for the poet to reveal His presence.

Both Stephens and Yeats considered poetry to be a medium for the expression of mythico-religious truth. Yet there are important differences in the artistry employed by each to embody mystical "truth" in his poetry; and in these differences one perhaps may recognize why in the last analysis Yeats must be regarded as the greater of the two poets. In his mature verse Yeats expresses eastern occult concepts within the framework of themes and imagery drawn from the Greco-Roman cultural tradition of Europe and from the Celtic tradition of Ireland. On the one hand, he intensifies objective reality with the spiritual passion of mysticism. He crowds Crazy Jane about with symbolism and elevates her from the commonplace life of rural Ireland to the spiritual permanence of his visionary Otherworld. He evokes the shade of Cú Chulainn to stalk through the Post Office and thereby transforms the Easter Rising from a historical event to a myth of terrible beauty. On the other hand, the visionary elements of Yeats' verse are given substance; his *anima mundi* is crowded with people and events—debased aristocrats, passionate lovers, great battles. His poetry effectively blends together objective and subjective, flesh and spirit.

Stephens is less successful than Yeats in applying the principle of *pars pro toto* to his poetry. Too frequently he fails to create a metaphor capable of absorbing his occult ideas and of communicating them to his reader. Too frequently he takes refuge in the circular rhetoric of abstraction. In "The Soul," for instance, Death describes for Young Nachiketas the nature of the soul:

> He is the Dreamer, and the Dream!
> He is the Frightened, and the Fear!
> He is the Hope! the Gloom! the Gleam!
> He is the Season, and the Year!
> —He is not This, nor That, nor Yon:
> He is Thyself! And Thou Art One!   (*Poems*, p. 256)

Despite the incantatory effect achieved by the use of initial rhyme (a device used in ancient Irish poetry as well as in the verse of eastern mysticism), an effect no doubt consciously contrived to suggest ritual, these lines lack vitality; they have about them the hollow sound of rhetoric rather than the intense sound of poetry. In another poem, "The Pit of Bliss (4)," Stephens adopts the Socratic method:

> What is Knowing?
> 'Tis to see!
> What is Feeling?
> 'Tis to be!
> What is Love? But, more and more,
> To See and Be! To be a Pour

> And Avalanche of Being, till
> Being ceases, and is still
> For very motion—What is Joy?
> —Being, past all earthly cloy
> And intermixture! Being spun
> Of Itself is Being won!
> That is Joy—and this is God,
> To be That, in cloud and clod:
> And, in cloud, and clod, to Sing
> Of Everything, and Anything!   (*Poems*, p. 260)

The headlong rush of the poem to its climax gives it a measure of lyric intensity; but whether such sententious mechanical technique—in this instance the extravagant use of capitalization and exclamation points—can compensate for the absence of sensuous imagery is at least questionable. The poem consists of little more than theosophical generalizations set to rhyme, and whatever their merit as philosophy, they do not necessarily make effective verse.[43]

There is implicit in Stephens' emphasis upon abstract values a rejection of Irish nationalism. In the later poetry one finds an occasional turn of phrase that is Irish in derivation, an isolated allusion now and again, a note of bitterness such as that sounded in "Tanist"; but there is no systematic treatment of Irish material. The poet has turned his gaze to the East, and Ireland and its people are excluded from his vision. The small wild creatures and the roguish human characters of Stephens' early work give way to the Demiurge and to Sarasvati, the Indian goddess of speech.[44] Why this should have happened—it did not happen with Yeats whose Irish symbols, aristocratic, peasant, and heroic, evolved step by step with his beliefs—must remain largely a matter of conjecture. Nevertheless, the evidence which is available, however sketchy it may be, points toward a disenchantment with Ireland and with the values of Irish society. In "Inis Fal," an adaptation of a seventeenth-century poem included in *Reincarnations* (1918), Stephens had written of his people and his nation:

> Our virtues, all, are withered every one!
> Our music vanished, and our skill to sing!
>
> Now may we quiet us and quit our moan!
> Nothing is whole that could be broke! [45] Nothing
> Remains to us of all that was our own.[46]

Whatever his reasons for doing so, Stephens divorced his art from Ireland in particular and from western civilization in general; and he gave himself and his art wholly to the East, to the theosophy of Madame Blavatsky and to the mystic philosophers of India. Indeed, if one is to believe Stephens' own testimony, he rejected completely the world of men: "... turning from all else that was not his, / He took himself to that which was his own / —He took him to his verse" (*Poems*, p. 267).

Despite such pronouncements, however, despite Stephens' professed intention to turn his heart and mind inward upon himself and to seek self-realization through the occult, he never managed to achieve the complete ascetic detachment that is the ideal of the mystic. There is always evident in his verse a deep and troubled sense of pity that has more relevance to man than to God. Stephens, like Yeats before him, took from eastern theosophical literature only those elements which gave substance and support to a philosophy of life which had long before ingrained itself upon his personality; and Stephens' personal philosophy of life begins and ends in the concept of humane love. In his later verse he does embroider his ideal of love with mystical symbols; in "For the Lion of Juda," for example, he refers to the Swan, the Dove, and the Phoenix, the first two, according to Madame Blavatsky, representing "the Universal Principle," the last expressing in its death and resurrection "the successive destruction and reproduction of the world." [47] Yet the aesthetic of this poem in particular and of Stephens' mature verse in general is not really mystical, for the poet's ultimate object is less religious than social; in "For the Lion of Juda" and in most of Stephens' esoteric poetry one finds a message for humanity:

Noble, Wise, and Kind are gone:
Men no more need muse upon
The Dove, the Phoenix, and the Swan!

(*Poems,* p. 325)

In other words, men living in a world or a nation governed by narrowness and hatred have little use for the symbols of the universal principle of love.

Nevertheless, as far as Stephens was concerned, love offered the only possible hope for the future of mankind and the one possible solution to the enigma of human existence. In a radio broadcast in 1948 Stephens said of Yeats' concept of love: "He worried about love, conceiving it as a passion, as a drama, and not the simplest, the most abundant thing in our otherwise bedevilled world, for love is complete trust, unremitting." [48] Stephens misinterprets Yeats, but in doing so he touches upon what is the essential difference between his own poetic vision and the vision of the older poet. For Yeats, passion is at the center of all, and love is but one of its manifestations; passion is for Yeats the "universal principle" by which unity of being may be achieved. For Stephens, on the other hand, the universal principle is love; love envelops passion and conflict, and brings unity and harmony. In his long poem defining the nature of love, "Theme with Variations," Stephens argues that

Love is love for everything,
Fly, spider,
Devil, God:
All that crawls
Or spreads a wing
Love doth love,
And praise, and sing:
Good, and bad,
Below, above
Beloved is,
Or love's not love.   (*Poems,* pp. 339–40)

This message, a message of deep-rooted, pervasive love, is the element that gives essential unity to Stephens' collected poems. Indeed, it is the underlying theme of all his published works; but while in his late poetry the message is presented as a philosophic discourse, in his early work, prose and verse, it is given the form of a parable. The rarified vision of *Kings and the Moon* finds its origin in the earlier volumes of poetry and the novels, in which the ideal of love is given shape and substance. In these early works Stephens' philosophy of life is expressed in terms of physical reality and with specific reference to Ireland and the Irish people; and within the context of these early works, Stephens' vision of the ideal nation emerges —a nation of love and kindness and joy.

Stephens' concept of love is given social application in *The Crock of Gold*. The Philosopher in the novel searches out Pan, the god of pleasure, who has carried off the daughter of Murrachu, and having found him, lectures him on morality. However, when the Philosopher asks rhetorically, "What is virtue?" Pan breaks in to say, "Virtue . . . is the performance of pleasant actions." Then, to the Philosopher's question, "And what, then, is vice?" Pan replies, "It is vicious . . . to neglect the performance of pleasant actions." Pan argues the case for natural physical pleasure against the repressive and unnatural morality of modern society, and (as the novel itself makes clear) of Irish society in particular. "Life is very simple," he tells the Philosopher; "it is to be born and to die, and in the interval to eat and drink, to dance and sing, to marry and beget children." [49] Stephens certainly would concur in Pan's rejection of conventional morality; but Pan represents self-love and, in Stephens' philosophy, self-love is not enough. Significantly, eventually Caitilin Ni Murrachu leaves Pan, the image of her own desires, in the company of Angus Óg, the ancient Irish god of love and youth, who has offered her something preferable to pleasure, namely, "the Happiness of the Divine Imagination." [50] This kind of happiness may be obtained only through a greater love than self-love, only through love that embraces all humanity. Living with Angus, Caitilin Ni Murrachu discovers "that no person can be happy for himelf alone. So she had come to understand the terrible sadness of the gods, and why Angus wept in secret; for often in the night she had heard him weeping, and she knew that his tears were for those others who were unhappy, and that he could not be comforted while there was a woeful person or evil deed hiding in the world." [51]

A Christ-like compassion for all mankind, especially the weak and oppressed—this is the essential love that informs Stephens' poetry as well as his prose. In "Optimist," an early poem included in *Insurrections*, Stephens preaches the ideal of brotherhood founded on love: "Naught can bind / Man closer unto man than that he feel / The trouble of his comrade!" (*Poems*, p. 216). The message remains the same in a later poem, "Strict Care, Strict Joy!" in which the poet first chronicles the sorrows of life and then identifies himself with the Irish bards, Raftery, O'Brien, and O'Rahilly: " . . . we cared naught that these were mournful things, / For, caring them, we made them beautiful." [52] Nowhere is Stephens' theme of compassion more movingly expressed than in his lyrics about the wild creatures of nature. In "The Snare" the poet, hearing the frightened cry of a rabbit caught in a snare, is overwhelmed by a desperate feeling of pity for the animal's plight (*Poems*, p. 22). In the prayer-like final appeal of "From Hawk and Kite," the frightened bird whose nest the poet has unwittingly disturbed becomes a symbol for all the helpless creatures of the earth, animal and human: "Shield the nests where'er they be! / In the house or in the tree! / Guard the poor from treachery!" (*Seumas Beg*, p. 58; *Poems*, p. 218).

Stephens' own early life probably had much to do with the shaping of his attitude toward society. Very little is known of his earliest years, so little, indeed, that as Birgit Bramsbäch remarks, "one may even have to reckon with the possibility that James Stephens is an assumed name." Nevertheless, if one is to judge by the poet's own occasional comments, his childhood was characterized by poverty and privation. One suspects there is more of truth than of myth in the curious biographical note inserted by someone into a gift copy of *The Crock of Gold* in 1912. Of Stephens' background the anonymous writer comments: "He was, I believe, a deserted child. His people are living somewhere, I think, but he does not know where. He has been hungry for weeks as a boy, has slept in parks, has fought with a swan for a piece of bread, has tramped the roads, has lived on the kindness of poor people who liked the queer little boy." [53] Stephens could claim kinship with the least fortunate of God's creatures; it is not surprising that he should become the champion of the impoverished but virtuous Mary Makebelieve or that he should send his angels to live among the tinkers. The final line of "From Hawk and Kite"—"Guard the poor from treachery"—accurately defines the social consciousness that pervades Stephens' prose and verse.

In his essay, "The Outlook for Literature," Stephens defines what he believed to be "the ideal attitude toward life" for a poet: "It is that he should be endlessly sensitive and insensitive. So sensitive that a cruelty or injustice to other people will set him mad; so insensitive that an injustice to himself will tickle him to death." This statement helps to explain the peculiar silence Stephens maintained concerning the biographical details of his childhood and with regard to his reason for leaving Ireland. The esoteric symbolism by which Stephens attempts to give his ideal of love universal significance limits the particular relevance of his mature verse to Ireland and the Irish people. However, in his earlier work Stephens treats of his ideal with reference to the human situation and especially the human situation of the Irish people; consequently, in the novels and earlier poetry Stephens most satisfactorily fulfills his own prescription, set down in "The Outlook for Literature," that the artist must be "not a self, but a national or communal conscience" (p. 812). The younger Stephens is always preaching to his people, castigating them for their sins, urging them toward a way of life upon which his ideal nation of love might be founded.

The social evil against which Stephens most persistently cries out is that of greed. It is on the count of greed that he attacks what he calls the "gombeen men," who may be roughly identified with Yeats' "paudeens," and it is on the count of greed that he condemns the hierarchical structure of society with its contrived castes of privileged and impoverished. "Civilization," he writes in *The Demi-gods*, "having built it-self at hazard upon the Right of Property, has sought on many occasions to unbuild itself again in sheer desperation of any advance, but from the great Ethic of Possession there never has been any escape, and there never will be until the solidarity of man has been created" (p. 53). A society founded upon greed inevitably separates humanity into two classes, the oppressors and the oppressed. This is the rule for personal relationships; so, for example, in *The Charwoman's Daughter* the police-man's emotional attitude toward Mary Makebelieve changes from love to lust when he learns of her poverty. It is the rule for group relationships as well; society protects the privileged and crushes the underprivileged. The hero of *The Charwoman's Daughter*, the young lodger, speaks for Stephens against social injustice: "Against all policemen and soldiers the young man professed an eager hostility, and with these bad people he included landlords and many employers of labor." [54] In "Irony" Stephens offers judgment on all those who would worship at the shrine of greed. He tells of a man who promises to believe in God's kindness and justice if He will only throw down a bag of gold:

> But when his wife rose from her bed
> To see what kept her man away,
> She found him, with a broken head:
> And on the ground beside him lay
> ...A bag of lead!   (*Poems*, p. 224)

For Stephens the "Ethic of Possession" represented the greatest obstacle to the achievement of a society founded upon natural virtue and humane love; but it was not the only obstacle. The poet regarded with suspicion, if not with outright hostility, the conventional religion and conventional morality of the Irish people, for he could not reconcile his observations of Christian doctrine (although one suspects his knowledge of Christian theology was superficial) and Christian practice as he found them in Ireland with his own obsessive belief in the universal principle of love. In his poem, "Besides That," Stephens comments that he would become a pig or a monkey if doing so would help him to reach heaven; but he cannot accept the way to salvation offered by Christianity, a way that bars pigs and monkeys and that "is very, very, difficult, / Besides that!" (*Poems*, p. 223). The tone of the poem is humorously ironic; yet its message is a serious one. Pigs and monkeys are innocent creatures which live in accord with natural law; despite this, however, or perhaps because of it, they are barred from the Christian heaven. Furthermore, the statement that the Christian way is "very, very, difficult" suggests that it involves a perversion of man's nature, for in Stephens' personal philosophy to live according to one's nature is the easiest and simplest and best way. Another poem, "The Fairy Boy," relates the story of a fairy child who sits upon a tree and sings a happy song about "a place where children play / In the sunlight every day." However, a priest, sprinkling holy water, drives the fairy to hell:

> So the tree is withered and
> There is sorrow on the land:
> But the devils milder grow
> Dancing gay
> Every day
> In that kinder land below:
> There the devils dance for joy
> And love that little wrinkled boy. (*Poems*, p. 153)

With Calvinistic zeal the Catholic Church in Ireland had driven natural joy from the land and replaced it with the "withered sorrow" of puritanism. As Stephens saw it, the

Church had imposed upon the Irish people a narrow code of social conformity which served only to stifle natural virtue and to substitute fear for love in men's hearts.

Stephens recognized other difficulties which would have to be overcome before his ideal nation could become a reality. For one thing, he believed that modern rationalism distorted man's understanding of life and kept him from fulfilling his nature. "Wisdom is all head and no heart," one Philosopher tells the other in *The Crock of Gold*. "Behold, brother, you are being crushed under the weight of your own head. You are dying of old age while you are yet a child." [55] In his poem, "Holiday," Stephens attempts to define his ideal society by listing those human perversities which would be excluded; he says that his heart's desire is to find a place

> Where there are no bounds at all
> Of hedge or stream or garden wall:
> No teacher, priest, or magistrate
> To scowl beside a bolted gate:
> Where no man could in his pocket
> Stick a sunny field and lock it:
> Where a draper wouldn't grin
> Sickly when you ventured in:
> Where a sage is never tied
> To a grocer at his side.   (*Poems*, p. 369)

That Stephens had Ireland in mind when he wrote this poem is evident from his use of the word "priest" to refer to the clergy and from his recurring allusion to land greed, a vice peculiar to a people who for centuries were denied all rights of property. Landowners, teachers, clergymen, lawyers, businessmen—these are the defenders of the status quo who make and enforce the rules and regulations which restrict human freedom in society, and all of these would be eliminated in Stephens' ideal state. Whether he seriously believed that such a society could evolve in Ireland, or indeed anywhere, is perhaps a moot question; yet the social system for which he argued would seem no more improbable in modern Ireland than those advocated by Yeats and Pearse.

However, Stephens' vision of the ideal nation differs from that of Yeats, who desired the re-establishment of an aristocratic autocracy, and from that of Pearse, who, under the influence of James Connolly, argued the cause of national socialism; both Yeats and Pearse recognized the social need for governing authority in one form or another. Stephens' nation, on the other hand—a nation without property rights or commerce, without education or religion, without law—is a nation without any authority whatsoever. In effect, Stephens rejects the concept of social order and advocates anarchy. His ideal nation is at best a practical absurdity, a never-never land. Yet who can read *The Crock of Gold* without half wishing that Stephens' dream were a reality? What reader can blame Angus Óg, the daughter of Murrachu, and the hosts of the Shee because "they took the Philosopher from his prison, even the Intellect of Man they took from the hands of the doctors and lawyers, from the sly priests, from the professors whose mouths are gorged with sawdust, and the merchants who sell blades of grass—the awful people of the Fomor"? What reader can refuse out of hand Stephens' invitation to join in "the Happy March": "Come away! for the dance has begun lightly, the wind is sounding over the hill, the sun laughs down into the valley, and the sea leaps upon the shingle panting for joy, dancing, dancing, dancing for joy." [56]

F. R. HIGGINS:

THE GOLD AND HONEY LAND

Yeats, A.E., Douglas Hyde, and Katherine Tynan had initiated
the Irish literary revival in the eighteen-eighties and eighteen-
nineties and they were followed in turn by a host of younger
writers—Pearse, MacDonagh, Synge, Joyce, Colum, and Stephens, to mention but a few. F. R. Higgins, whose first book of
verse appeared three decades after the founding of the Irish
Literary Society and the Gaelic League, represents yet a third
generation of Irish poets. Despite the passage of time and flow
of history, however, his avowed aesthetic purpose is essentially
the same as that of Yeats, George Russell, and Douglas
Hyde—to embody in his art the spirit of Cathleen Ní
Houlihan, to give poetic expression to the "indomitable
Irishry" of his race and nation. In Higgins' poem, "A Plea," a
personified Ireland speaks with romantic nostalgia of her past
glories. She refers to St. Patrick, who, according to a Fenian
story, recovered Caoilte's jeweled goblet from the mouth of a
salmon; to Fintan, a mythological creature who passed
through numerous incarnations and survived to give Gaelic
scribes an account of Ireland's prehistory; to Deirdre, the tragic
heroine of the Ulster cycle; to Aoife, who was transformed by
magic into a crane, the skin of which afterwards served as a

treasure bag for Mannan of the Sea; to the harp of Finn, which had three strings, one of which could conduce sorrow, another happiness, and the third sleep; and to the Fenian riders, their horses and hounds, who hunted wild boars across the mountains and glens of the countryside. Having evoked these images from the legendary past, Ireland addresses herself to the poets: "Come flush me with new praise, for I am Ireland, / Grown old and ashen with a touch of dawn!" [1]

In his earlier attempts to sing Ireland's glories, Higgins conforms in most respects to the established pattern for Irish writers, although now and again he strikes an original note. For example, like a hundred Gaelic and Anglo-Irish poets before him, he seeks poetic inspiration in the Irish countryside, where "soft rain is falling" and "plovers call" and "soft clouds are falling / Over all." [2] In such a setting of natural beauty one may "learn at the voice of a bird" or find wisdom "On a butterfly's wing." [3] Higgins' poetic landscape is crowded with small lakes overcast by "palest shadows" and dotted by sun-washed isles.[4] His imagery of nature, often reminiscent of the early Yeats, is used to proclaim the same pastoral ideal one finds expressed in Stephens' verse, in Colum's, and in Pearse's. His countryside is unique only in that it is identified with a particular landscape, that of Connemara, the Gaelic-speaking area in the counties of Galway and Mayo near the western sea. The scenic beauty of the West held a lasting fascination for Higgins, so much so that even in his later verse when he writes of the rich farmlands of County Meath on the far side of the island, his eye still wanders back to the "lean highlands" of the West "Where seas break silence and strip the yellow rocks / Of rich top-dressing." [5]

Higgins, like Padraic Pearse before him, perceived in those people who lived in the Irish countryside, and especially in those who lived in the Gaelic West, the true spirit of the Irish race and nation. Occasionally in his verse one finds a picture of peasant life as vivid and vigorous as those sketched by James Stephens; "The Woman of the Red-Haired Man," for exam-

ple, centers upon a bitter passion that is given final expression
in a curse worthy of Ó Bruadair: "Salt days at table, nights
without marriage / Leave milkless paps in your female clan." [6]
More often, however, the reality of life is hidden behind a
Celtic mist. "Death in the Mountain" is a monologue in which
the speaker is a man of the folk about to die:

> Pile on the brown fir over the fire,
> Green boughs on the withering blaze,—
> Wind to the flame that laps with a hiss,
> Sap full of leafy days;
> For now my old feet take no delight
> In crashing the frozen dew,
> When the dark is alone with the witchy moon
> Hung crooked in a yew. [7]

Higgins evidently has tried to harden his language in this
poem—the fire sounds with a "hiss"; the feet go "crashing";
the moon is "Hung crooked"—nevertheless, his treatment of
the theme of death is euphemistic. In "To a Hostel Keeper"
even the traditional curse is made more gentle: "But these
remembering hills shall leave your hostel / A field of stone to
shelter foreign peers." [8] Higgins' portrayal of Irish life in
general—except in certain of his late poems—is inevitably
softened and sentimentalized.

The people of Ireland also are subjected to romantic
distortion in Higgins' verse. They are represented not as
humble peasants but rather as "desperate / Most noble
men," [9] who number among their forebears Conn of the
Hundred Battles, Finn MacCumhaill and his comrades, and,
in the still remoter past, Cú Chulainn, Conchobhar, and
Medb. Higgins is concerned in particular with "the dark men"
of the western Gaeltacht, men who he believed were the direct
descendants of the aristocratic race of Mil and who were "bred
from the cold lean rock" of Connemara. [10] In "Island Blood"
the poet sets the scene near the coastal village of Renvyle at
twilight (p. 65):

> Soon dark men from the glenside
> And bare-limbed girls with creels

Shall wade along the ebb-tide
And rake the sand for eels—
With moonlight on the bare strand
They'll prong the bright sand-eels.

The romantic language—the traditional "creels" (baskets for carrying produce), the "glenside" and "bare strand" in the moonlight, the "bright sand-eels"—and the soft rhythm of the lines combine to give the verse a shadowy quality. The "dark men" and "bare-limbed girls" are not to be regarded as individualized human beings but rather as racial types, as living symbols of the ancient Gaelic race.

The current of racial consciousness runs strongly through modern Anglo-Irish verse; and, almost without exception, the poets have singled out the Irish peasant as the embodiment of the ancient racial strain of the Gael. In Yeats' verse the peasant is praised for his subservience, in Pearse's for his fighting spirit, in Colum's for his lowly virtue and his righteousness, in A.E.'s for his godliness; in Stephens' for his vitality and good humor. In Higgins' poetry, although the peasant ideal encompasses fighting spirit, lowly virtue, and, in some measure, vitality, it is vaguer and, in a romantic sense, more mystical than the verse of Stephens, Colum, or Pearse. In his "dark breed" of the West Higgins perceived both the past glory and future destiny of the Irish nation. His unpublished papers include some notes for a lecture that suggest his ideas concerning race were Nietzschean: "Let us just sing for that race of men who become immeasurably stronger, wiser, and subtler with the future, their bodies more harmonized, their movements more rhythmic, their voices more musical, when the forms of life become more dynamically dramatic. We may be the predessors [sic] of the race of supermen; it is within the conception of human intelligence, aye even Irish intelligence. Therefore 'be you lifted up! and cry to that great race that is to come!' " [11] Higgins' remarks may seem grotesque, even comic; yet they express accurately the popular Irish belief in racial purity and racial superiority—a myth utterly without foundation in history yet widely enough accepted in modern Ireland to make possible the fascistic Blue Shirt movement of General O'Duffy in the nineteen-thirties.

Certain of Higgins' poems can be termed overtly patriotic. "Celebration," for example, embodies a bitter attack upon the Orange Order, a Protestant Unionist organization, which was founded in 1795 and which during the nineteenth and twentieth centuries fought first against Catholic emancipation, then against agrarian reform, and finally against Irish home rule. The poem describes an Orange parade held on July 12th to commemorate the decisive defeat of the Jacobite Irish at the Battle of the Boyne in 1690.[12] Higgins sets the scene in Scarva, a village of County Down in Northern Ireland, where they "honour no saint's day"; he then contrasts the drunken barbarism of the marching Orangemen with the noble—and, one presumes, sober—dreams of loyal Irishmen:

> Their Orange drums are caned in blood
>   And savage factions join
> In drunken fealty to the crown
>   That's bearded on their coin—
> While our lost crown sends flighty dreams
>   Across the sleepy Boyne!   (*Dark Breed*, p. 24)

The poem has an unusual vigor that is perhaps attributable to the poet's genuine anger at what he regards as a national betrayal. In contrast, those poems which treat of the noble heroism of those Irish patriots who gave themselves to what Thomas MacDonagh termed "the cause that never dies" are characteristically soft and sentimental. In "Sword Makers," for example, Higgins describes a monastery where Irish soldiers could find refuge from their English pursuers during the struggle which preceded the "Flight of the Earls" in 1603. In the poem a monk welcomes the fleeing warriors to sanctuary: "Ah, worn-out kerns among the harried glens, / Here none can follow." One suspects this would be rhetoric enough in greeting battle-worn soldiers; but Higgins' monk, irrepressible, pushes onward with a torrent of affected imagery:

> Although the grey hawk hangs upon taut wing,
> He brooks no sorrow,
> With sunlight preening through an evening cloud.
>
> (*Dark Breed*, p. 59)

Such over-elaborate metaphor gives to Higgins' verse a flaccid quality that by modern aesthetic standards would be objectionable in any poem, but especially so in one purporting to be dramatic and treating of a martial theme. Nevertheless, the softening of the battle motif is probably deliberate. The Gaelic resistance against Elizabeth must be assimilated into the Irish racial memory, which in Higgins' poetry is a dreamlike repository for romantic sentiment.

Finn MacCumhaill and his *fianna* suffer the same fate as monk and soldiers; in Higgins' verse they become no more than fleeting specters in the racial memory of the Irish. In "The Return of Niamh" the poet lazily observes nature; he hears "the salmon waters leap the weirs of Ardnaree" and sees "three little foxes" rush through the grass; and then he remembers "why Finn rushed sunward to the sea / By sleepy wrens in hollow crannies, under crumbling woods" (*Island Blood*, p. 12). In "Eithne" an episode from the saga becomes an allusion in a lyrical address by a lover to his beloved:

> Now Caoilte goes spearing young salmon
> With javelins he borrowed from Finn;
> So come and close over your curtains,
> The slumber-musicians begin. (*Island Blood*, p. 48)

The third and fourth lines express succinctly Higgins' aesthetic approach to art; for, almost invariably in his earlier work, the poet seeks to lull the reader and then to draw him into the dream where the shades and shadows of the racial memory can be brought into play.

In "Dotage" Higgins makes use of historical material which had been absorbed into the popular tradition of the western Gaeltacht: the remarkable career of Gráinne Ní Mháille, queen of Clare Island and Clew Bay off the coast of Mayo, a woman who commanded war galleys and who was "for forty years the stay of all rebellions in the west" during the sixteenth century, and the episode of the Spanish Armada, which, after its defeat by the English, fled around the western coast of Ireland where many of its galleons foundered and sank.[13] The formula employed by the poet to give these traditions expression in his verse is essentially the same as that used in the case of the Fenian saga materials. The speaker in the poem is a homeless old man forced to wander the untamed countryside of Connemara, his only possession a "dream" of drinking from "the cups of Grace O'Maille, / When Spanish sails were mine." In the peasant's dream the legend of the fierce Gráinne Ní Mháille has been softened into nostalgic reminiscence; significant also is the fact that what is remembered is not the incessant plundering in which the queen of Clare Island reportedly engaged, but her famed hospitality. In a following stanza the old man speaks of the Armada. Although he duly records the fact of its destruction, his emphasis is upon the romantic grandeur of "the great fleet invincible":

> Or when the bold Armada.
>   Rode golden long ago,
> Through the clean waves plumbed with brightness
>   To the sun-washed rocks below;
> There every man's chest of treasure
>   Was a cask of sack and a gun,
> Until his full-sailed castle
>   Blazed down in a terrible sun.
>
> (*Island Blood*, pp. 10–11)

Higgins' imagery is controlled here; indeed, there is a kind of taut splendor about "clean waves plumbed with brightness" and ships that "Blazed down in a terrible sun"; yet the pattern of language—a past that is "golden," waves that are bright, rocks that are "sun-washed," a sack and gun that become a "treasure," and a ship that is a "full-sailed castle"—indicates clearly enough the poet's romantic intent. This account of the story of the Armada is not to be taken as literal history; it is the child of an Irishman's fancy. Indeed, Higgins' peasant is oblivious to the ironic fact that while certain of the Gaelic septs welcomed the Armada's survivors, others slaughtered them without mercy, so that some ten thousand Spaniards were lost or murdered on the western coast.[14]

What Robert Farren says of Higgins—that "every poem he wrote declares him an Irishman"—is certainly true with respect to the substance of his verse. It is true also with regard to his technique. Farren, in his *The Course of Irish Verse*, praises Higgins and Austin Clarke for their mastery of the device of assonance: "Hyde and some others were of course in a way before them; but their use of this central resource of Gaelic prosody, if not quite random, was certainly less systematic, determined and forceful than the use made by Higgins and by Clarke. They were Larminie's first-born, these two, and they held by father; their practice of assonance within and at the end of lines became almost instinctive." [15] Internal rhyme is, to be sure, the most striking feature of Higgins' prosody. In these lines from "Cattle Boats," for example, the sound patterns are obvious: "With an ear to the wind I've been hearing / On the way to the Graziers' Fair" (*Island Blood*, p. 49). Assonance and consonance—"With" and "wind," "ear" and "hearing," "way" and "Graziers' " and "Fair"—certainly determine the rhythm of the lines. Unfortunately, in doing so they also determine the tone of the verse and make it softer and more sentimental than it otherwise would be. Hyde's more restrained if "not quite random" use of assonance would have been preferable. The over-elaborate sound patterns in Higgins' verse contribute, in fact, to the vague romanticism of his racial dream.

In the nineteen-twenties Higgins identified himself with a group of writers described by Austin Clarke as "the new Irish school"; [16] In fact, however, there is very little new or original in Higgins' poetry. What emerges ultimately is the sentimental image of Ireland and the Irish people that had been fostered by the popular nationalist movement. Higgins' racial dream is much the same as Padraic Colum's, and, indeed, he employs much the same means to give that dream creative expression. In Colum's poetry one finds the same glorification of the peasant, the same romantic treatment of Irish history, the same nostalgia for Ireland's past greatness, and the same attempt to adapt the intricacies of Gaelic prosody to verse written in English. Occasionally Higgins may add a new note to an old theme; for instance, there is a fresh beauty in the wistful yearning of his poem, "Old Wine":

> But where's Beauty's joy,
> While Beauty's dust is clinging
> To a lonely cairn in Connacht
> And a burning wind from Troy. (*Island Blood*, p. 2)

More often, however, Higgins treats the conventional material in the conventional way. The poetry of *Salt Air, Island Blood,* and *The Dark Breed,* considered as a body of work, is quite obviously inferior to Colum's verse; yet there is much truth in a reviewer's comment, concerning the relationship between Colum's work and that of the younger Irish poets, including Higgins, that "it is often difficult to distinguish between the work of master and pupil." [17]

However, Higgins' approach to poetry differs from Colum's in one very important respect. Colum's work may be termed Philistine in that it proclaims values that are commonplace and conventional. Nevertheless, in him one must recognize a genuine craftsman. He is carefully precise in his technique and he is consistent in the development of his themes (whatever may be the initial fallacy inherent in any particular theme). Most important of all, his themes, his imagery, and his prosody all contribute in one way or another to an underlying intellectual pattern; in other words, his romantic vision of the ideal nation of peasants is given artistic unity. The same cannot be said of Higgins. His technique is often haphazard and his thematic development inconsistent. What is more, his approach to art is that of a dilettante; his aesthetic theory is always vague and frequently confused. In a lengthy note to his volume, *The Dark Breed* (p. 66), Higgins attempts to define the artistic objectives of the "new school" of Irish poets:

> The racial strength of a Gaelic aristocratic mind—with its vigorous colouring and hard emotion—is easily recognised in Irish poetry, by those acquainted with the literature of our own people. Like our Gaelic stock, its poetry is sun-bred; twilight for it is just the tremulous smoke of one day's fire. Not with dreams but with fire in the mind, the eyes of Gaelic poetry reflect a richness of life and the intensity of a dark people, still part of our landscape. Many qualities from such an ancestry may easily be detected in the poetry of younger Irish writers, who are working to-day in homely materials.
>
> The younger poets generally express themselves through idioms taken from Gaelic speech; they impose on English verse the rhythm of gapped music, and through their music we hear echoes of secret harmonies and sweet twists still turning to-day through many a quaint Connacht song. For indeed these poets, in the lineage of the Gaelic produce in Irish lyric—with its exuberance and wild delicacy—the memories of an ancient and rigorous technique. And yet it may be finally said that poetry forages no groundsel in a gilded cage, but having clamped the sod with a shoeless hoof, cleaves the wild air with liberal wings.

The worst sins of Irish critical prose are manifest in these two paragraphs—the questionable grammar and awkward sentence structure, the grotesque language, the disorganized clutter of ideas forced together into artificial paragraph units. More important, however, is Higgins' total disregard for objectivity and logical consistency. He describes the Irish people and Irish poetry as "sun-bred," yet the country's climate is invariably damp and overcast; [18] he praises the "hard emotion" of the "Gaelic aristocratic mind," yet the picture of the Gael one finds in his own verse is inevitably soft and sentimental. He denies that the "dreams" of "twilight" have any relevance to Irish poetry, yet his own poetry is crowded with such dreams and, indeed, the word "dream" itself recurs with obsessive regularity. Higgins is guilty of a kind of semantic irresponsibility that is characteristic of much contemporary Irish criticism; the very tone of his prose controverts everything he says about disciplined technique, fiery minds, and hard emotion. What could more conclusively give the lie to his claims for the "new school" of Irish writers than his own final metaphor, a collage of affectation, softness, and sentimentality?

The most significant elements in this passage, however, are its overtones of racial bias and Higgins' unquestioning acceptance of anything and everything Irish. The popular cultural ideals of Griffith's Sinn Féin movement and the nationalist cabals impregnated Higgins' mind and he took for his own the popular criteria for evaluating poetry, criteria which unfortunately have gained in contemporary Ireland widespread acceptance among writers, critics, and even scholars. One judges an Irish poem or, indeed, any work of art by an Irishman by asking two questions: first, is it Irish? and, second, is it good (or loyal) Irish? The final measure of a work of art depends upon whether it adequately reflects the conventional image of Ireland imposed on the particular medium by the nationalist movement. This narrow and no doubt naïve standard became for Higgins a first principle in evaluating not only Irish literature but the literature of any national or ethnic group. In a review in *The Irish Statesman* he finds fault with a book of verse by a Canadian because "it reveals no racial passion." "Too many Canadian poets," he writes, "show a colonial shallowness. . . . They look frequently on the Motherland and, as a result, sound its poetic echoes with all the fatuity of bad parody. These traits are noticeable in most colonial verse; and they are seen, even today, in portions of Anglo-Irish song!" [19] In such criticism as this, intellectual and aesthetic considerations, if they are not entirely ignored, must be subject to basically Philistine precepts spelled out by the popular cultural movement.

One need not be surprised that a strong current of obscurantism runs through the work of Higgins and that of other writers of the "new Irish school." Robert Farren in his book on Irish verse relates a conversation that once took place between Higgins and Louis MacNeice. Higgins asked, "Do poets of your school never sing?" and MacNeice asked in turn, "Do poets of *your* school never think?" [20] One is tempted to answer for Higgins, "Not too deeply." In both his prose and verse Higgins rejects intellectual and metaphysical probing as legitimate concerns of literature; like Colum, he proclaims the superiority of "simple bog wisdom" to more formal kinds of learning.[21] The poet, he argues, "must quarry in homely materials, work through a common idiom." [22] In "Evangelists" he makes much the same point:

> Let scribes leave these delights in
> Wise books of skin and horn
> I'll take my spoils of heaven
> From hooks of fish and corn.[23]

The language of Higgins' verse and prose is hardly that of a common idiom; yet certainly he consistently admires those Irish writers who successfully capture in their work the speech and the mentality of the folk. Pádraic Ó Conaire, for example, a storyteller in whom Higgins perceived true greatness, "had no sympathies with those writers who were suckling at literary pretence—on the contrary his vigorous mind, his humor and his sense of reality did much to wean many away from such skim milk." Ó Conaire was a man of the people who had accumulated much "bog wisdom" but to whom more sophisticated learning was anathema—"he left such decorative material," Higgins observes, "to those literary peacocks that preen their flashy feathers—and walk only in the preserves of poetic affectation." Ó Conaire's method of composition, as Higgins describes it, is of special interest: "Having seated himself at my table, with pen and paper, together with a pint bottle of porter, I left the room, [sic] and at his suggestion locked him in—only to return usually two hours later to liberate Padraic who then presented me with his new script. It was always written in perfect Gaelic lettering—without an alteration—beautifully lined and balanced on immaculately white pages. And he was always childishly proud of that clean script. It was the pride of a scribe before the days of the printing press." [24] Ó Conaire's spontaneous art is a case in point to support Higgins' belief that literature emerges naturally and inevitably from the racial memory—"To each tribe poetry exists"—and that no special intellectual effort is required of the writer. The poet perhaps has some responsibility to master his craft, yet even "the accomplishment of technique largely depends upon the verbal felicities of the language in which the poetry is composed." [25] What the writer must do, however, is steep himself in the living culture of the people, absorb their language and their lore, and by so doing make himself a fitting vehicle for the expression of racial ideals.

By the nineteen-twenties the ideals in the Irish racial memory had become stereotyped in the mold of conventional morals and mores. The Irish poet might, if he wished, proclaim the beauty of the Irish countryside. He might affirm his belief in the inherent nobility of the Irish peasant. He might praise Ireland's spirit of resistance through centuries of foreign oppression. He might sing the grandeur of ancient Ireland—although he would be wise to sing the Ireland of popular Fenian tradition, in which the influence of Christianity is apparent and more commonplace values are dominant, rather than the pagan and more sophisticated Ireland of the Ulster sagas. Whatever his subject, the poet's overall representation of Ireland must reflect the romantic and sentimental image of the popular mind; under no circumstances should he adulterate the accepted pattern with alien ideas or alien attitudes.

In general, such was the creed of the "new school" of Irish writers. Their faith in its tenets is evident in their own creative work and also in their intolerance toward anyone who deviated from the norm. The Irish tradition must be a thing undefiled. Higgins, for example, during the nineteen-twenties was determined to expose and counteract what a reviewer of his work terms "the nebulous mysticism" of A.E. and Yeats.[26] In a lecture on "Irish Poetry for the Past Thirty Years," Higgins observes that the later verse of James Stephens—the verse written after that poet exchanged conventional Irish material for Madame Blavatsky's theosophical profundities—"has grown thin and somewhat tricky. One feels that his agility has become a pose." [27] More remarkable is the stand taken by writers of the "new school" during the controversy which surrounded the production of Sean O'Casey's *The Plough and the Stars* at the Abbey Theatre. *The Irish Statesman* published letters from Liam O'Flaherty and Austin Clarke on February 20, 1926, and two weeks later a letter from Higgins. O'Flaherty admits O'Casey's right to his own opinions (which, one should note in fairness, are antithetical to his own) and concentrates his attack upon Yeats for having said in connection with the popular protest that the Irish people had been "cut to the bone." O'Flaherty comments: "Our people have their faults. It is a good thing that artists should point out their faults. But it is not a good thing that pompous fools should boast that we have been 'cut to the bone.'" In his letter Austin Clarke describes *The Plough and the Stars* as a "bad topical play, run flagrantly in the interests of the party politics of the [Marxist] movement," and then adds that the "writers of the new Irish school" believe O'Casey's work "is a crude exploitation of our poorer people in an Anglo-Irish tradition that is now moribund." [28] Higgins' letter is more moderate in tone, yet its central point is especially significant: "Mr. Sean O'Casey, in his new play, entirely lacks the sincerity of an artist." [29] In these three letters one may perceive the underlying objection to *The Plough and the Stars*. O'Flaherty and Clarke are indignant at what they regard as an insult directed against the Irish people; and Higgins defines the nature of that insult when he accuses

O'Casey of wanting sincerity; for the word "sincerity," as it is
commonly used by Irish writers and by Irishmen in general, is
synonymous with the word "sentimentality." O'Casey's sin,
like that of Synge in writing another play, was that he failed to
sweeten the Irish character with sentiment.

In *Salt Air, Island Blood,* and *The Dark Breed,* and in his
miscellaneous prose writings, Higgins dedicates himself to the
celebration of the popular romantic image of the Irish people
and nation that O'Casey saw fit to ignore. He sings the glory of
the Fenian heroes, of the Gaelic resistance to foreign rule, and,
most significantly, of the noble peasant, his traditions and
customs, and the countryside in which he lives. In many
respects, Higgins' vision of Ireland is similar to Colum's. Both
try to adapt Gaelic poetic technique to their verse in English;
both develop the same basic themes; and both attempt to
depict modern Ireland as a kind of latter-day Arcadia, a
survival of the Golden Age. Higgins' verse, however, lacks the
artistic discipline of Colum's; his imagery is often exorbitant,
his sentiment too often unrestrained. The ideal nation in
which his "dark men" and "bare-limbed girls" gather their eels
is "a gold and honey land"; [30] to such a land Higgins meant to
ride his "winged horse":

> If I could spare good money,
>   I would spread a sail and ride
> Toward lakes that glow like honey
> In a bloom of country-side.   (*Island Blood*, p. 65)

More often than not, Higgins' honeyed language and opulent
rhythms serve only to make his verse heavy, lethargic, and
unexciting. In any event, they are merely decorative. Beneath
the ornamentation one finds only the stereotyped ideals of the
popular nationalist movement. The passion of Cathleen Ní
Houlihan has been tamed by conventional morality. Ireland's
wine has been watered down with sentimentality. What are
truly lacking in Higgins' vision of the ideal nation are intellectual originality and emotional energy.

In a poem entitled "Repentance," published in *Arable Holdings* in 1933, Higgins passes judgment upon his own earlier poetry and rejects what he terms the "frailties of a bardic will." His repentance does not involve a rejection of Ireland; he does not mean to divorce his art from his nationality, as James Stephens had done. Indeed, at the very beginning of the poem Higgins makes clear that Ireland is to remain the focus of his art, for he places himself upon "Saint Patrick's hill." This is a reference to Croagh Patrick, a mountain retreat for penitents in western Ireland and for that reason a suitable setting in which to make an act of repentance; but in the context of the poem "Saint Patrick's hill" must also be recognized as a symbol for the Irish nation. Ireland will remain Higgins' subject; but his aesthetic attitude toward that subject will be radically changed:

> For I have diced in withered towns
> The true coin of the sun,
> And wasted crafts when plying at my ease
> The trickster's mental algebra
> Of nods and winks, with one
> Who brought no harvest to our knees.
>
> Men from the road's blue mouth know well
> Thoughts housed too long grow pale,
> Without hostilities from wind and rain;
> Yet moss and rheumy candlelight
> Were mine, until fierce hail
> Fell scolding on my window-pane.[31]

What his new attitude will be is fairly clear. He has left behind the "withered towns" where "Thoughts housed too long grow pale"; in other words, he has rejected the sentimental conventions of the popular tradition, those worn, effete conventions that permit the poet only a "trickster's mental algebra / Of nods and winks." He renounces also his soft, voluptuous imagery, which now seems to him like "moss and rheumy candlelight." In a subsequent stanza he again observes that he has turned away from the "twilight pools" of romanticism and then adds that he has done so in order to achieve in his verse "pure commerce with the sun," and he promises to "climb above the night, / That preys on mounds of holy stone." The tokens of his new aesthetic are "sun" and "wind and rain" and "fierce hail"; they point toward a harsher and more piercing quality in the thought and technique of Higgins' verse, and, in consequence, toward a new, more violent, and perhaps angry vision of Ireland.

What brought on so curious a change of outlook in a poet who previously had identified himself so closely with the cause of popular nationalism? The answer probably is to be found in the fact that Higgins had come under the influence of Yeats. Between the appearance of *The Dark Breed* in 1927 and that of *Arable Holdings* in 1933 he had won admission to the "inner circle" of the great Irish poet's friends and, according to Robert Farren, Higgins remained "Yeats's crony in the latter's old age." [32] Certainly Yeats looked upon the younger man as a kind of protégé. He was influential in having Higgins appointed a director of the Abbey Theatre and, when the Irish Academy of Letters was founded, he saw to it that Higgins was named secretary. Yeats also helped spread the younger poet's reputation among literary people outside Ireland.[33] For his part, Higgins became Yeatsian in all he undertook. His unpublished papers include a scenario for a ballet entitled "Puck Fair" and a typescript of another, entitled "Deuce O' Jacks." The former, described as a "pantomime ballet," is concerned with a conflict between the forces of respectability and the forces of passion; its characters include Lovely Girl, Black Coated Gentleman, and the Fiery Tinker whom Higgins represents as the "hero of them all." The latter is a one-act comedy with ballet, and of it Higgins comments in a note: "This production is not a play in the conventional structure— it is much more and a lot less. Primarily a genre painting, one darkened with age, it presents a sombre background to the first glimpse until with the increasing gesture and dance of its mellow figures, the characters, it becomes a succession of

moving pictures; only to complete itself in the grotesqueness of
its first sombre effect. Indeed to get a true perspective the
production should be seen a few times and from a distance!" [34]
Surely, Higgins could not have conceived of drama in such
exotic terms had it not been for Yeats' example.

The influence of Yeats upon Higgins' poetry in the nineteen-
thirties is more obvious; indeed, it is indisputable. In "Repentance" itself one finds language which certainly derives from
Yeats—"withered towns," for example, and "scolding on my
window pane." In other poems the pattern of imitation is
much more specific. In "East of Hy Breasail" Higgins experi-
ments with the theme of Yeats' "Sailing to Byzantium," [35] a
theme centering on the poet's quest for an ideal land of art:

> There is an isle I know
> Where we may go in the evening,
> Over the sea's white mearings,
> Through baronies of light;
> Waves brightly beckon us,
> A sailing wind invites us,
> And dream brings the isle into sight.
>
> There light is rustled by
> The grasshopper in his green kingdom—
> Little else stirs there,
> Only birds or the flow'r-mating bee;
> Summer grows lazy there—
> It merely suckles one bramble
> That's reaped by a wave of the sea.
>
> Surely it's on that isle
> We'll gather the airs of healing—
> Dews from the dead of night
> To perish age and pain;
> Eras of gold are seen there,
> To there the sunset is climbing
> Down flights of yellow rain.[36]

There are a number of close parallels between Higgins' poem
and that of Yeats. One must sail the seas to reach either
Higgins' "isle" or Yeats' "holy city" (or, for that matter, A.E.'s

"city of the gods" in "Mutiny"). Both places have treasure-
hoards of gold. "Eras of gold are seen" in Higgins' land; "To
there the sunset is climbing / Down flights of yellow rain." In
Yeats' city "Grecian goldsmiths" create forms "Of hammered
gold and gold enamelling / To keep a drowsy Emperor awake."
In both places one finds men of religious wisdom: In Higgins'
(in a subsequent stanza) figures from Irish myth and legend,
including the fabled sea-journeyer, Saint Brendan; in Yeats'
"sages standing in God's holy fire." Finally, both Higgins' isle
and Yeats' holy city promise the worthy traveler escape from
physical age and death.

Despite the parallels, however, the two poems are different
in a very basic sense. The object of Yeats' flight to Byzantium
is to escape the world of "dying generations," the world where
"Fish, flesh, or fowl, commend all summer long / Whatever is
begotten, born and dies." In the holy city, he tells his readers,
the creative spirit of man may find release from physical frailty,
from that part of man's nature which is "a dying animal"; the
creative spirit may be gathered into "the holy fire, perne in a
gyre," and there may be transformed into "the artifice of
eternity." In other words, man may find immortality only in
the creation of immortal art, art like that which Keats
perceived in a Grecian urn and then embodied in a poem of his
own. Higgins' isle, on the other hand, is a sensuous paradise; it
is green and summery and populated with grasshoppers and
birds and "flow'r-mating bee." What this isle offers is physical
rejuvenation through its "airs of healing"; Higgins promises to
eliminate death of the body, but he says nothing of the soul.
Whether Higgins altered the sense of Yeats' poem deliberately
or not is a matter for discussion. However, there is some reason
to suspect that he did not fully comprehend the underlying
meaning of "Sailing to Byzantium." In a later stanza he alludes
to "the mind's magnetic compass," a cold and fleshless image
that conveys something of Yeats' notion of the disembodied,
intuitive intellect; and the poem's final image, "in a blaze of
night," in its fusing of light and darkness suggests the Yeatsian
concept of passion as a unifying element. The difficulty is that

these images, hard and violent respectively, clash aesthetically with the softer, more sensuous imagery which sets the tone of the poem; the resulting incongruity weakens the poem's harmony. A comparison of "East of Hy Breasail" and "Sailing to Byzantium" demonstrates the way in which Higgins modeled his mature art upon Yeats' art; it shows also that he still had much to learn.

In other poems Higgins attempts to achieve the intensity of passion that informs Yeats' verse that is concerned with love, sexual or Platonic. In certain poems Higgins at first establishes a comparatively soft mood and then, in the end, transforms the tone of his verse with a cry of passion that is violent and jarring. In "Night Frenzy," for instance, he portrays a woman who is forced to share her bed with a husband she does not love. She recalls the words her true love used in wooing her; but the recollection serves only to drive her to bitterness and rebellion against her lot:

> Ah, what if I wish my bedded husband
> The scarecrow's fate in a ditch,
> Maybe with dreams of you I am souring—
> A fruit grown over-rich!
> Swoop down then, O love, lash up my body;
> And in an eagle's nest,
> Far from the cold tombstones of Irrus,
> Your brood shall drain my breast.[37]

In its rhythm and emotion this stanza resembles certain of the love complaints which Douglas Hyde gathered together into his *Love Songs of Connacht*. The first four lines especially, with the homely metaphor of ripened fruit and the colloquial phrasing—the initial sigh, the rhetorical question, the characteristic grammatical construction in the third line—give the stanza the flavor of a folk poem, even though the image of the ditch may have been drawn from Yeats' verse. The final picture of lover swooping down, lashing up his beloved, and carrying her off to his eagle's nest is certainly overdone, but there is a distinct Yeatsian quality in the final images of tombstones and drained breast.[38]

In some poems Higgins exploits the theme of sexual abandon which so obsessed Yeats as an old man. In "Glory O" he
serves up an "old, very old" woman who is intent on seducing a
young man, "a fellow that's high in his mettle." Like Chaucer's Wife of Bath, she boasts of the number of husbands she
has had in her time—"maybe your grand-dad was one of the
many"—and invites the youth to "the west of the ditch,"
which, she explains, "is the best of all settles." Finally, she
sings exultantly:

> O I'm old, very old, and I don't need a wattle,
> I'm old, very old, but I'm not a dry nettle;
> So you clout the pot and I'll clout the kettle,
> Glory O, glory O! And we'll both keep in time.[39]

No doubt Higgins intended his old woman to be another
Crazy Jane, and, indeed, in her own way, she is a lively enough
old crone. She shocks the reader certainly, just as Crazy Jane
does; but she does not teach the reader anything—intellectually, emotionally, spiritually. She is Crazy Jane, but without
Crazy Jane's mythic significance. Yeats created his ribald old
lady to preach his religion of passion and endowed her with
semi-divine status by crowding her about with symbols of the
supernatural. Higgins' portrayal of an "old, very old" woman
intent on sexual love lacks any serious meaning whatsoever; as
a result, although the crone's song jars the reader into attention, in the end it becomes merely vulgar.

In "Song for the Clatter-Bones" Higgins writes of Jezebel
of the Old Testament:

> God rest that Jewy woman,
> Queen Jezebel, the bitch
> Who peeled the clothes from her shoulder-bones
> Down to her spent teats.   (*Gap of Brightness*, p. 14)

There simply is no justification for Higgins' coarse language
in the context of the poem. Higgins describes Jezebel's demise
and the manner in which her "grey bones" were found by
"Hare-foot Mike" and given by him to the poet. In the poet's

hands the bones become a plaything: "So I'll just clack; though
her ghost lacks a back / There's music in the old bones yet."
The entire episode, with all its shock and violence, is converted
into a bawdy joke.

The promise of "Repentance" is never fulfilled in Higgins'
later verse. Indeed, he had set a hard task for himself: to follow
in Yeats' steps; and, unfortunately, he had neither the intellectual background nor the creative genius to achieve his objective. What is really lacking in the poetry of *Arable Holdings*
and *The Gap of Brightness* (1940) is an informing and
unifying attitude toward life and art. Yeats had worked out his
"system" in A *Vision* and, whatever one may think of that
curious work's merit as sociology, philosophy, or religion, it
nevertheless provides an intellectual frame of reference that
gives cogency and cohesion to even his most difficult verse and
drama. Higgins had no such master design from which his
poetry might draw broader significance. His mature aesthetic is
no more than a kind of inverted romanticism: what was gentle
in his earlier poetry is now bitter; what was soft is now hard;
what was sentimental is now cynical. Nowhere, however, is his
aesthetic turnabout given intellectual justification; indeed, one
still encounters in his prose work during this period an
occasional note of primitivist obscurantism. For example, in a
letter to Colonel Theodore Roosevelt in 1937, Higgins wrote
concerning a book of stories he hoped to write: "To be serious
I felt that all such stories should contain a certain amount of
simple bog wisdom such as the gods may give me in the belief
that simple truth is hidden from the wise and prudent when
revealed unto Babes." [40] However, to do the things Higgins
attempted in his late verse, to treat of the theme of sexual
abandon or to translate such language as "bitch" and "spent
teats" into poetry, a poet must be both wise and prudent;
Yeats, of course, was equal to the task; Higgins was not.

In *Arable Holdings* and *The Gap of Brightness* Higgins
rejects the sentimental image of the Irish nation which finds
expression in his earlier verse; however, he does not succeed in

his belated attempt to gain "pure commerce with the sun"; he fails to define the promised image of Ireland, new and more vital. Perhaps what Sean O'Faolain wrote a year after Higgins' death is a true judgment: "We knew all the faults of our friend—such as that he could sometimes mistake crudity for strength or, as so many developing poets do, confuse sentiment with emotion. We knew that he was given to fits of laziness and that his taste was not yet secure. But we knew also that the essential things were secure...we knew that his ultimate achievement was as much a certainty as anything can be that depends on unpredictable human nature." [41] Nevertheless, Higgins died before he could fulfill his friends' hopes; and the principal significance of his later poetry is that it represents a conscious attempt by an Irish poet to emulate and imitate Yeats.

Higgins' poetry has additional significance, perhaps, in that it sounds a note of protest against the increasing demand for conformity in Irish literature and art. "Exhortation," for instance, embodies Higgins' cry of dissent:

> You with the grace to give, come forth and allot
> Wicklow's raw gold for smith-work and flocks
>   to raise
> Books without censors; so shall our island be
> A shrine of living mightiness and not
> An Easter Island in the western sea.[42]

The allusion to "gold for smith-work" shows clearly enough the influence of Yeats' verse here. More important, however, is Higgins' attack upon censorship. In the nineteen-thirties Higgins, like many Irish writers, came to regard the censorship law—against which Yeats had vigorously protested as a senator in the Dáil, the Irish Parliament—as a singular threat to the continued flowering of Irish letters. That it was and remains such a threat few intelligent persons, in Ireland or elsewhere, will deny.[43] However, Higgins, like many Irish writers in the nineteen-thirties and thereafter, failed to recognize that their own anti-intellectual attitude toward art represented—and still represents—an even more effective curb than censorship to the creation of a literature of worth. By praising "bog wisdom" and denouncing sophisticated learning, by resisting the encroachment of new and different ideas—those of Madame Blavatsky, for example, or more recently, those of Freud or Marx or Jung—by insisting that Irish literature be a thing undefiled, Higgins and many other Irish writers like him have helped to stifle the development of a modern Irish literature, and the development of poetry in particular, and have helped bring about a cultural isolation which could indeed make Ireland "An Easter Island in the western sea."

10

AUSTIN CLARKE:
IRELAND OF THE BLACK CHURCH

Austin Clarke, like F. R. Higgins, belongs to a third generation of Irish poets to give themselves to the cause of national literary and cultural revival. He studied Gaelic briefly as a schoolboy, enduring the scorn of "more respectable school companions"; and he sampled the old Celtic literature by reading *Eisirt*, an ancient story from which Swift is said to have borrowed the idea for Lilliput. But his real conversion came as an undergraduate student at University College, Dublin. Clarke watched spellbound as Douglas Hyde, taking all the roles himself, acted out his Irish play, *Casadh an tSúgáin* (*The Twisting of the Rope*), and he listened as Hyde explained the "aims and ideals" of the language movement. In his autobiography Clarke paraphrases Hyde's remarks: "we were all equal, all united in the Gaelic movement. There was no vulgar competition, no showing off, no twopence-halfpenny looking down on twopence. Those plain words changed me in a few seconds. The hands of our lost despised centuries were laid on me." [1] Afterwards, he studied under Thomas Mac-Donagh, whom he greatly admired and from whom he absorbed the theory of an "Irish Mode" of literature that could develop "only when English had become the language of the

Irish people, mainly of Gaelic stock," the idea upon which MacDonagh expounds in *Literature in Ireland*.

Clarke's early poetry, though different in type from that of Higgins, is markedly influenced by the same conventional conception of art and poetry that finds expression in Higgins' *Salt Air, Island Blood*, and *The Dark Breed*. In his first four volumes of verse, *The Vengeance of Fionn* (1917), *The Fires of Baal* (1921), *The Sword of the West* (1921), and *The Cattledrive in Connaught and Other Poems* (1925), Clarke attempts epic-like narrative verse. *The Vengeance of Fionn* tells the story of Diarmuid and Gráinne; *The Fires of Baal* that of the death of Moses; and the last two, segments of the Ulster cycle, which at one point Clarke planned to retell in its entirety in English verse—a project which he abandoned just as James Stephens abandoned his plan to turn the saga into English prose. In commenting on these early works in his introduction to Clarke's *Collected Poems*, Padraic Colum praises them for their adherence to the conventions of peasant realism. He points out that *The Vengeance of Fionn* "renders happily abiding aspects of the Irish countryside and the dateless doings of a pastoral people." He says of *The Sword of the West* and *The Cattledrive in Connaught* that "the landscape ... is a great part of the story and there are details of action which belong to the countryside of to-day as they belonged to the countryside of a thousand years ago." Finally, Colum adds: "And as Austin Clarke does not lose sight of the actual Irish landscape, so he does not lose sight of the actual Irish character: he does not hesitate to make great Maeve talk like an assertive Connaught woman we might have known, while MacDara, the Ulster owner of the bull, talks like the tough particularist of to-day." [2] Colum's remarks are not entirely apt. There is, indeed, an unfortunate peasant quality about much of the dialogue of *The Cattledrive in Connaught*; [3] but in many ways Clarke's "epics" resemble English narrative verse of the nineteenth century much more closely than peasant poetry. The descriptions, especially in the earlier poems, are seemingly endless; the dialogue is artificial and unconvincing. In *The Vengeance of Fionn*, for example, one encounters such lines as these:

> The faery women spinning midnight wool
> By moonlight murmured sweetly: "Who is this?
> Shadow-haunted, mortal, yet so fair?"
> "O it is Grainne, the golden, the beautiful.
> O it is she by whom the wings of air
> Are brightened as they pass"—so the faery spinning
>   wheels
> Were crooning, crooning.[4]

Such verse is hardly in the tradition of peasant realism. Yet, at the same time, it is soft and sentimental, and so acceptable when judged by the aesthetic standards of the popular movement.

Were this the extent of Clarke's achievement, his work would hardly warrant serious consideration; much more than Higgins, however, Clarke developed as an artist. Indeed, of all the "new school" of Irish writers who gained a measure of recognition in the nineteen-twenties, only Austin Clarke may be said to have made an important contribution to modern Irish verse—a contribution deliberately ignored by most Irish intellectuals and virtually unknown outside of Ireland. For one thing, he succeeded, where so many others had failed, in making effective use of elements of Gaelic prosody in English-language verse. Colum and Higgins alike tried to combine assonance with the regular end-rhyme conventions of English verse; and in so doing they invariably softened and romanticized the tone of their verse. Clarke, too, in his earlier poetry is guilty of much the same sin of excess; in "Music Healers," for instance, a revised version of a poem that first appeared in *The Sword of the West*, he has Emer address her husband, the hero of the *Táin*: " 'Cuchullin, it is I / Without lie, though I cry' " (*Poems*, p. 69). In *The Cattledrive in Connaught*, the last of his narrative poems, however, Clarke ignores end-rhyme entirely and relies on assonance for his sound pattern.

In his more mature poetry he has come to regard end-rhyme as simply one device in the overall sound pattern, to be used or not according to need.[5]

Nor are Clarke's achievements limited to matters of prosody. He soon left behind the flaccid romanticism of his youthful verse and by 1929, with the publication of *Pilgrimage*, he was producing a harsher, much more potent kind of poetry. Clarke's poem, "The Young Woman of Beare"—the Old Woman of Beare, a well-known figure in folk stories, was reputed to have had seven periods of youth before age came upon her—may well have served as a prototype for Yeats' Crazy Jane poems. The peasant woman upon whom Clarke based his characterization resembles in some ways the old woman of Gort who, Yeats tells us, served as a model for Crazy Jane. In a note to his poem, Clarke comments: "In Glendalough, that holy place, a man told me of a poor old crone who had lived in the ruined settlement below the abandoned mines. She refused even the consolations of religion, for she remembered with great anger her own times of merriment and the strong mortals she had held" (*Poems*, p. 312). In certain of his ideas and images, too, Clarke seems to anticipate Yeats. In one stanza the woman says:

> I am the dark temptation
> Men know—and shining orders
> Of clergy have condemned me.[6]

In another she tells of the pleasures she has known with men who "gallop to my house":

> Half in a dream I lie there
> Until bad thoughts have bloomed
> In flushes of desire.
> Drowsy with indulgence,
> I please a secret eye
> That opens at the Judgment.[7]

Clarke's "The Young Woman of Beare" is long and lacks the masterful control which Yeats gave to his sequence of poems about Crazy Jane. Yet Clarke's poem was published in *Pilgrim-age* in 1929, a year before the first of Yeats' Crazy Jane poems were printed in *The New Republic* and *The London Mercury*. The elder poet never befriended or encouraged Clarke, as he did Higgins; yet surely he read Clarke's verse.

After 1930 Clarke turned his talents in new directions. His *Collected Poems* were published in 1936 and in 1938 he produced a small volume of new verse, *Night and Morning*. But during the same period he tried his hand at prose, publishing in 1932 a "romance," *The Bright Temptation*, and in 1936 another, *The Singing Men at Cashel*, both of them satiric attacks against the puritanism of the Irish Catholic Church, medieval and modern, and both banned in Ireland to this day.[8] More important in his development as a poet, he began to experiment with verse drama. This experience of writing for the theater benefited Clarke in much the same way that it had Yeats decades earlier: it gave him a sharper, more precise diction and a new sense of dramatic conflict, both of which were to serve him well when he returned to the writing of poetry. He also discovered in himself—something which Yeats never really found—a remarkable capacity for comic irony. His earliest play, *The Son of Learning*, portrays the sufferings of a medieval Irish king who has in his stomach a demon who is perpetually hungry. The king is convinced that a young scholar can drive out the evil sprite. He permits himself to be bound and, then, must watch in agony as the scholar, who is also hungry, devours his dinner. In desperation the king tries to pray; but because of the hungry demon crying for food, his words become confused: "I must say an act of nutrition," he says and, then, bows his head contritely: "Through my dumpling. Through / My dumpling. Through my most suety dumpling." [9]

After Yeats' death in 1939, Clarke returned to the theater with renewed enthusiasm. With another Irish poet, Robert Farren, he founded the Dublin Verse-Speaking Society, which afterwards became the Lyric Theatre Company;[10] and for eleven years he tried to keep alive the tradition of poetic drama that Yeats had insisted upon during his long tenure as director of the Abbey Theatre but which under his successors at the Abbey gave way to a popular demand for prose dramas and for what are disparagingly termed "country kitchen" comedies.[11] In his most recent volume of verse, *Flight to Africa and Other Poems*, Clarke writes of the fire which several years ago damaged the Abbey Theatre and led to a decision to build a new, larger Abbey Theatre—a theater which, as Clarke notes, will be wholly unsuited for the production of sophisticated verse drama:

> Stage, auditorium, escaped
> That fire but not from policy,
> Planning new theatre, old mirth.
> Yeats had not dreamed an unstubbed butt,
> Ill match, would bring his curtain down.[12]

Between 1939 and 1953 Clarke wrote nine plays, including one for radio broadcast. In most of his plays, including the earliest ones, *The Son of Learning* and *The Flame* (the heroine of which, Attracta, may have provided a model for Yeats' priestess in *The Herne's Egg*),[13] Clarke makes use of stories concerning medieval Christian Ireland, a source of material largely neglected by earlier writers, in order to satirize the influence of the Catholic Church upon the morals and mores of modern Ireland.

Clarke's work suffers deliberate neglect in his own country and remains virtually unknown elsewhere. Yet it is inevitable that he should begin to attract some critical attention. George Brandon Saul in a paper prepared for the American Committee for Irish Studies in the spring of 1963 traced Clarke's development as a poet and urged that he be given scholarly consideration.[14] An Irish writer, Douglas Sealy, also has examined Clarke's work, in a long article in *The Dubliner* magazine. Sealy's criticism is at times perceptive; but in the end he surrenders to the Irish penchant for exaggeration: "By concentration on ... two subjects, freedom of thought and

freedom of instinct, he produced the richest verse of any
Irishman of our age, not excepting Yeats. The Church is on
one side, freedom on the other. And both are in Clarke's mind.
The poetry is in the struggle. They are poems of a soul in
torment. Beside this agonizing, Yeats' occultism, astrology,
pernes and gyres and phases of the moon, despite the magnificent rhetoric of the poetry, seem shallow indeed." [15] Sealy
could not resist the temptation that at one time or another
seemingly besets every Irish critic—the temptation to cut
Yeats down to size. But Austin Clarke is no Yeats; the scope of
his poetic vision is simply too narrow to warrant the comparison. Nevertheless, the corpus of his creative work—and he is
still actively pursuing his art—represents a formidable achievement that does not deserve the critical neglect that has been
its lot.

The vision of Ireland which is given expression in Clarke's
work is determined by his intense and relentless rage against
the Irish Catholic Church. In his autobiography, *Twice
Round the Black Church*, Clarke implies that his disenchantment with Roman Catholicism, like that of James Joyce, was a
gradual thing, the result of a series of personal revelations. He
cites, for example (p. 132), a very early experience, his first
confession, during which the priest led him from the confes-
sional to the vestry and forced him to kneel down in terror
until he confessed to having committed masturbation—a sin
unknown to him at the age of seven. He notes, too, that as a
schoolboy he heard the same sermon on damnation which
Joyce describes in *A Portrait of the Artist as a Young Man*; and
he records his memories of beatings and book-burnings for the
sake of discipline and decency respectively.[16] Somehow,
though, the indictment is far less convincing than Joyce's.
Much of the bitterness seems more relevant to an angry poet

judging his early years in retrospect than to Clarke as a child. Stripped of Clarke's running exegesis, at any rate, his childhood seems to have been no more traumatic than that of any middle-class child.

Clarke's break with the Church more likely was the result of an episode that occurred much later, after he had completed his university education and was serving as an assistant in English on the faculty of University College, Dublin. Clarke became infatuated with a young woman, whose black hair hung almost to her knees and who was writing a novel, "Portrait of the Artist as a Young Woman," in imitation of Joyce. The two eventually decided to be married secretly—and outside the Church—at the Dublin Registry Office. When they arrived at the office, Clarke recalls, "we were informed that we must state the church which we had attended for one month before the date of our intended union or cause to be published in a local newspaper the name of the house or houses at which we had knelt in private worship. We chose the first alternative, which seemed to us quite safe, but in a few days anxious clergymen were hurrying to the flat in which Margaret was living. We persisted, nevertheless, in our design and, at the end of nine months, my University appointment, which was a yearly one, was not renewed." [17] Clarke went to London to find work as a book reviewer. He later returned to Ireland; but his alienation from the Catholic Church and the morality it imposes on the Irish people proved to be permanent.

Clarke's anger against what he regarded as the fanatical sexual puritanism of the Church increased and intensified as he grew older. There is more than a suggestion of anticlericalism in "The Young Woman of Beare"; in "Wandering Men," a poem also included in *Pilgrimage*, Clarke treats of "Great Brigid" not as a Christian saint but as the old pagan "goddess of Fire and Poetic Inspiration"; [18] and in *The Son of Learning* he carefully holds up to ridicule the abbot and monks of the Abbey of Corc. But much more direct and violent attacks on the Church may be found in his "romances," his prose renderings of stories of medieval Ireland. In *The Sun Dances at Easter*, for example, Enda, a former monastic student, recounts to Orla, a childless wife on a pilgrimage to St. Naal's well in hopes that a miracle will make her pregnant, his own search for the miraculous. Assigned to carry several manuscripts to the famous monastery at Clonmacnoise, he had wandered about seeking a firsthand account of a real miracle, but could find none. At last he learned of a wonder still occurring regularly. Each night an angel was said to stop at a pillarstone near Cluanmore and each morning one could see the holy dew at this spot. In consequence, the grass thereabout was always green. For three nights Enda waited by the pillarstone. On the first and second he fell asleep and awoke barely in time to see the disappearing drops of dew. On the third night he tied himself to the pillarstone, but fell asleep nonetheless. He woke up suddenly when a large dewdrop splattered on his head; and then he heard the rustling of the wings and looked up. " 'And you saw the angel?' " Orla asks. " 'Lady,' " the young man answers, " 'an enormous bird rose from the pillarstone into the moonlight with a croak. I tore up handfuls of the blessed grass and raved as I wiped the bird-filth from my head.' " [19] Afterwards in the story Orla discovers that the reason so many women return from the holy well with their prayers answered is that on the eve of the saint's feast the pilgrims, male and female, join in a celebration which, in Clarke's words, "is in fact a Bacchanal in the course of which the dancing partners take off for the bushes and copulate. It is on this night that children are conceived... usually by a male other than the husband." [20]

In *The Bright Temptation* Clarke suggests that masturbation was a most serious problem in the old monasteries: "Solitude, there, was to be avoided, for it leads to that self-sin which is still so common in Ireland. Hurley and other Irish games were encouraged among the students at Cluanmore, so that they might be wearied at night, and in this way the Devil was defeated." [21] In *The Singing Men at Cashel* he carries the Irish lust for chastity to the point of absurdity. Cormac, the scholar king, approaches Gormlai, his expectant bride, on their wedding night and proposes that they forego the sexual pleasure of marriage in order to keep to "the higher way" of virtue. "St. Ammon and his wife lived in this ideal state," he says, "as we are told in the books; St. Abraham and his wife parted on their nuptial night. I could tell you of many, indeed, who shared the same bed and board and kept their marriage unconsummated. St. Jerome expresses the noble ideal in an eloquent phrase when he tells us that the wood of matrimony may be cut down by the axe of virginity." [22]

If there is a major flaw in Clarke's prose "romances," it is that too often art surrenders to polemics. There are many passages of graceful, beautiful prose and many others of remarkable comic vigor. But, at the same time, there are far too many instances in which the prose becomes annoyingly shrill and dogmatic. Too often the characters' speeches degenerate into harangues. In one of the episodes of *The Sun Dances at Easter*, for example, the lovely and sensitive Eithne, a foster daughter of Angus Óg, who has been receiving religious instruction from a young disciple of St. Patrick, addresses her teacher in language that is hardly credible:

You have told me that the intellect without grace leads to heresy, that if all were converted there would be no further need of knowledge. When the holy orders increase, when monasteries and convents grow larger and more numerous, prayer alone will suffice. Have you not said that the simple prayer of an aged woman at night is worth more spiritually than learned and lifelong labour of scholars, that, since life is short, all things are transitory and nothing matters but the salvation of the soul? Have you not said that Ireland will be renowned in the future before all other lands, that faith will prosper there and be known by the threefold sign of obedience, simplicity and total ignorance? (p. 116)

In his verse Clarke argues for intellectual freedom with greater restraint. In "Night and Morning," for example, he urges a return to the spirit of inquiry and debate that characterized the early Church, a spirit which he believes had gradually given way to a debilitating obscurantism:

> O when all Europe was astir
> With echo of learned controversy,
> . . . .
> And in the pride that we ignore,
> The holy rage of argument,
> God was made man once more.[23]

But in his prose "romances" he too frequently engages in a kind of literary ventriloquism, forcing angry sermons through the lips of characters who in the context of his narrative are wholly unsuited to the task of preaching. Not only that, but in each of these prose works Clarke's relentless condemnation of what he regards as the moral perversity of the Irish Catholic Church gradually wears upon the reader and, unless he shares the author's intense aversion to Irish Catholicism, eventually bores him. One may be amused at first to have it suggested that Irish hermits taught "wild creatures, big and small, to behave themselves" sexually or that in Irish monasteries male and female animals were carefully segregated during mating season lest they be the cause of impure thoughts among the inmates.[24] But when the same observations are repeated again and again with little variation, the novelty loses its effect. In the end, perhaps, one is more convinced that the author has little affection for Christianity, especially as it is practiced in Ireland, than that the given "romance" is successful as a work of art.

Clarke's alternative to Irish Catholic puritanism is never clearly defined. In his dramas and prose stories about medieval Ireland, pagan naturalness is idealized and Christian asceticism condemned. Occasionally, there is a hint of AEism; so, in *The Sun Dances at Easter* (p. 111), St. Patrick's disciple, Ceasan, watching Eithne speak across the water to Angus Óg, is overcome by doubts: "Were there many worlds, each with their own order of invisible things, known in dream or delirium by the different races of mankind? His mind sank under unbooked thoughts that were too great for it and that only the intelligence of Eithne could understand." There is a touch of James Stephens' anarchism, too. In his autobiography Clarke records the story of a boy and girl who follow a magic ball from the city to the seaside where they play happily on the strand. But one day, against their own inner urgings, they argue with one another, "and immediately the shore grass was hidden by a mile-long promenade." With each argument the encroachments of urban society grow more numerous—a pier, a bandstand, terraces, hotels, and at last "the sudden personification of law and order, a policeman"—until the natural beauty of the strand and the happiness of the children are both destroyed.[25] But it is the question of sex that obsesses Clarke and it is to that question he inevitably returns. He frequently invokes Freud to support his contention that a nation like Ireland, in which sexual desires are systematically suppressed, is an unhappy nation. Conversely, a happy nation is one in which sexual pleasure is encouraged and blessed. In *The Son of Learning* (p. 56) the Scholar gives the reader a brief glimpse of this ideal nation:

> I know a bay where men are binding
> The cartwheel twice upon stone with fire
> And cold. There with the tide the blowing sails
> Have dropped; and hands that rowed with blessed Brendan
> Unload the chasubles from boats; nobles
> Hurry with women, whose red lips are cut
> By the salt dark, into a lighted house
> To talk, to dance; and when fire thickens the roof,
> White clergy bless their mirth in Latin, for
> Their grace is such a couple every night
> Is married and with candles, music, they
> Prepare those innocent delights.

It is noteworthy, too, that the heroes and heroines of the "romances" find happiness only when they have overcome their sense of guilt concerning sex and are able to follow their natural inclinations.

One does not find in Clarke's work, prose or poetry, any sustained intellectual justification of his art such as Yeats provides in A Vision. One could not accuse him of accepting the ideal of "bog wisdom," yet certainly the faith that motivates him is a simple one. He is for good, by which he means freedom of the individual, particularly in matters of sex but also in matters of intellect; and he is against evil, which takes in all the restrictive elements of Irish society but especially the Catholic Church. Clarke's reference to "the black church" in the title of his autobiography is significant. Literally the phrase refers to a Protestant church on Mountjoy Street in Dublin near Clarke's childhood home. But there is another, more important meaning as well. As a child Clarke had absorbed the street-lore about the grim, forbidding structure—"that anyone who ran round the church three times after dark would meet the Devil himself on the third round." Then, one Sunday two little Protestant girls, who were visiting his family, took him in hand and led him into the dreadful structure. "I was filled with astonishment," he comments, "for the interior of the church was as bright as its exterior was dark. I had known only the dimness of old city [Catholic] churches, the rich gleam of stained-glass windows in the transept with all their saints and instruments of torture.... But through the lancets of the Black Church came a plain and temperate daylight which showed all clearly." [26] "Black Church," as Clarke knows well, is a common street term used by Dubliners when referring to Protestant churches; and, as the anecdote of the church on Mountjoy Street and numerous other episodes in Twice Round the Black Church suggest, the term says much more of those who use it than of the Protestant places of worship to which it is applied. For Clarke, the Irish Catholic Church is "the Black Church," the church that destroys the light of intellectual and emotional freedom and that condemns the Irish people to the darkness of ignorance and puritanism.

Clarke is not a poet of great vision. No doubt the time was past when Irish poets might give themselves to the task of defining what the new Ireland might become. The British garrison had long since departed; the new Ireland was an established fact, a reality. For the poet determined to dedicate his art to his native country—and Clarke has been just as determined to do this as were Yeats and Pearse and Colum—there remained little choice but to look at the reality and to comment upon it. This is precisely what Clarke has done in his more recent verse, *Ancient Lights* (1955), *Too Great a Vine* (1958), *The Horse Eaters* (1960), and *Flight to Africa and Other Poems* (1963). The result is a sustained, bitter satire against the Irish Catholic Church and the ruling middle-class establishment. James Stephens had dabbled in satiric verse; and Yeats, in his poems about Parnell and Casement and in those inspired by the Abbey Theatre controversy in the first decade of the century and the Lane affair in the second decade, showed that he, too, could write in anger. But Stephens' satires are tempered by his humor, those of Yeats by his sense of aristocratic dignity and by the rhetorical discipline of his art. Clarke's later poetry knows no such restraint. Gone are the backdrop of medieval Ireland, the neopagan ideals, the occasional burst of comic humor. What remains is a savage rage that Ireland has not known since Swift in the seventeenth century and the Gaelic bards of an earlier age, Angus na n-aor Ó Dálaigh (Angus "of the Satires" O'Daly) and Tadhg Dall Ó Huiginn (Blind Teigue O'Higgin), both of whom were supposedly murdered by enraged victims of their satires.[27]

In a note appended to *Too Great a Vine* Clarke mentions one of his great-grandfathers who wore wigs of different color and amused himself by writing satires about his fellow tradesmen and hiring ballad-singers to recite them outside the shops of the victims.[28] Like his great-grandfather, Clarke has assumed the pose of an eccentric outsider. Almost all of his later poems are critical of some facet or other of Irish life, and many of them are topical.[29] In "The Common Market 1962," for example, he ridicules the Irish government for following England's lead in seeking admission to the European Economic Community: "The lion has been skinned: / War has a new whip for tradelets. Come back / Poor Twenty-sixer. Live on lack." [30] In "Right of Way" he complains of the growth of suburbs around Dublin. He can no longer wander along the bank of a small river that runs by his home in Templeogue because "Small owners have fenced the right of way, mere inches, / No wider than their graves." [31] In *The Horse Eaters* Clarke comments upon a controversy that arose in Dublin when the loss of forty-eight horses at sea drew public attention to the fact that Ireland was exporting horses to France to be butchered. The Irish government and local animal protection groups proposed as a solution the development of local abattoirs—so that the animals would not be subjected to the cruelty of a sea voyage. In one poem Clarke cries, "Don't ship, kill, can them / First"; and in another he urges the daughters of Dublin's rich to put on their most expensive riding habits and "straddle the meat / Dogs, foreigners, eat." [32]

Perhaps the Common Market, the phenomenon of surburban growth, and the morality of slaughtering horses are subjects too prosaic for poetry; yet Clarke's dramatic sense of rhythm and language give them a vigor that is difficult to gainsay. The effect is much more impressive, though, when the poet chooses for his subject a dramatic human situation. In "Street Game" he writes of an incident he witnessed in Dublin. A Bible teacher was leading a double file of small children, Protestant orphans, along a street.

> Suddenly Catholic joylets
> Darted from alleys, raggedy cherubs that dared them:
> "Luk, feckin' bastards, swaddlers, feckin' bastards!"
> Too well they knew the words their mothers, fathers,
> Used. Silent, the foundlings marched along the street-path
> With clink of boot-heel metal. We have cast
> Them out. Devotion, come to the man-hole at last,
> Bawls: "Feckin' bastards, swaddlers, feckin' bastards!" [33]

An Irish critic would no doubt dismiss this poem as offensive and crude; and one can certainly understand that Irish Catholics might be shocked. But however crude and offensive, "Street Game" is nevertheless a very powerful poem. The contrast between the silent Protestant orphans and the unruly street children, the broken rhythms, the incisive diction, and, most of all perhaps, the quoted phrase, all contribute to an effect that is violent and disturbing. The poet's years of writing for the theater had served him well; his mature technique has proved admirably suitable for the role of apostate and iconoclast which Clarke has chosen for himself.

Clarke's satires range over a variety of subjects—the use of corporal punishment in the schools, police brutality, the government's withdrawal of a plan to provide free medical care at childbirth.[34] But just as in the plays and "romances," his real enemy is the Irish Catholic Church; and whatever the ill under scrutiny, he invariably manages to place the ultimate blame upon the Church. The ruffians of "Street Game" he labels "Catholic joylets"; in "Right of Way" he notes that the home-owners who have fenced in their bit of river bank are following the example set by "our covetous religion"; and in "Mother and Child" he suggests that the legislation providing free obstetric care was killed to pacify "Bishops mitred." In "Burial of an Irish President" he records his sense of outrage that only two Catholics, himself and the French ambassador, attended the funeral of Douglas Hyde in St. Patrick's Cathedral, the church where Swift had served as dean. The Taoiseach (prime minister), his cabinet, and other dignitaries, as Irish Catholics, could not attend a Protestant service, even the funeral service for the republic's first president.

> Costello, his Cabinet,
> In Government cars, hiding
> Around the corner, ready
> Tall hat in hand, dreading
> *Our Father* in English. Better
> Not hear that "which" for "who"
> And risk eternal doom. (*Flight to Africa*, p. 18)

The poet's attacks on Irish Catholicism are usually more direct. "Miss Marnell" relates the story of an aged woman who squanders her fortune by supporting innumerable religious appeals and who in the end is left with only "litterings, flyblown, miced / In corners, faded notes of thanksgiving, / All signed—'Yours Gratefully, In Jesus Christ' " (*Too Great a Vine*, p. 13). In "The Wounds of Fodhla" Clarke comments on the brutal beating of a Protestant evangelist by Irish Catholics:

> Evangelist,
> Headlong, upset by farm-boot, fist,
> Two teeth knocked out, a bit o' twist,
> Bible kicked in the gutter but kissed
> Next morning. Bench did not insist
>   Too much on detail:
>   "Case dismissed"
>   Angelus rang.
>   "Next on the list." (*Flight to Africa*, p. 19)

In a poem entitled "Pilgrimage" he attacks the annual, organized excursions which bring many thousands of Irishmen to the shrine at Lourdes where, Clarke tells us, they purchase trifles at stalls and shops and try "To make a holiday of hope, / Then, stare at stretcher, limbs that grope" (*Too Great a Vine*, p. 24).

Clarke also rages against sexual puritanism, just as he had done in his prose stories and dramas. His poem, "Marriage," satirizes the system of rhythm advocated by the Church for Catholic couples: "Night school / Of love where all, who learn to cheat, grow pale / With guilty hope at every change of moon!" (*Ancient Lights*, p. 7). Another, "Living on Sin," suggests that the "hasty sin" of young couples "against a wall or crick-necked / In car" benefits only the religious orders of nuns that operate orphanages: "God-fearing State / Provides three pounds a week, our conscience money, / For every infant severed from the breast" (*Flight to Africa*, p. 45). In what is certainly the most savage poem in his canon, "Precautions,"

Clarke comments on a proposal made by several Catholic scholars, all of them priests, that missionary nuns be given contraceptive pills, so that if they are raped by Africans they will not become pregnant. Noting that such pills must be taken two hours before intercourse to be effective, Clarke asks rhetorically: "How will they know dread time or place / That leaves the soul still full of grace?" Then, he recommends that instead raped nuns "use / Syringe or douche away abuse, / Without a sin, trusting in God" (*Flight to Africa*, p. 24).

It may be argued that in "Precautions" Clarke has carried his hatred too far, that such a poem will repel even a sympathetic reader. Perhaps that is so. Yet much the same charge might be made against Swift for his account of Gulliver's first contact with the *yahoos* in the land of the *Houyhnhnms*. "They had no tails," says Gulliver, "nor any hair at all on the buttocks, except about the anus; which, I presume, nature had placed there to defend them as they sat on the ground. . . . The females were not so large as the males; they had long lank hair on their heads, and only a sort of down on the rest of their bodies, except about the anus, and pudenda. Their dugs hung between their fore-feet, and often reached almost to the ground as they walked." Then, a few lines later, the reader finds Gulliver, his back to a tree, defending himself against these creatures; and some of the *yahoos* leap into the tree and begin "to discharge their excrements" on Gulliver's head. Both Swift's prose and Clarke's poem offend our sense of decorum. But no doubt that is precisely what each of them intended; for the purpose of such satire is not to please men but to castigate them.

Clarke maintains that his comments on Irish life are accurate and just; and he can produce newspaper clippings to substantiate many of the incidents about which he writes.[35] No doubt the incidents of the poems are based on facts. Thousands of Irishmen do travel to Lourdes each year. Irish Catholics do molest Protestant evangelists, though they do not always escape justice as easily as Clarke would have it. The

Irish government did cancel legislation to provide free obstetric care—and fired the Minister of Health, Dr. Noel Browne,
who proposed it—after the Irish Catholic hierarchy denounced it as socialistic. But in Clarke's verse the incidents
are invariably subjected to ironic distortion and exaggeration.
Nor could one say that the composite picture of Ireland
which emerges from his poetry is a valid one. He is motivated
by an unrestrained personal hostility. His point of view is sav-
agely one-sided. Were he a historian, one could hardly credit
him.

But, of course, Clarke is not a historian but a poet. The
accuracy or inaccuracy of his social criticism is largely irrelevant to an objective judgment of his artistic achievement. His
art is not of the first order: its range is much too narrow, its
tone at times too shrill. Nevertheless, these late satires are
impressive; and what makes them so is the passionate rage that
informs them. Ireland and Irish verse had become, as James
Stephens predicted, "bitter and angry and defensive." Clarke is
the most bitter, most angry, most defensive of the Irish poets;
and his work, more than that of any other Irish writer,
proclaims the estrangement of the Irish artist from his society.
His poetry is not profound, but it is extraordinarily intense. He
sees only one "evil"—a monstrous religious establishment that
devours the country's wealth and condemns its people to
intellectual ignorance and sexual frustration. He is obsessed
with this violent vision of a black church and a bitter nation.

The final lines of the last poem in his most recent volume,
Flight to Africa and Other Poems (p. 123) consist of nonsense
rhymes he learned as a child:

> Up the hill,
> Hurry me not;
> Down the hill,
> Worry me not;
> On the level,
> Spare me not,

> In the stable,
> Forget me not.
>
> Forget me not.

Catholic Ireland may self-consciously ignore Austin Clarke; but it is not likely to forget him.

11

CONCLUSION

All of the poets considered in this study may be regarded as national poets in that all of them sought to identify their verse with the cultural heritage of the Irish people. The content of their verse is distinctive because it has been largely drawn from the various strands of Irish tradition—the long, tormented chronicle of Ireland's history, political and religious; the vast, unique literary inheritance of the old sagas; the popular traditions, cultural and literary, of the Irish countryside. The prosody of their verse is distinctive in some ways, too, because it has been influenced—to a greater or lesser degree—by both the technical peculiarities of the old Gaelic poetry and the eccentricities of the popular verse of town and country, whether written in Gaelic or English. Other influences, non-Irish influences, may be discerned easily enough in the work of Yeats and A.E., in that of the Rising poets, and in that of Colum, Stephens, Higgins, and Clarke. Nevertheless, one may ascribe to their work—and, indeed, to modern Anglo-Irish poetry taken as a whole—that somewhat vague concoction of sound and subject matter that Thomas MacDonagh has called "the Irish Mode."

In the last analysis, however, one must go beyond the observation that one or another Irish poet exploited the national heritage of the Irish people. One must pass judgment on the individual poet's aesthetic vision. What becomes of the Irish national heritage in his verse? What has he to say of and to Irishmen and other men living in the twentieth century? What relevance has his poetry to contemporary reality? How well does it answer the perplexing problems of an age pressed in by terror and doubt? The ultimate goal of poetry perhaps must remain undefined. But Yeats surely sensed the true nature of that goal when he exalted the moment of unity when "all nature murmurs in response if but a single note be touched"; and William Carlos Williams, the American poet, no doubt had much the same aesthetic ideal in mind when in his *Autobiography* he wrote of the poet's craft that "the difficulty is to catch the evasive life of the thing, to phrase the words in such a way that stereotype will yield a moment of insight. That is where the difficulty lies. We are lucky when the underground current can be tapped and the secret spring of all our lives will send up its pure water. It seldom happens. A thousand trivialities push themselves to the front, our lying habits of speech and thought are foremost, telling us that *that* is what 'they' want to hear. Tell them something else." [1]

In the last analysis, then, in that analysis which seeks to measure the worth of art, one must ask if the artist has broken through the commonplace "trivialities" of day-to-day existence and escaped the "lying habits" of commonplace speech and thought. Of the poets included in this study, only Yeats may be said to have done so; for only Yeats fashioned a unified design of poetry, drama, and prose, a masterwork of art born of his devotion to his nation and people but free from the restrictions which nation and people invariably seek to impose. Yeats did not reject nationality. True enough, he refused to submit to the dictates of ignorance and chauvinistic prejudice; yet his reverence for Ireland and for the Irish people is manifest in every line of his poetry and every sentence of his prose. His treatment of the national heritage is always arbitrary, often strange; yet, invariably, his underlying purpose is to create a fresh and vital image from which his people and his nation might draw new spiritual strength and achieve new spiritual nobility. For Yeats the poet, nothing of Ireland's heritage was sacrosanct, but everything was sacred. He brought to Irish tradition the fires of Byzantium and from the aesthetic union of the two created a literature that "taps the secret spring of all our lives" and achieves the enduring beauty of great art. The permanence of Yeats is surely beyond question.

None of the other poets considered in this study achieves this higher form of expression. This is not to suggest that they lacked talent, nor that they are undeserving of our notice. But their achievements are of a lesser sort.

Yeats no doubt had the advantage of greater genius. But it is also significant that whereas Yeats steadfastly refused to accommodate his aesthetic ideals to the popular conception of art, each of the others is hindered and limited, in different ways and to different degrees, by the pressures of middle-class Irish society. A.E., perhaps, was more a victim of his own vision, which he could never quite comprehend and, for that reason, could never satisfactorily objectify into art; yet he was also restricted by the circumstances that forced him to devote much of his intelligence and creative energy to the prosaic concerns of politics, economics, and journalism. Pearse, MacDonagh, and Plunkett, if only because of their roles in the revolutionary movement, were not subjected to the more stultifying impositions of popular nationalism; yet none of these three succeeded in fully detaching his artistic values from the relatively petty political and moral controversies that plagued the Irish movement from its beginnings. Pearse, one might argue, condemned Parnell's tormentors and defended Synge—and so he did. But for Pearse neither Parnell nor Synge was ever more than a public cause, an issue depending for its meaning on a specific crisis in the chronology of Irish history; for Yeats, on the other hand, the two martyrs, the one a statesman, the other a great dramatist, became symbols for the ideal of passion that informs his art. MacDonagh could not make up his mind whether the poet's first duty was to serve art, or God, or society; to resolve his doubts he turned to mechanical abstraction and, having done so, discovered he could write poetry no longer.[2] Plunkett was perhaps more successful in dissociating his art from the issues of the day; yet his verse, too, is designed to serve a social end: to justify the Catholic establishment against the heretical mysticism of Yeats and A.E. by creating a superior verse founded upon the orthodox occultism of Christian symbolism. The Rising poets adhered as best they could to the ideal of "a nobler form of art"; and one may recognize in their verse moments of insight; yet ultimately, pragmatic social and political values distort their art in some measure.

In the years preceding the Easter Rising of 1916 a wave of political hysteria enveloped the Irish cultural movement and made more and more difficult the poet's struggle to maintain his artistic integrity. The campaign against *The Playboy of the Western World* and the recurrent attacks upon Yeats were symptomatic of the times. Popular nationalism demanded conformity to its own values. Padraic Colum, a poet of considerable talent, devoted his art not to the task of seeking "the secret spring of all our lives" but to that of exalting the "common furniture" of life, the very "trivialities" and "lying habits" of everyday speech and thought that for centuries the greatest poets have sought to escape.

That the literary creed of popular nationalism affected the vision of James Stephens and F. R. Higgins is clear enough. Stephens was a child of the popular nationalist movement; but he was an artist of considerable genius as well. Inevitably, he found himself unable to reconcile his aesthetic belief and his allegiance to the popular movement. In the end he rejected nationalism; but in doing so he deliberately excluded Ireland and the Irish people from his art and gave himself to the expression of esoteric philosophy. His early verse, although it shows promise of a greater achievement to come, is hemmed in by the stereotypes of the convention. His later verse, stripped of the vital metaphor that might have given it substance, is at best an abstract, ethereal thing. The impact of popular nationalism on Higgins is more typical. He praises the peasant ideal in his early verse and condemns it in his later poetry; but in both periods his obscurantist faith in the "trivialities" and "lying habits" of commonplace thought remain constant.

Austin Clarke's place in the course of modern Anglo-Irish verse is an anomalous one. The Irish literary revival may be said to have died with Yeats. The dream that so fascinated the poets of the revival, the dream of an ideal nation that would be "a light unto the Gentiles," has since faded and disappeared. Only the reality of middle-class Ireland remains. And for Clarke that reality is a nightmare of ignorance, puritanism, and hypocrisy. He has become a classic study of the artist alienated from his society. He has become not a poet of vision but a satirist filled with a bitter, savage rage.

The relationship between the literary movement and popular nationalism in Ireland is not without a note of irony. In a very real sense, the poets who created the revival—Yeats, Hyde, and A.E.—begot the cultural and political movements that led to the Easter Rebellion and, eventually, to Irish independence; for the flood of poems, plays, stories, and essays, each celebrating one or another aspect of the folk culture of the Gaeltacht or of the ancient civilization of the Celts, and the founding of the Irish Literary Society, the National Literary Society, and the Gaelic League certainly gave to the intellectuals of a younger generation a sense of pride in race and nation at a moment when "the cause that never dies" seemed ready to expire. Nationalism, however, soon became a narrow creed reflecting the values of middle-class society; and its spokesmen inflicted upon Irish verse what Yeats would call "the wrong of unshapely things," "a wrong too great to be told." They demanded that the poet respect the forms of conventional morality and taste; and they demanded that he play the role of craftsman rather than magician. But when one considers the course of Anglo-Irish during the past seventy years, he must conclude that poetry deprived of its magic, deprived of its vision, is not likely to attain the level of universal art. The Irish poets too often have addressed their people and told them "what 'they' want to hear"; they might well have served their people better had they told them, as Yeats and the poets of the eighteen-nineties tried to tell them, of dreams of an ennobled Ireland, of an "image that blossoms a rose" deep in the heart.[3]

REFERENCE MATTER

NOTES

Chapter 1

1 J. G. O'Keefe, *The Frenzy of Suibhne*, Irish Texts Society (London, 1913), p. 63. Suibhne escapes the hag only by leaping from the summit of Dun Sobairce out into the sea. The hag leaps after him but falls to her death. Then Suibhne says:

> There came then to the strand
> the devil's crew to meet her,
> and they bore away her body;
> woe to the land of Erin in which it was buried!

2 Donal O'Sullivan, in his edition of *Songs of the Irish* (Dublin, 1960), comments (p. 142): "There is not much doubt that the original Caitilín Ní Uallacháin was the heroine of a (non-extant) love song." Toward the close of the eighteenth century, William Heffernan, a blind poet of County Tipperary, used the name as a synonym for Ireland in a patriotic ballad.

3 Sean O'Casey, *Inishfallen, Fare Thee Well* (New York, 1949), pp. 238–40.

4 Rev. Michael P. O'Hickey, *Language and Nationality* (Waterford, Ireland, 1918), p. 8. Douglas Hyde, in "The Necessity for De-Anglicizing Ireland," *The Revival of Irish Literature* (London, 1894), p. 138, cites an incident that supports O'Hickey's generalizations. While waiting for a train in Sligo, he conversed in Irish with a young girl until suddenly her brother interrupted them. " 'Arrah now, Mary,' said he, with what he intended to be a most bitter sneer; 'and isn't that a credit to you!' And poor Mary—whom I had with difficulty persuaded to begin—immediately hung her head and changed into English. This is going on from Malin Head to Galway, and from Galway to Waterford, with the exception possibly of a few spots in Donegal and Kerry, where people are wiser and more national."

5 Hyde, "De-Anglicizing Ireland," p. 124. Hyde's mention of Greece recalls the traditional story of the *Fir Bolg*, "men of bags," the people of Neimhead and the sons of Pamp, who

defeated the Fomorians but were themselves scattered; they returned to Ireland much later, after a period of bondage in Greece where, according to one account, they were forced to carry bags of earth to stony places. T. F. O'Rahilly, *Early Irish History and Mythology* (Dublin, 1946), pp. 46–52, notes this popular explanation for the name *Fir Bolg*, as well as these others: that the *Fir Bolg* carried bags of clay from Ireland to Greece as protection against snakes, that they sailed to Ireland in bag-like vessels, that *Bolg* really means "breeches" rather than "bags," that *Fir Bolg* means literally "burg-builders" and is not a racial name. O'Rahilly dismisses all of these and argues that *Bolg* derives from the name of the god of lightning and thunder, Bolga.

6   Hyde, "De-Anglicizing Ireland," p. 159.

7   O'Hickey, *Language and Nationality*, p. 51.

8   Geraldine Plunkett Dillon, Joseph Plunkett's sister, told me that neither Pearse nor her brother mastered Irish as a spoken language; MacDonagh, she said, who had a gift for learning "foreign" languages, was a fluent Gaelic speaker.

9   W. B. Yeats, *Autobiographies* (London, 1956), p. 199.

10 Thomas Davis, Gavin Duffy, and the other members of the "Young Ireland Party" who contributed to the *Nation*, quite clearly regarded literature as a vehicle for propaganda, and Gaelic culture as a means to the end of political liberty. Yeats recognized that the new movement would have to break with the tradition of "Young Ireland" if it was to create a national literature worthy of the name.

11 Una Ellis-Fermor, *The Irish Dramatic Movement* (London, 1919), p. 35.

12 Richard Ellmann, *James Joyce* (New York, 1959), p. 68.

13 In 1960 Ireland and England reached an agreement on the disposition of the pictures. Half the collection is now housed in the Municipal Gallery, Dublin; the other half in London.

14 Blanche Mary Kelly, *The Voice of Ireland* (New York, 1952), p. viii.

15 *Nationality*, Dublin, January 29, 1916.

16 P. J. Gannon, review of Joseph Hone, *W. B. Yeats*, in *Studies*, XXXII (March, 1943), 130.

17 W. B. Yeats, *Collected Poems* (New York, 1959), p. 204. (Hereafter referred to as *Poems*.)

18 Mary Colum, *Life and the Dream* (Garden City, 1948), pp.

105–6, mentions the vogue at the turn of the century for men to wear Gaelic kilts, especially to the Abbey Theatre. Several writers, she says, "affected them," including Darrell Figgis, Thomas MacDonagh, and the Pearse brothers, Padraic and William.

19 Yeats, *Poems*, p. 109.

20 Ethna Carbery's poetry covers much the same ground as Colum's, but her work lacks distinction.

21 John V. Kelleher, "Matthew Arnold and the Celtic Revival," *Perspectives of Criticism*, ed. Harry Levin (Cambridge, Massachusetts, 1950), p. 213.

22 Desmond Ryan, *The Sword of Light* (London, 1939), p. 239, lists other contributors to the Gaelic literature: Canon Peter O'Leary, Pádraic, Ó Conaire, "An Seabhac," Mícheál Breathnach, and Father P. S. Dinneen.

23 Ifan Kyle Fletcher, Jack Reading, and Sybil Rosenfeld, eds., *The Transactions of the International Conference on Theatre History* (London, 1957), p. 8. An Cómhar Drámuíochta (The Gaelic Dramatic Union), established in 1925 with a subsidy from the Irish Free State, received little public support and finally merged with the Abbey Theatre.

24 Thomas MacDonagh, *Literature in Ireland* (London, 1917), p. 58.

25 Y. O., review of David Morton's *The Renaissance of Irish Poetry*, in *The Irish Statesman*, XIII (December 28, 1929), 337–38. Y. O. was one of several pseudonyms used by George Russell in his newspaper writing.

26 Padraic Colum, *Three Plays: The Fiddler's House, The Land, Thomas Muskerry* (New York, 1925), p. 106.

27 Padraic Colum, *Collected Poems* (New York, 1953), p. 120 (title: "A Poor Scholar of the 'Forties"); *The Poet's Circuits* (London, 1960), p. 27 (title: "Poor Scholar").

28 F. R. Higgins, *The Gap of Brightness* (New York, 1940), p. 31.

29 Kathleen Hoagland, ed., *1000 Years of Irish Poetry* (New York, 1947), p. 730.

30 *The Bell*, I (April, 1940), 5.

31 Both Frank O'Connor and Mary Lavin attempted verse early in their careers. O'Connor has produced some remarkable translations of Gaelic poetry, but, for the most part, he devotes himself to writing fiction; Miss Lavin's early poems, published in *The Bell*, have most of the characteristics of the convention.

Chapter 2

1   Thomas Flanagan, *The Irish Novelists, 1800–1850* (New York, 1959), p. 7.

2   William J. O'Neill Daunt, *Personal Recollections of the Late Daniel O'Connell, M.P.* (London, 1848), I, 14–15. Flanagan, *Irish Novelists*, p. 45, quotes this passage and comments: "We have a deeper sense now of the interdependence of language and culture. We can appreciate that much which was rich and various, much which was uniquely Irish perished when Gaelic fell into disuse."

3   Daunt, *Daniel O'Connell*, II, 22–23, records the speech which O'Connell delivered after he put on his robes of office. A fuller excerpt is as follows: "I am now the guardian of your rights; it shall be my duty to promote and advance the interests of your city, to encourage morality, and discountenance vice. In doing so, one great means shall be, to use my utmost endeavours for the spread of teetotalism. Oh! give me my honest teetotaler." The whole speech is strongly Victorian in tone.

4   Quoted by André Malraux, *The Metamorphosis of the Gods*, trans. Stuart Gilbert (London, 1960), p. 2.

5   Yeats, *Poems*, p. 343.

6   Much of the information in this chapter concerning Irish political history has been drawn from Edmund Curtis, *A History of Ireland*, sixth ed. (London, 1961). More valuable for the pre-Norman period in Ireland are Eoin MacNeill's *Phases of Irish History* (Dublin, 1919) and Alice Stopford Green's *History of the Irish State to 1014* (London, 1925).

7   Padraic Colum, *A Treasury of Irish Folklore* (New York, 1954), pp. 222, 228.

8   David Morton, *The Renaissance of Irish Poetry: 1880–1930* (New York, 1929), p. 162.

9   Kelleher, "Matthew Arnold and the Celtic Revival," p. 204.

10 Colum, *Irish Folklore*, p. 577.

11 O'Neill and O'Donnell returned to their estates after the war, but soon found their position intolerable. In 1607 they abandoned Ireland with 97 other lords and went to Rome. In Irish tradition their departure is known as "the Flight of the Earls."

12 Padraic Colum, *The Legend of Saint Columba* (New York, 1935), pp. 106–17. In Yeats' play, *The King's Threshold, Collected Plays* (New York, 1953), p. 83, Seanchan uses essentially

the same argument to defend the right of the poets to a place at the council table.

13 James Carney, "The Impact of Christianity," *Early Irish Society,* ed. Myles Dillon (Dublin, 1959), p. 75.

14 Curtis, *History of Ireland,* p. 223.

15 Even today Bishop Walsh of Dublin and Bishop Croke of Cashel are remembered as "the patriot archbishops."

16 The principal source for scholarly translations of Old Irish literature is the series published by the Irish Texts Society. Myles Dillon, *Early Irish Literature* (Chicago, 1948), presents an excellent sampling of the best of the old literature. Tom Peete Cross, *Harper and Bard* (Chicago, 1931), provides imaginative (but inaccurate) renderings of tales from the three major cycles.

17 Aodh De Blácam, *Gaelic Literature Surveyed* (Dublin and Belfast, n.d.), p. 9.

18 Robert Graves, *The White Goddess* (New York, 1959), p. 188. Marie-Louise Sjoestedt, *Gods and Heroes of the Celts,* trans. Myles Dillon (London, 1949), pp. 24–37, discusses the mother-goddesses of Ireland.

19 Dillon, *Early Irish Literature,* p. 66.

20 *Ibid.,* p. 2. Dillon comments: "This literary form appears first in ancient India, and Oldenberg [Hermann Oldenberg, *Die Literatur des alten Indien* (Stuttgart, 1903)] has suggested that it is the earliest form of literature known to Indo-Europeans."

21 *The Ancient Irish Epic Tale Táin Bó Cúalnge,* trans. Joseph Dunn (London, 1914), pp. 190–91.

22 The account of Cú Chulainn's physical beauty (*Ibid.,* pp. 195–96) is as curious as that of his distortion: "Three heads of hair he wore; brown at the skin, blood-red in the middle, a golden yellow crown what thatched it [sic]. Beautiful was the arrangement of the hair, with three coils of hair wound round the nape of his neck, so that like a strand of thread of gold was each thread-like, loose-flowing, deep-golden, magnificent, long-tressed, splendid, beauteous-hued hair as it fell down over his shoulders. A hundred bright-purple windings of gold-flaming red gold at his neck. A hundred salmon-coloured (?) cords strung with carbuncles as a covering round his head. Four spots on either of his two cheeks, even a yellow spot, and a green spot, and a blue spot, and a purple spot. Seven jewels of the eyes brilliance was either of his kingly eyes. Seven toes to either of his two feet. Seven fingers to either of his two hands, with the clutch of

hawk's claw, with grip of hedgehog's talon in every separate one of them."

23 Sir James G. Frazer observes in *The Golden Bough* that the imposition of taboos on kings and priests is a practice found in many ancient societies.

24 Dillon, *Early Irish Literature*, pp. 42–43.

25 Padraic H. Pearse, *Songs of the Irish Rebels, Collected Works* (Dublin, 1924), p. 158.

26 David Greene, "Táin Bó Cúalnge," *Irish Sagas*, ed. Myles Dillon (Dublin, 1959), pp. 105–6.

27 *Ibid.*, pp. 95–96. Greene notes that the bull of Cooley is variously referred to as "*an Donn Cúalnge* and *an Dubh Cúalnge*; the name Donn is also that of the Old Irish god of the dead. Now, the word *bó* in Irish means only 'cow', but the corresponding word in other Indo-European languages—Sanskrit, for instance —can mean either 'bull' or 'cow.' " Greene adds: "It is plain that these [i.e., the dark bull and the white bull] are no mere animals, but heroic and god-like creatures; we have memories here, however altered, of a cult of bull-gods, such as is well known from the ancient civilisations of the Mediterranean."

28 Douglas Hyde, *Love Songs of Connacht* (Dublin, 1905), p. 5.

29 Morton, *Irish Poetry*, p. 240.

30 MacDonagh, *Literature in Ireland*, pp. 117–18.

31 Myles Dillon sets forth parallels between Old Irish and Old Indian literatures in *Archaism of Irish Tradition* (London, 1947).

32 James Stephens, "The Outlook for Literature with Special Reference to Ireland," *Century Magazine*, CIV (October, 1922), 813.

Chapter 3

1 W. B. Yeats, *Reveries over Childhood and Youth* (Churchtown, Dundrum, 1915), p. 81. According to Tadhg Kilgannon, *Sligo and Its Surroundings* (Sligo, 1932), p. 179, the island is small— "3 roods and 29 perches"—but is certainly adequate for a cabin, nine bean rows, and some hives for honeybees.

2 *Reveries*, pp. 88–89.

3 *Poems*, pp. 21–24. "The Ballad of Moll Magee" sentimentalizes the traditional Irish theme of the unfortunates who must walk

the roads for want of a home of their own. "The Ballad of Father O'Hart" celebrates a local Sligo story. Kilgannon, in *Sligo*, p. 249, notes that the Rt. Rev. John O'Hart, Bishop of Achonry, in an attempt to save the family estate from confiscation in penal days, had it transferred to a Protestant friend, "one Lawrence Bettridge." As soon as he had legal possession, Bettridge turned the O'Harts out. Catholics often transferred land to Protestant friends during the penal period, and, according to local belief, Bettridge's treachery was the only instance in which such a trust was violated in Sligo. The story clarifies the second stanza of Yeats' poem.

4   "Under Ben Bulben" (1939), *Poems*, p. 341.
5   Herbert Howarth, *The Irish Writers: 1880–1940* (London, 1958), p. 4.
6   Richard Ellmann, *Yeats: The Man and the Masks* (New York, 1948), p. 44.
7   *The Variorum Edition of the Poems of W. B. Yeats*, ed. Peter Allt and Russell K. Alspach (New York, 1957), p. 687—henceforth cited as *Var.*
8   W. B. Yeats, *The Trembling of the Veil* (London, 1922), p. 232. Oscar Wilde told Yeats that "if you carve a Cerberus upon an emerald and put it in the oil of a lamp and carry it into a room where your enemy is, two heads will come upon his shoulders and all three devour one another."
9   *Ibid.*, pp. 94–95.
10 *Ibid.*, pp. 101–2.
11 Padraic Pearse, *Political Writings and Speeches* in *Collected Works*, pp. 300–1, writes of the play: "When I was a child I believed that there was actually a woman called Erin, and had Mr. Yeats' Kathleen Ni Houlihan been written then and I had seen it, I should have taken it not as an allegory, but as a representation of a thing that might happen any day in any house."
12 Howarth, *Irish Writers*, p. 127.
13 *The Trembling of the Veil*, p. 211.
14 Howarth, *Irish Writers*, p. 11.
15 *Ibid.*, p. 111.
16 W. B. Yeats, *Estrangement* (Dublin, 1926), p. 29.
17 "The Municipal Gallery Revisited" (1937), *Poems*, p. 316.
18 *Var.*, p. 738. The last of four stanzas is quoted. The poem first appeared in *United Ireland*, October 10, 1891, and later was reprinted in *The Irish Weekly Independent*, May 20, 1893.

19 "On Those that Hated 'The Playboy of the Western World,'"
    Poems, p. 109, and "At the Abbey Theatre," *Poems*, p. 94.
    The first of these poems appeared in *The Irish Review*, December, 1911; the second in the same journal in December, 1912.

20 "To a Wealthy Man Who Promised a Second Subscription to
    the Dublin Municipal Gallery if it Were Proved the People
    Wanted Pictures," *Poems*, pp. 105–6. The poem first appeared
    in *The Irish Times*, January 11, 1913.

21 Sir Roger Casement was knighted by King George V in 1905 for
    his report on Belgian exploitation of Africans in the Congo; a
    decade later he was executed in Pentonville Prison, England,
    for the part he played in the Irish Easter Rising of 1916. The
    "black diaries"—supposedly written by Casement over a period
    of years—were documents used by British officials to insinuate
    a charge of homosexuality against him during his trial and in
    the period between the trial and his death. Most reputable
    scholars agree that the British government undertook a system-
    atic campaign to defame Casement, alienate sympathy for him,
    and thereby make a reprieve impossible. Shortly before the
    execution, Sir Ernly Blackwell, legal advisor to the Home Office,
    submitted to the British cabinet the following memorandum:
    "So far as I can judge, it would be far wiser from every point of
    view to allow the law to take its course and, by judicious means,
    to use these diaries to prevent Casement from achieving mar-
    tyrdom." The "diaries" or excerpts from them were shown
    privately to many influential persons—to King George V, for
    example, to the American Ambassador, and to Mr. Ben Allen,
    a correspondent for the Associated Press, who rejected an offer of
    exclusive publication rights when British officials refused to
    permit him to confront Casement with the manuscripts. British
    governmental duplicity in using the materials for political ends
    is difficult to gainsay. But it also has been charged that the
    "diaries" themselves were forged; and the question of their
    authenticity has yet to be answered satisfactorily. In 1959 the
    Home Office made the "diaries" available to scholars; but it
    has refused to submit the materials to examination by impartial
    technical experts to determine if they were written by Casement.
    Roger McHugh, "Casement: The Public Record Office Manu-
    scripts," *Threshold*, 1 (Spring-Summer, 1960), 28–57, provides
    a disturbing account of the numerous flaws in the official British
    position that the documents are authentic.

22 Joseph Hone, *W. B. Yeats: 1865–1939* (New York, 1943), p.
    481.

23 *Ibid.*, p. 401.
24 "To Ireland in the Coming Times" (1892), *Poems*, p. 50.
25 "The Fascination of What's Difficult" (1910), *Ibid.*, p. 91.
26 "Among School Children" (1927), *Ibid.*, p. 213.
27 "The Black Tower" (1939), *Ibid.*, p. 341.
28 Miss Olive Pollexfen Jackson and Mrs. Mabel Jackson Stewart, cousins of Yeats, told me in Sligo in August, 1960, that the poet was always reserved in his meetings with them. Their mother and the poet's mother were sisters, the youngest and eldest, respectively, in the Pollexfen family. By the time Miss Jackson and Mrs. Stewart came of age, the Abbey Theatre had been established and Yeats already was a literary figure of standing. The poet was a close associate of their father—both served together in the Senate of the Irish Free State—and the girls met him frequently when he visited their home in Sligo. Mrs. Stewart recalled that when they stayed in Dublin, Yeats would send them complimentary passes if ticket sales were slow. On one occasion, she said, she attended a play with Lily Yeats, the poet's sister, and afterwards the two women went to the Abbey's "Green Room," where celebrities gathered after a performance. Yeats himself entered and walked over to the spot where Lily and Mrs. Stewart were standing. Then, ignoring his cousin's presence, he asked Lily, "Is there anyone here I should know?" Both Miss Jackson and Mrs. Stewart felt greater affection for Jack Yeats than for W. B. Miss Jackson had a beautiful self-portrait given her by the artist; the only picture of the poet she had was a framed postcard. Both professed admiration for Yeats' poetry.
29 *W. B. Yeats: Letters to Katherine Tynan*, ed. Roger McHugh (New York, 1953), p. 149. On December 12, 1913, Yeats wrote to Katherine Tynan concerning her use of extracts from his letters in her autobiographical *Twenty-five Years* (1913): "No, you were not very indiscreet, though you were a little. There was a sentence about X that I would have crossed out but nothing that really mattered. However, if you are going to publish any more letters of mine, please let me see them first. I may even, in defiance of all right conduct, improve them."
30 "The Statues" (1939), *Poems*, p. 322.
31 Howarth, *Irish Writers*, p. 142.
32 Ellmann, *Yeats*, p. 142.
33 *Ibid.*, pp. 113–14.
34 W. B. Yeats, *If I Were Four-and-Twenty* (Dublin, 1940), p. 1.
35 "Fragments" (1931), *Poems*, p. 211. Hone, *Yeats,* p. 387,

notes that the purpose of "Leda and the Swan" was to show the cultural barrenness that followed the demagogic movement of Hobbes, the Encyclopedists, and the French Revolution.

36 Hone, in *Yeats*, p. 450, quotes from a letter Yeats wrote to an imaginary schoolmaster concerning the education of his son, Michael: "Do not teach him one word of Latin. The Roman people were the classic decadence, their literature form without matter. They destroyed Milton, the French seventeenth and our eighteenth century."

37 *Poems*, p. 106. In *Dramatis Personae, 1896–1902* (Edinburgh, 1936), pp. 49–50, Yeats relates materialism to English culture: "To transmute the anti-English passion into a passion of hatred against the vulgarity and materialism whereon England has founded her worst life and the whole life that she sends us, has always been a dream of mine."

38 *The Trembling of the Veil*, p. 38.

39 "Tom O'Roughley" (1918), *Poems*, p. 139.

40 P. W. Joyce, *The Origin and History of Irish Names of Places*, First Series (Dublin, 1870), pp. 374–75, explains that *Cruachan* is the diminutive of *cruach*, which means, literally, a rick or stack. The word is applied to many mountains in Ireland. Yeats is probably referring to *Cruachan-Bri-Eile*, the capital of Connacht in ancient times. T. F. O'Rahilly comments in *Early Irish History and Mythology* (pp. 525–26) that the word *goba* means "smith" and is the root word for the name of the divinity, Goibniu, the Otherworld artificer in Celtic mythology. Goibniu also is Lord of the Otherworld Feast: "Those who partook of his feast were preserved from age and decay, i.e., they became immortal." In Yeats' allusion the traditional "Goban's wine" is vulgarized to Goban's beer.

41 Hone, *Yeats*, p. 424, mentions the letter to Mrs. Yeats; the letter to Mrs. Shakespear is given in *The Letters of W. B. Yeats*, ed. Allan Wade (London, 1954), pp. 785–86.

42 "Ribh Denounces Patrick" (1934), *Poems*, p. 283. In his preface to *A Full Moon in March* (London, 1935), included in *Var.*, p. 857, Yeats' remarks: "The hermit Ribh in 'Supernatural Songs' is an imaginary critic of St. Patrick. His Christianity, come perhaps from Egypt like much early Irish Christianity, echoes pre-Christian thought." In a note included in *The King of the Great Clock Tower*, (Dublin, 1934), reprinted in *Var.*, pp. 837–38, he writes of a conversation which he had with another Irish poet concerning the early Irish Church: "I said

that for the moment I associated early Christian Ireland with India; Shri Purohet Swami, protected during his pilgrimage to a remote Himalyan shrine by a strange great dog that disappeared when danger was past, might have been that blessed Cellach who sang upon his deathbed of bird and beast; Bagwan Shri Hamsa's pilgrimage to Mount Kaílás, the legendary Meru, and to lake Manas Sarowa, suggested pilgrimages to Croagh Patrick and Lough Derg. . . . Saint Patrick must have found in Ireland, for he was not its first missionary, men whose Christianity had come from Egypt, and retained characteristics of older faiths that have become so important to our invention. Perhaps some man young enough for so great a task might discover there men and women he could honour—to adapt the words of Goethe —by conferring their names upon his own thoughts; perhaps I myself had made a beginning.

"While the book was passing through the press I wrote the poems for that old hermit Ribh. I did not explain the poems in *The King of the Great Clock Tower*, nor will I explain these. I would consider Ribh, were it not for his ideas about the Trinity, an orthodox man."

43   "Crazy Jane on the Day of Judgment," *Poems*, p. 252.
44   Denis Saurat, *Literature and Occult Tradition* (London, 1930), pp. 71–72, provides an excellent summary of Madame Blavatsky's system.
45   Ellmann, *Yeats*, p. 177.
46   From a recording played in connection with the Yeats' Society International Summer School in Sligo, August, 1960.
47   Yeats wrote a commentary on these songs for *Poetry* in 1934 explaining their origin and his decision to make them obscure so "that no party might sing them." In any event, neither version could have been sung to the traditional tune. Hone (*Yeats*, p. 466) tried to justify Yeats' brief association with the Blue Shirts and argues that the movement "appealed to the more conservative and orderly sections of the population." In fact the movement was demagogic and drew its strength from the strong-arm methods of hoodlum gangs. A plot to seize the government failed when De Valera posted heavily armed troops at key points in Dublin and the Blue Shirts backed down.
48   According to Hone (*Yeats*, p. 311), Yeats refused a tentative offer of a knighthood. Afterwards he wrote to his sister: "I do not wish anyone to say of me, 'only for a ribbon he left us.' "
49   W. B. Yeats, *The Bounty of Sweden* (Dublin, 1925), p. 8.

50   The cornucopia is associated with Amalthaea, whom Robert
     Graves (in *The White Goddess*, pp. 203, 392) identifies as the
     mother of Dionysus and perhaps of his follower, Pan. Sir James
     G. Frazer notes in *The Golden Bough* (p. 109) that "Apollo's
     prophetess ate the sacred laurel and was fumigated with it be-
     fore she prophesied."

51   *Dramatis Personae*, pp. 7-9.

52   W. B. Yeats, *The Death of Synge* (Dublin, 1928), pp. 3-5.

53   "Meditations in Time of Civil War" (1923), *Poems*, p. 198.

54   *The Collected Plays of W. B. Yeats*, p. 280 (hereafter cited as
     Plays).

55   "Meditations in Time of Civil War," *Poems*, p. 198.

56   W. B. Yeats, *On the Boiler* (Dublin, 1939), p. 10.

57   "The O'Rahilly" (1938), *Poems*, pp. 305-6.

58   *Plays*, p. 185. This song echoes in tone and movement the poem,
     "Easter 1916," which also is concerned with the heroic ideal.
     It should also be compared with "Under Ben Bulben," III,
     Poems, p. 342.

59   "I Am of Ireland" (1932), *Poems*, pp. 262-63. Yeats,
     Poems, p. 456, notes that he developed the poem from "an Irish
     fourteenth century dance song."

     Chapter 4

1   In 1902 in a letter to Lady Gregory, *The Letters of W. B. Yeats*
     (hereafter cited as *Letters*), p. 386, Yeats wrote: "These last
     few days I have been working particularly hard on the history
     of Allegory. I had no sooner begun reading at the British Mu-
     seum after my return when it flashed upon me that the Com-
     ing of Allegory coincided with the rise of the Middle Class. That
     it was the first effect on literature of the earnest spirit which
     afterwards created Puritanism."

2   William York Tindall, *The Literary Symbol* (Bloomington,
     1955), pp. 10, 31.

3   The composition of "Leda and the Swan" illustrates this move-
     ment from the objective world of experience to the subjective
     world of visionary art. Joseph Hone (*Yeats*, p. 387) observes that
     Yeats meant to write a political poem using the incident of Leda
     and the Swan as metaphor; "but as he wrote, bird and lady took
     such possession of the scene that all politics went out of it." A.

Norman Jeffares, *W. B. Yeats: Man and Poet* (London, 1949), p. 236, notes that the early drafts of "Sailing to Byzantium" are concerned with Ireland and that Yeats substituted the more exotic Byzantium while working on the poem.

4 Malraux, *Metamorphosis of the Gods*, p. 1.
5 *Ibid.*, pp. 6–7.
6 W. B. Yeats, *A Vision* (London, 1937), p. 27.
7 *Ibid.*, p. 8.
8 *Yeats: The Man and the Masks*, p. 162.
9 *Poems*, p. 78. "Adam's Curse" first appeared in *The Monthly Review*, December, 1902. In certain of the lines Yeats moves close to the idiom of everyday speech:

> Better go down upon your marrow-bones
> And scrub a kitchen pavement, or break stones
> Like an old pauper, in all kinds of weather.

10 *The Lonely Tower* (London, 1950), p. 110.
11 *The Identity of Yeats* (London, 1954), p. 171.
12 It should be noted that the image of Helen of Troy belongs also to the popular tradition of Irish poetry. It occurs, for example, in Douglas Hyde's translations, *The Love Songs of Connacht*, as well as in English verse of the peasantry.
13 *Poems*, p. 33. Thomas MacDonagh, *Literature in Ireland*, p. 50, criticizes Yeats for distorting Gaelic pronunciation and spelling in his verse through ignorance. Yeats, *Var.*, pp. 840–41, discusses the problem of pronunciation and spelling. Of possible mispronunciations of Gaelic words in his own poetry he writes: "I had hardly considered the question seriously."
14 *Language and Myth*, trans. Susanne K. Langer (New York, 1946), p. 33.
15 Letter to A.E., July, 1900, quoted from the Hone papers by Henn, *The Lonely Tower*, p. 122.
16 *Plays*, pp. 421–22. P. W. Joyce, *Irish Names of Places*, First Series, p. 159, notes that Slieve Fuadh, in County Armagh, was named for the Milesian chieftain Fuad, who was slain there during the pursuit of the defeated Tuatha Dé Danann.
17 Cassirer, *Language and Myth*, pp. 35–36.
18 *The Resurrection* is helpful in defining Yeats' conception of the myth-god and has for the reader the advantage of dealing with traditional Christian material. In essence the play is an attempt to express the nature of divinity. When the risen Christ enters the antechamber, the Syrian and Hebrew guards are gripped by

fear, but the Greek, who has regarded Christ alive and dead as a phantom, an illusion, remains calm and skeptical; he approaches the apparition and touches it:

> *The Greek.* . . . The heart of the phantom is beating!
> The heart of the phantom is beating!

Christ then passes into the inner chamber and the reader is told that Thomas has put his hand into the great wound in Christ's side. The Greek then exclaims: "O Athens, Alexandria, Rome, something has come to destroy you. The heart of the phantom is beating. Man has begun to die" (*Plays,* pp. 372–73). What we have here is a rejection of the conventional idealization of Christ risen in spiritual glory, an idealization which Yeats, like the Greek guard, would dismiss as a phantom, and the substitution of a Christ who reflects more accurately man's own nature and who resembles more closely the archetypal representations of divinity to be found in mythology. Yeats' Christ is not the abstraction of a prayer book; he is a physical experience. The point is stressed by repetition; the Greek feels the beat of Christ's heart, then Thomas places his hand in Christ's side. Here is a god with a gaping wound and a beating heart, a god who can embody flesh as well as spirit, terror as well as love, evil as well as good. The Dionysian revels in the street outside the chamber are not inappropriate, for Christ's coming, like that of the insane Dionysus, means turmoil and terror; it signals the end of one cycle, the beginning of another. In the Musicians' Song that ends the play we are told that the new god has emerged from the depths of man's own being: "Whatever flames upon the night / Man's own resinous heart has fed."

19 Cassirer, *Language and Myth,* p. 92.
20 "The Man and the Echo" (1939), *Poems,* p. 337.
21 Hone, *Yeats,* pp. 318–19.
22 "The O'Rahilly" (1938), *Poems,* p. 305.
23 *Poems,* p. 224.
24 In "At Galway Races" (1909), *Poems,* p. 95, the "horsemen" are contrasted favorably with "the merchant and the clerk" who breathe "on the world with timid breath." In "In Memory of Major Robert Gregory" (1918), *Poems,* p. 132, Lady Gregory's son is identified as a distinguished horseman; and in "On a Political Prisoner" (1920), *Poems,* p. 181, Con Markievicz is said to have ridden "Under Ben Bulben to the meet" in the years "before her mind / Became a bitter, an abstract thing." The

image of horseman is associated with Irish mythology in "Under Ben Bulben, I" (1939), *Poems*, p. 341, where Yeats invokes the horsemen and women whom

> Complexion and form prove superhuman,
> That pale, long-visaged company
> That air in immortality
> Completeness of their passions won;
> Now they ride the wintry dawn
> Where Ben Bulben sets the scene.

25 "The Two Trees (1892), *Poems*, pp. 47–48; "Cuchulain Comforted" (1939), *Poems*, pp. 339–40.

26 Frieda Fordham, *An Introduction to Jung's Psychology* (Bungay, Suffolk, 1939), p. 81, says that alchemy was taken seriously by such men as Thomas Aquinas and Isaac Newton and that it has "important connexions both with medieval philosophy and with religion. The alchemist is understood as one who tries to make gold, and certainly there were many of this type, but there were equally many others—high-minded and intelligent men—for whom the chemical processes they followed were largely symbolic, and the end in view was not the creation of gold, but discovery of the philosopher's stone. This mysterious stone—containing the whole secret of the 'art'—was on the one hand a product of their work and on the other a gift from God without which alchemy could not exist; it both held a spirit and was considered to be a spirit itself. In searching for it the alchemist was endeavouring to liberate the spirit he believed to be concealed in matter, and in so doing preserved the bridge to nature—i.e., the unconscious psyche—which the Church, with its emphasis on sinfulness, was steadily destroying." Yeats was not familiar with Jung and perhaps not with medieval alchemy at the time of the composition of "Easter 1916"; yet he was certainly aware of the significance of magic stones in various occult traditions. The magical stone of the Tuatha Dé Danann was one of the four treasures they brought with them to Ireland. Yeats uses the stone image as a symbol of immortality and permanence in "The Grey Rock" (*Poems*, pp. 101–4).

27 "The Black Tower" (1939), *Poems*, p. 340.

28 Hone, *Yeats*, p. 498. Pearse hung a picture of Cú Chulainn over the inside entranceway of St. Enda's School to inspire his students. Years after the Rising and after the composition of "Easter 1916" the Irish government commissioned a statue of

Cú Chulainn, tied to a pillar-stone and dying, as a monument to the leaders of the rebellion. The statue may be seen in the General Post Office, Dublin, which in 1916 served as head-quarters for the rebels.

29 "The Statues" (1939), *Poems*, p. 323.

30 "Sixteen Dead Men" (1920), *Poems*, p. 180.

31 The Count Goblet D'Alviella, *The Migration of Symbols* (New York, 1956), pp. 118–61.

32 Quoted by F. A. C. Wilson, *W. B. Yeats and Tradition* (London, 1958), p. 244.

33 "Sixteen Dead Men" (1920), *Poems*, p. 180; "The Statues" (1939), *Poems*, p. 323. The elevation is itself a mystical process. Cú Chulainn's purification is described in the difficult poem, "Cuchulain Comforted" (1939), *Poems*, pp. 339–40, in which the warrior-hero "leant upon a tree / As though to meditate on wounds and blood." But he is confronted by "bird-like things," which offer the hero both cowardice and godlike song. These spirits of poetry, of imagination, of pure intellect, are anti-thetical to the figure of heroic action. But it is only by the union of such opposites that spiritual perfection may be achieved. With the leaders of the 1916 Rising the converse may be true: they have already sung the poet's song; so, on Easter Monday, they summon Cú Chulainn's heroic passion to their side.

34 *The Trembling of the Veil*, p. 80.

35 In 1927 Lady Gregory was forced to sell Coole Park to the Free State government. As a condition, she was given permission to live on the estate during her life. She died in 1932. The Great House has since been dismantled to obtain building materials for workers' cottages. Remnants of what was the stable house may still be seen.

36 Yeats, *Estrangement*, p. 14.

37 John Unterecker, *A Reader's Guide to William Butler Yeats* (New York, 1959), p. 211.

38 In *Dramatis Personae*, p. 73, Yeats refers to Lady Gregory as a "centre of peace."

39 *Poems*, p. 239. Anthony Raftery was born *ca.* 1780 at Cilleadan, County Mayo, and died *ca.* 1840. Gerard K. Brady, Letter to *The Irish Times*, Sept. 13, 1960, notes that Raftery "came to Ballylee . . . one wet Sunday morning and found a warm welcome at the castle [i.e., Yeats' tower]. He was moved to praise the beauty of Mary Hynes after whom he called his poem, 'An Pabhsae Glégeal ó Bhéal Átha Liath" [i.e., "The Beautiful

Posy of Ballylee"]. There was still a family of her name living in the neighborhood when I last visited there a few years ago." Brady's family lived in the tower in the last half of the nineteenth century and his mother was born there. Douglas Hyde and Lady Gregory have translated versions of his poems that they found among the Gaelic-speaking people.

40 A summary of Hyde's account of the rediscovery of some forty-five of Raftery's poems is given in A Treasury of Irish Folklore, ed. Padraic Colum (New York, 1954), pp. 315–17.

41 The treatment given the Brown (or Dark) Bull of Cooley and Finnbheannach, the white bull, in the Táin indicates that the ancient Celts regarded the bull as a sacred animal.

42 Poems, p. 253. " 'All could be known or shown / If time were but gone.' "

43 In the Táin when Medb sets out with her armies to take the Bull of Cooley, all the warriors of the Ulaid, save only Cú Chulainn and his father, are stricken by a mysterious sickness which afflicts them periodically because of the curse of Macha, a fairy goddess whom they have wronged. Cú Chulainn slays one hundred of Medb's warriors each night and hides during the daylight hours. Finally, he agrees to fight in single combat against Medb's champions on the condition that her armies advance only while the struggle continues and halt from the moment her warrior is killed until another challenger is found. A long series of combats takes place at the ford of Ard Ciannacht and Cú Chulainn is always victorious. In the tale called "The House of the Quicken (Mountain Ash) Trees" of the Fenian cycle, Ficna, Finn's son, and his foster-son, Innsa, guard a narrow ford against the armies of Sinsar, King of the World, and his son Borba. They are slain; but Diarmuid takes up the defense until the fianna arrive to rout the foreigners.

Chapter 5

1 John Eglinton (William Kirkpatrick Magee), A Memoir of AE: George William Russell (London, 1937), pp. 26–27.

2 Ibid., pp. 34–35.

3 George Moore, Hail and Farewell (New York, 1925), I, 363–64.

4 Eglinton, Memoir of AE, p. 42.

5 Ibid., p. 52.

6 In 1904 the Theosophical Society issued a charter for a "Second

Dublin Lodge." Both A.E. and his wife were members. This group broke with the Society after another argument concerning leadership in 1909 and continued as the independent "Hermetic Society" until 1933 when A.E. left Dublin.

7 Alan Denson notes in *Printed Writings by George W. Russell (AE): A Bibliography* (Evanston, Illinois, 1961), p. 30, that the two plays were performed on April 2 at St. Teresa's Hall, Clarendon Street, Dublin. The Irish National Theatre Society had been formed earlier in the year. Yeats was named president, A.E., Douglas Hyde, and Maud Gonne vice-presidents.

8 Eglinton, *Memoir of AE*, pp. 88, 90. The mass meeting was held in the Royal Albert Hall. Among the other speakers were George Bernard Shaw and James Connolly, the Irish labor leader who afterwards shared with Padraic Pearse leadership of the 1916 rebellion.

9 *Ibid.*, p. 135.

10 *Ibid.*, pp. 275–79.

11 George William Russell (A.E.), *The National Being: Some Thoughts on Irish Polity* (New York, 1930), p. 150.

12 *AE's Letters to Mínanlábáin*, ed. Lucy Kingsley Porter (New York, 1937), p. 50.

13 Eglinton, *Memoir of AE*, p. 237.

14 George William Russell (A.E.), *Collected Poems* (London, 1926), p. 230 (hereafter cited as *Poems*).

15 Kathleen Hoagland, ed., *1000 Years of Irish Poetry*, p. 616.

16 In "Gods of War," *Poems*, pp. 236–38, A.E. expresses his belief that the "ancient gods" are gaining power because Christians have broken faith with the "Prince of Peace":

> How wanes Thine empire, Prince of Peace!
> With the fleet circling of the suns
> The ancient gods their power increase;
> Lo, how thine own anointed ones
> Make holy all Thy soul abhorred,
> The hate on which Thy love had warred.

Elsewhere he observes that the ancient gods, especially Zeus, "fit the dreams of power we hold."

17 *The National Being*, p. 125.

18 Yeats, *Autobiography*, p. 240.

19 Ernest A. Boyd, *Appreciations and Deprecations* (Dublin and London, 1917), p. 39.

20 Eglinton, *Memoir of AE*, p. 206.

21   *Ibid.*, p. 35.
22   *Ibid.*, pp. 9, 27.
23   *Letters to Mínanlábáin*, p. 49.
24   St. John Ervine, *Some Impressions of My Elders* (London, 1923), p. 41.
25   George William Russell (A.E.), *The Candle of Vision* (London, 1931), pp. 10–11.
26   In his "Commentary on the Secret of the Golden Flower," C. G. Jung, *Psyche and Symbol* (Garden City, New York, 1958), p. 325, comments with regard to the particular kind of visionary experience A.E. seems to have had: "As far as I have been able to understand it, the phenomenon seems to have to do with an acute state of consciousness, as intensive as it is abstract, a 'detached' consciousness, which, as Hildegard pertinently remarks, brings up to consciousness regions of psychic events ordinarily covered with darkness. The fact that the general bodily sensations disappear during such an experience shows that their specific energy has been withdrawn from them, and apparently has gone toward heightening the clarity of consciousness. As a rule, the phenomenon is spontaneous, coming and going on its own initiative. Its effect is astonishing in that it almost always brings about a solution of psychic complications, and thereby frees the inner personality from emotional and intellectual entanglements, creating thus a unity of being, which is universally felt as 'liberation.'"
27   Eglinton, *Memoir of AE*, p. 9.
28   Yeats, *Autobiography*, pp. 245–46.
29   Eglinton, *Memoir of AE*, pp. 260–61.
30   In *The Candle of Vision*, pp. 166–67, A.E. records a vision of the legendary treasure of the Tuatha Dé Danann: "I saw rising out of deep water seven shiny and silvery figures, and three on one side and three on another side and one beneath, they held uplifted hands on the hilt of a gigantic sword of quivering flame, and they waved that mighty sword in air and sank again beneath the waters. And after that seven others rose up and they held a great spear, and it they pointed skywards and sank below; and after that arose two carrying a cauldron, and, when they had vanished, one solitary figure arose and it held in its hands a great and glittering stone."
31   Eglinton, *Memoir of AE*, pp. 37–38.
32   See pp. 28–29.
33   Graves, *The White Goddess*, pp. 409, 449.

34 *Autobiography*, p. 240.
35 George William Russell (A.E.), *The House of Titans and Other Poems* (New York, 1934), pp. 3–35.
36 Dillon, *Early Irish Literature*, pp. 59–60, recounts the overthrow of the Fomorians by the Tuatha Dé Danann. The episode is crowded with suggestions of pagan belief. In general, it is possible to recognize the Tuatha Dé Danann as symbolic of the forces of good, the Fomorians as symbolic of the forces of evil. The supernatural Lug enters the battle on the side of the Tuatha Dé Danann and slays Balor of the Poisonous Eye. Balor may be identified as a sun deity in that his glance, like the sun's lightning, brings destruction. Lug is the son of Balor's daughter and Cian Mac Diancécht of the Tuatha Dé Danann. Thomas F. O'Rahilly, *Early Irish History and Mythology*, pp. 58–61, notes that in mythology the sun god is slain with his own weapon; so, Lug slays Balor with the lightning spear.
37 Moore, *Hail and Farewell*, I, 370–71.
38 Eglinton, *Memoir of AE*, pp. 132–33.
39 *The National Being*, p. 122.
40 Boyd, *Appreciations and Deprecations*, p. 30.
41 Robert Farren, *The Course of Irish Verse* (New York, 1947), p. 81.
42 *Ibid.*, p. 79.

Chapter 6

1 There is reason to suppose that the leaders of the Rising literally "sacrificed" themselves. In *Easter Fires: Pages from Personal Record of 1916*, ed. Allen Downey (Waterford, Ireland, 1943), pp. 29–30, Dr. James Ryan recalls having been told by Sean MacDermott of the decision to surrender: "What terms did he think Pearse and Connolly had agreed to at the castle? That the signatories would be shot and the rest of us set free, he thought." Thomas J. Clarke and Joseph Plunkett told the doctor much the same thing. The signers of the proclamation of the Irish Republic were seven: Clarke, Seán MacDiarmada (MacDermott), Pearse, James Connolly, MacDonagh, Éamonn Ceannt, and Plunkett.
2 See Robert Farren, *The Course of Irish Verse*, pp. 118–23.
3 St. John Ervine, *Bernard Shaw* (New York, 1956), p. 466.
4 Another poet, John Francis MacEntee, whose work includes

propagandist ballads and some lyrics written in imitation of Elizabethan poetry, also participated in the Rising. He survived and has become a minister in the Irish government. Sir Roger Casement, captured before the rebellion began, also wrote verse. James Connolly, the labor leader and commanding general of the rebels, composed ballads, and Éamonn Ceannt wrote several militant songs.

5   James Stephens, in his introduction to *The Poetical Works of Thomas MacDonagh* (Dublin, 1916), p. xi, notes that three weeks before the rebellion MacDonagh asked him "to talk to some of his boys about the poetry of William Blake."

6   *The Poets of 1916* (Dublin and Cork, 1931), pp. 5–6.

7   *Easter Fires*, p. 7.

8   Much of Pearse's work was written first in Gaelic, afterwards translated into English by himself. All of his stories, written in Irish, were translated by another bilingual poet, Joseph Campbell.

9   *The Poetical Works of Thomas MacDonagh: Lyrical Poems*, p. 135. Separate pagination is given in this volume for *Songs of Myself* and *Lyrical Poems*. Subsequent references will be given as *Poetical Works: Songs of Myself* or *Poetical Works: Lyrical Poems*.

10 *An Macaomh*, I, 2 (Christmas, 1909), p. 50. Hyde made the remarks in a lecture at St. Enda's. *An Macaomh* was the school magazine.

11 Copies of the magazine shipped to England were twice seized, once during the labor trouble of 1913 and again in 1914 when Plunkett devoted much of an issue to insurrectionary propaganda. The loss resulting from the second seizure forced Plunkett to give up publication.

12 *An Macaomh*, I, 1 (Midsummer, 1909), pp. 8–9.

13 *Poetical Works of Thomas MacDonagh*, p. xii.

14 Arthur E. Clery, "Pearse, MacDonagh, Plunkett: an Appreciation," in *Poets of the Insurrection* (Dublin and London, 1918), p. 50.

15 Padraic H. Pearse, *Collected Works: Plays, Stories, Poems* (Dublin, 1924), p. 313.

16 *Ibid.*, pp. 312–13.

17 *Ibid.*, p. 333. The poet's sister, Mary Brigit Pearse, *The Home Life of Padraig Pearse* (Dublin, Belfast, etc. [1934]), p. 49, describes the relationship between Pearse and "the little mother of his heart." Among other things Miss Pearse records what

supposedly was her mother's reaction to Pearse's promise to think of her at the moment of his death: "Oh! What inexpressible consolation this beautiful promise has been to me! What greater happiness or exultation could any mother's soul contain!"

18   Pearse, *Plays, Stories, Poems*, pp. 316, 326, 341.

19   Padraic H. Pearse, *Collected Works: The Story of a Success* (Dublin, 1924), pp. 18, 232. A similar belief is expressed by MacDonagh in "Of My Poems," *Poetical Works: Lyrical Poems*, p. 9:

> I've found wise books but never such
> As could teach me a single word
> To set by what my childhood heard.

20   MacDonagh dedicated to Yeats his first volume, *Through the Ivory Gate* (Dublin, 1902). Yeats' influence is clear in such a poem as "Cuchulain" (p. 95), in which MacDonagh invokes the shade of the *Táin's* hero—"oh! we need a mighty soul like thee"—to watch over Ireland's fortunes. But in *April and May* (Dublin, 1903), p. 1, it is for a military rather than a spiritual resurgence that MacDonagh calls:

> Some speak of victories, of battles fought,
>> With never a gun's loud pealing;
> Of freedom won and rights long sought,
>> With never a life-blood's sealing:—
> Oh! with ring of steel, the *bearna baoghail*
> Ever echoes the Nation's calling;
> And he loves her best who with dauntless breast
> Dies there, for Ireland falling.

The phrase, *beárna baoghail*, means "gap of danger" and is pronounced "barna bweel."

21   Thomas MacDonagh, *Literature in Ireland*, pp. 33–34.

22   MacDonagh, *Poetical Works: Lyrical Poems*, pp. 96–97.

23   The use of ellipsis in this poem satisfies the theory of metrics developed by MacDonagh. In *Thomas Campion and the Art of English Poetry* (Dublin and London, 1913), p. 78, he denies the importance of unstressed syllables for the scansion of English language verse: "The [metrical] unit is the time-space, the period, in which are embedded syllables and pauses. Accent marks off the periods from one another. In a falling meter the stress is on the first syllable of the foot, in a rising meter on the last; and all forms are reducible to these two, the so-called accentual amphibrach and the like being unnecessary."

24 Archaisms, especially survivals of Elizabethan speech, are not uncommon in contemporary Anglo-Irish dialects.

25 MacDonagh, *Poetical Works: Lyrical Poems*, p. 107.

26 Peter McBrien, "Joseph M. Plunkett," in *Poets of the Insurrection*, p. 32.

27 Rev. James F. Cassidy, *Visions of Ireland Old and New* (Dublin, 1933), p. 43.

28 *The Poems of Joseph Mary Plunkett* (Dublin, 1916), pp. 17–19.

29 Plunkett's sister includes an example of this patriotic verse in her introductory essay to *Poems*, pp. xiii–xiv, and describes it as "an extremely good imitation of the old topical ballad, with all its beautiful badnesses." The poem is clearly in the tradition of popular Irish protest verse:

> On my father's lands there are many mansions
> With sheep and cattle and pigs go leór,
> Until the Saxon came over the border
> With detention orders that raked him sore.
> His herds they plundered and killed five hundred,
> And the rest they sundered north, east and south,
> Saying, keep the hides and the woolly fleeces
> For the beasts have diseases of the foot and mouth!

Miss Plunkett wisely excluded the ballad from her brother's collected poems on the ground that it would be "out of place in the text. . . ."

30 *An Macaomh*, I, 1 (Midsummer, 1909), pp. 26–27. In *Collected Works: Songs of the Irish Rebels* (Dublin, 1924), p. 35, Pearse translated a quatrain composed by a dispossessed Irishman after seeing an Englishman hanging upon a tree:

> Good is thy fruit, O tree!
> The luck of thy fruit on every bough;
> Would that the trees of Innisfail
> Were full of thy fruit every day!

Innisfail is a traditional name for Ireland. In a pamphlet, *Ghosts* (Dublin, 1916), p. 10, Pearse quotes these lines, but dissociates himself from the vengeful sentiment expressed; "I do not defend this blood-thirstiness any more than I apologize for it. I simply point it out as the note of a literature."

31 Clery, "Pearse, MacDonagh, Plunkett," p. 55.

32 "Lullaby of a Woman of the Mountain," *Plays, Stories, Poems*, p. 311.

33 Cathaoir O'Braonain, "Padraic H. Pearse," in *Poets of the Insurrection*, p. 11. In the second part of a folklore series, "The Wood," *The Irish Review*, IV (September-November, 1914, pp. 306–17, Pearse tells the story of a nature-child called Mac an Chuill (i.e., son of the hazel) who is brother to "the birds of the air and the creatures of the plain." Mac an Chuill so identifies himself with nature that he refuses to wear clothing made for him by his foster parents.

34 MacDonagh's "John-John," *Poetical Works: Songs of Myself*, pp. 41–43, is a humorous peasant ballad. Father Cassidy, *Visions of Ireland*, p. 43, notes the echo of the traditional keen in Plunkett's "1841–1891," [sic] commemorating the death of O'Connell:

> The wind rose, the sea rose,
> A wave rose on the sea
> Swelled by mournful singing
> Of a sad centenary.

The title of this poem is probably the result of a typographical error. O'Connell died in 1847. A list of poems included in Plunkett's papers, National Library of Ireland MS. 10,999, gives the title as "1847–1891."

35 Plunkett, *Poems*, p. 56. See note 20, p. 308, for MacDonagh's treatment of Cú Chulainn. Pearse in "I am Ireland," *Plays, Stories, Poems*, p. 323, includes in Ireland's racial heritage both Cú Chulainn's heroism and the betrayal of the country by Diarmuid and Dervorgilla.

36 Padraic Colum, ed., *A Treasury of Irish Folklore*, pp. 124–27, gives St. Colmcille's account of Patrick's promised intercession.

37 A Gaelic-speaking Irishman may greet another by saying, *Dia dhuit* (i.e., God be with you); the second person replies, *Dia is Muire dhuit* (i.e., God and Mary be with you). But if the first speaker invokes both God *and* Mary, then the second must add St. Patrick's name to his reply; and if all three are initially invoked, then the response must include a fourth name—*Dia is Muire dhuit is Pádraig is Bríd* (i.e., God and Mary and Patrick and Brigid be with you).

38 Padraic H. Pearse, "Some Aspects of Irish Literature," in *Collected Works: Songs of the Irish Rebels* (Dublin, 1924), p. 157.

39 Pearse, *Political Writings and Speeches*, p. 25.

40 Plunkett, *Poems*, p. 91.

41 Thomas MacDonagh, *Metempsychosis: or A Mad World, The*

Irish Review, I (February, 1912), pp. 585–99. The play ridicules the notion that the soul passes through a series of reincarnations from one race to another, upward or downward. It is notable in that it aligns MacDonagh with the orthodoxy and against theosophy.

42 Pearse, *Songs of the Irish Rebels*, p. 149.

43 Padraic H. Pearse, *Collected Works: Political Writings and Speeches* (Dublin, 1924), pp. 145–46, comments on the Synge episode: "Ireland in our day as in the past, has excommunicated some of those who have served her best, and has canonized some of those who have served her worst. We damn a man for an unpopular phrase; we deify a man who does a mean thing gracefully.... When a man like Synge, a man in whose sad heart there glowed a true love of Ireland, one of the two or three men who have in our time made Ireland considerable in the eyes of the world, uses strange symbols which we do not understand, we cry out that he has blasphemed and we proceed to crucify him.... This is really a very terrible symptom in contemporary Ireland."

44 Padraic H. Pearse, *Ghosts*, p. 3.

45 Pearse, *An Macaomh*, II, 2 (May, 1913), 8.

46 Johann Tauler, *The Following of Christ*, trans. J. R. Morell (London, 1910), pp. 2–3 [Nos. 3–4].

47 Cassidy, *Visions of Ireland*, p. 40.

48 Thomas MacDonagh, "Language and Literature in Ireland," *The Irish Review*, IV (March-April, 1914), 176–82.

49 Pearse, *Plays, Stories, Poems*, p. 324.

50 Plunkett, *Poems*, p. 9.

51 MacDonagh, *Poetical Works: Lyrical Poems*, p. 29.

52 Plunkett, "Obscurity and Poetry," in *Poems*, p. 95.

53 Cassidy, *Visions of Ireland*, p. 33, says of Plunkett that "Stoneyhurst made keen his visionary powers and gave a signal impetus to a mind already hot on the trail of the mysteries and intangibles." Geraldine Plunkett, *Poems*, p. vii, observes that "his most constant companions were St. John of the Cross, St. Teresa, St. Francis, and John Tauler." It would seem, on the evidence of his poetry, that Plunkett drew most consistently from Tauler's *The Following of Christ* for his mature work.

54 Plunkett, *Poems*, p. 1.

55 *Ibid.*, p. 70.

56 *Ibid.*, p. 83.

57 *The Works of St. John [de Yèpes] of the Cross*, trans. David

Lewis (London, 1891), II, 243, 255, 257. In Apoc. viii: 1, when the seventh seal is broken, "there followed a silence in heaven for about the space of half an hour."

58   MacDonagh, *Poetical Works: Songs of Myself*, pp. 32–37.

59   MacDonagh, *Poetical Works: Lyrical Poems*, pp. 10–11. The two notions are not very far apart; for the Original Sin consisted of eating of the fruit of the tree of knowledge of good and evil.

60   Professor O'Neill, "Thomas MacDonagh," in *Poets of the Insurrection*, p. 20, notes that many of MacDonagh's poems "reflect the troubles of a mind to which religious difficulties were a keen perplexity. Of mixed religious and racial ancestry (his mother's name, Parker, spoke of English descent, and she had been received as a convert in the Catholic Church), the scenes of his early life may have familiarized him with religious dissent. Brought up a Catholic and in a Catholic college, he became for a time a member of a religious order. Quitting, however, that anchorage, he became a roamer on the wide seas of experience and doubt."

61   MacDonagh, *Poetical Works: Lyrical Poems*, pp. 30–33. The final lines of this poem warrant favorable comparison with the third movement of Yeats' "Easter 1916":

> And I hear the trampling of hooves
> Thundering up with a plough,
> And a team of horses moves
> In splendour over the rise
> Of the ridge, and into the light.

62   Mary Pearse, *The Home Life*, p. 67. Pearse's story, "The Priest," *Plays, Stories, Poems*, pp. 247–57, concerns a boy, Paraig, who plays at saying Mass dressed in his mother's bodice.

63   Mary Pearse, *The Home Life*, p. 149.

64   *Ibid.*, p. 56.

65   *Ibid.*, p. 148. According to Mary Hayden, a friend, Pearse spoke on "Our Brothers and Sisters": "The subject was kindness to animals. He maintained that . . . the modern Irish were far behind the English; and that this was especially true in the Irish speaking districts. 'The Gaels are too poor to attend to animals!' one man interrupted. 'Does it cost more to pat a dog than to kick it?' was Pearse's retort."

66   Pearse, *Plays, Stories, Poems*, pp. 324, 341.

67   Croagh Patrick was the site of one of the more fabulous legends concerning Patrick. P. W. Joyce, *The Origin and History of Irish*

Names of Places, First Series, p. 190, attributes to a twelfth-century life of the saint the story that Patrick brought "all the serpents and venomous creatures and *demons* of Ireland" to the top of the mountain and then drove them into the sea.

68 Padraic H. Pearse, *The Spiritual Nation* (Dublin, 1916), pp. 4–5.

69 *Ibid.*, p. 4. Pearse identifies the person who believed in the "mystical entity" of Ireland's soul only as "a friend of mine."

70 MacDonagh, *Literature in Ireland*, p. 14.

71 Pearse, *Ghosts*, p. 4.

72 Pearse, *Plays, Stories, Poems*, pp. 337–38.

73 Exod. v–vi.

74 Gen. iii: 21–24.

75 Plunkett, *Poems*, p. 56. Light is an attribute of God and of the soul in a state of blessedness. See Tauler, *The Following of Christ*, pp. 121–22 [Nos. 142–43]. In an unpublished poem, "Big Talk," National Library of Ireland MS. 10,999, Plunkett equates political freedom with spiritual grace:

> Everywhere I see chains
> And slaves hugging them
> For fear of freedom
> The unsensed to them is full of fear
> How much more so the supersensible
> Liberty
> Therefore they cling to chains
> Of the body and of the spirit
> Holding the body back from bravery
> The spirit from good
> The soul from God
> And the heart from seeking the beloved
> Slaves construct their own chain
> Out of themselves.

This is not, of course, a finished poem.

76 MacDonagh, *Poetical Works: Lyrical Poems*, p. 138.

77 S. of Sol. ii: 1.

78 One of the best known poems using the rose as symbol for Ireland is Aubrey De Vere's "The Little Black Rose." Plunkett, *Poems*, pp. 59–60, uses as the title for a sonnet the first line of De Vere's poem—"The Little Black Rose shall be red at last." Yeats' "The Rose Tree" also deals with the same theme. Donal O'Sullivan, *Songs of the Irish*, pp. 130, 133, points out that

Róisín Dubh, like Cathleen Ní Houlihan, was the heroine of an old Gaelic love song and that James Clarence Mangan correctly translated the name as "Dark Rosaleen." But a patriotic song was written to the same tune; and all of the poets of the revival regarded the "dark rose" as a symbol of the Irish nation under English rule.

79 Francis Sheehy-Skeffington, the pacifist, whom the British murdered during Easter Week, 1916, regarded MacDonagh as a moderate and published an open letter to him in *The Irish Citizen*, May 22, 1915, urging him to renounce the "militarist" aims of the Irish Volunteers.

80 MacDonagh, *Poetical Works: Lyrical Poems*, p. 48.

81 *Ibid.*, p. 128.

82 *Ibid.*, p. 130.

83 Plunkett, *Poems*, p. 81.

84 Pearse, *Plays, Stories, Poems*, pp. 324–25.

85 Quoted by Pearse in *Ghosts*, p. 22. The reference is to John Mitchel, *Jail Journal* (Dublin, 1918). The work originally was published in Mitchel's paper, *The Citizen*, in New York (where he was an exile) from January 14 to August 19, 1854. Mitchel's influence upon Pearse's prose writing was very strong. For example, in a speech urging the Irish people to arms, "The Coming Revolution," *Political Writings and Speeches*, pp. 98–99, Pearse said: "We must accustom ourselves to the thought of arms, to the sight of arms, to the use of arms. We may make mistakes in the beginning and shoot the wrong people; but bloodshed is a cleansing and a sanctifying thing, and the nation which regards it as the final horror has lost its manhood. There are many things more horrible than bloodshed; and slavery is one of them." Sean O'Casey makes effective dramatic use of this speech in *The Plough and the Stars*.

86 Quoted by Pearse, *The Separatist Idea* (Dublin, 1916), p. 1. Wolfe Tone's battle cry echoes the motto of the British royal family: "Dieu et Mon Droit."

87 Plunkett, *Poems*, p. 56. In an unpublished poem, National Library of Ireland MS 10,999, Plunkett gives a curious twist to the idea of the divine right of kings:

> Out of tempestuous night
> Into the luminous morn
> With the seal of Divinity's Kingly right
> The National Leader is born.

> He will come with the call of the hour
> He will come with the sealing of light
> He will carry the Pike of the People's power
> And mow with the Scythe of their right[.]

88 Pearse, *Plays, Stories, Poems*, p. 323.

89 W. B. Yeats, *Collected Poems*, p. 321.

90 Colum, *A Treasury of Irish Folklore*, p. 376.

91 Pearse, *Plays, Stories, Poems*, pp. 319-20.

92 MacDonagh, *Poetical Works: Lyrical Poems*, p. 27.

93 MacDonagh, *Poetical Works: Songs of Myself*, p. 20.

94 Plunkett, *Poems*, p. 73.

95 *An Macaomh*, II, 2 (May, 1913), pp. 6-7.

96 Pearse, *Plays, Stories, Poems*, pp. 43-44.

97 Tauler, *The Following of Christ*, p. 159.

98 Plunkett, *Poems*, pp. 11-12.

99 *Ibid.*, pp. 6-7.

100 *Ibid.*, p. 4.

101 *Works of St. John of the Cross*, II, 385.

102 That Plunkett himself identified the red rose with the sacrifice of the cross is suggested by his sonnet, "I See His Blood Upon the Rose," *Poems*, p. 50.

103 Plunkett, *Poems*, pp. 59-60.

104 In "Big Talk," National Library of Ireland MS. 10,999, Plunkett uses the imagery of spiritual love to define the relationship between national leader and nation:

> He shall know his bride
> To be the bride of God
> And his love
> To be the love of God
> And he shall hear St. Paul's precept:
> "Husbands love your wives
> As Christ also loved the Church"
> And he shall know that he is not
>   God
> And shall be afraid
> He shall hear St. Paul accuse him
> That he has made the members of Christ
>   the members of a harlot
> And he shall be terrified
> For that he has lain with the world
> In apathy.

105 MacDonagh, *Poetical Works: Lyrical Poems,* p. 142.

106 MacDonagh, *Poetical Works: Songs of Myself,* p. 7.

107 *Ibid.,* pp. 46–47.

108 MacDonagh, *Pagans: A Modern Play in Two Conversations* (Dublin and London, 1920), p. 40.

109 MacDonagh, *When the Dawn Is Come* (Dublin, 1908), p. 43.

110 Mary Pearse, *The Home Life,* p. 141.

111 Pearse, *Plays, Stories, Poems,* p. 328.

112 *An Macaomh,* I, 1 (Midsummer, 1909), p. 5. The picture is used as a frontispiece for the first issue of the school publication.

113 Mary Pearse, *The Home Life,* p. 105. Mary Colum, *Life and the Dream,* p. 157, writes that the play "caused a minor dramatic sensation so that accounts of it were not only in the London but in the Continental papers."

114 Mary Pearse, *The Home Life,* p. 130.

115 Pearse, *Plays, Stories, Poems,* pp. 335–36.

116 *Ibid.,* p. 339.

117 *Ibid.,* p. 333.

118 Desmond Ryan, *The Rising: The Complete Story of Easter Week* (Dublin, 1949), pp. 97–98. Ryan himself participated in the insurrection.

119 Pearse's essays on education and economics are included in *Political Writings and Speeches.* Eimar O'Duffy, *The Wasted Island* (Dublin, 1919), p. 421, implies that many of the rank and file of the Volunteers disapproved of the Rising because it could be nothing more than a sacrifice. He describes a group of Volunteers talking together; one of them reads a poem, "Ignis Immortalis," which resembles the poetry of Pearse, MacDonagh, and Plunkett:

    " 'It means that they don't hope for success, but mean the whole thing as a blood-sacrifice to restore the national spirit.'

    " 'What's wrong with the national spirit? It's coming along fine as far as I can see.'

    " 'Poetical impatience, my boy. They like the thing done dramatically.'

    " 'Well, Mallow and Co. are welcome to make a blood-sacrifice of themselves if they like, but I object to their playing the game on me. I'll be no bleeding corpse in a slaughtered heap for Pearse to die on.' "

    O'Duffy was himself involved in the Volunteer movement.

120 Ryan, *The Rising*, p. 260.
121 W. B. Yeats, *Collected Plays*, p. 56.

Chapter 7

1 Several years ago Colum completed a biography of Griffith for which most of the research had been carried out by Seán Milroy. *Arthur Griffith* (Dublin, 1959) was published under Colum's name. The American edition is entitled *Ourselves Alone!* (New York, 1959). Griffith died before the Free State was formally established.

2 "Odysseus: In Memory of Arthur Griffith," *The Collected Poems of Padraic Colum*, pp. 205-6.

3 "Roger Casement," *Collected Poems*, p. 207.

4 Padraic Colum, *The Poet's Circuits*. This phrase serves as subtitle for the volume.

5 Mary C. Sturgeon, *Studies of Contemporary Poets* (London, 1916), pp. 170-71.

6 L. A. G. Strong, *Personal Remarks* (London and New York, 1953), pp. 80-81.

7 *Collected Poems*, pp. 8-10. "Reminiscence" is not included in full in *The Poet's Circuits*. However, the sixth poem of the original sequence, the poem concerned with "Nell the Rambler," is reprinted in the volume of Irish poems, pp. 111-12, under the title, "The Mountain Thrush." Subsequent notes to Colum's verse will include page references to both *The Collected Poems* and *The Poet's Circuits* if the poem in question is printed in both volumes.

8 In *Thomas Muskerry, Three Plays: The Fiddler's House, The Land, Thomas Muskerry*, pp. 159-60, Colum compares a city pauper with a country pauper. Felix Tournour, who was born in the workhouse and never lived in the country, is "an ugly figure": "His scanty beard is coal black. He has a wide mouth and bony teeth. His forehead is narrow and bony." By contrast, Myles Gorman, the blind piper who is also a pauper, "is a Gael of the West of Ireland, with a face full of intellectual vigour."

9 Colum told me in Dublin on January 18, 1961, that part of his childhood was spent in Sandycove, part in a provincial workhouse where his father was master, and part in a peasant cottage in County Longford. He himself does not regard his personal

background as so important as his "deliberate decision in favor of the Irish peasantry." His concern with the "characters and situations" of the countryside is explicitly stated in *The Poet's Circuits*, p. v.

10　*The Poet's Circuits*, p. vi. The *ceilidhe* is a country social evening of song and story.

11　Padraic Colum, ed., *Broad-Sheet Ballads* (Dublin and London, 1913), p. xv.

12　Padraic Colum, *The Story of Lowry Maen* (New York, 1937). The name of Colum's hero deserves comment. "Maen" in Irish means "speechless," and "Lowry" (in Irish, "Lahaid") means "speaks": hence, his name literally means "the speechless speaks." As a boy the young prince is struck dumb at the horror of his father's murder by his uncle. His speech returns when he bests his uncle's son on a playing field. Colum intended that his long poem should be suitable for oral recitation in modern Ireland. But he told me he regarded the poem, except the first book of it, as less than satisfactory.

13　A number of Colum's poems were set to music by Herbert Hughes before the latter's death. Nine of these are included in Padraic Colum and Herbert Hughes, *Songs From Connacht* (Dublin, 1913).

14　Strong, *Personal Remarks*, p. 84.

15　Sturgeon, *Contemporary Poets*, pp. 164-65.

16　Similarly, in Colum's *The Adventures of Odysseus and the Tale of Troy* (London, 1920), p. 20, two eagles appear above a council of nobles to support Telemachus' threats against those who abuse the hospitality of his father's house.

17　Padraic Colum, *The Frenzied Prince* (Philadelphia, 1943), pp. 110-22; *The Collected Plays of W. B. Yeats*, pp. 405-28.

18　John O'Donovan, trans. and ed., *The Banquet of Dún Na N-Gédh and the Battle of Magh Rath: an Ancient Historical Tale*, Irish Archaeological Society (Dublin, 1842), pp. vii, 35-37.

19　The most startling innovation is the ravishing of Attracta by Congal and his men. Yeats also has Congal emerge victorious in the battle, whereas in the old tale he loses the battle and his life as well. Yeats used as the source for his play Sir Samuel Ferguson's *Congal: A Poem in Five Books* (Dublin and London, 1893) rather than O'Donovan's text. Ferguson's version follows the original tale closely. One must also note that Yeats was probably writing from memory, rather than with the text of Ferguson's poem close at hand.

20 O'Donovan, *Banquet of Dún Na N-Gédh, etc.*, p. 21.

21 Sturgeon, *Contemporary Poets*, p. 164.

22 Colum, *My Irish Year* (New York, 1913), pp. 72–73.

23 *Collected Poems*, pp. 117–18; *The Poet's Circuits,* pp. 78–79. Douglas Hyde, "The Brow of the Red Mountain," *Love Songs of Connacht*, pp. 21–23.

24 In January, 1961, Colum spoke to me of his verse in terms of these three influences.

25 Colum, *My Irish Year*, p. 69, comments on the difficulties of adapting Gaelic poetic technique to English verse.

26 National Library of Ireland MS. 3904 (*ca.* 1904–6). In *My Irish Year*, p. 69, he gives Moore credit for the musical quality of Irish verse.

27 Thomas MacDonagh in *Literature in Ireland* discusses at considerable length the grammatical peculiarities of the Anglo-Irish dialect. P. W. Joyce, *English As We Speak It in Ireland* (London, 1910), lists hundreds of Anglo-Irish language and grammatical variants. See also P. L. Henry, *An Anglo-Irish Dialect of North Roscommon* (Dublin, n.d. [1958?]).

28 Colum discussed his debt to Ibsen at a seminar meeting in the National University of Ireland, Dublin (U.C.D.), in February, 1961.

29 *Collected Poems*, p. 91; *The Poet's Circuits*, p. 109. In *Irish Names of Places*, Second Series, p. 391, P. W. Joyce identifies Innishore (literally "big island") as an island in Lough Erne in County Fermanagh.

30 Rev. James F. Cassidy, *Visions of Ireland*, p. 85.

31 Colum presents Owen Paralon as the ideal Irish peasant. Paralon is the hero of Colum's "Fore-Piece" to *The Poet's Circuits*.

32 Colum, *Castle Conquer* (London, 1923), p. 93.

33 *Collected Poems*, pp. 92–93; *The Poet's Circuits*, p. 31. *The Land*, in *Three Plays*, pp. 111–14.

34 Padraic Colum, *The Big Tree of Bunlahy: Stories of My Own Countryside* (New York, 1933), pp. 1–2.

35 Colmcille, or Columba, the Irish saint, is traditionally remembered for his love of defenseless animals. His love for nature's creatures is the theme of the opening pages of Colum's *The Legend of Saint Columba*.

36 Colum told me in January, 1961, that the underlying motif of his work has always been the heroism of the peasantry. At a seminar at the National University of Ireland, Dublin (U.C.D.), in February, 1961, Colum while talking of heroism used the

phrase, "Plutarch lied," by which he meant to suggest that Plutarch was wrong in identifying heroism with great and noble men. Some notes in National Library of Ireland MS. 9453 (*ca.* 1910) suggest that as a young man Colum read Plutarch differently and found in him support for his notion of peasant heroism: in these notes he tries to define Plutarch's "conception of biography": "he looks on life as one who has read Plato.... The aristocratic form of government is most pleasing to this student of Plato, but he is no more a hero-worshipper than Gibbon is." (These were notebook jottings and often did not follow grammatical form.) In a National Library of Ireland MS. Autograph, a letter dated December 25, 1914, Colum asks a friend, William Ryan, in Dublin to send to him in New York his set of Plutarch to which he refers as "very precious possessions." It is likely that Plutarch had a formative influence upon Colum, both on his idea of heroism and his conception of art as the expression of character.

37 Padraic Colum, *A Boy of Eirinn* (London, 1915).
38 *The Poet's Circuits*, p. 9. Conn Ced-Cathach (Conn of the Hundred Battles), according to the old genealogies, was one of the kings of Tara.
39 Honor Tracy's *The Straight and Narrow Path* (Middlesex, 1960) provides an antidote for Colum's romantic view of Ireland, although its satire is at times grotesque. O'Faolain has published a number of essays in *The Bell* criticizing the social conformity imposed on Irish life by the Catholic Church. In *The Bell*, XVIII (February, 1953), 517–27, he describes an incident which took place at a meeting of the International Affairs Association in Dublin. After a paper on Communist persecution in Yugoslavia had been read, Mr. Hubert Butler, a guest of Dr. Owen Sheehy-Skeffington, suggested that Archbishop Stepinac had been "duped or deceived" by the German puppet government during World War II. The Papal Nuncio, who was present, left the meeting in protest. A furor resulted. The Association apologized for Mr. Butler's conduct. Afterwards Butler was forced to resign as honorary secretary of the Kilkenny Archeological Society and Sheehy-Skeffington, son of the pacifist who was murdered by the English in 1916, was banned from a public debate on the subject, "Can the Individual Survive?" In another essay, "Ireland after Yeats," *The Bell*, XVIII (Summer, 1953), 38–39, O'Faolain criticizes what he calls the "nervy, sensitive, touchy, defensive-aggressive, on-

guard mentality" of the Church and government in Ireland. O'Faolain is himself a Roman Catholic, but remains critical of the Irish Catholic clergy.

40   *Collected Poems*, pp. 117–18; *The Poet's Circuits*, pp. 78–79. Hyde, *Love Songs of Connacht*, pp. 21–23.

41   *Collected Poems*, p. 97; *The Poet's Circuits*, p. 106. Joyce, *Irish Names of Places*, First Series, p. 510, notes that Bunratty is a town in County Clare. The name means literally the "mouth" (*bun*) of the river once called the Ratty, now called Owen Ogarney River. Cruckmaelin means "little bare hill," and Carricknabauna means "the rock of whiteness."

42   *The Collected Poems of W. B. Yeats*, p. 236.

43   Epigraph to Honor Tracy's *The Straight and Narrow Path*, on title page.

44   Sturgeon, *Contemporary Poets*, pp. 168–69.

Chapter 8

1   It is true that the poets and writers of the *Nation* made use of much traditional Irish material; yet in doing so their primary concern was the propagandistic value of such material rather than its artistic value. W. B. Yeats, *The Trembling of the Veil*, pp. 87–88, asserts that "Young Ireland had sought a nation unified by political doctrine alone, a subservient art and letters aiding and abetting. The movement of thought, which had in the 'fifties and 'forties at Paris and London and Boston, filled literature, and especially poetical literature, with curiosities about science, about history, about politics, with moral purpose and educational fervour—abstractions all—had created a new instrument for Irish politics, a method of writing that took its poetical style from Campbell, Scott, Macaulay, and Beranger, with certain elements from Gaelic, its prose style—in John Mitchell [sic] the only Young Ireland prose-writer who had a style at all—from Carlyle. To recommend this method of writing as literature without much reservation and discrimination I contended was to be deceived or to practice deception."

2   Griffith published an essay by Stephens in *Sinn Féin* on April 20, 1907; thereafter the young solicitor's clerk became a regular contributor.

3   Birgit Bramsbäch, *James Stephens: A Literary and Bibliographical Study* (Copenhagen, Dublin and Cambridge, Massachusetts,

1959), p. 28. Stephens apparently could read Irish, but he did not master the spoken language.

4   It was printed in *Sinn Féin*, November 26, 1910. Hurriedly written, it is a bad poem.

5   James Stephens, *Arthur Griffith: Journalist and Statesman* (Dublin, *ca.* 1922), p. 4.

6   *Sinn Féin*, May 7, 1910. Stephen's only published play, *Julia Elizabeth* (New York, 1929), was produced in 1911 by the Theatre of Ireland, a company founded by Edward Martyn, Joseph Plunkett, and Padraic Colum in competition with the Abbey Theatre.

7   "Irish Englishmen," *Sinn Féin*, June 1, 1907; "The Seoinin," *Sinn Féin*, April 20, 1907. The word, "seóinín," is the diminutive of Seán and translates literally as "little John." The name was applied disparagingly to persons affecting English ways.

8   *Sinn Féin*, May 11, 1907. Banbha, originally an ancient Irish goddess, became a traditional name for Ireland in peasant stories and songs."

9   James Stephens, *The Adventures of Seumas Beg* and *The Rocky Road to Dublin* (London, 1915), p. 50.

10   *Sinn Féin*, August 3, 1907.

11   James Stephens, *Collected Poems* (London, 1954), p. 45. Hereafter cited as *Poems*.

12   Dorothy M. Hoare, *The Works of Morris and Yeats in Relation to Early Saga Literature* (Cambridge, England, 1937), p. 133.

13   James Stephens, "The Outlook for Literature with special Reference to Ireland," *Century Magazine*, CIV (October, 1922), 813.

14   Vivian Mercier, "James Stephens: His Version of Pastoral," *Irish Writing*, 14 (March, 1951), 53.

15   Hoare, *Morris and Yeats*, pp. 172-73.

16   James Stephens, *In the Land of Youth* (London, 1924), pp. 14, 18.

17   Mercier, "James Stephens: His Version of Pastoral," p. 54.

18   Typical of the ballads and elegies for the sixteen executed leaders of the Rising is this one, "Vengeance," cited by Donagh MacDonagh, "Ballads of 1916," *The Bell*, II, 1 (April, 1941), 22:

> In Dublin town they murdered them, like dogs
>   they shot them down,
> God's curse be on you England, God strike you
>   London town,

And cursed be every Irishman alive and yet to live
Who dare forget the death they died, who ever dare
    forgive.

19 *Poems,* p. 107. Joyce, *Irish Names of Places,* First Series, p. 157,
    notes that the Paps of Dana are two mountains in County Kerry
    and that their name honors a Princess Danu; more likely the
    name derives from the ancient goddess Danu.

20 James Stephens, *The Demi-gods* (London, 1914), p. 63.

21 *Ibid.,* pp. 57–58.

22 James Stephens, *Reincarnations* (London, 1918), p. 37: *Poems,*
    p. 185.

23 *Reincarnations,* pp. 55–56; *Poems,* p. 186. The final line of
    the poem may be contrasted with the nuns' prayer cited by
    Yeats' in *The Bounty of Sweden*: "Daughter of a Queen, grand-
    daughter of a Queen, great-grand-daughter of a Queen, great-
    great-grand-daughter of a Queen."

24 According to Douglas Hyde, *A Literary History of Ireland* (Lon-
    don, 1910), p. 592, David Ó Bruadair, a Gaelic poet of the late
    seventeenth century, was noted for his verse on the Williamite
    wars and the decline of the Jacobite cause. His poetry has been
    published by the Irish Texts Society, Vols. XI, XIII, XVIII.

25 John M. Synge, *Poems and Translations* (Dundrum, Ireland,
    1909), p. viii.

26 *Ibid.,* p. 2.

27 James Stephens, *Insurrections* (Dublin, 1909), p. 7; *Poems,*
    p. 79.

28 Synge, *Poems and Translations,* p. 5.

29 Robert Farren, *The Course of Irish Verse,* pp. 124–25.

30 In *Arthur Griffith,* p. 14, Stephens records a conversation in
    which he asked Griffith:
        " 'If, by touching a button on the lamp-post, you could kill
    a person living in China and get all his goods without fear of
    detection or punishment either here or in hell, would you touch
    the button?'
        "Mr. Griffith laughed, but focussed the problem.
        " 'I would not touch the button,' he averred.
        " 'Would Connolly?' I urged. 'Would Russell? or Mont-
    gomery, or Gogarty?'
        " 'Yeats would,' said Mr. Griffith, for at that time he felt
    that there was nothing good about Mr. Yeats except his poetry:
    but he would perhaps not now maintain these mutually destruc-
    tive postulates."

31 *Poems*, pp. 143–45. "The Peeler and the Goat," *National Comic Song Book* (Dublin, n.d.), pp. 10–11, was written by Darby Ryan, of County Tipperary, in the nineteenth century when the "peelers" were a new police force in Ireland. The song ridicules the peelers' officiousness. Stephens' implied identification between God and the peeler gives a final note of irony to the poem.

32 James Stephens, *The Insurrection in Dublin* (Dublin and London, 1916), pp. 17–18.

33 A frequently offered explanation for Stephens' departure is that his wife wished to move into London society. In later years Stephens was in great demand in England and America because of his reputation as a conversationalist. Stephens suffered poor health during most of his mature years; one doubts, however, that he would have sought a better climate in England, and especially in London.

34 James Stephens, "Thomas Moore, Champion Minor Poet," *Poetry Ireland*, XVII (April, 1952), 4. The talk first was transmitted by the B.B.C. on August 17, 1944.

35 Edmund Curtis, *A History of Ireland* (London and New York, 1961), p. 124, notes that Tanistry was a relatively late development in Irish law of succession and represented an attempt to "attain that primogeniture which gave the Norman feudal class much of its stability." Under Tanistry a chief could appoint a successor to rule until his own son came of age. Under the older "Derb-fine" law, all male descendants of a chief, or king, to the fourth degree, could succeed them.

36 George Moore, *Hail and Farewell*, III, 170.

37 H. P. Blavatsky, *The Key to Theosophy* (London and New York, 1893), pp. 132, 224.

38 Thomas MacDonagh, *Metempsychosis*, pp. 585–99.

39 *Journal and Letters of Stephen MacKenna*, ed. E. R. Dodds (London, 1936), p. 289. In a letter dated April 12, 1932, MacKenna wrote to Margaret Nunn: "I have never succeeded like you and J. S. in taking Yoga so seriously, as an approach to the divine; in fact I don't think we ought."

40 H. P. Blavatsky, *The Secret Doctrine* (London, 1888), I, 292–93. (Mme. Blavatsky's italics.) Stephens, *On Prose and Verse* (New York, 1928), p. 40, remarks that "an artistic failure is rarely traceable to an incapacity for thinking. Such a failure is always attributable to a failure of the will."

41 *Poems*, p. 234. In an introduction to Ruth Pitter, *A Trophy of*

Arms: Poems 1926–1935 (London [1936]), p. ix, Stephens argues that "a something is exhaustively nominated by the uttering of itself and its logical opposite."

42   On Prose and Verse, p. 25.

43   There are, of course, instances in which Stephens communicates his message in powerful and effective language; for example, in "Variations," 10 (Poems, pp. 283–84), Stephens defines the destructive principle (the antithesis of the principle of love) which is manifest in all living creatures: "Look you, the fly, come to the spider's web, / Quick-clutched is, parcelled is, and is devoured!" Spider in turn is devoured by bird, bird by cat, cat by dog, and dog by another creature, presumably man: "Eater and eaten, / Murdered and murderer, goes murdering down!" In Yeats' verse a similar pattern is used to express Ribh's notion of sexuality in man, beast, fly, and God.

44   "Sarasvati" (Poems, p. 263), like "The Demiurge" takes its theme from occult lore. Madame Blavatsky, The Secret Doctrine, pp. 94–95, records an allegory in which Mind and Speech (i.e., Sarasvati) ask Self of Being which of them has precedence. When Mind is exalted, Sarasvati protests and the Lord, Self, then differentiates between two "minds," the "movable" and the "immovable"; the former is the dominion of Sarasvati, the latter the dominion of Self.

45   Cf. Yeats' lines, "For nothing can be sole or whole / That has not been rent," in "Crazy Jane Talks with the Bishop," Collected Poems, p. 255.

46   Poems, p. 199. This poem appeared first in Reincarnations, p. 33; but Stephens made important changes in stanzaic pattern and punctuation—as he did with much of his earlier verse—before including it in his Collected Poems. His intent apparently was to make his poetry more stylized and thus further removed from temporal reality.

47   Blavatsky, The Secret Doctrine, I, 354, 357; II, 617.

48   From a broadcast made in January, 1949. Cited by T. R. Henn, The Lonely Tower, p. 65.

49   James Stephens, The Crock of Gold (London, 1922), pp. 97–98.

50   Ibid., pp. 143–48.

51   Ibid., pp. 287–88.

52   Poems, pp. 268–69. Egan O'Rahilly was a poet of the late seventeenth and early eighteenth centuries. I have been unable to identify O'Brien.

53 Bramsbäch, *James Stephens*, p. 15.
54 James Stephens, *The Charwoman's Daughter* (London, 1928), p. 185.
55 *The Crock of Gold*, p. 16. At one point (p. 6) Stephens' Philosophers wish to abolish all sound ("by a bird, a breeze, a shower of rain") except their own conversation.
56 *Ibid.*, pp. 297–98.

Chapter 9

1 F. R. Higgins, *The Dark Breed* (London, 1927), pp. 64–65, 68–69.
2 F. R. Higgins, *Island Blood* (London, 1925), p. 8.
3 *Ibid.*, p. 13.
4 F. R. Higgins, *The Gap of Brightness*, p. 15.
5 F. R. Higgins, *Arable Holdings* (Dublin, 1933), p. 23; *The Gap of Brightness*, p. 56.
6 *Arable Holdings*, p. 18; *The Gap of Brightness*, p. 49.
7 *Island Blood*, pp. 19–20. In this poem Higgins tries to achieve a more physical atmosphere by alluding to certain folk customs: in the second stanza he mentions the traditional wake with "pipes for the neighbors and drink" and in the third he refers to the custom of closing the eyes of the dead with two pennies.
8 *Island Blood*, p. 31.
9 *The Dark Breed*, p. 9.
10 *Ibid.*, p. 2.
11 National Library of Ireland MS. 10,864.
12 The Battle of the Boyne was fought on July 1, 1690; after his defeat King James fled Ireland. On July 12th of the following year the Irish fought a last stand at Aughrim.
13 Edmund Curtis, *A History of Ireland*, pp. 196, 204. In a note for *The Dark Breed*, pp. 66–67, Higgins writes that "Gran Uaile, or Grace O'Maille, was a famous female sea rover, who commanded extensive free-booting along the western seaboard. Her main base was at Clew Bay, where she liberally contributed to the support of the Abbey at Murrisk. The ballad-makers used 'Gran Uaile' as a secret name for Ireland." Following this practice, Higgins himself used the name as a personification of Ireland in "A Petition," *The Dark Breed*, p. 1.
14 Curtis, *History of Ireland*, p. 204.
15 Robert Farren, *The Course of Irish Verse*, p. 145. William Larminie (1850–99) in his essay, "The Development of English

Metres," *The Contemporary Review*, LXVI (November, 1894), describes the Gaelic system of assonance, observes a similarity in the prosody of ancient Greece, and advocates the use of assonance in Irish verse written in English.

16 Letter by Austin Clarke, *The Irish Statesman*, V (February 20, 1926), 740.

17 Review of *Island Blood*, *The Irish Statesman*, IV (April 4, 1925), 118.

18 The adjectival "sun-bred" has moralistic connotations. The Irishman is morally better than other people because he is closer to nature. Pearse had much the same notion in mind when he wrote in *Songs of the Irish Rebels* (Dublin, 1924), pp. 223–24, concerning non-Irish literature: "There is no healthy out-of-door attitude."

19 *The Irish Statesman*, IX (October 8, 1927), 112. Robert Farren, *The Course of Irish Verse*, pp. 131–32, makes the same point in more picturesque language: "The making of a national poetry...may well be a labour in the mines; but the Jones who goes down with his pick for coal is the Jones who comes up with his paw for pay; while your cosmopolitan writing is more like Nirvana: you pay for its absence of pain by its absence of you. It has always seemed to the Western man to be better to be silly than extinct; just so you had better be a national ass—a frivolous Frenchman, we'll say, or a muzzy German, a blockheaded Englishman or even a priestridden Irishman—than merely to rejoice as a grey, indiscriminate bubble in the thickest, hottest, most mouth-watering cosmopolitan stew."

20 Farren, *The Course of Irish Verse*, p. 144.

21 Letter to Colonel Theodore Roosevelt, of Doubleday, Doran and Co., dated February 18, 1937, in National Library of Ireland MS. 10,864.

22 Notes by Higgins for a lecture on poetry, in National Library of Ireland MS. 10,864.

23 *Arable Holdings*, p. 5; *The Gap of Brightness*, p. 44.

24 Draft of an essay on Pádraic Ó Conaire, in National Library of Ireland MS. 10,864.

25 Notes by Higgins for a lecture on poetry, in National Library of Ireland MS. 10,864.

26 Review of *The Dark Breed*, *Studies*, XVII (September, 1928), 513.

27 Notes by Higgins for a lecture on poetry, in National Library of Ireland MS. 10,864.

28 *The Irish Statesman*, V (February 20, 1926), 739–40.

29   *The Irish Statesman*, V (March 6, 1926), 798.

30   *Island Blood*, p. 55.

31   *Arable Holdings*, pp. 30–31; *The Gap of Brightness*, pp. 70–71.

32   Farren, *The Course of Irish Verse*, p. 147.

33   Higgins' position as secretary to the Irish Academy placed him in correspondence with most of the prominent Irish writers of the time, including Bernard Shaw, Louis MacNeice, and, oddly enough, T. E. Lawrence. Many of these letters are preserved in the collection of Higgins' papers at the National Library of Ireland, Dublin.

34   National Library of Ireland MS. 10,864. A fragment of a third play, *The Fortune Teller*, also is preserved. It is a peasant farce and includes the following dialogue between Raftery, the poet, and Le Po, an Irish harper:

> Raftery: Shush! You're too touchy
> Le Po (indignant): Where there's itch there's touch
> Raftery: Then scratch!

35   *The Collected Poems of W. B. Yeats*, pp. 191–92.

36   *Arable Holdings*, p. 33; *The Gap of Brightness*, p. 72.

37   *Arable Holdings*, pp. 37–38; *The Gap of Brightness*, pp. 74–75. The name Irrus could refer to any one of a number of peninsulas in Connacht. P. W. Joyce, *The Origin and History of Irish Names of Places*, Second Series, p. 208, comments: "There can be no doubt that the word was applied to a peninsula; for all the iorruses of Galway are peninsulas."

38   Yeats uses the image of the ditch often, usually to suggest social criticism. In "On a Political Prisoner," *Collected Poems*, p. 181, he links "the foul ditch" with "Blind and leader of the blind"; in "A Dialogue of Self and Soul," p. 232, he alludes to the "blind man's ditch"; in "The Old Stone Cross," p. 314, he tells us that "this age and the next age / Engender in the ditch." In "Crazy Jane Talks with the Bishop," *Collected Poems*, p. 254, Yeats' prelate admonishes Jane: " 'Those breasts are flat and fallen now, / Those veins must soon be dry.' "

39   *The Gap of Brightness*, p. 55. In the summer of 1963 Austin Clarke suggested to me that Higgins may have influenced Yeats to develop the ribald, earthy themes which one finds in Yeats' later verse. He said that once the older poet accompanied Higgins to a working class pub. After only a few minutes Yeats, complaining of the noise and the smoke, insisted they leave.

40   Letter to Colonel Theodore Roosevelt, of Doubleday, Doran

and Co., dated February 18, 1937, in National Library of Ireland MS. 10,864.

41 Sean O'Faolain, *The Bell*, III (January, 1942), 251–52.

42 *Arable Holdings*, pp. 35–36. "Easter Island" had a double allusion: to the lost civilization of the South Pacific and to the Easter Rising of 1916, an event which Irish Philistines invoke as justification for their own ideals of nationalism.

43 Several years ago the composition of the Censorship Board of Appeal in Ireland was altered so that persons in the academic professions constitute a majority. As a result, the board has become more lenient, especially in dealing with established writers. The works of Graham Greene, for example, banned earlier, can now be purchased in Ireland. Curiously, the board seems to be most severe in passing upon the works of Irish writers. Several of Austin Clarke's prose works, for example, remain under the censor's ban.

Chapter 10

1 Austin Clarke, *Twice Round the Black Church* (London, 1962), p. 169.

2 Austin Clarke, *The Collected Poems of Austin Clarke* (London, 1936), pp. 11–13 (hereafter cited as *Poems*).

3 Austin Clarke, *The Cattledrive in Connaught and Other Poems* (London, 1925). On pp. 60–61, MacDara, angered that Medb's envoy has driven MacDara's own men out of the house, rejects Medb's offer of wealth in exchange for the great bull:

> "By god, now, you have driven
> My men out of my house but it was yours
> That horned the knives. I see all clearly now
> And you will never have this bull of mine
> On hire to fill your cows. Now take your money
> Out of my lands for by the kindly laws
> Of hospitality it is your own
> To carry to that meddlesome red woman
> In the west."

4 Austin Clarke, *The Vengeance of Fionn* (Dublin and London, 1917), p. 21.

5 Robert Farren, *The Course of Irish Verse*, pp. 155–58, analyzes Clarke's expert use of assonance.

6   *Poems*, p. 105. In "Crazy Jane and the Bishop," *Collected Poems of W. B. Yeats*, pp. 251–52, the Bishop condemns the sexual love of Crazy Jane and Jack the Journeyman.

7   *Poems*, p. 99. Cf. "Crazy Jane on the Day of Judgment," *Collected Poems of W. B. Yeats*, pp. 252–53.

8   Clarke published a third "romance," *The Sun Dances at Easter*, in 1952. All three are banned in Ireland. Clarke told me in the summer of 1963 that although many works by non-Irish writers, previously banned, could now be purchased in Ireland, censorship was still being used by the government to enforce conformity on Irish writers. He suggested that the sale of James Joyce's works is now permitted because Joyce has become a factor in the tourist trade.

9   Austin Clarke, *The Son of Learning* (London, 1927), p. 44.

10 Farren, *The Course of Irish Verse*, p. 161.

11 The plot interest in "country kitchen" comedies is usually nil, the humor almost invariably of a slapstick sort.

12 Austin Clarke, *Flight to Africa and Other Poems* (Dublin, 1963), p. 17. This passage and subsequent citations from this volume were taken from the prepublication "proof copy" of the book, which Mr. Clarke kindly loaned to me.

13 Austin Clarke, *The Flame* (London, 1930). The play is set in the convent in Kildare where for many centuries nuns tended the flame of St. Brigid.

14 Saul's paper will shortly be published along with other papers read at the 1963 meeting of the American Committee for Irish Studies as part of the Purdue Humanities Series.

15 Douglas Sealy, "Austin Clarke: A Survey of His Work," *The Dubliner*, No. 6 (January-February, 1963), 17.

16 *Twice Round the Black Church*, pp. 123, 147–50. Clarke distinguishes between the indiscriminate beatings he received from the Christian Brothers and the systematically impersonal punishment doled out by the Jesuits; but he cannot decide which was worse.

17 *Ibid.*, pp. 89–90. A member of the faculty of University College, Dublin, suggested to me in the summer of 1963 that Clarke's marriage outside the Church had nothing to do with the university's failure to renew his contract. The Catholic hierarchy have always exerted a strong influence upon the National University, however, and it is difficult to believe that Clarke's marriage would have passed unnoticed by the administration.

18 *Poems*, pp. 87–98, 312. There also are overtones of paganism in
    Clarke's treatment of Brigid's sacred fire in *The Flame*.
19 Austin Clarke, *The Sun Dances at Easter*, pp. 51–52.
20 *Ibid.*, p. 152.
21 Austin Clarke, *The Bright Temptation* (London, 1932), p. 122.
    In *The Sun Dances at Easter*, p. 50, Clarke implies that homo-
    sexuality also posed a problem in the monasteries. Enda recalls
    that " 'I was happier indeed at Favoria than some of my fellow
    students, who were much tormented by the Adversary. Some
    of them, indeed, dreamed at night of their younger companions
    and woke up with cries of distress.' "
22 Austin Clarke, *The Singing Men at Cashel* (London, 1936),
    pp. 135–36. Clarke's references to St. Ammon and St. Abraham
    are accurate. St. Ammon, who pioneered monasticism in Egypt,
    was forced into marriage, lived with his wife for twenty-two
    years without consummating the union, then retired to the Nit-
    rian desert where he founded many monasteries. Abraham of
    Kidunja in Mesopotamia left his young wife on their wedding
    day and fled to the Syrian desert where he spent twelve years in
    a hut. He was then ordained a priest.
23 Austin Clarke, *Later Poems* (Dublin, 1961), p. 30.
24 In the second episode of *The Sun Dances at Easter*, "The
    Only Jealousy of Congal More," Clarke explains that Irish
    saints undertook to train the wild animals "so that the good
    might walk even in remote places without offense to eye or im-
    modesty of thought."
25 *Twice Round the Black Church*, pp. 124–25.
26 *Ibid.*, pp. 23–24.
27 Vivian Mercier, *The Irish Comic Tradition* (Oxford, 1962),
    pp. 134–35, writes that Ó Dálaigh was reportedly killed by a serv-
    ant of one of his victims, Ó Huiginn by six men of the O'-
    Haras whom he had satirized for raiding his house. Lady Greg-
    ory, *Poets and Dreamers* (London, 1903), p. 3, says that Ó
    Dálaigh was killed when the servant of an Irish chief stuck a
    knife in his throat and that Ó Huiginn had his tongue cut out.
28 Austin Clarke, *Too Great a Vine: Poems and Satires* (Temple-
    ogue, County Dublin, 1957), p. 27.
29 Some of the poems in Clarke's new book, *Flight to Africa and
    Other Poems*, are not satires. Clarke told me in the summer of
    1963 that he has decided to turn to other, less bitter subjects. In
    one poem in the new volume, "Mount Parnassus," he records

his impressions on visiting the mountain sacred to Apollo and
the Muse in Greece:

> Never have I been in the south
> So far from self and yet I must
> Learn, straight from the horse's mouth,
> To kick up my own dust.
> Here is the source. Here was our must.
> I see no flowers to grass us,
> Only the scale of Mount Parnassus:
> Simplicity of snow
> Above, the pillared drouth,
> The worn-out, below.
> I stray from American, German, tourists,
> Greek guide, feel in my two wrists
> Answer for which I have come,
> The Oracle, not yet dumb.

Clarke told me that when he returned from Greece he wrote
steadily for twelve weeks.

30 *Flight to Africa and Other Poems*, p. 15. "Twenty-sixer" refers
to the Republic of Ireland, which has twenty-six counties.
Northern Ireland, which remains a part of the British Isles, consists of six counties.

31 *Ibid.*, p. 59.

32 Austin Clarke, *The Horse Eaters: Poems and Satires* (Templeogue, County Dublin, 1960), pp. 9–10. Clarke's information is
correct. Abattoirs subsequently were established in Ireland.

33 *Flight to Africa and Other Poems*, p. 26. "Swaddlers," Clarke
told me, is an old Dublin word that in the nineteenth century
was used to refer to proselytizing Protestants who placed foundlings in their own orphanages. In street usage, apparently, the
word came to mean the foundlings themselves.

34 In "Corporal Punishment," *Flight to Africa and Other Poems*,
p. 44, Clarke concludes with the line: "Let Queen Victoria still
reign here." In a poem entitled "Christmas Eve: Dublin, 1959"
in *The Horse Eaters*, p. 13, he describes a Christmas eve riot
on O'Connell Street in the center of Dublin. The guards, he
writes, "scoring with stripes and licks, / Batoned their fellow-
Catholics." In "Mother and Child," *Ancient Lights: Poems and
Satires* (Templeogue, County Dublin, 1955), p. 17, he comments ironically on the government's attitude toward the bill
to give free care at childbirth: "Common help is harmful / And
state-control must starve the soul."

35 Clarke showed me a number of these clippings when I visited him in Dublin.

Chapter 11

1 *The Autobiography of William Carlos Williams* (New York, 1948), p. 359.
2 Geraldine Plunkett Dillon, sister of Joseph Plunkett, told me in April, 1961, that before the Easter Rising MacDonagh had decided to give up writing poetry and devote himself to critical prose.
3 *The Collected Poems of W. B. Yeats,* p. 54.

BIBLIOGRAPHY

Primary Materials

Clarke, Austin. *Ancient Lights: Poems and Satires*. Dublin, 1955.
———. *As the Crow Flies*. Dublin and London, 1943.
———. *Black Fast*. Dublin, 1941.
———. *The Bright Temptation*. London and New York, 1932.
———. *The Cattledrive in Connaught and Other Poems*. London, 1925.
———. *Collected Plays*. Dublin, 1963.
———. *The Collected Poems of Austin Clarke*. London, 1963.
———. *The Fires of Baal*. Dublin and London, 1921.
———. *First Visit to England and Other Memories*. Dublin and London, 1945.
———. *The Flame*. London, 1930.
———. *Flight to Africa and Other Poems*. Dublin, 1963.
———. *Forget Me Not*. Dublin, 1962.
———. *The Horse Eaters: Poems and Satires*. Dublin, 1960.
———. *Later Poems*. Dublin, 1961.
———. Letter to the Editor, *The Irish Statesman*, V (February 20, 1926), 740.
———. *The Moment Next to Nothing*. Dublin, 1963.
———. *Night and Morning*. Dublin, 1938.
———. *Pilgrimage and Other Poems*. London, 1929.
———. *The Plot Succeeds*. Dublin and London, 1950.
———. *Poetry in Modern Ireland*. Dublin, 1951.
———. *The Second Kiss*. Dublin and London, 1946.
———. *The Singing Men at Cashel*. London, 1936.
———. *Sister Eucharia*. Dublin and London, 1939.
———. *The Son of Learning*. London, 1927.
———. *The Sun Dances at Easter*. London, 1952.
———. *The Sword of the West*. Dublin and London, 1921.
———. *Two Great a Vine: Poems and Satires*. Dublin, 1957.
———. *Twice Round the Black Church*. London, 1961.
———. *The Vengeance of Fionn*. Dublin and London, 1917.

―――. *The Viscount of Blarney and Other Plays*. Dublin, 1944.

Colum, Padraic. *The Adventures of Odysseus and the Tale of Troy*. London, 1920.

―――, ed. *Anthology of Irish Verse*. New York, 1922.

―――. *Arthur Griffith*. Dublin, 1959.

―――. *The Big Tree of Bunlahy: Stories of My Own Countryside*. New York, 1933.

―――. *A Boy of Eirinn*. London, 1915.

―――, ed. *Broad-Sheet Ballads*. Dublin and London, 1913.

―――. *Castle Conquer*. London, 1923.

―――. *The Collected Poems of Padraic Colum*. New York, 1953.

―――. *Crossroads in Ireland*. New York, 1931.

―――. *The Frenzied Prince*. Philadelphia, 1943.

―――. *A Half-day's Ride or Estates in Corsica*. New York, 1932.

―――. "James Clarence Mangan." National Library of Ireland MS. 3904.

―――. *The Legend of Saint Columba*. New York, 1935.

―――. Letter to William Ryan, dated December 25, 1914. National Library of Ireland MS. Autograph.

―――. *My Irish Year*. New York, 1913.

―――. Notes on Plutarch, National Library of Ireland MS. 9453.

―――. "Padraic Colum Comments on Irish Verse," *The Irish Times*, December 31, 1960.

―――, and Edward J. O'Brien, eds. *Poems by the Revolutionary Brotherhood*. Boston, 1916.

―――. *The Poet's Circuits*. London, 1960.

―――. *Songs from Connacht*, music by Herbert Hughes and lyrics by Padraic Colum. Dublin, 1913.

―――. *The Story of Lowry Maen*. New York, 1937.

―――. *Three Plays: The Fiddler's House, The Land, Thomas Muskerry*. New York, 1925.

―――. *A Treasury of Irish Folklore*. New York, 1954.

Higgins, F. R. *Arable Holdings*. Dublin, 1933.

―――. *The Dark Breed*. London, 1927.

―――. Correspondence of F. R. Higgins as Secretary for the Irish Academy of Letters. National Library of Ireland MS. 10,864.

―――. "Deuce O'Jacks" (typescript). National Library of Ireland MS. 10,864.

―――. Essay on Poetry (draft). National Library of Ireland MS. 10,864.

―――. "The Fortune Teller" (fragment). National Library of Ireland MS. 10,864.

Higgins, F. R. *The Gap of Brightness*. New York, 1940.

———. "Irish Poetry for the Past Thirty Years." National Library of Ireland MS. 10,864.

———. *Island Blood*. London, 1925.

———. Letter to Colonel Theodore Roosevelt of Doubleday, Doran, and Company. National Library of Ireland MS. 10,864.

———. Letter to the Editor, *The Irish Statesman*, V (March 6, 1926), 798.

———. "Literature and Life: from Paradise to Puck Fair," *The Irish Statesman*, VIII (March 19, 1927), 37–39.

———. "Maire of Magdala," *The Irish Statesman*, V (October 3, 1925), 106.

———. Notes for a Lecture on Poetry. National Library of Ireland MS. 10,864.

———. "Pádraic Ó Conaire." National Library of Ireland MS. 10,864.

———. "Puck Fair" (scenario). National Library of Ireland MS. 10,864.

———. Review of A. M. Stephen's *The Land of Singing Water* and *The Poems of Duncan Campbell Scott*, *The Irish Statesman*, IX (October 8, 1927), 112–13.

———. Review of Humbert Wolfe's *Requiem*, *The Irish Statesman*, IX (September 24, 1927), 65.

———. *Salt Air*. Dublin, 1923.

———. "The Undoing of Dandy Dhu." National Library of Ireland MS. 10,864.

———. "Yeats and Poetic Drama," in *The Irish Theatre*, ed. Lennox Robinson. London, 1939.

MacDonagh, Thomas. *April and May*. Dublin, 1903.

———. "The Art and the Craft," *The Irish Review*, I (January, 1912), 557–59.

———. *The Golden Joy*. Dublin, 1906.

———. "Language and Literature in Ireland," *The Irish Review*, IV (March-April, 1914), 176–82.

———. *Literature in Ireland*. London, 1917.

———. *Lyrical Poems*. Dublin, 1913.

———. "Metempsychosis or a Mad World," *The Irish Review*, I (February, 1912), 585–99.

———. "The New Anthology," *The Irish Review*, IV (July-August, 1914), 278–80.

———. *Pagans: a Modern Play in Two Conversations*. Dublin, 1920.

———. *The Poetical Works of Thomas MacDonagh*. Dublin, 1916.

———. *Songs of Myself*. Dublin, 1910.

———. *Thomas Campion and the Art of English Poetry*. Dublin and London, 1913.

———. *Through the Ivory Gate*. Dublin, 1902.

———. *When the Dawn Is Come*. Dublin, 1908.

Pearse, Padraic H. *An Macaomh*, I–II. Dublin, 1909–13.

———. *Collected Works: Plays, Stories, Poems*. Dublin, 1924.

———. *Collected Works: Political Writings and Speeches*. Dublin, 1924.

———. *Collected Works: Songs of the Irish Rebels and Three Lectures on Gaelic Topics*. Dublin, 1924.

———. *Collected Works: The Story of a Success*. Dublin, 1924.

———. *Ghosts*. Dublin, 1916.

———. *The Separatist Idea*. Dublin, 1916.

———. *The Spiritual Nation*. Dublin, 1916.

———. "The Wood," *The Irish Review*, IV (September-November, 1914), 306–17.

Plunkett, Joseph Mary. "Big Talk." National Library of Ireland MS. 10,999.

———. *The Circle and the Sword*. Dublin, 1911.

———. *The Poems of Joseph Mary Plunkett*. Dublin, 1916.

Russell, George William (A.E.). *AE's Letters to Mínanlábáin*, ed. Lucy Kingsley Porter. New York, 1937.

———. *The Avatars*. New York, 1933.

———. *The Candle of Vision*. London, 1931.

———. *Collected Poems*. London, 1926.

———. *The Earth Breath and Other Poems*. New York and London, 1897.

———. *The House of Titans and Other Poems*. New York, 1934.

———. *Imaginations and Reveries*. Dublin, 1915.

———. *The Living Torch*. London, 1937.

———. *The National Being: Some Thoughts on Irish Polity*. Dublin and London, 1919.

———. *The Nuts of Knowledge, Lyrical Poems Old and New*. Dundrum, Ireland, 1903.

———. Review of David Morton's *The Renaissance of Irish Poetry*, *The Irish Statesman*, XIII (December 28, 1929), 337–38.

———. Review of F. R. Higgins' *Salt Air*, *The Irish Statesman*, I (November 17, 1923), 310.

———. Review of James Stephens' *Collected Poems*, *The Irish Statesman*, VII (November 6, 1926), 205–6.

Russell, George William. *Voices of Stone*. London, 1925.

Stephens, James. *The Adventures of Seumas Beg* and *The Rocky Road to Dublin*. London, 1915.

————. *Arthur Griffith: Journalist and Statesman*. Dublin, *ca.* 1922.

————. "Builders," *Sinn Féin*, May 11, 1907.

————. *The Charwoman's Daughter (Mary, Mary)*. London, 1928.

————. *Collected Poems*. London, 1954.

————. *The Crock of Gold*. London, 1922.

————. *Deirdre*. New York, 1923.

————. *The Demi-gods*. London, 1914.

————. "Epithalamium," *Sinn Féin*, November 26, 1910.

————. *The Insurrection in Dublin*. Dublin and London, 1916.

————. *Insurrections*. Dublin, 1909.

————. *In the Land of Youth*. London, 1924.

————. "Irish Englishmen," *Sinn Féin*, June 1, 1907.

————. *Irish Fairy Tales*. London, 1920.

————. "Irish Idiosyncrasies," *Sinn Féin*, May 7, 1910.

————. *Julia Elizabeth*. New York, 1929.

————. *Kings and the Moon*. New York, 1938.

————. *On Prose and Verse*. New York, 1928.

————. "The Outlook for Literature with Special Reference to Ireland," *Century Magazine*, CIV (October, 1922), 811–18.

————. *Reincarnations*. London, 1918.

————. "The Seoinin," *Sinn Féin*, April 20, 1907.

————. "Thomas Moore, Champion Minor Poet," *Poetry Ireland*, No. 17 (April, 1952), 3–5.

Yeats, William Butler. *The Autobiography of William Butler Yeats*. New York, 1958.

————. *The Bounty of Sweden*. Dublin, 1925.

————. *The Collected Plays of W. B. Yeats*. New York, 1953.

————. *The Collected Poems of W. B. Yeats*. New York, 1959.

————. *The Death of Synge*. Dublin, 1928.

————. *Dramatis Personae, 1896–1902*. Edinburgh, 1936.

————. *Estrangement*. Dublin, 1926.

————. *If I Were Four-and-Twenty*. Dublin, 1940.

————. *The Letters of W. B. Yeats*. Allan Wade, ed. London, 1954.

————. Letter to John O'Leary, *The Irish Booklover*, XXVII (November, 1940), 248.

————. *Mythologies*. New York, 1959.

————. *On the Boiler*. Dublin, 1939.

————. *Per Amica Silentia Lunae*. London, 1918.

————. *Reveries over Childhood and Youth*. Churchtown, Dundrum, Ireland, 1915.

————. *The Trembling of the Veil*. London, 1922.

————. *The Variorum Edition of the Poems of W. B. Yeats*. Peter Allt and Russell K. Alspach, eds. New York, 1957.

————. *A Vision*. London, 1937.

————. *W. B. Yeats: Letters to Katherine Tynan*. Roger McHugh, ed. New York, 1953.

Secondary Materials

Allt, Peter, and Russell K. Alspach, eds. *The Variorum Edition of the Poems of W. B. Yeats*. New York, 1957.

Anonymous. *The National Song Book*. Dublin, n.d.

————. *The Poets of 1916*. Dublin and Cork, 1931.

————. Review of F. R. Higgins' *The Dark Breed*, *Studies* (Dublin), XVII (September, 1928), 513–14.

————. Review of F. R. Higgins' *Island Blood*, *The Irish Statesman*, IV (April 4, 1925), 116, 118.

————. Review of J. H. Pollock's *William Butler Yeats*, *Studies*, XXIV (September, 1935), 493.

Arnold, Matthew. *On the Study of Celtic Literature and Other Essays*. London and New York, n.d.

Bate, Walter Jackson. *Criticism: The Major Texts*. New York, 1952.

Bentley, Eric. "Yeats as a Playwright," *Kenyon Review*, X (Spring, 1948), 196–208.

Bjersby (Bramsbäch), Birgit. *The Interpretation of the Cuchulain Legend in the Works of W. B. Yeats*. Upsala, 1950.

Blavatsky, H. P. *The Key to Theosophy*. London and New York, 1893.

————. *The Secret Doctrine: The Synthesis of Science, Religion, and Philosophy*. London, 1888.

Boyd, Ernest A. *Appreciations and Deprecations*. Dublin and London, 1917.

————. *Ireland's Literary Renaissance*. Dublin, 1916.

Bramsbäch (Bjersby), Birgit. *James Stephens: A Literary and Bibliographical Study*. Upsala, 1959.

Campbell, Joseph. *The Masks of God: Primitive Mythology*. New York, 1959.

Carney, James. *Studies in Irish Literature and History*. Dublin, 1955.

Cassidy, Rev. James F. *Visions of Ireland Old and New*. Dublin, 1933.

Cassirer, Ernst. *Language and Myth*. Susanne K. Langer, trans. New York, 1946.

Charles, Dr. R. H. *A Critical and Exegetical Commentary on the Revelation of St. John*. 2 vols. Edinburgh, 1920.

Clark, James M. *The Vocabulary of Anglo-Irish*. St. Gallen, Ireland, 1917.

Colum, Mary. *From These Roots*. New York and London, 1938.

——. *Life and the Dream*. Garden City, 1948.

Connolly, James. *Labour and Easter Week*. Dublin, 1948.

——. *Socialism and Nationalism*. Dublin, 1948.

——. *The Workers' Republic: A Selection from His Writing*. Desmond Ryan, ed. Dublin, 1951.

Corkery, Daniel. *The Hidden Ireland: A Study of Gaelic Munster in the Eighteenth Century*. Dublin, 1925.

Cross, Tom Peete. *Harper and Bard: The Beauties of Irish Literature*. Chicago, 1931.

Curtis, Edmund. *A History of Ireland*. London, 1961.

D'Alviella, The Count Goblet. *The Migration of Symbols*. New York, 1956.

Daunt, J. O'Neill. *Personal Recollections of the Late Daniel O'Connell, M.P.* London, 1848.

De Blácam, Aodh. *Gaelic Literature Surveyed*. Dublin and Belfast, n.d.

Denson, Andrew, comp. *Writings by George W. Russell (AE)*. Evanston, Illinois, 1961.

Dillon, Myles. *Archaism of Irish Tradition*. London, 1947.

——. *The Cycles of the Kings*. London and New York, 1946.

——. *Early Irish Literature*. Chicago, 1948.

——, ed. *Early Irish Society*. Dublin, 1959.

——, ed. *Irish Sagas*. Dublin, 1959.

Downey, Allen, ed. *Easter Fires: Pages from Personal Records of 1916*. Waterford, Ireland, 1943.

Dunn, Joseph, trans. *The Ancient Irish Epic Tale Táin Bó Cúalnge*. London, 1914.

Ellis-Fermor, Una. *The Irish Dramatic Movement*. London, 1919.

Ellmann, Richard. *The Identity of Yeats*. London, 1954.

——. *James Joyce*. New York, 1959.

——. *Yeats: The Man and the Masks*. New York, 1948.

Engleberg, Edward. "The Herald of Art: a Study of W. B. Yeats' Criticism and Aesthetic," unpubl. diss. Wisconsin, 1958.

——. "Picture and Gesture in the Yeatsian Aesthetic," *Criticism*, III (Spring, 1961), 101–20.

Ervine, St. John. *Bernard Shaw*. New York, 1956.

————. *Some Impressions of My Elders*. New York, 1922.

Farren, Robert. *The Course of Irish Verse*. New York, 1947.

Ferguson, Sir Samuel. *Congal: A Poem in Five Books*. Dublin and London, 1893.

Figgis, Darrell. *AE (George W. Russell): A Study of a Man and a Nation*. New York, 1916.

————. *The Return of the Hero*. New York, 1930.

Fitzhenry, Edna C., ed. *Nineteen-Sixteen: An Anthology*. Dublin and London, 1935.

Five Great Modern Irish Plays. New York, 1941.

Flanagan, Thomas. *The Irish Novelists, 1800–1850*. New York, 1959.

Fletcher, Ifan Kyle, Jack Reading, and Sybil Rosenfeld, eds. *The Transactions of the International Conference on Theatre History*. London, 1957.

Fordham, Frieda. *An Introduction to Jung's Psychology*. Bungay, Suffolk, 1959.

Frazer, Sir James G. *The Golden Bough*. Abr. ed. New York, 1958.

Gannon, P. J. Review of Joseph Hone's *W. B. Yeats, Studies*, XXXII (March, 1943), 130–31.

Gaynor, Frank, ed. *Dictionary of Mysticism*. New York, 1953.

Gibbon, Monk. *The Masterpiece and the Man: Yeats as I Knew Him*. London, 1959.

Girodias, Maurice, and Peter Singleton-Gates, eds. *The Black Diaries*. Paris, 1959.

Gogarty, Oliver St. John. *As I Was Going Down Sackville Street*. New York, 1937.

————. *A Week End in the Middle of the Week and Other Essays on the Bias*. New York, 1958.

Graves, Robert. *The White Goddess*. New York, 1958.

Gregory, Lady Isabella Augusta. *Gods and Fighting Men*. London, 1914.

————. *The Kiltartan History Book*. London, 1910.

————. *Poets and Dreamers*. Dublin and London, 1903.

Green, Alice Stopford. *History of the Irish State to 1014*. London, 1925.

Gwynn, Dennis. *The Life and Death of Roger Casement*. London, n.d.

Gwynn, Stephen, ed. *Scattering Branches: Tributes to the Memory of W. B. Yeats*. New York, 1940.

Hall, James, ed. *The Permanence of Yeats*. New York, 1950.

Hartog, Marcus, and Mary Hayden. "The Irish Dialect in English," *Fortnightly Review*, XCI (1909), 775–76.

Henn, T. R. *The Lonely Tower: Studies in the Poetry of* W. B. *Yeats.* London, 1950.

Highet, Gilbert. *The Classical Tradition.* New York, 1957.

Hoagland, Kathleen, ed. *1000 Years of Irish Poetry.* New York, 1947.

Hoare, Dorothy M. *The Works of Morris and Yeats in Relation to Early Saga Literature.* Cambridge, England, 1937.

Hone, Joseph. W. B. *Yeats: 1865–1939.* New York, 1943.

Howarth, Herbert. *The Irish Writers: 1880–1940.* London, 1958.

Hull, Eleanor, ed. *The Poem-book of the Gael.* London, 1912.

Hyde, Douglas. *A Literary History of Ireland.* London, 1920.

——. *Love Songs of Connacht.* Dublin, 1905.

——. "The Necessity for De-Anglicizing Ireland," in *The Revival of Irish Literature.* London, 1894.

Jeffares, A. Norman. W. B. *Yeats: Man and Poet.* New Haven, 1949.

Jeffrey, William. "In Memoriam: F. R. H.," *The Dublin Magazine,* V (April-June, 1941), 1.

Joyce, James. *A Portrait of the Artist as a Young Man.* New York, 1928.

Joyce, P. W. *English as We Speak It in Ireland.* London, 1910.

——. *The Origin and History of Irish Names of Places.* First Series. Dublin, 1870.

——. *The Origin and History of Irish Names of Places.* Second Series. Dublin, 1875.

Jung, C. G. *Collected Works of C. G. Jung. Vol. XII: Psychology and Alchemy.* Herbert Read, Michael Fordham and Gerhard Adler, eds. London, 1953.

——. *Psyche and Symbol.* Garden City, 1958.

Kelleher, John V. "Matthew Arnold and the Celtic Revival," in *Perspectives of Criticism,* ed. Harry Levin. Cambridge, Massachusetts, 1950.

Kelly, Blanche Mary. *The Voice of Ireland.* New York, 1952.

Kermode, Frank. *Romantic Image.* London, 1957.

Kilgannon, Tadhg. *Sligo and Its Surroundings.* Sligo, Ireland, 1932.

Knott, George H., ed. *Trial of Roger Casement.* Philadelphia, 1917.

Krutch, Joseph Wood. "The Tragic Fallacy," in *European Theories of Drama,* ed. Barrett H. Clark. New York, 1947.

Larminie, William. "The Development of English Metres," *The Contemporary Review,* LXVI (November, 1874), 717–36.

Lewis, David, trans. *The Works of St. John [de Yèpes] of the Cross.* London, 1891.

Loftus, Richard J. "Yeats and the Easter Rising: A Study in Ritual," *Arizona Quarterly,* XVI (Summer, 1960), 168–77.

MacColl, René. *Roger Casement: A New Judgment.* New York, 1956.

MacDonagh, Donagh. "Ballads of 1916," *The Bell*, II (April, 1941), 21–25.

McHugh, Roger. "Casement: The Public Record Office Manuscripts," *Threshold*, 1 (Spring-Summer, 1960) 28–57.

———, ed. W. B. *Yeats: Letters to Katherine Tynan*. New York, 1953.

MacKenna, Stephen. *Journal and Letters of Stephen MacKenna*, ed. E. R. Dodds. London, 1936.

Mac Neill, Eoin, ed. *The Book of the Lays of Fionn*. Irish Text Society. London, 1908.

———. *Phases of Irish History*, Dublin, 1919.

Magee, William Kirkpatrick (John Eglinton). *Anglo-Irish Essays*. New York, 1918.

———. *A Memoir of AE: George William Russell*. London, 1937.

Malraux, André. *The Metamorphosis of the Gods*. Trans. Stuart Gilbert. London, 1960.

Melchiori, Georgio. *The Whole Mystery of Art: Pattern into Poetry in the Work of W. B. Yeats*. London, 1960.

Mercier, Vivian. *The Irish Comic Tradition*. Oxford, 1962.

———. "James Stephens: His Version of Pastoral," *Irish Writing*, No. 14 (March, 1951), 48–57.

Mitchel, John. *Jail Journal*. Dublin, 1918.

Moore, George. *Hail and Farewell*. 3 vols. London, 1911–14.

Moore, Virginia. *The Unicorn: William Butler Yeats' Search for Reality*. New York, 1954.

Morton, David. *The Renaissance of Irish Poetry*. New York, 1929.

Murphy, Gerard. *The Ossianic Lore and Romantic Tales of Ireland*. Dublin, 1955.

Neil, Crawford. *Happy Island: Child Poems*. Dublin, 1916.

The Nineteen-Sixteen Song Book. Dublin, 1959.

Noyes, Alfred. *The Accusing Ghost or Justice for Casement*. London, 1957.

O'Braonain, Cathaoir, Professor George O'Neill, S.J., Peter McBrien, Padraic Gregory, and Professor Arthur Clery. *Poets of the Insurrection*. Dublin and London, 1918.

O'Brien, James Howard. "Theosophy and the Poetry of George Russell (AE), William Butler Yeats, and James Stephens," unpubl. diss. University of Washington, 1956.

Ó Bruadair, David. *The Poems of David Ó Bruadair*. Part I, trans. Rev. John C. Mac Erlean, S.J. Irish Texts Society. London, 1910.

———. *The Poems of David Ó Bruadair*. Part II, trans. Rev. John C. Mac Erlean, S.J. Irish Texts Society. London, 1913.

Ó Bruadair, David. *The Poems of David Ó Bruadair.* Part III, trans. Rev. John C. Mac Erlean, S.J. London, 1917.

O'Casey, Sean. *The Green Crow.* New York, 1956.

———. *I Knock at the Door.* New York, 1939.

———. *Inishfallen, Fare Thee Well.* New York, 1949.

———. *Selected Plays of Sean O'Casey.* New York, 1954.

———. *The Story of the Irish Citizen Army.* Dublin and London, 1919.

———. *Sunset and Evening Star.* New York, 1955.

Ó Conaire, Pádraic. *Field and Fair: Travels with a Donkey in Ireland,* trans. Cormac Breathnach. Dublin, 1930.

O'Conor, Norreys Jephson. *Changing Ireland: Literary Backgrounds of the Irish Free State, 1889–1922.* Cambridge, Massachusetts, 1924.

O'Donoghue, E. J., ed. *Poems of James Clarence Mangan.* Dublin, 1910.

O'Donovan, John, ed. and trans. *The Banquet of Dún Na N-Gédh and the Battle of Magh Rath: An Ancient Historical Tale.* Irish Archaeological Society. Dublin, 1842.

O'Duffy, Eimar. *The Wasted Island.* Dublin, 1919.

O'Faolain, Sean. Editor's Statement, *The Bell,* I (April, 1940), 5–6.

———. "F. R. Higgins," *The Bell,* III (January, 1942), 251–52.

———. "Ireland after Yeats," *The Bell,* XVIII (Summer, 1953), 38–39.

———. "A Pilgrim Has Been among Us," *The Bell,* XIX (February, 1954), 5–9.

O'Flaherty, Liam. *Insurrection.* London, 1950.

———. Letter to the Editor, *The Irish Statesman,* V (February 20, 1926), 740.

O'Hanlon, Cecil. Review of F. R. Higgins' *Island Blood, Dublin Magazine,* II (April, 1925), 683–85.

O'Hickey, Rev. Michael P. *Language and Nationality.* Waterford, Ireland, 1918.

O'Keefe, J. G., trans. *The Frenzy of Suibhne.* Irish Texts Society. London, 1913.

O'Rahilly, T. F. *Early Irish History and Mythology.* Dublin, 1946.

O'Sullivan, Donal, ed. *Songs of the Irish.* Dublin, 1960.

Pearse, Mary Brigit. *The Home Life of Padraig Pearse.* Dublin and Belfast, 1934.

Porter, Lucy Kingsley, ed. *AE's Letters to Mínanlábáin.* New York, 1937.

Praeger, R. Lloyd. *Irish Landscape.* Dublin, 1953.

Price, Alan. *Synge and the Anglo-Irish Drama.* London, 1961.

Read, Herbert, Michael Fordham, and Gerhard Adler, eds. *Collected Works of C. G. Jung. XII: Psychology and Alchemy.* London, 1953.

Robinson, Lennox, ed. *The Irish Theatre Lectures Delivered during the Abbey Theatre Festival Held in Dublin in August 1938.* London, 1939.

Ryan, Desmond. *The Man Called Pearse.* Dublin, 1924.

———. *The Rising: The Complete Story of Easter Week.* Dublin, 1949.

———. *The Sword of Light.* London, 1939.

Saul, George Brandon. *The Shadow of the Three Queens.* Harrisburg, Pennsylvania, 1953.

———. *Stephens, Yeats, and Other Irish Concerns.* New York, 1954.

———. "Yeats' Verse Before Responsibilities," *Arizona Quarterly,* XVI (Summer, 1960), 158–67.

Saurat, Denis. *Literature and Occult Tradition.* London, 1930.

Sheehy-Skeffington, Francis. Open Letter to Thomas MacDonagh, *The Irish Citizen,* May 22, 1915.

Sigerson, George. *Bards of the Gael and Gall.* Dublin and London, 1925.

Sjoestedt, Marie-Louise. *Gods and Heroes of the Celts,* trans. Myles Dillon. London, 1949.

Smith, Hallett. *Elizabethan Poetry.* Cambridge, Massachusetts, 1952.

Songs and Recitations of Ireland. Cork, 1959.

Starkey, James (Seumas O'Sullivan), *Poems of Seumas O'Sullivan.* Boston, 1923.

Strong, L. A. G. "James Stephens the Poet," *Poetry Ireland,* No. 1 (April, 1948), 15–18.

———. *Personal Remarks.* London and New York, 1953.

Sturgeon, Mary C. *Studies of Contemporary Poets.* London, 1916.

Synge, John M. *The Playboy of the Western World.* Dublin, 1907.

———. *Poems and Translations.* Dundrum, Ireland, 1909.

Taylor, Estella Ruth. *The Modern Irish Writers: Cross Currents of Criticism.* Lawrence, Kansas, 1954.

Taylor, T. N., ed. *Soeur Thérèse of Lisieux.* London, 1913.

Tindall, William York. *The Literary Symbol.* Bloomington, Indiana, 1955.

Torchiana, Donalt T. "Senator Yeats, Burke, and Able Men," *The Newberry Library Bulletin,* V (July, 1961), 267–81.

Tracy, Honor. *The Straight and Narrow Path.* Middlesex, England, 1960.

Unterecker, John. *A Reader's Guide to William Butler Yeats.* New York, 1959.

Valéry, Paul. *Paul Valéry: Selected Writings*. New York, 1950.
Williams, William Carlos. *The Autobiography of William Carlos Williams*. New York, 1948.
Wilson, F. A. C. *W. B. Yeats and Tradition*. London, 1958.
———. *Yeats's Iconography*. London, 1960.
Winters, Yvor. *The Poetry of W. B. Yeats*. Denver, 1960.
Woulfe, Rev. Patrick. *Irish Names and Surnames*. Dublin, 1923.
Yonge, Charlotte M. *History of Christian Names*. 2 vols. London, 1863.

INDEX